IMMIGRATION APPEAL REPORTS
[2024 - 2nd Issue] Imm AR 251-453

Editorial Board:
The Honourable Mr Justice Dove (President of the UT, IAC),
The Honourable Mr Justice Swift, Sir Peter Lane,
Mr CMG Ockelton (Deputy High Court Judge),
Ms M Plimmer (President of the FtT, IAC), Professor A Grubb
(Retired Judge of the UT, IAC), Mr DK Allen (Retired Judge of the
UT, IAC) and Mr J Rintoul (Judge of the UT, IAC)

Contributing Editors:
Rebeccah Sheen (Sub Editor), Laura Cogman and
Georgia Boyle (Legal & Research Unit, IAC)

LONDON: TSO

Published by TSO (The Stationery Office), part of Williams Lea, and available from:

Online
www.tsoshop.co.uk

Mail, Telephone & E-mail
TSO
PO Box 29, Norwich, NR3 1GN
Telephone orders/General enquiries: 0333 202 5070
E-mail: customer.services@tso.co.uk
Textphone: 0333 202 5077

Published for the Ministry of Justice under licence from the Controller of His Majesty's Stationery Office.

© Crown Copyright 2024.

This is a Value Added product which is outside the scope of the HMSO Core Licence.

Applications to reuse, reproduce or republish extracts of material in the publication should be sent to the Information Policy Team, The National Archives, Kew, Richmond, Surrey, TW9 4DU.

First published 2024

ISBN 9780117851740

Printed in the United Kingdom by The Stationery Office.

SD000195

Table of Cases

In [2024] Imm AR

Pages 1 – 250 are in the first issue
Pages 251 – 504 are in the second issue

Azizi (Succinct credibility findings; lies) [2024] UKUT 65 (IAC)	251
FXJ v Secretary of State for the Home Department and Home Office [2023] EWCA Civ 1357	260
Abdi and Others v Entry Clearance Officer [2023] EWCA Civ 1455	283
Secretary of State for the Home Department v AA (Poland) [2024] EWCA Civ 18	298
Geddes v Secretary of State for the Home Department [2024] EWHC 66 (Admin)	321
Secretary of State for the Home Department v Okafor [2024] EWCA Civ 23	332
XY v Secretary of State for the Home Department [2024] EWHC 81 (Admin)	348
MD and Others ('joining' – Appendix EU Family Permit) Ghana [2024[UKUT 64 (IAC)	380
Yalcin v Secretary of State for the Home Department [2024] EWCA Civ 74	393
R (on the application of Zhou, Fei and Zhou) v Secretary of State for the Home Department [2024] EWCA Civ 81	420
R (on the application of VLT (Vietnam)) v Secretary of State for the Home Department (Trafficking, DL policy, transitional provisions, deportation) [2024] UKUT 67 (IAC)	434
Abdullah & Ors (EEA; deportation appeals; procedure) [2024] UKUT 66 (IAC)	453

Decisions of the Upper Tribunal, Immigration and Asylum Chamber can be found at https://tribunalsdecisions.service.gov.uk/utiac

Alphabetical Table of Cases

In [2024] Imm AR

Pages 1 – 250 are in the first issue
Pages 251 – 504 are in the second issue

Abdi and Others v Entry Clearance Officer [2023] EWCA Civ 1455 ...   283

Procedure and process – procedural irregularities – fairness – adverse credibility findings not put to witness – credibility not raised in refusal letters – Secretary of State not represented at the hearing

Abdullah & Ors (EEA; deportation appeals; procedure) [2024] UKUT 66 (IAC) ...   453

Procedure and process – deportation – EEA nationals – scope of protection under the Withdrawal Agreement – scope of protection under domestic law – rights of appeal

Azizi (Succinct credibility findings; lies) [2024] UKUT 65 (IAC)...   251

Evidence – credibility of the claimants – lies in previous asylum appeal – Devaseelan principles applied – explanation for telling lies considered – procedure and process – conduct of appeal – consideration of principal contentious issues – succinct credibility findings

FXJ v Secretary of State for the Home Department and Home Office [2023] EWCA Civ 1357 ...   260

Human rights – Article 8 of the ECHR – private and family life – delay – impact of delay on mental health – questions 4 and 5 of Razgar *[2004] UKHL 27*

Geddes v Secretary of State for the Home Department [2024] EWHC 66 (Admin) ...   321

Procedure and process – deportation – construction of section 104 of the NIAA 2002 – pending permission to appeal before the Supreme Court – impact on a deportation order – meaning of 'finally determined'

MD and Others ('joining' – Appendix EU Family Permit) Ghana [2024] UKUT 64 (IAC) ...   380

European Union law – family members – paragraph FP6.(1)(c) & FP6.(1)(d) of Appendix EU (Family Permit) to the Immigration Rules – 'joining them in the UK' – cancellation of leave to enter – change of circumstances – proportionality

R (on the application of VLT (Vietnam)) v Secretary of State for the Home Department (Trafficking, DL policy, transitional provisions, deportation) [2024] UKUT 67 (IAC) 434

Immigration – Home Office policies and concessions – victims of trafficking – discretionary leave policy – transitional provisions – deportation exception

R (on the application of Zhou, Fei and Zhou) v Secretary of State for the Home Department [2024] EWCA Civ 81 420

Human rights – Article 8 of the ECHR – family and private life – overstayers – 'hostile environment' – no unlawful interference with rights – immigration – leave to remain – deferral of substantive decision on application – pending criminal investigation – delay lawful and rational – paragraph 34BB(1) of the Immigration Rules – variation of first application – appeal academic

Secretary of State for the Home Department v AA (Poland) [2024] EWCA Civ 18 298

European Union law – expulsion – serious sex offender – long residence in the United Kingdom – period of imprisonment – sufficiency of integration prior to deportation decision – paragraph 4 of Schedule 1 to the Immigration (EEA) Regulations 2016 – double discounting of mitigating measures – human rights – Article 8 of the ECHR – private and family life – proportionality – application of EEA Regulations legally distinct

Secretary of State for the Home Department v Okafor [2024] EWCA Civ 23 332

European Union law – exclusion – public policy grounds – foreign criminals – failure to disclose past conviction – regulation 27 of the Immigration (EEA) Regulations 2016 – BF (Portugal) [2009] EWCA Civ 923 followed – Bouchereau exception not met – cumulative assessment – post-conviction behaviour – low risk of re-offending

VLT (Vietnam), R (on the application of) v Secretary of State for the Home Department (Trafficking, DL policy, transitional provisions, deportation) [2024] UKUT 67 (IAC) 434

Immigration – Home Office policies and concessions – victims of trafficking – discretionary leave policy – transitional provisions – deportation exception

XY v Secretary of State for the Home Department [2024] EWHC 81 (Admin) 348

Human rights – Article 8 of the ECHR – private life – substantive and procedural breach – Article 14 of the ECHR – prohibition of discrimination – difference of treatment under unpublished policy not justified – procedure and process – Home Office procedures – pause in decision-making following R (on the application of KTT) [2021] EWHC 2722 (Admin) – unpublished policy unlawful

Yalcin v Secretary of State for the Home Department [2024] EWCA Civ 74 393

Human rights – Article 8 of the ECHR – family and private life – proportionality – best interests of the child – loss of financial support – procedure and process – deportation – foreign criminal – exceptions in section 117C(4) and (5) of the Nationality, Immigration and Asylum Act 2002 – proportionality assessment – section 117C(6) – NA (Pakistan) [2016] EWCA Civ 662 applied

Zhou, Fei and Zhou, R (on the application of) v Secretary of State for the Home Department [2024] EWCA Civ 81 420

Human rights – Article 8 of the ECHR – family and private life – overstayers – 'hostile environment' – no unlawful interference with rights – immigration – leave to remain – deferral of substantive decision on application – pending criminal investigation – delay lawful and rational – paragraph 34BB(1) of the Immigration Rules – variation of first application – appeal academic

Subject Index of Cases Reported

In [2024] Imm AR

Pages 1 – 250 are in the first issue
Pages 251 – 504 are in the second issue

ASYLUM

Article 1D

HA v United Kingdom (Application no. 30919/20) ECtHR (Fourth Section) 230
Article 1D – sufficiency of protection – availability of UNRWA protection – human rights – Article 3 of the ECHR – prohibition of torture – risk on return – non-state actors – stateless Palestinian living in Lebanese refugee camp – forced recruitment – rival paramilitary factions

EUROPEAN UNION LAW

Exclusion

Secretary of State for the Home Department v Okafor [2024] EWCA Civ 23 332
Exclusion – public policy grounds – foreign criminals – failure to disclose past conviction – regulation 27 of the Immigration (EEA) Regulations 2016 – BF (Portugal) [2009] EWCA Civ 923 followed – Bouchereau exception not met – cumulative assessment – post-conviction behaviour – low risk of re-offending

Expulsion

Secretary of State for the Home Department v AA (Poland) [2024] EWCA Civ 18 298
Expulsion – serious sex offender – long residence in the United Kingdom – period of imprisonment – sufficiency of integration prior to deportation decision – paragraph 4 of Schedule 1 to the Immigration (EEA) Regulations 2016 – double discounting of mitigating measures – human rights – Article 8 of the ECHR – private and family life – proportionality – application of EEA Regulations legally distinct

Family Members

Allaraj (EEA EFMs; admission; IO's stamps) [2023] UKUT 277 (IAC) ... 48
Family members – extended family members – lawful admission – regulation 7(3) of the 2016 Regulations – powers of Immigration Officers – stamp in passport not a relevant document – Article 10(2)-(3) of the Withdrawal Agreement – facilitation of residence – immigration – leave to remain – EU Settlement Scheme – Appendix EU of the Immigration Rules – durable partner

MD and Others ('joining' – Appendix EU Family Permit) Ghana [2024] UKUT 64 (IAC) ... 380
Family members – paragraph FP6.(1)(c) & FP6.(1)(d) of Appendix EU (Family Permit) to the Immigration Rules – 'joining them in the UK' – cancellation of leave to enter – change of circumstances – proportionality

EVIDENCE

Assessment of Evidence

ASO (Iraq) v Secretary of State for the Home Department [2023] EWCA Civ 1282 ... 145
Assessment of evidence – credibility of the claimants – standard of proof – protection claim – availability of direct evidence from country of origin – risk on return – honour killings – illicit relationship – Iraq

NC v Secretary of State for the Home Department [2023] EWCA Civ 1379 ... 194
Assessment of evidence – state protection – family connections – failure to consider objective evidence – risk on return – non-state actors – paragraph 276ADE(1)(vi) of the Immigration Rules – reintegration to home country – consideration of obstacles – subjective fear

Burden of Proof

Ram v Secretary of State for the Home Department [2023] EWCA Civ 1323 ... 87
Burden of proof – reliance on findings in DK & RK (ETS: SSHD evidence; proof) India [2022] UKUT 112 (IAC) – immigration – leave to remain – proficiency in English – TOEIC certificate – fraud – refusal on suitability grounds

Credibility of the Claimants

ASO (Iraq) v Secretary of State for the Home Department [2023] EWCA Civ 1282 ... 145
Credibility of the claimants – standard of proof – protection claim – availability of direct evidence from country of origin – assessment of evidence – risk on return – honour killings – illicit relationship – Iraq

Azizi (Succinct credibility findings; lies) [2024] UKUT 65 (IAC)... ... 251
Credibility of the claimants – lies in previous asylum appeal – Devaseelan principles applied – explanation for telling lies considered – procedure and process – conduct of appeal – consideration of principal contentious issues – succinct credibility findings

Standard of Proof

ASO (Iraq) v Secretary of State for the Home Department [2023] EWCA Civ 1282... 145
Standard of proof – protection claim – availability of direct evidence from country of origin – assessment of evidence – credibility of the claimants – risk on return – honour killings – illicit relationship – Iraq

HUMAN RIGHTS

Article 3 of the ECHR

AMA v The Netherlands (Application no. 23048/19) ECtHR (Third Section) 95
Article 3 of the ECHR – subsequent asylum application – 'last-minute' proceedings – failure to discharge procedural obligation during risk assessment

HA v United Kingdom (Application no. 30919/20) ECtHR (Fourth Section) 230
Article 3 of the ECHR – prohibition of torture – risk on return – non-state actors – stateless Palestinian living in Lebanese refugee camp – forced recruitment – rival paramilitary factions – asylum – Article 1D – sufficiency of protection – availability of UNRWA protection

Article 8 of the ECHR

Dani (non-removal human rights submissions) [2023] UKUT 293 (IAC) 128
Article 8 of the ECHR – non-removal human rights submissions – refusal of leave under the EUSS – 'new matter' regime not applicable – 'relevant to the substance of the decision appealed against' – regulation 9(4) of the Immigration (Citizens' Rights Appeals) (EU Exit) Regulations 2020 – no jurisdiction to consider free-standing human rights claims – section 7(1)(b) of the Human Rights Act 1998

FXJ v Secretary of State for the Home Department and Home Office [2023] EWCA Civ 1357 260
Article 8 of the ECHR – private and family life – delay – impact of delay on mental health – questions 4 and 5 of Razgar *[2004] UKHL 27*

R (on the application of Zhou, Fei and Zhou) v Secretary of State for the Home Department [2024] EWCA Civ 81 420
Article 8 of the ECHR – family and private life – overstayers – 'hostile environment' – no unlawful interference with rights – immigration – leave to remain – deferral of substantive decision on application – pending criminal investigation – delay lawful and rational – paragraph 34BB(1) of the Immigration Rules – variation of first application – appeal academic

Said v Secretary of State for the Home Department [2023] NICA 49 ... 24
Article 8 of the ECHR – private life – no engagement or interference – Article 14 of the ECHR – other status – analogous situation – procedure and process – Home Office procedures – Application Registration Card – failed asylum seeker – paragraph 359 of the Immigration Rules – exercise of discretion

Secretary of State for the Home Department v AA (Poland) [2024] EWCA Civ 18 298
Article 8 of the ECHR – private and family life – proportionality – application of EEA Regulations legally distinct – European Union law – expulsion – serious sex offender – long residence in the United Kingdom – period of imprisonment – sufficiency of integration prior to deportation decision – paragraph 4 of Schedule 1 to the Immigration (EEA) Regulations 2016 – double discounting of mitigating measures

XY v Secretary of State for the Home Department [2024] EWHC 81 (Admin) 348
Article 8 of the ECHR – private life – substantive and procedural breach – Article 14 of the ECHR – prohibition of discrimination – difference of treatment under unpublished policy not justified – procedure and process – Home Office procedures – pause in decision-making following R (on the application of KTT) [2021] EWHC 2722 (Admin) – unpublished policy unlawful

Yalcin v Secretary of State for the Home Department [2024] EWCA Civ 74 393
Article 8 of the ECHR – family and private life – proportionality – best interests of the child – loss of financial support – procedure and process – deportation – foreign criminal – exceptions in section 117C(4) and (5) of the Nationality, Immigration and Asylum Act 2002 – proportionality assessment – section 117C(6) – NA (Pakistan) [2016] EWCA Civ 662 applied

Article 14 of the ECHR

Said v Secretary of State for the Home Department [2023] NICA 49 ... 24
Article 14 of the ECHR – other status – analogous situation – Article 8 of the ECHR – private life – no engagement or interference – procedure and process – Home Office procedures – Application Registration Card – failed asylum seeker – paragraph 359 of the Immigration Rules – exercise of discretion

XY v Secretary of State for the Home Department [2024] EWHC 81 (Admin) 348
Article 14 of the ECHR – prohibition of discrimination – difference of treatment under unpublished policy not justified – Article 8 of the ECHR – private life – substantive and procedural breach – procedure and process – Home Office procedures – pause in decision-making following R (on the application of KTT) [2021] EWHC 2722 (Admin) – unpublished policy unlawful

Proportionality

Secretary of State for the Home Department v AA (Poland) [2024] EWCA Civ 18 298
Proportionality – application of EEA Regulations legally distinct – Article 8 of the ECHR – private and family life – European Union law – expulsion – serious sex offender – long residence in the United Kingdom – period of imprisonment – sufficiency of integration prior to deportation decision – paragraph 4 of Schedule 1 to the Immigration (EEA) Regulations 2016 – double discounting of mitigating measures

Yalcin v Secretary of State for the Home Department [2024] EWCA Civ 74 393
Proportionality – best interests of the child – loss of financial support – Article 8 of the ECHR – family and private life – procedure and process – deportation – foreign criminal – exceptions in section 117C(4) and (5) of the Nationality, Immigration and Asylum Act 2002 – proportionality assessment – section 117C(6) – NA (Pakistan) [2016] EWCA Civ 662 applied

IMMIGRATION

Citizenship

Kolicaj (Deprivation: procedure and discretion) [2023] UKUT 294 (IAC) 160
Citizenship – deprivation – section 40(2) of the British Nationality Act 1981 – condition precedent – conducive to the public good – published policy – future risk of re-offending – procedural fairness – discretion

Home Office Policies and Concessions

R (on the application of VLT (Vietnam)) v Secretary of State for the Home Department (Trafficking, DL policy, transitional provisions, deportation) [2024] UKUT 67 (IAC) 434
Home Office policies and concessions – victims of trafficking – discretionary leave policy – transitional provisions – deportation exception

Leave to Remain

Allaraj (EEA EFMs; admission; IO's stamps) [2023] UKUT 277 (IAC) ... 48
Leave to remain – EU Settlement Scheme – Appendix EU of the Immigration Rules – durable partner – European Union law – family members – extended family members – lawful admission – regulation 7(3) of the 2016 Regulations – powers of Immigration Officers – stamp in passport not a relevant document – Article 10(2)-(3) of the Withdrawal Agreement – facilitation of residence

R (on the application of Zhou, Fei and Zhou) v Secretary of State for the Home Department [2024] EWCA Civ 81 ... 420
Leave to remain – deferral of substantive decision on application – pending criminal investigation – delay lawful and rational – paragraph 34BB(1) of the Immigration Rules – variation of first application – appeal academic – human rights – Article 8 of the ECHR – family and private life – overstayers – 'hostile environment' – no unlawful interference with rights

Ram v Secretary of State for the Home Department [2023] EWCA Civ 1323 ... 87
Leave to remain – proficiency in English – TOEIC certificate – fraud – refusal on suitability grounds – evidence – burden of proof – reliance on findings in DK & RK (ETS: SSHD evidence; proof) India [2022] UKUT 112 (IAC)

Sonkor (Zambrano and non-EUSS leave) [2023] UKUT 276 (IAC) ... 1
Leave to remain – non-EUSS leave – definition of 'person with a Zambrano right to reside' – Annex 1 to Appendix EU of the Immigration Rules

Long Residence

R (on the application of Afzal) v Secretary of State for the Home Department; R (on the application of Iyieke) v Secretary of State for the Home Department [2023] UKSC 46 ... 206
Long residence – paragraph 276B(v) of the Immigration Rules – invalid application – failure to pay Immigration Health Surcharge – application of section 3C of the 1971 Act – periods of overstaying – meaning of 'disregarded' and 'the previous application'

Right of Abode

R (on the application of Murugason) v Secretary of State for the Home Department [2023] EWCA Civ 1336... 185
Right of abode – statutory interpretation – section 2(1) of the Immigration Act 1971 – qualifying words 'in the United Kingdom' applicable to birth, adoption, naturalisation and registration

PROCEDURE AND PROCESS

Conduct of Appeal

Azizi (Succinct credibility findings; lies) [2024] UKUT 65 (IAC)... ... 251
Conduct of appeal – consideration of principal contentious issues – succinct credibility findings – evidence – credibility of the claimants – lies in previous asylum appeal – Devaseelan *principles applied – explanation for telling lies considered*

Deportation

Abdullah & Ors (EEA; deportation appeals; procedure) [2024] UKUT 66 (IAC) 453
Deportation – EEA nationals – scope of protection under the Withdrawal Agreement – scope of protection under domestic law – rights of appeal

Geddes v Secretary of State for the Home Department [2024] EWHC 66 (Admin) 321
Deportation – construction of section 104 of the NIAA 2002 – pending permission to appeal before the Supreme Court – impact on a deportation order – meaning of 'finally determined'

Yalcin v Secretary of State for the Home Department [2024] EWCA Civ 74 393
Deportation – foreign criminal – exceptions in section 117C(4) and (5) of the Nationality, Immigration and Asylum Act 2002 – proportionality assessment – section 117C(6) – NA (Pakistan) *[2016] EWCA Civ 662 applied – human rights – Article 8 of the ECHR – family and private life – proportionality – best interests of the child – loss of financial support*

Home Office Procedures

Said v Secretary of State for the Home Department [2023] NICA 49 ... 24
Home Office procedures – Application Registration Card – failed asylum seeker – paragraph 359 of the Immigration Rules – exercise of discretion – human rights – Article 8 of the ECHR – private life – no engagement or interference – Article 14 of the ECHR – other status – analogous situation

XY v Secretary of State for the Home Department [2024] EWHC 81 (Admin)... 348
Home Office procedures – pause in decision-making following R (on the application of KTT) *[2021] EWHC 2722 (Admin) – unpublished policy unlawful – human rights – Article 8 of the ECHR – private life – substantive and procedural breach – Article 14 of the ECHR – prohibition of discrimination – difference of treatment under unpublished policy not justified*

Procedural Irregularities

Abdi and Others v Entry Clearance Officer [2023] EWCA Civ 1455 ... 283
Procedural irregularities – fairness – adverse credibility findings not put to witness – credibility not raised in refusal letters – Secretary of State not represented at the hearing

Rights of Appeal

Abdullah & Ors (EEA; deportation appeals; procedure) [2024] UKUT 66 (IAC) ... 453
Rights of appeal – deportation – EEA nationals – scope of protection under the Withdrawal Agreement – scope of protection under domestic law

RISK ON RETURN

Honour Killings

ASO (Iraq) v Secretary of State for the Home Department [2023] EWCA Civ 1282 ... 145
Honour killings – illicit relationship – Iraq – evidence – assessment of evidence – credibility of the claimants – standard of proof – protection claim – availability of direct evidence from country of origin

Non-State Actors

HA v United Kingdom (Application no. 30919/20) ECtHR (Fourth Section)... 230
Non-state actors – stateless Palestinian living in Lebanese refugee camp – forced recruitment – rival paramilitary factions – asylum – Article 1D – sufficiency of protection – availability of UNRWA protection – human rights – Article 3 of the ECHR – prohibition of torture

NC v Secretary of State for the Home Department [2023] EWCA Civ 1379 ... 194
Non-state actors – paragraph 276ADE(1)(vi) of the Immigration Rules – reintegration to home country – consideration of obstacles – subjective fear – evidence – assessment of evidence – state protection – family connections – failure to consider objective evidence

AZIZI (SUCCINCT CREDIBILITY FINDINGS; LIES)

UPPER TRIBUNAL (IMMIGRATION AND ASYLUM CHAMBER)

Dove J (President), CMG Ockelton (Vice President) and Blum UTJ

[2024] UKUT 65 (IAC)
13 August 2023

Evidence – credibility of the claimants – lies in previous asylum appeal – Devaseelan principles applied – explanation for telling lies considered – procedure and process – conduct of appeal – consideration of principal contentious issues – succinct credibility findings

    The Claimant, a citizen of Iraq, arrived in the United Kingdom in December 2007 and applied for asylum. He claimed that he was in fact a citizen of Iran and that his father was a member of the KDPI, who had been arrested and tortured. The Claimant had also carried out duties for the KDPI. He claimed that if he was returned to Iran, he would be arrested, ill-treated, and imprisoned for his KDPI activities. The Secretary of State for the Home Department refused the application. In 2010, the First-tier Tribunal ('FtT') dismissed the Claimant's appeal against that decision, finding that his account was not credible and that he was an unreliable witness. He became appeal rights exhausted in January 2012 and thereafter returned to Iraq.

    In August 2019, the Claimant returned to the United Kingdom. He lodged further submissions in his case explaining that he would be at risk of being traced and killed by his in-laws on return to Iraq due to having married their daughter without their approval. The Secretary of State refused the claim, relying on the principles in *Devaseelan (Second Appeals – ECHR – Extra-Territorial Effect) Sri Lanka** [2002] UKIAT 702 and the comprehensive adverse credibility findings which had been made in the 2010 decision. On appeal before the FtT, the Claimant admitted that when he came to the United Kingdom in 2007, he had lied about his true nationality and reasons for seeking asylum. He said that he had feared returning to Iraq because of potential violence from his future wife's family but had been advised by other migrants to change his story. When he returned to Iraq in 2012, the family reached a settlement and he married his wife in 2013. He claimed, however, that he had to move around Iraq driven by his fear of his wife's family and their persistent threats against him. That fear led him to flee Iraq again leaving his wife and children with his mother-in-law.

    In February 2023, the FtT Judge dismissed the appeal, finding that the Claimant was completely incapable of belief as a result of his actions in his previous claim. Moreover, the Judge concluded that the evidence did not support the Claimant's assertion that he was at risk. Finally, the Judge found the claim implausible as the marriage was arranged by both families and the couple had lived together for a non-insignificant period of time and had children. It was highly unlikely that the Claimant would be at risk considering the marriage was agreed.

Before the Upper Tribunal, the Claimant submitted that the FtT Judge had failed to administer what was known in the context of a criminal case as a *Lucas* direction, namely, to ask why, if a person had admitted to lying about something, he had done so, since simply lying about one matter would not necessarily imply that he had lied about everything or indeed other matters. Moreover, he submitted that the Judge had failed to adopt a proper approach to credibility by examining the details, consistency and plausibility of the Claimant's account prior to arriving at his conclusions and had applied the wrong standard of proof. Finally, he submitted that the Judge had failed to assess the potential corroborative value from available country evidence.

Held, dismissing the appeal:

(1) There was no substance to the criticisms of the FtT's decision. Under the *Devaseelan* principles, the starting point was whether there were reasons to depart from findings reached in the 2010 decision in order to conclude that the Claimant was credible in relation to his current account, or which would justify reaching a different conclusion. The Claimant had previously told lies to seek to persuade the authorities to grant him protection on an entirely false basis to avoid being returned to Iraq. They were not lies which arose from some unrelated motivation, such as shame, humiliation, or confusion. Therefore, the administration of a *Lucas* direction was of very limited assistance to the Claimant. Moreover, the FtT Judge had addressed the Claimant's explanation for lying on the earlier occasion and rejected it on the basis that if he had been genuinely at risk then he should have said so (*paras 14 – 15*).

(2) The FtT Judge did not fail to have regard to the detail, consistency and plausibility of the Claimant's case. Whilst the reasons which the Judge gave were brief, they addressed each of the points in the Claimant's evidence upon which reliance was placed to suggest that his current account might establish a genuine claim for asylum. Furthermore, the Judge had reasonably concluded that the Claimant would not be at risk from his wife's family given that her family had arranged the marriage, they had lived together for a period of time and had children together. Given the background of the earlier 2010 appeal, and the Judge's concerns in relation to the quality of the evidence the Claimant had produced in the current appeal, it was open to the Judge to conclude as he did that the Claimant was 'completely incapable of belief'. There was no evidence that the Judge had applied the wrong standard of proof (*paras 16 – 18*).

(3) Although the FtT Judge did not expressly refer to an extract of country evidence referenced in the Claimant's skeleton argument, that could not amount to an error of law in the particular circumstances of the case. The Judge had focused on the principal controversial issues in the appeal related to whether the Claimant's account of his own circumstances based on his own evidence and supporting documents was to be found credible. Bearing in mind the fundamental difficulties that the Claimant faced, a reference to selected gobbets of country information from sources suggesting that wrongdoing against a family's honour did not diminish over time was peripheral and provided very little assistance to save the credibility of the Claimant's case which was already fundamentally undermined. It was not a necessary requirement for the FtT Judge to engage with each and every point that was made on behalf of a claimant, but rather in reaching a reasoned conclusion to

address the principal contentious issues which required to be resolved. The FtT Judge was not required to give reasons for his reasons and had adequately explained in a succinct determination why the appeal had been dismissed. In short, the determination was of adequate length to serve the purpose of explaining the decision in the case *(paras 19 – 20)*.

Cases referred to:

AU v Secretary of State for the Home Department [2020] EWCA Civ 338; [2020] 1 WLR 1562; [2020] Imm AR 1008
Devaseelan (Second Appeals – ECHR – Extra-Territorial Effect) Sri Lanka* [2002] UKIAT 702; [2003] Imm AR 1
MAH (Egypt) v Secretary of State for the Home Department [2023] EWCA Civ 216; [2023] Imm AR 713

Representation

Mr M Symes instructed by Barns Harrild & Dyer, for the Claimant;
Mr D Clarke, Senior Home Office Presenting Officer, for the Secretary of State.

Judgment

MR JUSTICE DOVE:

Introduction

[1] The appellant is a national of Iraq who was born on 14th October 1979. He appeals with permission from a decision of the First-tier Tribunal ("FtT") dated 11th February 2023.

The Appellant's First Asylum Claim

[2] The appellant initially arrived in the United Kingdom on 5th December 2007 and claimed asylum on the same date. That asylum claim was eventually refused on 23rd April 2010. The appellant appealed to the FtT, and his appeal was dismissed by a determination dated 25th August 2010. The appellant's claim to refugee status, which was supported by the evidence which he gave in that appeal, was that he was in fact a citizen of Iran (although this was explicitly not accepted by the respondent). The appellant claimed that his father was a member of the KDPI, who had been arrested and tortured and who had involved the appellant in carrying out duties for the KDPI. These duties included travel to a nearby settlement to support the distribution of propaganda and the hanging of posters and the writing of slogans upon walls. Having been warned by his father that the person who he had assisted had been arrested he went into hiding, following which he received a message that his father had been arrested and held as hostage for the appellant. This led to the appellant departing Iran and claiming that if he were returned there, he would be arrested, ill-treated, and imprisoned for his KDPI activities.

[3] In addition to the appellant giving evidence, he called a witness who he had encountered by chance in the United Kingdom and who claimed that he knew the appellant's father from party meetings between 2000 and 2004. This witness was called to support the appellant's account that he came from the village that he claimed as his home and that his family were involved in the KDPI.

[4] Having heard this evidence the FtT Judge concluded that the evidence of the appellant's witness was wholly unreliable and lacking credibility. The FtT Judge went on to conclude, based on errors in the appellant's understanding of the Farsi calendar, the implausibility of his story, his account in relation to contact with his family and the fact that he could have claimed asylum in France, that the appellant's account was also not credible and that he was an unreliable witness. He concluded that "his story is a fabrication and that he has never been involved with the KDPI and is not known to, or wanted by, the authorities in Iran". On this basis the appeal was dismissed.

[5] Whilst the appellant was granted permission to appeal to the Upper Tribunal on 9th December 2011 the Upper Tribunal dismissed his appeal on all grounds. The appellant therefore became appeal rights exhausted on 11th January 2012 and although further submissions were lodged on his behalf on 6th August 2012 these were refused on 21st August 2012. Following this it appears that the appellant returned to Iraq.

The Current Proceedings

[6] The appellant claims that he left Iraq in August 2019, and then travelled via Turkey, Greece and Italy to France, prior to coming to the UK by lorry. On 3rd January 2020 the appellant lodged further submissions in his case explaining in particular that he would be at risk of being traced and killed by his in-laws on return to Iraq due to having married their daughter without their approval. This claim was refused by the respondent in a detailed refusal letter addressing a number of potential issues, but commencing from the application of the principle established by the starred case of *Devaseelan* [2002] UKIAT 00702, and in particular relying upon the comprehensive adverse credibility findings which had been made in the earlier appeal by the FtT Judge who had found that he was not a reliable witness. The respondent was not able to identify any basis upon which the appellant's claim could be allowed.

[7] For the purposes of the FtT hearing the appellant produced a witness statement in which he explained that in fact when he came to the UK for the first time it was as a result of fear for his life as a result of potential violence from his wife's family which had forced him to flee Iraq. He said this in the witness statement in relation to his earlier account:

"5. I did not tell the Home Office my true reason for claiming asylum previously. When I was in France on my way to the UK, I met some Kurdish migrants who asked me where I was from. They said that if I was from Iraq then I would definitely be sent back to my home country once I got to the UK. As I was fearful, at my asylum interview, I lied about my nationality and the reasons that I feared returning home to Iran. I thought that if I said I was from Iraq then I would be sent back to Raina and my problem with the other family was still ongoing and they had not been resolved yet.

6. I was advised to say that I supported the Democratic party and that I was from Iran. I did not mean to mislead the authorities, but I relied on other people who spoke my language in the UK. I genuinely believed that if I told the Home Office what my true nationality was, then I would be sent back to Iraq."

[8] The witness statement went on to explain that having fled Iraq in 2007, his wife had first got married in 2008 but her family were unhappy because of her earlier relationship with the appellant and the fact that she was not a virgin at the time of this wedding. This led to the failure of the marriage. Her first husband became violent, leading to the grant of a divorce. The appellant provided a copy of the divorce document which he furnished to the hearing. There followed a "Sullah" in which a negotiated family settlement was arrived at permitting the appellant to return to marry his wife and leading to him returning to Iraq in 2012 and marrying her in 2013. The witness statement went on to describe the appellant continuing to move around Iraq driven, he stated, by his fear of his wife's family and their persistent threats and pursuit of him. This fear led him to flee Iraq again leaving his wife and children with his mother-in-law. The fear that he has would not permit him to relocate anywhere within Iraq.

[9] In addition to the documentation relating to the divorce, the appellant produced identity documentation with respect to his wife and children along with text messages from 2020 threatening him and his wife and children.

[10] A skeleton argument was submitted on behalf of the appellant which made reference to objective evidence related to the resolution of tribal matters, and the risk to family members of reprisals, which identified as follows:

"A also accepts that he accepted voluntary return to Iraq but only after his father spoke to his wife's family and they agreed to accept the marriage between A and his wife [AB: WS: para 9]. A instructs that there was still animosity because in the meantime the family had arranged a marriage between his wife and a third party but this marriage ended in divorce once the husband was made aware of A's relationship with his wife before her marriage. A instructs that the family still believe that he brought shame and dishonour on their family and so A's life and the life of his children are at risk as intimated by the messages received by A.

- It is submitted that despite the resolution of *tribal matters that objective evidence still point to the risk of family members of reprisals. In Honour Crimes against Men in Kurdistan Region of Iraq (KRI) and the Availability of Protection, 'Report from Danish Immigration Service's fact-finding mission to Erbil, Sulemaniyah and Dahuk, KRI' dated 6 to 20 January 2010* at page 5 states that: Mahdi M. Qadr and Fakhir Ibrahim, PAO, Erbil, stated that the concern of a wrongdoing against a family's honour does not diminish over the years. Wrong-doing against honour is considered unforgivable.

And:

Sardasht Abdulrahman Majid, Director, and Aree Jaza Mahmoud, Lawyer, Democracy and Human Rights Development Center (DHRD), Sulemaniyah, emphasized that honour is not a short-term matter. Honour is eternal in the sense that the offended family may seek retribution for years to come, or even for generations.

Issue 2 – *Whether A can obtain sufficient protection from his aggressors.*

- In *Honour Crimes against men* in KRI, it states: *Possibility for protection for heterosexual men*[.] There are no shelters for men in KRI. ... There are very few actors protecting men in conflicts; one source pointed to an organisation called 'Men's Union Organisation'; the same source said that this organisation will not be able to protect men in a broader sense. ... A man might be protected by friends, or he has to run away. For a man who flees abroad, sometimes Interpol will be contacted in case he is accused of rape or killing. The threat against him will remain, but he can easily survive. A man can easily change his name, which makes it easier to survive."

[11] The determination of the FtT Judge commenced with setting out the appellant's immigration history, and then the observations in the reasons for refusal letter from the respondent in respect of the earlier FtT Judge's findings that the appellant was not a credible witness. The FtT Judge recorded the basis of the appellant's claim and his reliance upon the witness statement which he provided and which has been summarised above. He also recorded the nature of the documentation which the appellant relied upon. The FtT Judge recorded that the appellant was cross-examined, and that despite him being married to his wife with her family's agreement he persisted in his claim that her family were not happy with him, even though she was a divorced woman at the time he married her. He continued to claim that her family sought to harm him. The FtT Judge then recorded his findings and conclusions in paragraph 10 of his decision as follows:

"10. The appeal is dismissed. The appellant is not entitled to any relief in the UK. I reach this conclusion for the following reasons;

A. The appellant has shown himself to be completely incapable of belief as a result of his actions in his previous claim. He admits lying about his nationality and lied about the reasons he sought protection. That is unforgiveable in terms of his credibility. He is, in my view, completely incapable of belief after those actions. I reject in its entirety his reasoning for giving completely false information on the last occasion. He is a grown man and if he was genuinely at risk then he should have said so. It shows he is capable of lying to serve his own means and endeavours.

B. The messages he relies upon are not in the remotest persuasive. They could be from anyone. They could even be from the appellant himself using another phone. I place no weight and reliance upon them.

C. The marriage documents do not assist him in his claim. They do not show that he is at risk.

D. His claim is not even plausible. The marriage was arranged by her family and his family and they have lived together for a non-insignificant period of time and had children. It seems highly unlikely that the appellant would be at risk considering it was all agreed."

[12] The FtT Judge went on to conclude that the appellant had and could obtain the necessary documentation to be returned to Iraq and that on the basis of his rejection of the appellant's account the FtT Judge concluded that there was no basis to grant him any form of protection or conclude that there would be any unlawful infringement of his human rights.

Submissions and Conclusions

[13] Mr Symes on behalf of the appellant submits that the determination in this case lapses into errors of law associated with a failure to have regard to material considerations in reaching the conclusions which the judge did, and also failing to provide adequate reasons. The particular points raised in connection with this ground are, firstly, that the reasoning provided needed to show that every factor which might tell in favour of the applicant had been properly taken into account consistent with the understanding of anxious scrutiny in asylum claims provided by Carnwath LJ in *YH* [2010] EWCA Civ 116. Secondly, following the decision in *Uddin* [2020] EWCA Civ 338 there was a failure by the judge to administer to himself what would be known in the context of a criminal case as a *Lucas* direction, namely to ask why, if a person has admitted to lying about something, they had done so, since simply lying about one matter would not necessarily imply that they had lied about everything or indeed other matters. Mr Symes submits that the judge failed to take this approach. Thirdly, the judge failed to adopt a proper approach to credibility examining the details, consistency and plausibility of the appellant's account prior to arriving at his conclusions. Fourthly, it is submitted by Mr Symes that the judge failed to assess the potential corroborative value from available country evidence. Fifthly, it is submitted that following the recent decision of the Court of Appeal in *MAH (Egypt)* [2023] EWCA Civ 216 the reasoning betrays that the judge failed to apply the correct standard of proof.

[14] Having carefully considered each of these criticisms of the judge's decision we are unable to accept that there is any substance to them. As both the reasons for refusal letter and also the FtT Judge identified, the starting point for the consideration of the appellant's appeal was, in accordance with the well-known *Devaseelan* principles, the previous decision reached in 2010. In that first decision the FtT Judge concerned had reached the conclusion, having analysed the appellant's account, that he was not a credible witness, and indeed that he had adduced further evidence from another witness also lacking credibility in relation to the key issues. The starting point was, therefore, whether there were reasons to depart from those earlier findings in order to conclude that the appellant was credible in relation to his current account or which would justify reaching a different conclusion.

[15] As is evident from what is set out above, in that the appellant accepted that his previous account had been completely false it follows that in fact the judge in 2010 had been entitled to conclude that that account was lacking in credibility. It turns out that this is the appellant's case in the current appeal. This perhaps then brings into focus the appellant's submission in relation to the need for a *Lucas* direction in respect of those earlier lies. It appears to us that there are two difficulties for the appellant in making that submission. Firstly, if one enquires as to why the appellant previously told lies, then the reason for doing so was to seek to persuade the authorities to grant him protection on an entirely false basis so as to avoid being returned to Iraq. They were not lies which arose from some unrelated motivation, such as shame, humiliation, or confusion. Indeed, his observation in his witness statement that he did not mean to mislead the authorities by giving them a false account does not assist in this connection either. In the particular circumstances of this case, therefore, the administration of a *Lucas* direction is of very limited assistance to the appellant. The second difficulty which lies in the way of this submission is that the judge addressed his explanation for lying on the earlier occasion in paragraph 10a, and rejected it on the basis that if he had been genuinely at risk then he should have said so. Thus, the judge did consider the question of why the appellant lied on the previous occasion whether the motivation or explanation for those lies was of any assistance to him and, in our view understandably, rejected the appellant's submission.

[16] Given the particular circumstances of this case, and in particular the earlier findings in the 2010 appeal, we are unable to accept the submission that the judge failed to have regard to the detail, consistency and plausibility of the appellant's case. Whilst the reasons which the judge gave were brief, they addressed each of the points in the appellant's evidence upon which reliance was placed to suggest that his current account might establish a genuine claim for asylum. As set out above the judge dealt with the appellant's explanation for why he had lied in his previous claim and dismissed that for the reasons he gave.

[17] The judge went on to consider both the messages upon which the appellant relied and also the marriage document explaining why, in his view, neither of those pieces of evidence were material which persuaded him of the appellant's account. The judge then went on to consider plausibility and, again, for the reasons which he gave, concluded that bearing in mind the marriage had been arranged by the appellant's wife's family, and that they had lived together for a period of time and had children together, it was highly unlikely the appellant would be at risk. This led to the judge concluding that the claim was not plausible.

[18] The appellant's contention that it may be that the judge had applied the wrong standard of proof is not supported by the reasoning which the judge gives for his decision. Bearing in mind the background of the earlier 2010 appeal, and his concerns in relation to the quality of the evidence the appellant had produced in the current appeal, it was open to the judge to conclude as he did that the appellant was "completely incapable of belief". Having considered the judge's reasons we are unable to identify any evidence that the wrong standard of proof was applied.

[19] Finally, whilst it is correct to observe that an extract of country evidence was referred to in the appellant's skeleton argument, and not expressly referenced by the judge, we are not satisfied that this could amount to an error of law in the particular circumstances of this case. In reaching his conclusions in paragraph 10 of the determination the judge had in our view focused on the principal controversial issues in the appeal related to whether the appellant's account of his own

circumstances based on his own evidence and supporting documents was to be found credible. Bearing in mind the fundamental difficulties that the appellant faced, a reference to selected gobbets of country information from sources suggesting that wrongdoing against a family's honour did not diminish over time was peripheral and provided very little assistance to save the credibility of the appellant's case which was already fundamentally undermined. It is not a necessary requirement for the FtT judge to engage with each and every point that is made on behalf of an appellant, but rather in reaching a reasoned conclusion to address the principal contentious issues which require to be resolved. It was not an error for the judge not to address this point directly against the background of the strength of his other conclusions in relation to the credibility of the appellant's account. Whilst in his skeleton argument Mr Symes references other aspects of the country evidence which he submits would be of relevance to risk on return, in so far as it is suggested they provide further context to the appellant's account they were not matters which it appears were drawn to the judge's attention and relied upon in the presentation of the appellant's case.

[20] Having considered each of the points raised on behalf of the appellant as criticisms of the FtT judge's credibility findings we are satisfied that none are of substance and, in reality, the judge engaged with and took account of all of the matters which might have told in favour of the appellant in the particular circumstances pertaining to this case. As we have stated, he dealt with all of the principal controversial issues upon which the decision in this case turned, and thus no lengthier decision was required. The FtT judge was not required to give reasons for his reasons, and had adequately explained in this succinct determination why he had dismissed this appeal. In short, the determination was of adequate length to serve the purpose of explaining the decision in the case.

[21] Mr Symes accepted during the course of argument and indeed at paragraph 9 of his skeleton argument that ground 2, namely the assessment of risk on return, followed from the establishment of flaws in the FtT judge's credibility findings under ground 1. For the reasons that we have given we are not satisfied that there is any error of law in the FtT judge's credibility findings for the reasons which we have given and, therefore, it follows that ground 2 does not arise. For all of these reasons, therefore, this appeal must be dismissed.

Notice of Decision

The appeal is dismissed.

FXJ v SECRETARY OF STATE FOR THE HOME DEPARTMENT AND HOME OFFICE

COURT OF APPEAL

Underhill LJ (Vice President of the Court of Appeal (Civil Division)), Lady Simler and Andrews LJ

[2023] EWCA Civ 1357
20 November 2023

Human rights – Article 8 of the ECHR – private and family life – delay – impact of delay on mental health – questions 4 and 5 of Razgar *[2004] UKHL 27*

The Claimant was a national of Somalia who suffered from serious mental illness including psychotic and depressive symptoms. He arrived in the United Kingdom in October 2001 and sought asylum. His application was refused, but he was granted a period of exceptional leave. The Secretary of State for the Home Department refused a subsequent asylum application in January 2014. The Upper Tribunal ('UT') allowed the Claimant's appeal against that decision in December 2015.

In July 2016, the Secretary of State granted the Claimant refugee status with five years' leave to remain. During the delay between the time for appealing the UT decision expiring in February 2016 and the Claimant being granted refugee status in July 2016, the Claimant's mental health deteriorated. In May 2016 he was arrested and admitted to hospital under the Mental Health Act 1983. After discharge from hospital, and despite confirmation that he had leave to remain in the United Kingdom, the Claimant continued to abuse substances and failed to comply with his medication regime. Expert psychiatric evidence stated that the delay in granting refugee status was an aggravating factor which had made the schizophrenic relapse longer and more severe.

In 2017 the Claimant brought proceedings in the County Court against the Secretary of State. He claimed damages alleging negligence and breach of his rights under Article 8 ECHR because of the five-month delay in granting him refugee status. The County Court rejected the negligence claim. It held that the Claimant's pleadings had alleged that the Secretary of State had failed to confer a benefit on him, rather than that her actions had harmed him. Accordingly, the Secretary of State had owed the Claimant no duty of care to make a prompt decision on his immigration status. The Court also rejected the Article 8 claim, holding that the delay of five months was a short period and any interference with Article 8 rights was justified by the public interest in immigration control. The High Court upheld the Country Court's decision.

Before the Court of Appeal, the Claimant argued that the County Court's conclusion that no duty of care was owed by the Secretary of State was wrong. The Claimant also challenged the conclusion that there had been no breach of Article 8 ECHR and asserted that the balancing exercise conducted by the High Court was flawed.

Held, dismissing the appeal:

(1) The County Court had not erred in characterising the claim as a failure to confer a benefit. As a matter of pleading, the case had been advanced on the sole basis of a failure to make prompt decisions about the Claimant's immigration status, leading to delay in the grant of leave to remain. The Secretary of State had been under no duty to exercise appeal rights in a particular way, still less to make a status decision within a particular timeframe. The County Court's starting point was, correctly, the pleaded case as set out in the Particulars of Claim, which alleged a duty of care to confer on him a prompt immigration status decision and that a failure to do so caused harm. The courts below were amply entitled to understand the pleaded case as limited to a failure to confer a benefit (paras 36 – 40).

(2) The decision in *R v Secretary of State for the Home Department ex parte Razgar* [2004] UKHL 27 listed five questions to be considered when a removal decision was challenged on Article 8 ECHR grounds. While the questions in *Razgar* related to the specific context of a proposed removal, they could be adapted to deal with conduct and interference in a particular case and provided a structured basis for analysing an Article 8 claim. In the instant appeal, the focus was on questions four and five (paras 52 – 53 and 57).

(3) In most cases, the interference relied on was a positive act on the part of the state, such as a removal or deportation decision. In the instant appeal, the interference flowed from an inaction on the part of the state. Although inaction could amount to an interference, it was less obvious how questions four and five in *Razgar* might be analysed in the context of inaction or delay as delay could never have a legitimate aim or in itself be justified. A broader judgement was required. First, where a case alleged delay, it was necessary to identify the period of culpable delay. Reasonable, robust decision-making took time and delay in the sense of a lapse of time was unavoidable. Hindsight was unlikely to be a reliable basis to determine what was reasonable in a particular case. Secondly, there could come a point where the lapse in time was so significant with regard to its length, seriousness and culpability that the gravity of its consequences could be regarded as a lack of respect for the individual's private life rights. Thus, it was necessary to weigh the culpability of the delay and the severity of its consequences to determine whether the operation of the administrative system in a particular case had been proportionate to its public aims or whether it had reached the threshold of being disproportionate: *Anufrijeva v London Borough of Southwark* [2003] EWCA Civ 1406 applied (paras 58 – 61).

(4) In the instant case, the courts below found the five-month delay to be relatively short. It involved no breach of legal duty and there was no finding of any intention to cause delay, nor had any separate element of culpability been identified. The parties agreed that the impact of the delay on the Claimant's mental health had been a significant aggravating factor that rendered his schizophrenic relapse more severe and longer in duration. However, that agreed description offered no means of assessing the quality of the aggravation or its severity in the context of the Claimant's already bad mental health. In fact, the expert evidence showed that the Claimant was on a downward spiral before the UT hearing at which his appeal was allowed. There was no evidence, nor means of assessing, how and in what way his symptoms were more severe or for how much longer they lasted as a consequence of the delay. The courts below had been entitled to conclude that the effect of the delay on the Claimant's mental health was not disproportionate (paras 64 – 65).

FXJ v SSHD

Cases referred to:

Advocate General for Scotland v Adiukwu [2020] CSIH 47; [2021] Imm AR 413
Anufrijeva and Another v London Borough of Southwark; R (on the application of 'N') v Secretary of State for the Home Department; R (on the application of 'M') v Secretary of State for the Home Department [2003] EWCA Civ 1406; [2004] QB 1124; [2004] 2 WLR 603; [2004] 1 All ER 833
Customs and Excise v Barclays Bank plc [2006] UKHL 28; [2007] 1 AC 181; [2006] 3 WLR 1; [2006] 4 All ER 256
FXJ v Secretary of State for the Home Department and Home Office [2022] EWHC 1531 (QB); [2023] QB 390; [2022] 3 WLR 881; [2023] 2 All ER 489
H v United Kingdom 1987 ECHR 9580/81, ECtHR; (1988) 10 EHRR 95
Home Office v Mohammed and Others [2011] EWCA Civ 351; [2011] 1 WLR 2862
Michael and Others v Chief Constable of South Wales Police and Another [2015] UKSC 2; [2015] AC 1732; [2015] 2 WLR 343; [2015] 2 All ER 635
Poole Borough Council v GN (through his litigation friend 'The Official Solicitor') and Another [2019] UKSC 25; [2020] AC 780; [2019] 2 WLR 1478; [2019] 4 All ER 581
R v Secretary of State for the Home Department ex parte Razgar [2004] UKHL 27; [2004] 2 AC 368; [2004] 3 WLR 58; [2004] 3 All ER 821; [2004] Imm AR 381; [2004] INLR 349
Robinson v Chief Constable of West Yorkshire Police [2018] UKSC 4; [2018] AC 736; [2018] 2 WLR 595; [2018] 2 All ER 1041
W v Home Office [1997] EWCA Civ 1052; [1997] Imm AR 302

Legislation and international instruments judicially considered:

European Convention on Human Rights, Article 8
Human Rights Act 1998, section 7

Representation

Mr *D Chirico* and Ms *A Nicolaou* instructed by Wilsons Solicitors LLP, for the Claimant;
Mr *R Cohen* instructed by the Government Legal Department, for the Respondents.

Judgment

This judgment was handed down remotely at 10.30am on 20 November 2023 by circulation to the parties or their representatives by e-mail and by release to the National Archives.

LADY SIMLER:

Introduction

[1] This appeal raises the question whether the Secretary of State for the Home Department, the respondent, owed a duty of care in tort to the appellant and/or breached his article 8 rights, in circumstances where a delay in making a refugee status decision in his case (during which a late appeal was withdrawn) were significant aggravating factors that rendered a relapse in the appellant's mental health more severe and longer in duration.

[2] The appellant is a Somali national (now recognised as a refugee in the United Kingdom in consequence of his well-founded fear of persecution in Somalia). He suffers from a severe and enduring mental illness that includes psychotic and depressive symptoms pre-dating the events that are the subject of this appeal. He first entered the United Kingdom on 1 October 2001 and applied for asylum. His application was refused and his appeal dismissed, but he was granted exceptional leave to remain until 2003. A subsequent application for asylum was also refused and an appeal dismissed but meanwhile, in August 2007, he was convicted of robbery and sentenced to 18 months' imprisonment. As a result, the respondent served him with a deportation order once his appeal rights were exhausted in February 2009. The appellant did not leave but remained as an overstayer. His immigration status was finally determined by the respondent on 27 January 2014, rejecting his asylum claim. The appellant challenged the respondent's decision and was ultimately successful in his appeal on article 3 grounds.

[3] This appeal and the underlying proceedings arise out of the events that followed the appellant's successful appeal against the respondent's refusal of asylum, starting with his asylum appeal being allowed by the Upper Tribunal by a decision promulgated on 4 December 2015, and concluding with the grant of refugee status with five years' leave to remain on 23 July 2016. In particular, the appellant challenged the respondent's delay in granting him status as a refugee from 10 February 2016 (when time for appealing the Upper Tribunal decision expired), together with the respondent's decision to initiate and then withdraw a late application to appeal to the Court of Appeal against the Upper Tribunal's decision.

[4] The appellant brought proceedings for damages in negligence, misfeasance in public office and under section 7 of the Human Rights Act 1998. The negligence claim alleged, in summary, that the respondent owed him a common law "duty to make a prompt decision on the implementation of his successful appeal and on the grant of leave to remain in the UK", particularly in light of his known vulnerabilities as an asylum seeker suffering from serious mental illness. He alleged that the duty was breached (among other things) by the failure to act properly and expeditiously when taking decisions regarding his immigration status and by making and then withdrawing a late application (characterised as futile) for permission to appeal out of time in the period 10 February to 23 July 2016. The claims were all denied by the respondent.

[5] At the trial (on liability only), the parties' psychiatric experts agreed that:

"the Home Office appeal and the resultant delay in his being granted refugee status were significant aggravating factors that rendered his 2016–7 episode of schizophrenic relapse more severe and longer in duration."

[6] The trial judge, HHJ Baucher, dismissed all three claims. In summary:

i) *Negligence*: she held that no common law duty of care was owed by the respondent to the appellant in the circumstances of this case: the true relationship between the parties during the material period was one of litigation, and as a litigant the respondent owed no duty to the appellant. But even if the respondent was exercising statutory responsibility for immigration control, the pleaded allegations were directed at omissions rather than actions, and the respondent had not voluntarily assumed responsibility in any sense. No duty of care arose on this basis either accordingly.

ii) Judge Baucher found in the alternative, that there was no breach of duty: although provided with extracts from file notes passing between the respondent's officers at the material time, she did not have a complete picture of what the respondent was doing or thinking, and the file notes were made while the case was the subject of litigation and that formed part of the context. She held that there was no evidence on which she could properly find that the respondent failed to have adequate systems of communication, either internally or with legal representatives. She was not provided with details of exactly what passed internally or externally and observed that litigation privilege would inevitably apply. She also held that there was no evidence that the respondent failed to act expeditiously. Moreover, in relation to the aborted attempt to appeal out of time, the discussions about this case did not disclose any breach of duty.

iii) *Misfeasance*: Judge Baucher rejected this claim based on untargeted malice in the pursuit of a futile appeal against a known Somali refugee suffering from serious mental illness, and in the sending of misleading correspondence about the appeal. She held that the respondent was entitled to consider the merits of a late appeal and that none of the matters complained of in relation to the appeal, even taken at their highest, could properly be considered unlawful; nor did they disclose subjective recklessness. Likewise, she rejected the claim that the correspondence and application were misleading, but even if they were, there was no unlawful conduct.

iv) *Article 8*: Judge Baucher held that the respondent's delay in implementing the appellant's grant of status was not substantial. She continued:

"118. ... On any consideration, five months was a short period and I am satisfied that period of delay does not engage a breach of Article 8.

119. Even if I am wrong I am satisfied, in any event that any interference would be justified. There is important public interest in immigration control, the deportation of offenders and parties being able to seek permission to appeal so as to engage Article 8(2)."

[7] The appellant appealed unsuccessfully against all of those conclusions (judgment of Choudhury J, reported as [2022] EWHC 1531 (QB), [2023] QB 390). I shall return to both the judgment of Choudhury J and HHJ Baucher below.

[8] There are three grounds of appeal. The first two challenge Judge Baucher's conclusion that no duty of care was owed by the respondent to the appellant in the circumstances of this case. Ground two (which is logically anterior to ground one) argues that the case falls within an exception to the general rule that public bodies do not ordinarily owe a duty of care when fulfilling their public functions, because the case is properly characterised as involving conduct that caused harm or made things worse. Ground one is only relevant if the appellant succeeds in establishing a *prima facie* duty on ground two. It contends that once a statutory appeal was under way (with the express function of determining the United Kingdom's responsibilities under international law), the respondent had a dual role as both primary immigration decision-maker and litigant, and so is not caught by the well-established exception identified by the judge. This is a special category of litigation which is exempt from the rule that litigants do not owe any duty of care to one another. The third ground of appeal challenges the conclusion that there was no breach of article 8. The appellant contends that the balancing exercise conducted by Choudhury J was flawed because it failed to adopt an individualised approach to the question of proportionality. There is no challenge to the dismissal of the claim for misfeasance.

The facts

[9] The facts were helpfully set out by HHJ Baucher in her judgment at paragraphs 10 to 15 dealing with events before the material period, and paragraphs 16 to 49 dealing with the material period. They were summarised by Choudhury J and I gratefully adopt much of his summary in what follows.

[10] As indicated, the appellant exhausted his immigration appeal rights in February 2009 at which point the respondent made an order to deport him as a foreign national criminal. On 4 March 2009, the appellant made further representations seeking revocation of the deportation order. The respondent refused those representations on 27 January 2014. That was the respondent's final immigration decision in this matter before litigation ensued.

[11] The appellant appealed the respondent's refusal decision to the First-tier Tribunal (Immigration and Asylum Chamber) ("the FtT"). The respondent resisted the appeal. By a decision dated 15 May 2015, the FtT dismissed the appeal, but granted permission to appeal to the Upper Tribunal ("the UT"). By a decision dated 16 October 2015, the UT set aside the FtT's decision on the ground that it contained a material error of law and ordered a rehearing. In doing so, UT Judge Finch observed that it was "clear from the medical evidence that any ongoing delay in resolving this case is likely to be detrimental to the appellant's mental health".

[12] The rehearing took place very promptly on 16 November 2015, and the UT allowed the appeal by a decision promulgated on 4 December 2015. In an internal post-hearing note, the respondent acknowledged that the appeal would be allowed,

in part on the basis of evidence which the respondent had herself provided about the likely poor treatment in Somalia of people suffering from serious mental illness.

[13] By an application dated 17 December 2015, the respondent sought permission to appeal the UT's decision from the UT itself. That application was refused by the UT by a decision dated 5 January 2016. The respondent was then entitled to renew the application for permission to appeal directly to the Court of Appeal. The deadline for doing so was 10 February 2016. That deadline expired without any such application to this court being made.

[14] By letter dated 19 February 2016, the appellant's solicitors, Wilson Solicitors LLP, entered into correspondence with the respondent requesting that the appellant be granted settled status "forthwith" following his successful appeal. They reminded the respondent of the serious mental health problems he suffered and made clear that delay in granting him status "is likely to have a detrimental effect on his mental health". In the absence of any substantive response, the solicitors issued a pre-action letter dated 1 March 2016.

[15] On 15 April 2016, more than two months after the expiry of the appeal time limit, the respondent filed a notice of appeal with the Court of Appeal together with an application for an extension of time.

[16] Although a late appeal was lodged, internal file notes dated 26 and 27 April 2016 record the views of one of the responsible Home Office officers that "no further challenge [was] proposed" and that a "final sign off [was awaited] from Mike Wells". This suggested that the respondent was considering withdrawing the appeal.

[17] The appeal was reviewed by Mr Wells (a senior Home Office official with authority to "sign off" on the appeal) on 10 May 2016. He concluded:

> "I agree that we should not pursue this case. I have previously expressed concerns about the Home Office position with regards to Somalis with mental illness. The UT finding – extract below – is clear (a) that those with mental health disorders are often subject to humiliating conditions including that they are often chained; and (b) that the chaining of mental health patients amounts to inhuman and degrading treatment.
>
> As I have previously stated, unless we wish to challenge one or other of these findings it follows that Somalis whom we accept have serious mental health issues cannot normally be returned. There would have to be exceptional factors such as a strong family network in the Mogadishu area to have even a chance of overcoming that presumption that Article 3 applies.
>
> Given that, where we accept that a Somali has serious mental health issues and does not have a strong family support network in Mogadishu, I do not understand why we would not grant leave nor why we would incur taxpayers' money on futile attempts to deport."

The respondent's withdrawal of the appeal very shortly afterwards was confirmed by a court order sealed on 13 May 2016. By letter dated 19 May 2016, the respondent wrote to the appellant's solicitors confirming that he would be granted leave to remain for five years. There was then a delay until 16 June when the appellant completed a biometric residence permit application. On 23 July 2016, the respondent granted the appellant refugee status and leave to remain for five years.

[18] During the period leading up to the withdrawal of the respondent's late application for permission to appeal the UT decision, the appellant's mental health deteriorated. The psychiatric report from Professor Katona MD FRCPsych, dated 15 October 2017, served with the Particulars of Claim, stated that even before the UT hearing at which his appeal was allowed, the appellant became less compliant with medication and his behaviour became more irritable and aggressive. He started expressing persecutory ideas and had resumed heavy drinking by that time. Professor Katona expressed the view that the combination of increased alcohol and illicit drug use, poor medication compliance and the stress of the impending tribunal hearing were likely to have triggered that deterioration. Professor Katona said the deterioration became more marked after the UT decision and as it became clear to the appellant that he might after all not be granted leave to remain in the UK. By January 2016 his deterioration and threatening behaviour had become very marked. He was seen on about 17 May 2016, by Dr Hewitt, consultant forensic psychiatrist, and appeared irritable and expressed a number of psychotic beliefs. He was recorded as having made serious threats. Dr Hewitt was sufficiently concerned to contact the police. The appellant was arrested on 17 May 2016 and admitted to hospital on 18 May 2016, under the provisions of section 2 of the Mental Health Act 1983. He remained in hospital for 43 days.

[19] After his discharge from hospital and despite confirmation that he then had leave to remain in the UK, the appellant was recorded by Professor Katona as having resumed and maintained his alcohol and drug use; his mental state had deteriorated; he was hearing voices again, and his self-care had become quite poor. Professor Katona expressed the clinical opinion that:

> "the delay in the Home Office granting him refugee status and the fact that they made a late appeal to the Court of Appeal were important stressors for [him]. In people with schizophrenia, relapse tends to occur at times of stress.
>
> I would therefore conclude that the Home Office's late appeal and the delay in the granting of refugee status were important contributors to [the appellant's] relapse which occurred between July 2015 and his hospitalisation in May 2016. His poor medication compliance, his resumption of alcohol and illicit drug use and the ongoing stress of his immigration uncertainty were however also important contributors. Given that his relapse appears to have had its onset well before the Tribunal decision which the Home Office challenged, neither the Home Office appeal against the Tribunal decision nor the resultant delay in his being granted refugee status can be regarded as causative of his relapse (which was already happening). They were however significant aggravating factors."

[20] I also note that the appellant had at least one further relapse after the material period, leading to a 28 day period of hospitalisation in early 2019. In his 10 October 2019 report, Professor Katona said factors such as the appellant's poor medication compliance, continued heavy use of alcohol and continued use of cannabis, "had been the main 'drivers' of his persistent (albeit fluctuating) psychotic and depressive symptoms and of his 2019 hospitalisation". Professor Katona said that the appellant continued to have a severe and enduring mental illness, requiring ongoing support and medication.

The judgments below

[21] Although this is an appeal from the order of Choudhury J dismissing the first appeal, this court is primarily concerned with the correctness or otherwise of the judgment and reasoning of the trial judge, HHJ Baucher.

[22] In relation to the duty of care question, the judge analysed the relationship between these parties as one of being in litigation against each other following the respondent's determination of the appellant's immigration status on 27 January 2014. From then, she held that the entire matter depended on the progress of his appeals and their determination by the courts. She held that the "whole tenor of the claimant's pleaded claim and the allegations of breach of alleged duty related entirely to the litigation process" and there was "not one single allegation challenging the actual original decision to deport because that was the substance of the litigation". She rejected the contentions that the conduct of the litigation and the conduct of the decisions about the appellant's immigration status were so interlinked that the decision to pursue the appeal could not be viewed as separate from the respondent's immigration responsibilities. The case was indistinguishable from *Customs and Excise Commissioners v Barclays Bank* [2006] UKHL 28, [2007] 1 AC 181 and *Business Computers International Ltd v Registrar of Companies* [1988] Ch 229, where there was held to be no duty of care owed by one litigant to another about how litigation is conducted. Neither the fact that those cases involved pure economic loss whereas this involved personal injury, nor the respondent's special role in making immigration decisions afforded any basis on which to distinguish them.

[23] As for whether the respondent owed the appellant a duty of care in the exercise of her statutory immigration duties, the judge regarded *Advocate General for Scotland v Adiukwu* [2020] CSIH 47, [2020] SLT 861 as highly persuasive and concluded that there was no relevant distinction between that case and this one. She was satisfied that the appellant's pleaded allegations were all directed at omissions, and that the respondent had done nothing to justify any inference that she had assumed responsibility for making an earlier decision. The question whether the respondent had harmed (rather than failed to protect) the appellant did not arise. Accordingly, no duty of care was owed on either of the bases advanced by the appellant.

[24] Choudhury J dismissed the appeal against those findings. He concluded that there was no error in the judge's characterisation of the parties' relationship as one of parties in litigation and agreed that they were in litigation once an appeal challenging the respondent's refusal to grant leave to remain in January 2014 was commenced. The fact that the respondent had an ongoing responsibility for immigration control in relation to the appellant did not alter that position and indeed if it were the case that the existence of an ongoing public law power or duty in respect of a person nullified what would otherwise be a litigation based relationship, then there would be few if any instances of a public authority ever being in such a relationship. Nor was the judge wrong to conclude that this was an omissions case rather than one involving a positive act. Careful analysis of the pleaded claim showed it was directed at omissions rather than actions, and HHJ Baucher also "stood back" to assess what the case was really all about. She considered permissibly that, as in *Adiukwu*, this was a claim about a failure to confer a benefit.

[25] In rejecting the claim under article 8, HHJ Baucher accepted the significance of the five questions identified as relevant to determining an article 8 claim by Lord Bingham in *R (Razgar) v Secretary of State for the Home Department* [2004] UKHL 27, [2004] 2 AC 368, but said they had to be set in context, and "did not need to be determined in that format" in this case. The claim as pleaded was directed only at delay in granting immigration status rather than at the impact on the appellant's mental health; and the delay of five months was a short period. She held that the period of delay did not engage a breach of article 8, and even if she was wrong about that, any interference was justified by the "important public interest in immigration control, the deportation of offenders and parties being able to seek permission to appeal".

[26] Choudhury J identified flaws in the judge's approach to and analysis of the article 8 claim:

"89. There are two flaws in that analysis: first, Mr Chirico was not seeking through his submissions to 'turn the argument' from delay to the effect of that delay. It had clearly been pleaded that the delay in implementing the Appellant's grant of status 'amounted to an interference in his right to respect for his private life (including his mental integrity)'. Thus the *effect* of the delay, i.e. the consequences for the Appellant's mental health, was always part of his case under Article 8. Following a structured approach would have enabled the Judge to identify the distinction between the act complained of (i.e. the delay) and the resultant interference with Article 8 rights (i.e. the effect on the Appellant's mental health). Second, the phrase, 'does not engage a breach of Article 8' conflates two separate issues: the first being whether Article 8 is engaged by reason of the alleged interference; and the second being whether Article 8 is breached, which requires a consideration of whether any interference was justified."

[27] However, he observed that the errors would not warrant any interference by an appellate court if the ultimate conclusion reached by the judge was plainly and unarguably correct. Notwithstanding the flaws he had identified, he concluded that the judge's ultimate analysis was focused on the question of justification and whether the effect of the delay amounted to a proportionate means of achieving a legitimate aim. That question was considered by the judge, albeit briefly, in paragraph 119 of her judgment, as an alternative to her earlier conclusions. Though not as well expressed as perhaps it could have been, Choudhury J understood the judge's conclusion on justification as a finding that the delay and its consequential effects amounted to a proportionate means of achieving the legitimate aim of having effective immigration control systems with rights of appeal for both parties. In any lawful system of immigration control, an adverse decision or an appeal against a positive decision, would be likely to result in anxiety and stress for affected individuals, and delays in the relevant processes would be likely to add to that stress. Such delays are an occasional, unavoidable feature of any system dependent on individual decision-making. He concluded that the judge was entitled to find that the effect of delay, which was not substantial or serious, was not disproportionate. There was no error in her approach which was sufficiently specific in the context of this case.

[28] Choudhury J rejected the argument that by stating that article 8(2) was not engaged, the judge asked herself the wrong question. He found nothing in this point: the judge clearly intended to state that the interference was justified within the meaning of article 8(2). The infelicitous reference to the language of "engagement" did not render that conclusion incorrect.

The appeal: common law duty of care

[29] Against that background I shall start my consideration of this appeal with ground two and whether HHJ Baucher was wrong to characterise the matters complained of as the failure to confer a benefit (or failing to make things better) rather than conduct that caused harm (or made things worse).

[30] There is no dispute that the statutory scheme giving immigration powers to and imposing duties on the respondent does not create a statutory cause of action that sounds in damages. It is common ground that to recover damages in tort the appellant must establish that the events relied on (including any period of delay during which the respondent attempted to pursue a futile appeal to this court) give rise to a common law duty of care.

[31] It is also uncontroversial that the legal principles that apply in answering the question whether the law imposes a concurrent common law duty of care on a public body exercising statutory powers and duties were set out in three decisions of the Supreme Court: *Michael v Chief Constable of South Wales* [2015] UKSC 2, [2015] AC 1732; *Robinson v Chief Constable of West Yorkshire Police* [2018] UKSC 4, [2018] AC 736; and *Poole Borough Council v GN and another* [2019] UKSC 25, [2020] AC 780. It is sufficient for present purposes to refer only to what Lord Reed (with whom the other members of the court agreed) said in his review of the established principles in *Poole* at paragraphs 63 to 65:

"63. Most recently, the decision of this court in 2018 in the case of *Robinson v Chief Constable of West Yorkshire Police* drew together several strands in the previous case law. The case concerned the question whether police officers owed a duty to take reasonable care for the safety of an elderly pedestrian when they attempted to arrest a suspect who was standing beside her and was likely to attempt to escape. The court held that, since it was reasonably foreseeable that the claimant would suffer personal injury as a result of the officers' conduct unless reasonable care was taken, a duty of care arose in accordance with the principle in *Donoghue v Stevenson* [1932] AC 562. Such a duty might be excluded by statute or the common law if it was incompatible with the performance of the officers' functions, but no such incompatibility existed on the facts of the case. The court distinguished between a duty to take reasonable care not to cause injury and a duty to take reasonable care to protect against injury caused by a third party. A duty of care of the latter kind would not normally arise at common law in the absence of special circumstances, such as where the police had created the source of danger or had assumed a responsibility to protect the claimant against it. The decision in *Hill v Chief Constable of West Yorkshire* was explained as an example of the absence of a duty of care to protect against harm caused by a third party, in the absence of special circumstances. It did not lay down a general rule that, for reasons of public policy, the police could never owe a duty of care to members of the public.

64. *Robinson* did not lay down any new principle of law, but three matters in particular were clarified. First, the decision explained, as *Michael* had previously done, that *Caparo* did not impose a universal tripartite test for the existence of a duty of care, but recommended an incremental approach to novel situations, based on the use of established categories of liability as guides, by analogy, to the existence and scope of a duty of care in cases which fall outside them. The question whether the imposition of a duty of care would be fair, just and reasonable forms part of the assessment of whether such an incremental step ought to be taken. It follows that, in the ordinary run of cases, courts should apply established principles of law, rather than basing their decisions on their assessment of the requirements of public policy. Secondly, the decision reaffirmed the significance of the distinction between harming the claimant and failing to protect the claimant from harm (including harm caused by third parties), which was also emphasised in *Mitchell* and *Michael*. Thirdly, the decision confirmed, following *Michael* and numerous older authorities, that public authorities are generally subject to the same general principles of the law of negligence as private individuals and bodies, except to the extent that legislation requires a departure from those principles. That is the basic premise of the consequent framework for determining the existence or nonexistence of a duty of care on the part of a public authority.

65. It follows (1) that public authorities may owe a duty of care in circumstances where the principles applicable to private individuals would impose such a duty, unless such a duty would be inconsistent with, and is therefore excluded by, the legislation from which their powers or duties are derived; (2) that public authorities do not owe a duty of care at common law merely because they have statutory powers or duties, even if, by exercising their statutory functions, they could prevent a person from suffering harm; and (3) that public authorities can come under a common law duty to protect from harm in circumstances where the principles applicable to private individuals or bodies would impose such a duty, as for example where the authority has created the source of danger or has assumed a responsibility to protect the claimant from harm, unless the imposition of such a duty would be inconsistent with the relevant legislation."

[32] A critical distinction is therefore to be drawn between causing harm (or making things worse) where a common law duty of care might arise if fair, just and reasonable to impose it; and failing to confer a benefit (or not making things better), where no such duty will ordinarily be imposed. Despite the fact that there can be difficulties in drawing or applying this distinction in borderline cases, it reflects a recognition that there is a fundamental difference between requiring a person to take care, if they embark on a course of conduct which may harm others, not to create a risk of danger; and requiring a person, who is doing nothing, to take positive action to protect others from harm for which they were not responsible, and to hold them liable in damages if they fail to do so. The law of negligence generally imposes duties not to cause harm to other people or their property and does not generally impose duties to provide them with benefits, which are, in general, voluntarily undertaken rather than being imposed by the common law. As in the case of private individuals, however, a duty to protect from harm or confer some other benefit might arise in particular circumstances, for example where the public body has

created the source of danger or has assumed a responsibility to protect the claimant from harm. Lord Reed explained that drawing the distinction in this way rather than the more traditional distinction between acts and omissions, better conveys the rationale of the distinction drawn in the authorities, and might be easier to apply.

[33] Mr Chirico accepted below and in this court, that the distinction was and remains fundamental to the determination of whether a common law duty of care was owed to the appellant in this case. In his submission, the respondent engaged in positive conduct (by lodging a futile appeal) that made things worse and this was not (as the judge found) simply a case of failing to confer a benefit (the grant of immigration status) or a "pure omissions" case. He accepted however, that if, as HHJ Baucher held, the claim is properly characterised as one involving the failure to confer a benefit, then it would have been necessary for the appellant to show some additional basis for establishing a duty of care (such as the respondent creating the danger of harm or voluntarily assuming responsibility toward him). But since the appellant fairly accepts that no such additional basis exists, the viability of this claim depends on at least some material element being one of conduct causing harm (or making things worse).

[34] Mr Chirico submitted that on a correct application of the principles in *Poole* to the circumstances of this case, the bringing of a late, futile appeal, and the conduct leading to it, amounted to or included conduct causing harm (or making things worse). The fact that this occurred in the context of or alongside a wider series of omissions or failures to confer a benefit does not negate the fact that the respondent also caused harm, and does not deprive the positive conduct of that status. This was a mixed omissions and actions case and HHJ Baucher was wrong to conclude otherwise. Mr Chirico submitted that it is only if, in reality, no event is identified in which a defendant causes harm that the claim can be treated as falling entirely on the "failing to confer a benefit" side of the line. The error made by the judges below was in concluding that if the overall context of a claim was failure to confer a benefit, then isolated actions causing harm can and should be subsumed into that overall context.

[35] There are two ways in which Mr Chirico submits that the respondent caused harm or made things worse for the highly vulnerable appellant in the particular circumstances of this case, where the respondent was on notice that delay was foreseeably likely to cause a deterioration in his mental health. First, the respondent was under a duty not to embark on an active course of action that delayed the grant of immigration status by bringing a futile appeal. Secondly, in the course of the delay in conferring immigration status on the appellant, the respondent brought a futile appeal that caused foreseeable personal injury. Both involved the respondent *conducting* an activity (she decided to bring, and brought, an appeal) and this part of the claim relates to the way in which she did so (including considering whether she took reasonable steps to ensure that she was aware of the merits of the underlying asylum/human rights claim and of the proposed appeal, before bringing it). The conduct caused personal injury by significantly aggravating the appellant's mental illness.

[36] Persuasively as these submissions were advanced, I do not accept that there was any error by either judge below in characterising this as a failure to confer a benefit case. I recognise that the distinction between causing harm and failing to confer a benefit can sometimes be difficult to apply. Indeed, as Choudhury J observed, most conduct relied upon as amounting to negligence can be said to comprise acts and omissions that fall on both sides of the line. However, by

considering the purpose of the distinction it is possible to come to a common sense conclusion as to which side of the line the impugned conduct falls. As Lord Reed said in *Robinson*:

> "4. The distinction between careless acts causing personal injury, for which the law generally imposes liability, and careless omissions to prevent acts (by other agencies) causing personal injury, for which the common law generally imposes no liability, is not a mere alternative to policy-based reasoning, but is inherent in the nature of the tort of negligence. For the same reason, although the distinction, like any other distinction, can be difficult to draw in borderline cases, it is of fundamental importance. The central point is that the law of negligence generally imposes duties not to cause harm to other people or their property: it does not generally impose duties to provide them with benefits (including the prevention of harm caused by other agencies). Duties to provide benefits are, in general, voluntarily undertaken rather than being imposed by the common law, and are typically within the domain of contract, promises and trusts rather than tort. It follows from that basic characteristic of the law of negligence that liability is generally imposed for causing harm rather than for failing to prevent harm caused by other people or by natural causes. It is also consistent with that characteristic that the exceptions to the general non-imposition of liability for omissions include situations where there has been a voluntary assumption of responsibility to prevent harm (situations which have sometimes been described as being close or akin to contract), situations where a person has assumed a status which carries with it a responsibility to prevent harm, such as being a parent or standing in loco parentis, and situations where the omission arises in the context of the defendant's having acted so as to create or increase a risk of harm."

Where a course of conduct involves features that are capable of being analysed in both ways, the real nature and purpose of the distinction must be kept in mind in coming to a common sense decision about how the matters complained of as causing the harm should properly be characterised. These are questions of fact and degree. There may be cases where, as a matter of fact, the significance of one aspect of the course of conduct leads to the conclusion that it was positive conduct that caused harm notwithstanding that other aspects involve failures to act or confer benefits. That however, is not this case.

[37] HHJ Baucher's starting point was, correctly, the pleaded case as set out in the appellant's Particulars of Claim. There can be no doubt that the appellant's claim in negligence alleged a duty of care to confer on him a prompt immigration status decision, and that the failure so to act caused harm. The duty is expressly pleaded in paragraphs 49 and 50 as follows:

> "49. ... there was a delay of over 5 months, from the final determination of the Upper Tribunal allowing his appeal, in granting C leave to remain in the United Kingdom. As a result, C suffered loss and damage, including psychiatric harm ...
>
> 50. At all material times, D owed C a duty of care. In particular, and in light of C's particular vulnerability ... which was known to D, and in light of the specific finding of the Upper Tribunal about the likely impact of a delay on C's mental health, D owed C a duty to make a prompt decision on the implementation of his successful appeal and on the grant of leave to remain in the UK."

[38] The particulars of breach of that duty are pleaded at paragraph 51. They refer to (a) failures to have in place adequate systems for communication between the respondent's officers and/or departments charged with implementing the status decision; (b) failure to operate systems adequately and promptly; (c) failure to have in place adequate systems for communication with legal representatives to ensure they were given expeditious and adequate instructions, or to operate such systems adequately and promptly; (d) failure to act with reasonable care and expedition in response to triggers which should have ensured awareness of relevant time limits for appealing. True it is, as Mr Chirico submitted, that the lodging of the appeal is expressly pleaded at paragraph 51(e) and (f). However, the allegations are expressly that (e) the respondent failed to ensure that a full and informed decision was taken about the merits of an appeal and/or whether there was a serious intention of pursuing it before it was lodged and/or withdrawn; and (f) if the respondent had acted with reasonable competence and expedition, she would have decided no later than 10 February 2016 not to pursue an appeal to the Court of Appeal and the delay of over three months from then to 13 May 2016, when the appeal was withdrawn, would have been entirely avoided.

[39] In other words, the alleged duty and the breaches are all focussed on the requirement to make prompt and timely decisions touching on the implementation of the UT decision allowing the appellant's appeal, by granting him status in the United Kingdom. The additional period of delay from 10 May (when the appeal was withdrawn) to 23 July 2016 was also pleaded as involving further failure to act with utmost expedition in implementing the decision to grant leave to remain in light of the earlier delays. This analysis does not involve subsuming isolated actions that caused the appellant harm into an overall omissions context, as Mr Chirico sought to argue. The pleaded case identifies the gravamen of the appellant's complaint: the respondent was under a duty to act promptly but took too long in deciding and implementing the immigration status decision and this caused the appellant harm. In these circumstances it seems to me that the judges below were amply entitled to understand the pleaded case as limited to failure to confer a benefit on this appellant.

[40] Accordingly, as a matter of pleading, the case was advanced on the sole basis of a failure to make prompt decisions about the appellant's immigration status, leading to delay in the grant of leave to remain. That is what is said to have caused him harm. Unsurprisingly, there is no pleaded allegation that the conduct of lodging a futile appeal, and doing so out of time, itself caused harm to the appellant.

[41] Looked at as a matter of substance, it is artificial to view this claim in any other way. As a matter of common sense, this case is about the respondent, in her role as immigration status decision-maker, failing to make prompt and timely decisions about the appellant's immigration status. The respondent was under no duty to exercise or refrain from exercising appeal rights in a particular way, still less to make a status decision within a particular timeframe. Her conduct as a litigant in appeal proceedings was regulated by court rules, but the common law has no role to play in regulating that activity, and as a litigant, the respondent owed no duty of care to the opposing party. Nor did any of the exceptions to the general non-imposition of liability for omissions apply: the respondent did not voluntarily assume responsibility for expediting the implementation of the UT decision, or undertake to make a status decision by a certain date or within a certain period of time. Nor did any of the alleged failures arise in the context of the respondent having acted so as to create or increase a risk of harm.

[42] The duty on the respondent was the duty to exercise her discretion to grant leave to remain. It was this benefit that was not conferred promptly and which is alleged to have led to the loss and damage claimed. The lodging of the appeal prolonged the period over which that benefit was not conferred. It is part of the reason for the delay. However, it cannot be viewed as an isolated act that caused harm, and nor was the case pleaded in this way. To do so would be to ignore the purpose of the distinction identified in *Robinson* and *Poole* between a positive act that makes things worse and a failure to confer a benefit, namely to distinguish between regulating the way in which an activity may be conducted and imposing a duty to act upon a person who is not carrying on any relevant activity. As a matter of pleading and substance, it is clear that what caused harm to the appellant was the delay in complying with the duty to exercise discretion in this case by granting a period of leave to remain. The respondent could have delayed for the same period without taking any steps to issue a late appeal and the same harm as now alleged would no doubt have been caused; and on those facts, as Mr Chirico accepted, the case would have been an omissions case only. The decision to appeal could have been handled differently, and with greater clarity and speed. But the act of issuing the appeal late and in an "unregulated" way cannot realistically be viewed as having caused harm. There was nothing about the act of issuing the appeal itself, that involved, gave rise to or created a source of harm, even on the particular facts of this case.

[43] As well as relying on the pleading to conclude that this was an omissions case rather than one involving any positive acts, HHJ Baucher also "stood back" in order to assess what this case was really all about, and in doing so, concluded that, as in *Adiukwu*, this was a claim about a failure to confer on the appellant the benefit of leave to remain status.

[44] In *Adiukwu*, A claimed damages for financial loss suffered as a result of the failure of the Secretary of State for the Home Department over a period of 20 months, to issue a "status letter" confirming leave to remain following a successful appeal. The analogy with this case is clear, although the delay in that case was substantially longer and the damages claim appears to have been based on pure economic loss rather than including personal injury. The Scottish Court of Session (Inner House) analysed the duty of care question by reference to *Robinson* and *Poole*, concluding in summary that the case was not one of causing harm to the complainant but of failing to confer a benefit on her (the grant of immigration status), and therefore fell within the established principle that a duty of care did not arise save in very limited exceptions. Those exceptions (where the defender had created the source of the danger or where there had been a voluntary assumption of responsibility) equally did not apply. A was in no worse position following the decision of the First-tier Tribunal as a result of the Home Secretary's actions; the point of her claim was that the Home Secretary did not take action to put her in a better position. This did not begin to amount to creating a source of danger for her, and there was no voluntary assumption of responsibility.

[45] Mr Chirico was critical of the reliance below on *Adiukwu*, which was accepted to be persuasive rather than binding. There is nothing in this criticism. The factual similarities with the present case and the detailed analysis undertaken by the court lend it particularly persuasive weight. As already stated, HHJ Baucher analysed the pleaded case, and then stood back to assess what the case was really about. Her conclusion that, like in *Adiukwu*, this was not a case of making things worse, but was one of failing to confer a benefit reflects a proper application of the

principles set out in *Poole*. *Adiukwu* is not distinguishable as a pure omissions case for the reasons set out above. To the contrary, I can see no error in the judge's reference to it as an analogous case.

[46] HHJ Baucher placed no substantive reliance on the two earlier cases of *Home Office v Mohammed and others* [2011] EWCA Civ 351, [2011] 1 WLR 2862 and *W v Home Office* [1997] Imm AR 302 that are criticised by Mr Chirico as outdated and inconsistent with *Poole*; and to the extent that they were referred to by Choudhury J, it was in a passage that Mr Chirico accepts as *obiter* to his judgment. In these circumstances, and since we were not fully addressed on the question, I regard it as unnecessary to consider whether and to what extent they can still be relied on as limiting the liability of the respondent (beyond the limits identified in *Poole*).

[47] For all these reasons, ground two fails. The respondent's conduct was properly characterised as a failure or series of failures to confer a benefit, rather than as causing harm or making things worse. Since the viability of the appellant's claim that the respondent owed him a duty of care in negligence depended on him establishing that at least some material element of his claim involved the respondent causing him harm, this conclusion means that no duty of care was owed. Standing back, this is a claim about the respondent's failure to act promptly and timeously in circumstances that might have given rise to a public law duty but are not susceptible of giving rise to any common law duty of care being owed.

[48] This conclusion makes it unnecessary to consider the litigation exception in ground one, and I prefer to express no view about it.

Ground 3: article 8

[49] This ground of appeal contends that the judges below erred in concluding that the interference with the appellant's right to respect for his private life was justified. Mr Chirico contended, in summary, that there was an overall failure to conduct a particularised analysis of the respondent's conduct and its impact on the appellant for the purposes of a lawful article 8 balancing exercise, and in the unusual factual context of this case.

[50] Before addressing the arguments advanced by Mr Chirico, it is helpful to record the appellant's pleaded article 8 claim. The pleading was brief. It focussed entirely on the alleged delay:

> "D's delay in implementing C's grant of status amounted to an interference in his right to respect for his private life (including his mental integrity). For the reasons set out above, that interference was unjustified (because arbitrary and therefore disproportionate)."

Damages were claimed in respect of that breach of his article 8 rights pursuant to section 7 of the Human Rights Act 1998.

[51] HHJ Baucher rejected this claim, finding that the delay in this case was not substantial and was insufficient to "engage a breach of article 8". In the alternative, she held that any interference with article 8 rights was justified.

[52] Choudhury J accepted that article 8 can potentially be engaged in the circumstances of this case. He referred to paragraphs 10 and 17 in *Razgar* (cited above) where Lord Bingham stated:

"10. ... [T]he rights protected by article 8 can be engaged by the foreseeable consequences for health of removal from the United Kingdom pursuant to an immigration decision, even where such removal does not violate article 3, if the facts relied upon by the applicant are sufficiently strong.

...

17. In considering whether a challenge to the Secretary of State's decision to remove a person must clearly fail, the reviewing court must, as it seems to me, consider how an appeal would be likely to fare before an adjudicator, as the tribunal responsible for deciding the appeal if there were an appeal. This means that the reviewing court must ask itself essentially the questions which would have to be answered by an adjudicator. In a case where removal is resisted in reliance on article 8, these questions are likely to be: (1) will the proposed removal be an interference by a public authority with the exercise of the applicant's right to respect for his private or (as the case may be) family life? (2) If so, will such interference have consequences of such gravity as potentially to engage the operation of article 8? (3) If so, is such interference in accordance with the law? (4) If so, is such interference necessary in a democratic society in the interests of national security, public safety or the economic well-being of the country, for the prevention of disorder or crime, for the protection of health or morals, or for the protection of the rights and freedoms of others? (5) If so, is such interference proportionate to the legitimate public end sought to be achieved?"

[53] Whilst the *Razgar* questions relate to the specific context of a proposed removal that is resisted, they can be adapted to deal with the specific conduct and interference in a particular case, providing a structured basis for analysing an article 8 claim. Here, Choudhury J held that the conduct said to give rise to the interference is the five month delay in granting immigration status; and the interference is the impact of the delay on the appellant's mental health which engaged article 8. Mr Cohen did not seek to go behind these conclusions. In particular, he accepted that article 8 is potentially engaged in answer to question 1, and conceded that the consequences of the interference were of sufficient gravity for question 2 to be satisfied as well. I therefore proceed on the basis of these concessions without considering their correctness or otherwise.

[54] Choudhury J concluded that HHJ Baucher failed to distinguish between the conduct which caused an interference and the interference itself. That meant she asked the wrong question (namely, whether the delay was substantial) and failed to ask the correct question (whether the interference was justified). However, he held that her ultimate conclusion, that any interference was justified, was plainly and unarguably correct, as he explained:

"90. However, the failure to take a structured approach to the analysis would not warrant any interference by the appellate court if it transpires that the ultimate conclusion reached was plainly and unarguably correct. It seems to me that, notwithstanding the flaws identified above, the Judge's analysis was, as Mr Cohen submits, essentially focused on the question of justification and whether the effect of delay amounted to a proportionate means of achieving a legitimate aim. That question was considered by the Judge, albeit very briefly, in the penultimate paragraph of the Judgment, which provides:

'119. Even if I am wrong I am satisfied, in any event that any interference would be justified. There is important public interest in immigration control, the deportation of offenders and parties being able to seek permission to appeal so at (*sic*) to engage Article 8(2).'

91. This is a decision in the alternative to what has gone before; in other words, if the Judge was wrong that there is no engagement or interference with Article 8 rights, the Judge considered whether that interference was justified. Having determined that the delay of five months was 'a short period', the Judge's conclusion that the interference was justified 'so as to engage Article 8(2)', amounted to a truncated and somewhat infelicitous way of stating that the delay and its consequential effects amounted to a proportionate means of achieving the legitimate aim of having effective immigration control systems with rights of appeal for both parties. In any lawful system of immigration control, an adverse decision or an appeal against a positive decision, would be likely to result in anxiety and stress for affected individuals, and delays in the relevant processes would be likely to add to that stress. However, delays are an occasional unavoidable feature of any system dependent on individual decision-making. The Judge was entitled to conclude that the effect of delay, which was not substantial or serious, was not disproportionate.

92. Mr Chirico submits that the conclusion on justification was inadequate because it is based on 'generalities' (namely the important public interest in the deportation of offenders) rather than on the evidence that the attempts to deport were considered by the Respondent's own chief decision-maker as 'futile, unlawful, and waste of tax payer's money'. I do not accept that submission. Having a system of immigration controls in place (including the deportation of offenders) with appeal rights for both parties is undoubtedly a legitimate aim. The fact that the aim is expressed in high-level and general terms is neither surprising nor unlawful. Furthermore, the pleaded case on Article 8 merely complains that the interference was 'unjustified (because arbitrary and disproportionate)'; it makes no reference expressly to Mr Wells' views as giving rise to arbitrariness or disproportionality. Indeed, given that the principal complaint was, as the Judge found, about delay, it is reasonable to infer that it was that factor (i.e. delay) that was complained about as being arbitrary and disproportionate. The Judge's clear conclusion was that the delay was relatively short, and, it may be inferred, that delay and/or its effect was not disproportionate. Furthermore, given that Mr Wells' email resulted in the withdrawal of the appeal within a matter of days of the email being sent, it can hardly be said that the content of that email contributed significantly to the allegedly disproportionate delay.

93. Mr Chirico's final complaint is that by stating that Article 8(2) was not engaged, the Judge asked herself the wrong question. There is nothing in this point: the Judge clearly intended to state that the interference was justified within the meaning of Article 8(2). The infelicitous reference to the language of 'engagement' does not render that conclusion incorrect."

[55] In developing this ground of appeal, Mr Chirico made clear his acceptance that there is a legitimate aim in preventing disorder and crime and in protecting the economic interests of the United Kingdom and that, for present purposes at least,

having a system of immigration controls with rights of appeal for both parties is a means which is capable of furthering that aim. He also accepts that at the level of generality, delays are an occasional, unavoidable feature of any system dependent on individual decision making and that in any lawful system of immigration control, an adverse decision or an appeal against a positive decision would be likely to result in anxiety and stress for affected individuals. These general observations form part of the background against which the proportionality of an individual interference may be assessed.

[56] However he submitted that they do not begin to answer the question which must be answered in this case, namely whether the specific interference with the appellant's rights is a proportionate means of achieving the legitimate aim pursued. In order to answer that question it is necessary, he submitted, to have regard to the degree of interference in this particular case and to identify the weight to be attached to the public interest in this particular case. Mr Chirico submitted that Choudhury J did neither: this was not a mere complaint about anxiety or stress, but psychiatric harm which contributed to a deterioration in the appellant's mental health sufficient to require his detention in a psychiatric hospital. Further, in terms of the weight to be attached to the legitimate aim in this particular case, particular regard should have been paid to the known urgency about the appellant's case, and the risk to his mental health of delay; the respondent's own assessment of the merits of the appeal; and whether the five month delay was justified. This resulted in an overall failure to conduct an individualised analysis of the proportionality of the interference, having regard to the aims in this case and the impact on the appellant.

[57] The respondent's concession that questions 1 and 2 of *Razgar* are satisfied, and there being no dispute that question 3 is satisfied, means that the focus is on questions 4 and 5.

[58] In most cases the interference relied on is a positive act by the state: a removal or deportation decision, detention or some other similar act. Here, the interference flows from inaction by the state. I do not suggest that inaction cannot amount to an interference, but it is less obvious how the *Razgar* questions 4 and 5 are to be analysed in the context of inaction or delay because delay (culpable or otherwise) can never have a legitimate aim or in itself be justified. I therefore have some sympathy with HHJ Baucher's view that the *Razgar* questions did not need to be "determined in that format for the purpose of this cause of action". On one view it might be thought that in answering questions 4 and 5 in a case of delay, a broader judgment is required.

[59] First, in a case alleging delay, it is necessary to identify the period of culpable delay. Reasonable, robust decision-making takes time and delay (in the sense of lapse of time) is an unavoidable feature of any system dependent on individual decision-making. Hindsight is not likely to be a reliable basis on which to determine what is reasonable in a particular case; and I reject Mr Chirico's argument that the period of nine days taken from the point of withdrawing the appeal to the date of the decision to afford five years' leave to remain, is a reliable yardstick against which to assess what was a reasonable time for an immigration status decision in this case. Apart from anything else, the nine day period inevitably built on what had been happening in the period before that. Nor is it necessarily the case that exceeding a time limit of, say, 28 days for lodging an appeal, means that any additional time taken inevitably constitutes culpable delay. There may be good reason for additional time being necessary, as the power to extend time in an appropriate case makes clear. Biometric residence permit applications also take

time, as demonstrated by what happened in this case. Thus although the appellant relies on the whole five month period as a period of what is in effect culpable delay, the respondent contends that anything up to six months is well within the time reasonably taken for decision-making of this kind, and there was no culpable delay at all.

[60] Secondly, since any administrative system of decision-making takes time and can involve undesirable lapses of time, there may come a point where the lapse is so significant having regard to its length, seriousness and culpability and the gravity of its consequences in the particular case as to be regarded as involving a lack of respect for the individual's private life rights. Thus it is necessary to weigh the culpability of the delay and the severity of its consequence to determine whether the operation of the administrative system in a particular case remains proportionate to the public aims of such a system, or has reached the threshold of being disproportionate.

[61] This broader approach finds some support in *Anufrijeva v London Borough of Southwark* [2003] EWCA Civ 1406, [2004] 2 WLR 603 where this court reviewed the Strasbourg authorities dealing with maladministration as a breach of article 8. It held that the failure by a public body, in breach of duty, to provide an individual with a benefit or advantage to which he or she is entitled under public law is capable of breaching the individual's human rights. It will constitute an actual breach of article 8 if it amounts to a lack of respect for private and family life because of an element of culpability by the public body. *Anufrijeva* confirms that culpable delay in the administrative processes necessary to determine and to give effect to an article 8 right, as well as outright failure to provide a benefit, is capable of infringing article 8 where substantial prejudice has been caused to the applicant. In cases involving custody of children, procedural delay has been held to amount to a breach of article 8 because of the prejudice such delay can have on the ultimate decision – thus in *H v United Kingdom* (1987) 10 EHRR 95 (at paragraph 89) the court held article 8 was infringed by delay in the conduct of access and adoption proceedings because the proceedings "lay within an area in which procedural delay may lead to a *de facto* determination of the matter at issue", which was precisely what had occurred. This court also referred to the fact that the Strasbourg court had rightly emphasised the need to have regard to resources when considering the obligations imposed on a state by article 8: the demands on resources would be significantly increased if states were to be faced with claims for breaches of article 8 simply on the ground of administrative delays.

[62] At paragraph 48, this court said that in considering whether there has been a breach of article 8:

"it is necessary to have regard both to the extent of the culpability of the failure to act and to the severity of the consequence. Clearly, where one is considering whether there has been a lack of respect for article 8 rights, the more glaring the deficiency in the behaviour of the public authority, the easier it will be to establish the necessary want of respect."

[63] Alternatively, and adapting the *Razgar* questions to suit the particular circumstances before the court, both Mr Chirico and Mr Cohen agree that the question is not whether the period of culpable delay has a legitimate aim and is justified. Rather, the immigration decision-making system has the legitimate aims identified above and requires a process to be followed that involves allowing

decision-makers the time to make robust immigration decisions, including where appropriate taking decisions about whether to appeal. The question in those circumstances is whether when the system allows or leads to delay, the delay is serious enough in context to be viewed as culpable and has a sufficiently grave effect on the individual's private or family rights to breach article 8.

[64] Adopting either approach here, on the findings of the judges below, and treating the whole period of five months as the delay period, the period was found by HHJ Baucher to be relatively short. It involved no breach of legal duty, and there was no finding of any intention to cause delay, nor was any separate element of culpability identified.

[65] As for the impact of the delay on the appellant's mental health, the parties agreed that the delay was a significant aggravating factor that rendered his schizophrenic relapse more severe and longer in duration. However, this agreed description afforded no means of assessing the quality of the aggravation, or its severity in the context of the appellant's already bad mental health. On the contrary, Professor Katona's evidence was that even before the UT hearing at which the appellant's appeal was allowed, the appellant was on a downward spiral: he was not complying with his medication regime, his behaviour was increasingly irritable and aggressive, with persecutory ideas, and he had resumed heavy drinking and illicit drug use. This together with the stress of the impending UT hearing triggered a deterioration in his mental health which became more marked after the UT decision, and as early as January 2016 (well before the impugned delay period) had become very marked. There was no evidence about (and no means of assessing) how and in what way his symptoms were more severe, or for how much longer he experienced them, as a consequence of the delay. In these circumstances, the limited material available simply did not begin to justify a finding that the delay had a substantial or serious impact on the appellant's mental health or caused the appellant substantial prejudice. On the contrary, the judges below were entitled to conclude, that the effect of the delay (which was neither substantial nor serious) on the appellant's already bad mental health, was not disproportionate.

[66] I do not accept Mr Chirico's criticism that the conclusion on justification failed to balance the degree of interference in the particular case against the weight to be attached to the public interest in this particular case. Although neither judge expressed themselves in quite the same way as I have done, the findings made and conclusions reached reflect a judgment made about proportionality on an individualised basis by reference to the particular circumstances of this case. First, there can be no doubt that Choudhury J recognised that the *effect* of the delay, in other words, the consequences for the appellant's mental health, was always part of his case under article 8. That was his express conclusion at paragraph 89, and there is nothing to suggest that he overlooked it when conducting the proportionality exercise in the context of a recognition that delay is an unavoidable feature of individual decision-making and can cause stress and anxiety. Further, as I have explained, the actual impact of the delay on the appellant was agreed in the sense that it contributed to an already markedly bad mental health state that involved a relapse and hospitalisation, but was otherwise incapable of any qualitative assessment on the limited material available. There can be no doubt that the judges below were fully cognizant of the appellant's undoubted vulnerabilities and the agreed medical position. However, there was, as a matter of fact, no material to justify a conclusion that the delay had a serious or substantial impact on the appellant's mental health. For the reasons already given, there was nothing perverse

in this conclusion. Secondly, the pleaded case on article 8 complained that the interference was "unjustified (because arbitrary and disproportionate)". In other words, the impact of the delay, its effect on the appellant, was arbitrary and disproportionate. Again, even in the context of a vulnerable refugee, immigration status decisions take time and can involve delay. The respondent could have acted with greater speed and clarity, but the lapse of time in context, was not substantial or serious. Nor was there any other feature that supported a conclusion that it was culpable. The pleading made no reference to the respondent's internally expressed views about the merits of the aborted appeal. But even if it had, Mr Wells' email setting out his view of the merits of the appeal resulted in the withdrawal of the appeal within a matter of days of the email being sent, and it is difficult to see how the content of that email could arguably have contributed significantly to the seriousness or culpability of the delay.

[67] For these reasons, I agree with Choudhury J that the judge's ultimate conclusion that there was no breach of article 8 was one she was entitled to reach on the material placed before her, and reflected no error. Choudhury J's own analysis also reflected a proper approach to the balancing exercise required by article 8. His conclusion that there was no breach of article 8 involved no error. This ground of appeal therefore also fails.

ANDREWS LJ:

[68] Had this appeal turned on Ground 1, I would have held that the litigation exception ceased to apply as soon as the prescribed time for seeking permission to appeal from this Court elapsed. From then onwards, the appellant and respondent were no longer parties to litigation. To all intents and purposes the litigation had been resolved, and the appellant and his legal advisers were entitled to treat the Upper Tribunal's decision as final. I cannot see how it can be possible for the unsuccessful party to seek permission to appeal two months after the prescribed time limit for doing so, and then use that application as justification for re-characterising the relationship between the parties with retrospective effect.

[69] However, nothing turns on this because, having had the benefit of seeing my Lady, Lady Justice Simler's judgment in draft, I agree with everything she says on Grounds 2 and 3. Ground 1 therefore does not arise.

UNDERHILL LJ:

[70] I agree with both judgments.

[2024] Imm AR 2

ABDI AND OTHERS v ENTRY CLEARANCE OFFICER

COURT OF APPEAL

King, Arnold and Popplewell LJJ

[2023] EWCA Civ 1455
7 December 2023

Procedure and process – procedural irregularities – fairness – adverse credibility findings not put to witness – credibility not raised in refusal letters – Secretary of State not represented at the hearing

The first and second Claimants were brother and sister, aged 21 and 22 respectively. The third Claimant was the sister's three-year-old child. All the Claimants were nationals of Somalia living in Kenya. The siblings' eldest brother, Ashkir, was a Dutch national who lived in England at all material times. The Claimants applied for EEA Family Permits to join Ashkir in England. They sought to bring themselves within the definition of an extended family member in regulation 8 of the Immigration (European Economic Area) Regulations 2016 which required them to establish, *inter alia*, that they were dependent on the EEA national in that they needed his material support to meet their essential living needs. The Secretary of State for the Home Department refused the applications on the grounds that there was sporadic evidence of money transfers from Ashkir and the Claimants had not provided evidence of their financial circumstances.

On appeal before the First-tier Tribunal ('FtT'), Ashkir gave evidence regarding his financial circumstances and about the remittances he had made to support the Claimants. The FtT Judge dismissed the appeal as she was not satisfied that Ashkir was the source of the funds used by the Claimants and therefore they were not financially dependent on him. The Judge based her conclusion on calculations of purported payments from Ashkir and draft tax returns showing his profits, which would have left him with virtually nothing to live on. The Secretary of State was not represented at the hearing.

On appeal to the Upper Tribunal ('UT'), the Claimants argued that the FtT had acted unfairly by not putting the adverse credibility findings to Ashkir and without them having been relied on in the refusal letters. Moreover, the FtT had failed to make findings as to whether some of the money sent contributed to the Claimants' essential living needs. The UT dismissed the appeal. It concluded that, although it would have been better if the FtT had raised concerns about Ashkir's ability to remit funds at the hearing, there was no procedural unfairness and, even if there was, it had made no material difference to the outcome given the evidence that there were no other sources of income available to Ashkir at the relevant time. The UT rejected the second ground, finding that none of the funds emanated from Ashkir and the claim of dependency therefore failed.

Before the Court of Appeal, the Claimants submitted, *inter alia*, that the UT had erred in law in finding that there had been no material procedural unfairness in the FtT notwithstanding that the FtT had decided the appeal on the basis of a matter that had not been raised by the Secretary of State and of which it had given the Claimants no notice. The Secretary of State submitted by way of a Respondent's Notice that there was no evidence before the UT as to what had occurred during the FtT hearing, such as a transcript or recording. Accordingly, it was not open to the Claimants to submit that the FtT hearing had been unfair and there was no evidential basis on which the UT could have reached that conclusion. In response to the Respondent's Notice, the Claimants provided a transcript of the FtT hearing.

Held, allowing the appeal:

(1) The point raised in the Respondent's Notice was hopeless. The Secretary of State had conceded before the UT that the FtT had not raised any concern that Ashkir had not made the payments that he said he had made. That issue was at the forefront of the appeal to the UT and the allegation of procedural unfairness. If the Secretary of State had wished to dispute the factual basis on which the Claimants appealed to the UT, namely what happened at the FtT hearing, she should have served a notice under rule 24 of the Tribunal Procedure (Upper Tribunal) Rules 2008 in response to the notice of appeal. The UT decision recorded the Secretary of State's submissions in terms that were inconsistent with any dispute having been raised. Where the point relied on was simply that a matter had not been raised at the hearing, and there was no reason to anticipate a dispute, there had been no need for the Claimants to adduce evidence in the form of a transcript or witness statement from counsel before the UT hearing. In any event, the Claimants had adduced a transcript of the FtT hearing for the instant appeal which confirmed beyond doubt that the point about Ashkir's payments was not raised at the hearing. Reasonable diligence did not require the transcript to have been obtained before the UT hearing, and until the Respondent's Notice raised the point the Claimants could not reasonably have anticipated that it would be necessary to adduce the transcript to make good their procedural unfairness argument (*paras 19 – 27*).

(2) Whether there was procedural unfairness was fact sensitive. A failure to put to a party a point that was decided against him could be grossly unfair and lead to injustice because he had to have a proper opportunity to deal with the point. Problems could arise as to how the tribunal could avoid giving an appearance of bias where, as often happened, the Secretary of State was not represented at the hearing and so the usual adversarial testing of the claimant's evidence by cross-examination did not take place. Where credibility was not raised in the refusal letter but from reading the papers the tribunal considered that issues of credibility arose, it should point them out to the representative and ask that they be dealt with, either in examination of the claimant or in submissions: Guideline 5 of *MNM (*Surendran *guidelines for adjudicators) Kenya** [2000] UKIAT 5 applied. Fairness generally required that if a witness's evidence was to be rejected, it should be challenged at the hearing to give him an opportunity to address the challenge: *Griffiths v TUI UK Ltd* [2023] UKSC 48 followed (*paras 28 – 33*).

(3) The failure by the FtT Judge to give the Claimants and Ashkir an opportunity to address the point upon which she decided the case was unfair. The refusal letters had not challenged Ashkir's payments to the Claimants. They were supported by remittance receipts with Ashkir's name and personal details on them. Neither of the points raised in the refusal letters gave rise to questions of credibility. There had been no reason to anticipate an issue as to whether Ashkir had made the remittances. That had been reinforced in the Judge's decision, where she indicated that she treated the Secretary of State's submissions as those set out in the refusal letters.

Contrary to the Secretary of State's submission, it would not have been obvious to the Claimants' representatives without any prompting from the tribunal that the issue of the source of the remittances needed to be addressed. There was no reason to anticipate a focus on how Ashkir had been able to afford to remit the money. There was not some obvious inconsistency in the evidence that should foreseeably have been addressed without the tribunal specifically raising it (*paras 34 – 36*).

(4) The suggestion that the failure to raise the point had no material impact on the outcome was not accepted. The test to establish such a point was a high one: namely whether remission would be pointless because the result would invariably have been the same: *SH (Afghanistan) v Secretary of State for the Home Department* [2011] EWCA Civ 1284 considered. In the instant case, it was not clear that the only outcome was obvious. There were a number of reasons why net receipts in a given tax year, in the form of disposable income, might not match those shown in draft accounts. The outcome upon remission would depend upon the explanation given, the facts found and, possibly, the application of disputed issues of law on the relevance of the source of the funds. Resolution of such legal issues was best left until the relevant facts were found. The matter was remitted to the FtT (*paras 37 – 39*).

Cases referred to:

BW (witness statements by advocates) Afghanistan [2014] UKUT 568 (IAC)
Griffiths v TUI UK Ltd [2023] UKSC 48; [2023] 3 WLR 1204
HA and TD v Secretary of State for the Home Department [2010] CSIH 28; 2010 SC 457; [2010] Imm AR 599
Hickman v Berens [1895] 2 Ch 638
Jia v Migrationsverket (Case C-1/105); [2007] QB 545; [2007] 2 WLR 1005; [2007] 1 CMLR 41; [2007] All ER (EC) 575; [2007] Imm AR 439; [2007] INLR 336
Ladd v Marshall [1954] EWCA Civ 1; [1954] 1 WLR 1489; [1954] 3 All ER 745
*MNM (*Surendran *guidelines for adjudicators) Kenya** [2000] UKIAT 5
Mahad (previously referred to as AM) (Ethiopia) and Others v Entry Clearance Officer; Muhumed (previously referred to as AM (No. 2)) (Somalia) v Entry Clearance Officer [2009] UKSC 16; [2010] 1 WLR 48; [2010] 2 All ER 535; [2010] Imm AR 203; [2010] INLR 268
SH (Afghanistan) by Litigation Friend The Official Solicitor v Secretary of State for the Home Department [2011] EWCA Civ 1284
SM (India) v Entry Clearance Officer (Mumbai); OQ (India) and NQ (India) v Entry Clearance Officer (Mumbai) [2009] EWCA Civ 1426; [2010] Imm AR 351; [2010] INLR 324
Secretary of State for the Home Department v Maheshwaran [2002] EWCA Civ 173; [2002] All ER (D) 184 (Feb)
*WN (*Surendran*; credibility; new evidence) Democratic Republic of Congo* [2004] UKIAT 213; [2005] INLR 340

Legislation judicially considered:

Immigration (European Economic Area) Regulations 2016, regulations 8 & 12
Tribunal Procedure (Upper Tribunal) Rules 2008, rules 2 & 24

Representation

Mr *R Toal* and Ms *U Dirie* instructed by Wilson Solicitors LLP, for the Claimants; Mr *P Skinner* instructed by the Government Legal Department, for the Secretary of State.

Judgment

This judgment was handed down remotely at 10.00am on 7 December 2023 by circulation to the parties or their representatives by e-mail and by release to the National Archives.

LORD JUSTICE POPPLEWELL:

Introduction

[1] The first and second appellants ("Dahir" and "Ubah") are brother and sister. They are aged 21 and 22 respectively. The third appellant ("Mahrez") is Ubah's son, now aged 3. They are all nationals of Somalia. They live together in Kenya, their Kenyan visas having expired.

[2] Dahir and Ubah's eldest unmarried brother is Ashkir Elmi Abdi ("Ashkir"). He is a national of the Netherlands, having been granted asylum there, and has been, at the material times, living in England. Dahir, Ubah and Mahrez applied for EEA Family Permits to join Ashkir in England. Their applications were refused by the Respondent. They appealed to the First tier Tribunal. In a decision by FtT Judge Bartlett dated 25 February 2022 ("the FtT Decision") their appeal was dismissed. They appealed, with leave, to the Upper Tribunal. By a decision dated 10 November 2022 ("the UT Decision"), Upper Tribunal Judge Norton-Taylor dismissed their appeal. They appeal to this Court with permission from Carr LJ, as she then was.

EEA Family Permits

[3] EEA Family Permits are issued under Regulation 12 of the Immigration (European Economic Area) Regulations 2016 SI 2016/1052 ("the Regulations"). Different provisions apply to "family members" and to "extended family members". The appellants do not fall within the definition of family member in Regulation 7 but seek to bring themselves within the definition of extended family member contained in Regulation 8. So far as relevant, this required them to establish that they are a relative of an EEA national, that they were residing in a country other than the UK, and that they were dependent upon the EEA national. There is no dispute that they are relatives of Ashkir and that they are residing outside the UK. The issue which arises is whether in the words of Regulation 8(2)(b) they are "dependent upon the EEA national", i.e. Ashkir. If so, an EEA family permit falls to be granted in accordance with Regulation 12(4) if they want to join Ashkir in the UK.

[4] In this context "dependent" means that the applicant needs the material support of that EEA family member to meet their essential living needs: *SM (India) v Entry Clearance Officer (Mumbai)* [2009] EWCA Civ 1426, [2010] Imm AR 351; and C-1/105 *Jia v Migrationsverket* [2007] QB 545. In order to establish dependence, it is not necessary to establish that the EEA family member is the sole source of funds from which the applicant meets essential living needs. The support must be "material", in the sense that without it the applicant could not meet their essential needs. This is recognised in the Home Office guidance published on 27 March 2019 which at page 18 provides:

> "The Applicant does not need to be dependent on the EEA national to meet all or most of their essential needs. For example, an applicant is considered dependent if they received a pension which covers half of their needs and money from their EEA national sponsor which covers the other half."

The Refusal Letters

[5] The applications by Ubah and Mahrez were dismissed by the Respondent's refusal letters dated 22 January 2021, each in identical terms ("the Refusal Letters"). The letters accepted that Ashkir was a Dutch national but refused the application on the following two grounds:

- On your application you state that you are financially dependent on your sponsor. As evidence of this you have provided money transfer remittance receipts from your sponsor to you, however, it is noted that these transfers are dated sporadically from 2019 to 2020. Unfortunately, this limited amount of evidence in isolation does not prove that you are financially dependent on your sponsor. I would expect to see substantial evidence of this over a prolonged period.

- I would also expect to see evidence which fully details yours and your family's circumstances. Your income, expenditure and evidence of your financial position which would prove that without the financial support of your sponsor your essential living needs could not be met.

[6] A separate refusal letter was sent to Dahir dated 25 February 2021. This refused the application on the basis that no supporting documents had been provided. That was an error. The FtT treated his appeal as raising the same issues as that of Ubah and Mahrez, and it was agreed before the UT and before us that the same approach should be adopted. For convenience I shall therefore refer to the Refusal Letters as if they applied to all three appellants.

The FtT Decision

[7] Before the FtT, the appellants were represented by counsel, Ms Dirie, who was acting pro bono. No one appeared to represent the respondent. The hearing took place via CVP. There were two witness statements from Ashkir, who attended by CVP and gave evidence in accordance with his witness statements, supplemented by a few questions by Ms Dirie. Because the respondent was not represented there

was no cross-examination. Judge Bartlett herself asked Ashkir some questions. Ashkir's evidence, as summarised at paragraph 3 of the FtT Decision was as follows:

> "(i) He fled to the Netherlands in 2008 where he was granted asylum and in April 2015 he became a Dutch national. In September 2015 he came to the United Kingdom and has settled status here. He works as a self-employed taxi driver mainly with Uber but also with Bolt;
>
> (ii) He sponsored his mother to come to the United Kingdom in 2019. She obtained an EEA Family Permit and lives with the sponsor;
>
> (iii) He has a younger brother and sister Huseen and Jasmine who have lived in the Netherlands since around 2016. They are both married with children of their own. Huseen has five children and Jasmine has three children;
>
> (iv) Jasmine works part time as a cleaner and Huseen works part time as a postman;
>
> (v) He and his mother live with his sister Kin and her family including five children [in the] United Kingdom. He does not pay anything towards his accommodation costs so that he can send as much money as possible to the first two Appellants;
>
> (vi) He is the eldest son of the family and has been supporting his mother and the first and second Appellants since he went to the Netherlands in 2018;
>
> (vii) He made an application for his mother first and then later the Appellants to this appeal because he was told by the Somali community that his applications would be more likely to succeed if they were made one at a time;
>
> (viii) After living for a short time in Kenya in 2018 the first two Appellants returned to Mogadishu. Ubah married in July 2019 and her husband moved into the house. He supported them all because none of them were working. In late 2019 Ubah's husband [ran away] because he was threatened by Al-Shabaab, later threats were made to the first two Appellants and so they decided to apply to come to the United Kingdom;
>
> (ix) The Appellants are currently living undocumented in Kenya. Their rent is equivalent to approximately $270 to $300 pm. They pay around $40pm for utility bills and spend about $250pm on food;
>
> (x) Recently their visas for Kenya expired and about two weeks ago they were stopped by police on the street and asked for their papers. When they could not provide them the police required a bribe of $10."

[8] The bundle before the FtT contained receipts evidencing the money transfers said to have been made by Ashkir to Dahir and Ubah between 2019 and 2021, confirming Ashkir's evidence as to the payments made to Dahir and Ubah over that period. The money transfer receipts bore his name and personal details as the transferor. Ms Dirie had helpfully produced in her skeleton argument a table of all those payments.

[9] Ms Dirie made submissions on behalf of the appellants. At paragraph 7 of the FtT Decision, Judge Bartlett said that she took the Refusal Letters as being the respondent's submissions.

[10] Judge Bartlett concluded at paragraph 10 of the Decision that "I am not satisfied that [Ashkir] is the source of the funds either sent to or used by the appellants for their essential living needs". She explained her reasons for that conclusion in the paragraphs which followed. They were that the bundle included tax returns for Ashkir for 2019 and 2020, and as to 2021: "there is also a tax return in respect of 2021 which may not be complete but is also accompanied by an accountant's letter confirming the figures." This last set of documents, for the 2020/21 tax year, showed "net business profit also described as total taxable profit of £5627".

[11] The Judge then analysed the payments made by Ashkir to Dahir and Ubah during the tax year 2020/21, as set out in the tables in Ms Dirie's skeleton argument, and calculated that in total they amounted to payments of $6,875 and 75,374 Kenyan Shillings. She then used exchange rates to convert those figures into Pounds Sterling and came to a total of £5,500. She compared that with the total business profit of £5,627, and said that that would mean that Ashkir had only £127 for the entire year to meet his own essential living expenses. She went on to say that even if different exchanges rates were used this would not have a material effect on her findings because it would still remain that the amount it is claimed was paid to the appellants would be very close to Ashkir's income and therefore he would have had virtually nothing to live on. On that basis, she concluded that "I am not satisfied that the funds which allegedly came from the sponsor actually came from the sponsor. In the circumstances, I am not satisfied that the appellants are financially dependent on the sponsor".

The Appeal to the Upper Tribunal

[12] The appellants appealed to the Upper Tribunal relying on three grounds of appeal, Ground 2 is no longer pursued and can be ignored. Grounds 1 and 3 were that:

(a) in deciding that Ashkir was not the source of the funds, the FtT Judge made adverse credibility findings against Ashkir without these being put to Ashkir and without them having been relied on by the respondent in its Refusal Letters; it was therefore unfair to rely on this reasoning;

(b) the Judge failed to make findings as to whether some of the money sent contributed to the appellants' essential living needs.

[13] At the hearing before UT Judge Norton-Taylor, Ms Dirie again appeared for the appellants, pro bono. On this occasion the respondent was represented by Ms Willocks-Briscoe, a senior Home Office Presenting Officer.

[14] In the UT Decision, the UT Judge concluded that it would have been much better if the FtT Judge had specifically raised at the hearing any concern with Ashkir's ability to remit funds but concluded that there was no procedural unfairness such that the decision should be set aside. His reasons were that there was significantly more evidence provided before the FtT than in the original applications, so that the FtT Judge had to consider additional evidence which had not been before the original decision-maker. The FtT Judge's figure of £127 was a finding which was open to her. The question was then what would have happened if the FtT Judge's concern had been raised at the hearing. The UT Judge said that it had been accepted by Ms Dirie at the hearing that there was no evidence before the FtT Judge of any other sources of income available to Ashkir, and that there had in fact been no other sources of income for Ashkir at the relevant time. In those circumstances, the UT Judge concluded that there was no procedural unfairness on the Judge's part, or that even if there was, by virtue of a failure to raise an issue at the hearing, it could not have made a material difference to the outcome. Although he expressed his conclusion in this alternative form, the essence of his reasoning was that the failure to raise the point at the hearing had made no material difference to the outcome.

[15] The UT Judge rejected the second ground of appeal on the basis that the FtT Judge's finding was that none of the funds received by the Appellants had emanated from Ashkir, and so the dependency claim fell at the first stage.

The issues in the appeal

[16] Two grounds of appeal are advanced on behalf of the appellants:

(1)   Ground 1: the Upper Tribunal erred in law by holding that there had been no or no material procedural unfairness before the FtT notwithstanding that the FtT decided the appeal against the appellants on the basis of a matter that had not been raised by the respondent and of which the FtT gave the appellants no notice.

(2)   Ground 2: the FtT erred in law by failing to determine (a) whether Ashkir contributed to the remittances to the appellants even if he did not provide the whole of the amount remitted and (b) whether the appellants were dependent on that contribution. The Upper Tribunal erred in law by holding that the FtT had not been required to determine those issues.

[17] In relation to Ground 1, the respondent advances essentially two points. The first, which is taken by way of a Respondent's Notice, is that there was no evidence before the Upper Tribunal as to what had occurred during the hearing before the FtT, such as the transcript, a recording, a note from the FtT Judge, or a witness statement from Ms Dirie; and that accordingly it was not open to the appellants to submit that the hearing before the FtT was not fair and there was no evidential basis on which the UT Judge could have reached that conclusion. The second answer to Ground 1 put forward by the respondents, in the alternative, is that procedural fairness did not require the FtT Judge to put her doubts as to the credibility of Ashkir to the appellants at the hearing. In relation to Ground 2, the respondent supports the holding by the UT Judge that the FtT Judge found that none of the funds had been sent by Ashkir.

[18] In response to the Respondent's Notice, the appellants obtained a transcript of the hearing before the FtT Judge and made an application to this court to rely upon it. The respondent resists that application. At the hearing of the appeal, we allowed the transcript to be put before us *de bene esse*, subject to determining its admissibility in our judgment.

The Respondent's Notice point

[19] In my view this is hopeless because it is clear that it was conceded before the UT that the FtT Judge had not raised any concern that Ashkir had not made the payments he said he had made, and had not raised the point comparing the total of payments allegedly made by Ashkir against the profit in the draft tax accounts which formed the ground on which she decided that they had not been. The appellants' contention that those matters had not been raised at the hearing was at the forefront of ground 1. Ground 1 was set out at paragraphs 14 to 16 of the grounds, which asserted unequivocally that the point on which the FtT Judge rested her decision had not been relied on by the respondent and had not been raised at the hearing. This was the central factual premise for the allegation of procedural unfairness.

[20] Rule 24 of the Tribunal Procedure (Upper Tribunal) Rules 2008 ("the UT Rules") provides that a respondent must serve a response to a notice of appeal if the respondent – (a) wishes the Upper Tribunal to uphold the decision for reasons other than those given by the tribunal; or (b) relies on any grounds on which the respondent was unsuccessful in the proceedings which are the subject of the appeal; and that in other circumstances may do so. The Rules also contain in Rule 2 the overriding objective to deal with cases fairly and justly, which includes dealing with them at proportionate cost and without unnecessary delay. Rule 2(4) requires the parties to help the Upper Tribunal to further the overriding objective. Although the terms of Rule 24 did not make service of a notice mandatory in this case, Rule 2 dictates that one should be served where the notice of appeal contains a complaint as to what happened at the hearing as the factual basis of a ground of appeal. A Rule 24 notice ought then to be served identifying whether that factual basis is in issue, and if so, highlighting the nature of the controversy. Only in that way can any dispute be identified in a way which enables orderly preparations to be made for it to be resolved at the appeal hearing, if necessary by evidence, so as to avoid unnecessary delay and expense. If resolution of any dispute necessitates a witness statement from counsel, that will give rise to particular consequences which may include new counsel being instructed to conduct the appeal: see *BW v Secretary of State for the Home Department* [2014] UKUT 00568 (IAC) at [5]. No such Rule 24 notice was served in response to the grounds of appeal in this case.

[21] The assertion that the point had not been raised at the hearing was not only the central premise of the written grounds of appeal but the central premise of the ground advanced orally by Ms Dirie in argument. She must have said so in the course of argument.

[22] In those circumstances it was incumbent on Ms Willocks-Briscoe to say whether the factual premise was disputed, not least because Rule 2 of the UT Rules requires the parties to help the UT to further the overriding objective there set out. It is clear enough that Ms Willocks-Briscoe did not do so. That is clear from the terms of the UT Decision, which record her submissions in terms which are inconsistent with any such dispute having been raised, and treat it as an undisputed fact that the point was not raised at the FtT hearing.

[23] Mr Skinner submitted that there is a distinction to be drawn between not disputing a matter and making an express concession; and that there was no basis for treating Ms Willocks-Briscoe as having made an express concession. I would accept that in some circumstances there can be a material distinction between not disputing a matter and conceding it, but there is no such distinction to be made on the facts of this case. In the circumstances, Ms Willocks-Briscoe's failure to say that the point was disputed amounted to a concession.

[24] Mr Skinner also suggested that it was incumbent on the appellants to adduce evidence in the form of a transcript or a witness statement from Ms Dirie at the permission to appeal stage, or at latest prior to the UT hearing. Had a witness statement been provided, it is said, Ms Dirie would then have had to withdraw and other counsel be instructed. I cannot accept this submission. There would be no conflict between counsel acting as a witness and acting as an advocate unless and until a dispute was identified about what had happened. No doubt there are some cases where what is said to have happened at the FtT hearing is likely to be in dispute and where the evidential basis for rival contentions should be dealt with formally by evidence in the form of a witness statement in the way suggested in *BW*. Where allegations of conduct amounting to apparent bias are made it may often be important both to address exactly what happened and to make an evaluative judgment of its effect, in circumstances where a dispute can be readily anticipated. Sometimes a transcript will not be conclusive. However where, as in this case, the point relied on is simply that a matter was not raised at the hearing, in circumstances where there is no reason to anticipate a dispute, the convenient way of dealing with it is that which was adopted in the present case. Requiring the appellants to apply and pay for a transcript, or Ms Dirie to make a witness statement, before there was any reason to suspect that the point might be in dispute, would simply have led to additional expense and delay to no useful purpose.

[25] Moreover, even if I were wrong that Ms Willock-Briscoe's conduct amounted to conceding the point, I would not accept that there was no evidence before the Upper Tribunal that the point had not been raised at the FtT hearing. There was evidence to that effect in each of two forms. First there was the FtT decision itself, which it is reasonable to suppose would have included in its summary of Ashkir's evidence whatever response he would have made had the point been raised. The absence of any record of a response to the point in the evidence recited in the FtT Decision is persuasive evidence that it was not raised. Secondly the UT had Ms Dirie's statement from the bar as to what had happened. That is evidence upon which a Court is entitled to rely (*Hickman v Berens* [1895] 2 Ch 638). It happens frequently that courts or tribunals sitting on appeal inquire as to what happened below and are told the position by counsel. In the absence of any reason to question what counsel says, the court can proceed on the basis of what they are told by counsel in fulfilment of their professional duty.

[26] I would, in any event accede, to the application by the appellants to adduce the transcript in evidence before us, which confirms beyond doubt that the point was not raised at the hearing. Indeed it is clear from that transcript that the FtT Judge led Ms Dirie to believe that the matters in issue which she needed to address in relation to dependency were those set out in the Refusal Letters, which did not involve any dispute about whether Ashkir had made the payments he said he had made.

[27] Mr Skinner submitted that this required fulfilment of the familiar criteria laid down in *Ladd v Marshall* [1954] 1 WLR 1489, and that they were not fulfilled in this case. I have some doubt whether a record of what happened at first instance in the form of a transcript attracts the stringency of these criteria; but if it does I would hold that they are fulfilled. Reasonable diligence did not require the transcript to have been obtained before the hearing took place before the Upper Tribunal, and until the Respondent's Notice raised the point the appellants could not reasonably have anticipated that it would be necessary to adduce the transcript to make good their procedural unfairness argument.

Ground 1

[28] There is a wealth of authority on the circumstances in which a failure to raise a point at a hearing amounts to procedural unfairness, both generally and in the context of immigration cases. It is only necessary to refer to a few.

[29] *HA v Secretary of State for the Home Department (No 2)* [2010] SC 457 [2010] CSIH 28 was a decision of an Extra Division of the Inner House of the Court of Session presided over by Lord Reed (now PSC), who delivered the Opinion. It made a number of general points about procedural fairness in the context of immigration cases, amongst which the following emerge at [4]–[13]. Subject to the procedural rules governing first instance tribunals, the tribunal has power to decide the procedure it adopts, but in doing so must act fairly. What fairness requires is essentially an intuitive judgment which is dependent on the context of the decision; although it is possible to identify a number of general principles, they cannot be applied by rote identically in every situation. An overall judgment must be made in the light of all the circumstances of a particular case. Whether there is procedural unfairness is fact-sensitive. See [4] and [13]. The tribunal may identify an issue which has not been raised by the parties to the proceedings, but it will be unfair, ordinarily at least, for it to base its decision upon its view of the issue without giving the parties an opportunity to address it upon the matter (see [7]). As an expert body, the tribunal is entitled to reject evidence notwithstanding that the evidence has not been challenged before it. Fairness may, however, require it to disclose its concerns about the evidence so as to afford the parties an opportunity to address them (see [8]). There is, on the other hand no general obligation on the tribunal to give notice to the parties during the hearing of all the matters on which it may relay in reaching its decision (see [10]). Where an applicant can generally be expected to be aware that the tribunal will have to assess their credibility, there will generally be no unfairness in a tribunal proceeding without drawing attention to a point which the applicant could reasonably expect to be plainly relevant to that assessment (at [11]–[12]).

[30] In *The Secretary of State for the Home Department v Maheshwaran* [2002] EWCA Civ 173 [2004] 176 Imm AR, Schiemann LJ delivered the judgment of this court. He drew attention to the difficulties often faced by those sitting at first instance in immigration cases. Of relevance to the present appeal are the following observations. There are innumerable decisions which have stressed that the requirements of fairness are very much conditioned by the facts of each case (at [6]). A failure to put to a party a point which is decided against him can be grossly unfair and lead to injustice because he must have a proper opportunity to deal with the point (at [4]). Where much depends on the credibility of a party which has made several inconsistent statements, that party has a forensic problem as to whether to

confront them or focus attention elsewhere. Fairness may in some such circumstances require the inconsistencies to be put to the witness but that will not usually be the case. Usually the tribunal can remain silent, especially if the party is represented, and see how the case unfolds (at [5]).

[31] Problems often arise as to how the tribunal can avoid giving an appearance of bias where, as has increasingly happened, the respondent is not represented at the hearing and so the usual adversarial testing of the applicant's evidence by cross-examination does not take place. In June 1999, the Immigration Appeal Tribunal gave guidance in what have come to be known as the Surendran Guidelines, given emphasis by the Immigration Appeal Tribunal in *MNM v Secretary of State for the Home Department* [2000] UKIAT 00005. Paragraph 5 of the Surendran Guidelines is of direct application in this case. It provides:

"5. Where no matters of credibility are raised in the letter of refusal but, from a reading of the papers the special adjudicator himself considers that there are matters of credibility arising therefrom, he should similarly point these out to the representative and ask that they be dealt with, either in examination of the appellant or in submissions."

[32] In *WN v Secretary of State for the Home Department* [2004] UKIAT 00213, Ouseley J (President) emphasised that a failure to follow the Surendran Guidelines was not itself conclusive of procedural unfairness. At [34] he said that paragraph 5 needs also to cover the position where no issue of credibility has been raised in the Refusal Letter and yet it may be obvious that further material provided to the adjudicator raises issues of credibility. They should be raised or put to the appellant so that he may answer them, but it does not mean that the hearing is unfair where that does not take place, at least where the appellant is represented. That depends on whether the points are obvious ones going to the appellant's credibility which he could be expected to realise needed addressing in any event, such as inconsistencies with previous statements or a failure to raise a particular matter earlier.

[33] The recent decision of the Supreme Court in *TUI UK Ltd v Griffiths* [2023] UKSC 48 reemphasises the principle that fairness generally requires that if the evidence of a witness is to be rejected, it should be challenged at the hearing so as to give them an opportunity to address the challenge; and that that is a matter of fairness to the witness as well as fairness to the parties, and necessary for the integrity of the court process in enabling the tribunal to reach a sound conclusion: see especially at [42]–[43], [55], and [70]. The rule is subject to certain exceptions and is to be applied flexibly in the circumstances of any individual case in application of the criterion of the overall fairness of the trial ([61]–[69] and [70(vii) and (viii)].

[34] Applying those principles, I have little hesitation in concluding that the failure by the FtT Judge to give the appellants and Ashkir an opportunity to address the point on which she decided the case was unfair. The Refusal Letters had not challenged that the payments which Ashkir said he had made to Ubah had been made by him. They were supported by remittance receipts with Ashkir's name and personal details on them. Rather, two points had been made in the Refusal Letters, one being that the number of payments was "sporadic" and the other being a lack of information about the recipient's financial circumstances. Neither of those raised any question about the credibility of Ashkir. The matter requiring to be addressed, so far as his involvement was concerned, was simply the extent of the payments

made by him. Although the evidence adduced before the FtT included a greater number of payments than had been advanced in the initial application to the respondent, with similar supporting documentation, there was no reason to anticipate an issue as to whether Ashkir had made them. This was reinforced by the comments of the FtT Judge at the hearing that the issue of dependency in dispute was that identified in the Refusal Letters, which was echoed in para 7 of her Decision that she treated the respondent's submissions as those set out in the Refusal Letters.

[35] Mr Skinner submitted that the point which emerged in the FtT Decision as determinative was one which it would have been obvious to those advising the appellants needed to be addressed without any prompting from the tribunal. I cannot agree. The remittance receipts made clear that the money had come from Ashkir. There was no reason to anticipate a focus on how Ashkir had been able to afford to remit the money. Mr Skinner does not suggest that the point the FtT Judge made is sufficient to outweigh the evidence of the documented remittance receipts which evidenced that Ashkir was the sender of the payments. Rather, he submits, in the terms set out at paragraph 39 of his skeleton argument, that

> "there is no other realistic inference to be drawn other than that the Sponsor was in effect a conduit for others' money, whether directly or by being provided for in kind by others freeing up the money he earned to send to the Appellants, and that any support provided to the Appellants is accordingly not the support *from him*". [emphasis in original]

I shall address below whether this is the inevitable inference, but assuming it to be so, it reinforces the point that it would not have been obvious that the appellants needed to address the source of the monies prior to their despatch by Ashkir. There is, to put it at the lowest, considerable doubt whether as a matter of law the source of the money is of any relevance to the question of dependency: see *Mahad v Entry Clearance Officer* [2009] UKSC 16 [2010] 1 WLR 48 *per* Lord Brown at [34]–[36] and Lord Kerr at [56], in which using the sponsor as a conduit was held not to affect dependency under the immigration rules. Ashkir's evidence made clear that he was living with his sister's family who charged him no rent in order to enable him to remit funds to the greatest extent possible to the appellants. If it be the case that they were also supporting his other living needs, as is suggested to be one of two inevitable inferences, it does not seem right, at least at first blush, to describe that as Ashkir acting "as a conduit for others' money": he would be sending his own money.

[36] In those circumstances this is not a case in which some obvious inconsistency in the evidence which was being put forward should foreseeably have been addressed without the tribunal specifically raising it.

[37] Nor can I accept Mr Skinner's submission that the failure to raise the point had no material impact on the outcome, which was in essence the ground on which the Upper Tribunal dismissed the appeal. The test is a high one. In *SH (Afghanistan) v Secretary of State for the Home Department* [2011] EWCA Civ 1284, this court was concerned with procedural unfairness in failing to grant an adjournment for further expert evidence as to the age of the applicant, and the question arose as to whether the judge had been right to conclude that even if the report had been obtained it was reasonably likely that the decision would have been the same. Moses LJ, giving the judgment of the court, said at [15]:

"15. The judge, on that issue, concluded that even if that report had been obtained, 'it is reasonably likely' that Immigration Judge Froom would have reached the same decision. This was not the correct test .... Tribunals, like courts, must set aside a determination reached by the adoption of an unfair procedure unless they are satisfied that it would be pointless to do so because the result would inevitably be the same. Both Simon Brown LJ and Dyson LJ reminded themselves, as all faced with the argument that the result would inevitably be the same must remind themselves, of Megarry J's evocation of the essence of justice in *John v Rees* [1970] Ch 345,402:

> 'It may be that there are some who would decry the importance which the courts attach to the observance of the rules of natural justice. "When something is obvious," they may say, "why force everyone to go through the tiresome waste of time involved in framing charges and giving an opportunity to be heard? The result is obvious from the start". Those who take this view do not, I think, do themselves justice. As everybody who has anything to do with the law well knows, the path of the law is strewn with examples of open and shut cases which, somehow, were not; unanswerable charges which, in the event, were completely answered; of inexplicable conduct which was fully explained; of fixed and unalterable determinations that, by discussion, suffered a change. Nor are those with any knowledge of human nature who pause to think for a moment likely to underestimate the feelings of resentment of those who find that a decision against them has been made without their being afforded any opportunity to influence the course of events.'"

[38] The test is whether remission would be pointless because the result would inevitably have been the same.

[39] I would not accept that the only inference from the material relied on by the FtT Judge is that asserted by Mr Skinner at paragraph 39 of his skeleton argument, namely that Ashkir was a conduit for others' money directly or by being provided for in kind by others freeing up the money he earned to send to the appellants. We do not have the draft tax return documents for 2020/21 which were before the FtT, but it is not obvious to me that a draft tax return by a self-employed taxi driver giving an operational profit is conclusive of disposable income. His evidence to the FtT Judge was that his gross receipts were of the order of £5,000 to £6,000 per month, and there are a number of reasons why net receipts in the given tax year, in the form of disposable income, might not match those shown in draft accounts. For example capital allowances on a vehicle purchased prior to the relevant tax period would not diminish his cash flow in that period. Many deductions from income may legitimately be made on a broad brush basis, such as allowances per mile for vehicle expenses, or use of a mobile phone for business purposes. All that is speculation so far as these draft accounts are concerned, but it means that this court cannot say with the necessary degree of certainty that remitting the matter would be pointless because the result would *inevitably* be the same. The outcome will depend upon the explanation given and the facts found, and, quite possibly, the application of disputed issues of law on the relevance of the source of the sponsor's funds and/or living support from others. Resolution of such legal issues is best left until the relevant facts have been found.

[40] For these reasons I would allow the appeal on ground 1. Ground 2 does not therefore arise for decision. The parties are agreed that the appropriate form of relief is to remit the matter to the First tier Tribunal.

Postscript

[41] By way of postscript, I should make two things clear. First, I am not expressing any view as to whether it formed a proper part of the FtT Judge's role, in adversarial proceedings, to take the point which formed the basis for her Decision when that point had not been taken by the respondent. We are concerned only with the consequences of her having done so. Secondly, Mr Skinner's submissions at times strayed into general propositions which lost sight of the facts of this case, perhaps through an anxiety that if the appeal were allowed, it would have a widespread effect on FtT decisions in immigration cases more generally. However, my conclusions have been reached very much on the facts of this particular case, which illustrates the point emphasised in both *HA* and *Maheshwaran*, that questions of procedural unfairness depends upon the context and are fact-sensitive and case-specific.

LORD JUSTICE ARNOLD:

[42] I agree.

LADY JUSTICE KING:

[43] I also agree.

SECRETARY OF STATE FOR THE HOME DEPARTMENT v AA (POLAND)

COURT OF APPEAL

Baker, Elisabeth Laing and Warby LJJ

[2024] EWCA Civ 18
19 January 2024

European Union law – expulsion – serious sex offender – long residence in the United Kingdom – period of imprisonment – sufficiency of integration prior to deportation decision – paragraph 4 of Schedule 1 to the Immigration (EEA) Regulations 2016 – double discounting of mitigating measures – human rights – Article 8 of the ECHR – private and family life – proportionality – application of EEA Regulations legally distinct

The Claimant, a citizen of Poland, moved to the United Kingdom in 2006. He met his wife, K, in 2007 and they married in 2012. His daughter, V, was born in July 2014. Police attended the Claimant's home in February 2016 and found 1,450 indecent images of children on his devices including some 300 in category A, the most serious. Some of the category B and C images were of V. In June 2018, the Claimant was sentenced to a total of five years' imprisonment and made subject to a wide-ranging Sexual Harm Prevention Order ('SHPO') for ten years. He was released on licence in December 2020. The Secretary of State for the Home Department decided to deport him pursuant to the Immigration (European Economic Area) Regulations 2016 ('the EEA Regulations') on the basis that he constituted a genuine, present, and sufficiently serious risk to the public to justify his deportation on grounds of public policy and public security, and that it was proportionate to order his removal to Poland on those grounds ('the Decision').

In a supplementary decision letter dated April 2021, the Secretary of State accepted that the Claimant had a right of permanent residence and that he had resided in the United Kingdom for a period of at least ten years. It was not accepted, however, that he was entitled to 'imperative grounds' protection pursuant to Article 28(3) of Directive 2004/38/EC ('the Directive') or regulation 27(4) of the EEA Regulations because he was insufficiently integrated into the United Kingdom. The Secretary of State considered that, although the case fell within the 'serious grounds' category pursuant to Article 28(2) of the Directive and regulation 27(3) of the EEA Regulations, that threshold was met because of the real risk of reoffending and the risk of harm if that occurred. The Claimant's human rights claim was rejected on the basis that, although the Nationality, Immigration and Asylum Act 2002 ('the 2002 Act') did not apply directly because the Claimant was an EEA national, the provisions of Part 5A were relevant because Article 8 ECHR applied equally to everyone regardless of nationality. The Secretary of State concluded that the Claimant had not shown that either of the exceptions in section 117C(4) and (5) of the 2002 Act were applicable or that there were 'very compelling circumstances' over and above those exceptions within the meaning of section 117C(6).

On appeal, the First-tier Tribunal ('FtT') held that the Claimant was entitled to 'imperative grounds' protection because his offending and imprisonment had led to his earlier integration being 'weakened but not so broken as to mean that he ceased to be entitled to the highest level of protection'. In relation to the level of threat the Claimant represented, the FtT held that, while he posed a genuine and present risk to public security, it could not be said that that was particularly serious such as to justify his removal on imperative grounds of public security. Had it been necessary to decide the issue, the FtT stated that it would have found the Claimant's removal disproportionate, mainly because of the effect it would have on his rehabilitation and risk of future offending. The FtT allowed the Claimant's appeal on human rights grounds on the basis that that outcome was dictated by the answer to the other grounds of appeal. The FtT held that the Claimant's integrative links to the United Kingdom meant that Article 8(1) ECHR was engaged by the deportation decision and that, removal being contrary to the EEA Regulations, applying section 117B(1) of the 2002 Act the decision was incapable of justification under Article 8(2). That established the very compelling circumstances required by section 117C(6). The Upper Tribunal ('UT') upheld the FtT's decision on further appeal.

Before the Court of Appeal, the Secretary of State submitted that the FtT had erred in law by misapplying the EEA Regulations and treating the application of the EEA Regulations as effectively decisive of the human rights claim.

Held, allowing the appeal:

(1) The issue for consideration was the degree of integration achieved by the Claimant in the ten years prior to the Decision. For the last 30 months of that period, he was in prison serving a sentence for serious sexual offending. For a period before that he was committing the offences. On the evidence, it was legitimate to infer that the Claimant had a long history of accessing child pornography and that the offending for which he was sentenced in 2018 spanned a period of at least a year before his arrest. It was fair to conclude that any integrating links formed in the 12-month period from February 2015 onwards were formed at or around the same time as the commission of a criminal offence (*para 48*).

(2) The instant case did not involve particularly strong features that would allow the tribunal to depart from the general normative guidance laid down by regulation 27(8) and paragraph 4 of Schedule 1 to the EEA Regulations. Accordingly, the FtT was duty bound to attribute 'little weight' to any integrating links formed by the Claimant during 42 of the 68 months immediately preceding the Decision. The FtT had in fact attributed significant weight to integration during the period when the Claimant was offending. The FtT had placed reliance on outward manifestations of integration at a time when the offending was 'going on in the background' and had attached real and significant weight to his conduct when in prison. Offending counted against the proposition that a person was integrated into society because it showed a disregard for fellow citizens and the rejection of core values of United Kingdom culture: *Binbuga v Secretary of State for the Home Department* [2019] EWCA Civ 551 applied. Serious sexual offending involved a stark rejection of fundamental societal norms. The rejection of United Kingdom values inherent in offending of that kind was not rendered less significant by the fact that the offending had not involved physical violence, or was conducted in secret. Nor was it appropriate to draw distinctions based on public activities that gave the superficial

appearance of integration. Further, it was arguable that the FtT should have attached little weight to any integrative links formed during the 28-month period between the Claimant's arrest and sentence. Although he was no longer offending at that time and at liberty, he was subject to criminal proceedings, on stringent bail conditions and the delay appeared largely due to the fact that he was falsely denying his guilt of the offences involving V *(paras 49 – 51)*.

(3) Measures such as imprisonment, licence conditions on release, SHPOs and notification requirements were all put in place because a person posed a threat to one of the fundamental interests of society. The existence of such measures was relevant because they involved a recognition of that threat and the need to prevent, manage, or mitigate it. The preventative or mitigating effects that such measures might have were not, however, themselves material to the question of what level of threat existed. The FtT's 'real world' approach in the instant case therefore involved the same error as was perpetrated by the FtT in *Restivo (EEA – prisoner transfer)* [2016] UKUT 449 (IAC). The seriousness of the threat that the Claimant's personal conduct represented should have been assessed without regard to the mitigating measures on which the FtT had placed weight. The FtT's approach to the OASys report had involved 'double discounting' which had fed into its overall conclusion that the risk could not be said to be 'particularly serious' and led to an under-estimate of the seriousness of the threat that the Claimant posed to the fundamental interests of society *(paras 54 – 59)*.

(4) The FtT had erred in stating that a balance was to be struck between the Claimant's personal conduct and the risk of compromising his rehabilitation. The relevance of the Claimant's 'personal conduct' was that it posed a threat to one of the fundamental interests of society in the United Kingdom which was serious enough to justify his removal to Poland on at least 'serious grounds'. His personal interest in rehabilitation was relevant on the other side of the balance, in the context of his private life rights. The key question in that context, however, was whether and to what extent his rehabilitation would be compromised by deportation. The FtT had no adequate basis for concluding that that would be so. It had no basis for finding that there was some public interest that counted against removing the Claimant and instead ensuring his rehabilitation within the context of United Kingdom society *(paras 64 – 66)*.

(5) The application of the EEA Regulations was a legally distinct exercise from the assessment of a human rights claim. Where both arose, they should be addressed separately and in turn: *Badewa (ss.117A–D and EEA Regulations) Nigeria* [2015] UKUT 329 (IAC) approved. The EEA Regulations should be addressed first, including the assessment required by regulation 27(5)(a) as to whether deportation would comply with the EU principle of proportionality. The provisions of Part 5A of the 2002 Act had no part to play at that stage. They must, however, be addressed as part of the human rights assessment, if the public interest question arose. If deportation would interfere with Article 8 ECHR rights, the question would arise as to whether it would be in accordance with the law. That would not be so if deportation would be contrary to the EEA Regulations. In such a case the human rights analysis need go no further. If deportation would be consistent with the EEA Regulations and otherwise lawful, the tribunal should address the public interest question in the way that Parliament had prescribed in Part 5A of the 2002 Act. Given the FtT's conclusions on the first two issues, it was unnecessary for it to address Part 5A. In doing so, however, it had adopted a flawed approach, first by placing weight on section 117B(1), and secondly by treating its conclusion that deportation

would breach the principle of proportionality as making out the 'very compelling circumstances' required by section 117C(6). It should have explicitly asked and answered the question of whether the case featured any and if so what 'very compelling' circumstances over and above those specified in section 117C(4) and (5) (*paras 71 – 73*).

Cases referred to:

B v Land Baden-Württemberg; Secretary of State for the Home Department v Vomero (Cases C-316/16 and C-424/16); [2019] QB 126; [2018] 3 WLR 1035; [2018] 3 CMLR 24; [2018] Imm AR 1145; [2018] INLR 399

Badewa (ss. 117A–D and EEA Regulations) [2015] UKUT 329 (IAC); [2015] Imm AR 1150; [2016] INLR 165

Binbuga v Secretary of State for the Home Department [2019] EWCA Civ 551; [2019] Imm AR 1026; [2019] INLR 403

KO (Nigeria) v Secretary of State for the Home Department; IT (Jamaica) v Secretary of State for the Home Department; NS (Sri Lanka) and Others v Secretary of State for the Home Department; Pereira v Secretary of State for the Home Department [2018] UKSC 53; [2018] 1 WLR 5273; [2019] 1 All ER 675; [2019] Imm AR 400; [2019] INLR 41

Land Baden-Württemberg v Tsakouridis (Case C-145/09); [2012] All ER (EC) 183; [2011] 2 CMLR 11; [2011] Imm AR 276; [2011] INLR 415

Mullarkey and Goodman v Broad [2009] EWCA Civ 2

Notting Hill Finance Limited v Sheikh [2019] EWCA Civ 1337; [2019] 4 WLR 146

R (on the application of Lumsdon and Others) v Legal Services Board [2015] UKSC 41; [2016] AC 697; [2015] 3 WLR 121; [2016] 1 All ER 391; [2015] 3 CMLR 42

Restivo (EEA – prisoner transfer) [2016] UKUT 449 (IAC); [2017] Imm AR 188

Rhuppiah v Secretary of State for the Home Department [2018] UKSC 58; [2018] 1 WLR 5536; [2019] 1 All ER 1007; [2019] Imm AR 452; [2019] INLR 233

Secretary of State for the Home Department v AA 5 July 2022 (DA/00003/2021) UTIAC (unreported)

Secretary of State for the Home Department v Viscu [2019] EWCA Civ 1052; [2019] 1 WLR 5376; [2020] 1 All ER 988; [2019] Imm AR 1298

Singh v Dass [2019] EWCA Civ 360

Legislation and international instruments judicially considered:

Charter of Fundamental Rights, Article 7
Citizens' Rights (Restrictions of Rights of Entry and Residence) (EU Exit) Regulations 2020, Schedule 1
Directive 2004/38/EC ('the Citizens Directive'), Articles 27 & 28
European Convention on Human Rights, Article 8
Immigration (European Economic Area) Regulations 2016, regulations 2, 23(6) & 27; paragraph 4 of Schedule 1
Nationality, Immigration and Asylum Act 2002, sections 32, 117A(2), 117B & 117C
UK Borders Act 2007, sections 32 & 33

Representation

Mr M Pilgerstorfer KC instructed by the Government Legal Department, for the Secretary of State;
Ms L Hirst instructed by Turpin Miller, for the Claimant.

Judgment

This judgment was handed down remotely at 10.30am on 19 January 2024 by circulation to the parties or their representatives by e-mail and by release to the National Archives.

LORD JUSTICE WARBY:

Introduction

[1] This appeal is about a decision made by the Secretary of State (SSHD) to deport AA, an EU citizen who had committed serious sexual offences in this country.

[2] The First-tier Tribunal (FtT) allowed AA's appeal against the SSHD's decision, holding that AA's removal would infringe his rights under the EU Treaties as implemented by the *Immigration (European Economic Area) Regulations 2016* (the 2016 Regulations) and his right to respect for private and family life under Article 8 of the European Convention on Human Rights (the Convention). The Upper Tribunal (UT) dismissed an appeal by the SSHD, holding that the FtT had made no error of law and that its conclusions were sufficiently reasoned. The SSHD brings this second appeal with the permission of Asplin LJ.

[3] The grounds of appeal raise two main issues: did the FtT err in law by (1) misapplying the 2016 Regulations and (2) treating the application of the 2016 Regulations as effectively decisive of AA's claim to remain in the UK on the basis of his human rights?

[4] AA is anonymised as he has been throughout the proceedings. That is not for his own sake but only because it is a necessary measure for the protection of his daughter (V). v was, as an infant, a victim of the relevant offending and benefits from the right to lifetime anonymity provided for by the Sexual Offences (Amendment) Act 1992.

The facts

[5] AA is a Polish national, born on 29 May 1981. In 2006 he moved to the UK. In April 2007 he met his wife K who had moved to the UK from Poland earlier that year. They were married in 2012. In January 2014, AA gained a Master's degree in Aeronautical Engineering. In July of the same year v was born. At this point AA began openly questioning his gender identity. (I use male pronouns because AA has indicated he prefers this).

[6] On 23 February 2016, police attended AA's home with a search warrant, acting on intelligence that someone at the address had used the internet to access indecent images of children. On AA's devices the police found some 1,450 such images, including some 300 in Category A, the most serious. Some of the Category

B and C images were of v AA was arrested and charged. He pleaded guilty to three counts of making indecent images but contested charges of sexually assaulting his daughter, taking two indecent Category B images of her, and taking 17 indecent Category C images of her including a video. On 4 May 2018, in the Crown Court at Isleworth, he was convicted of all those charges.

[7] On 18 June 2018, AA was sentenced to a total of five years' imprisonment comprising four years in respect of the sexual assault on V, concurrent terms for the other offending against V, and 12 months consecutive for the offences to which he had pleaded guilty. The sentencing judge made a wide-ranging Sexual Harm Prevention Order (SHPO) for 10 years. As a further consequence of his conviction AA was subject to the sex offender registration and notification requirements for 10 years and was liable to be placed on the barring list by the Disclosure and Barring Service.

[8] On 2 July 2018, AA was warned by the SSHD that he could be liable to deportation pursuant to the 2016 Regulations and invited to submit representations. On 16 December 2020, the custodial portion of AA's sentence came to an end and he was released on licence. On 20 December 2020, having considered AA's representations that his deportation would be contrary to the 2016 Regulations and his Article 8 rights, the SSHD decided that he should be deported (the Decision). A supplementary decision letter of 6 April 2021 affirmed the Decision on slightly different grounds.

The legal framework

[9] Section 32 of the UK Borders Act 2007 requires the SSHD to make a deportation order in respect of a person who is not a British Citizen and is convicted in the UK of an offence and sentenced to at least 12 months' imprisonment (a "foreign criminal") unless the case falls within an exception under s 33 of the 2007 Act. At the material times this case would have fallen within one of the exceptions if AA's removal would breach his right to respect for private and family life under Article 8 (Exception 1, s 33(2)(a)) or his rights under the EU Treaties (Exception 3, s 33(4)).

[10] The main focus of attention in this case has been on AA's rights under the EU Treaties.

[11] The expulsion of EU citizens by Member States is governed by Directive 2004/38/EC, known as the Citizens' Rights Directive. Article 27 of the Directive authorises restrictions on freedom of movement on grounds of public policy, public security or public health, subject to certain preconditions. Among these are that the measure must comply with the principle of proportionality and be based exclusively on the personal conduct of the individual concerned which "must represent a genuine, present and sufficiently serious threat affecting one of the fundamental interests of society."

[12] Article 28 sets out three levels or tiers of protection against expulsion. In every case the Member State must take account of "considerations such as how long the individual concerned has resided on its territory, his/her age, state of health, family and economic situation, social and cultural integration into the host Member State and the extent of his/her links with the country of origin" (Article 28(1)). If the individual concerned has the right of permanent residence in the host State an expulsion decision must not be taken against them "except on serious grounds of public policy or public security" (Article 28(2)). If the individual has "resided in the

host Member State for the previous ten years" an expulsion decision must not be taken against them "except if the decision is based on imperative grounds of public security, as defined by Member States" (Article 28(3)).

[13] Decisions of the CJEU have made clear that the ten-year residence provision in Article 28(3) is not to be interpreted or applied literally or mechanically. It is not just a question of arithmetic. The factors specified in Article 28(1) are relevant. Where the individual in question has been subjected to a period of imprisonment that may break integrative links previously forged with the host Member State; to decide whether that is so it is necessary to conduct an overall assessment of the situation at the time of the relevant decision: see *Land Baden-Wurtemburg v Tsakouridis* (Case C-145/09) [2011] 2 CMLR 11 [33], *B and Vomero* [2019] QB 126 [72]–[75]. In *Secretary of State for the Home Department v Viscu* [2019] EWCA Civ 1052 [44] Flaux LJ identified the following points as established by the European jurisprudence:

"... (i) that the degree of protection against expulsion to which a Union national resident in another member state is entitled under the Directive is dependent upon the degree of integration of that individual in the member state; (ii) that, in general, a custodial sentence is indicative of a rejection of societal values and thus of a severing of integrative links with the member state but (iii) that the extent to which there is such a severing of integrative links will depend upon an overall assessment of the individual's situation at the time of the expulsion decision."

[14] The 2016 Regulations transposed the provisions of the Citizens' Rights Directive into domestic law with added details. Although the 2016 Regulations have now been revoked, they continue to apply to this case because AA was protected at the time of the Decision: see regulation 2(3) and Schedule 1 of the *Citizens' Rights (Restrictions of Rights of Entry and Residence) (EU Exit) Regulations* 2020.

[15] Regulation 23(6) of the 2016 Regulations authorises the removal of an EEA national who has entered the UK if the SSHD "has decided that the person's removal is justified on grounds of public policy, public security or public health in accordance with regulation 27". Such a decision is termed a "relevant decision".

[16] Regulation 27 contains the following provisions about such decisions:

"(3) A relevant decision may not be taken in respect of a person with a right of permanent residence under regulation 15 except on serious grounds of public policy and public security.

(4) A relevant decision may not be taken except on imperative grounds of public security in respect of an EEA national who –

(a) has a right of permanent residence under regulation 15 and who has resided in the United Kingdom for a continuous period of at least ten years prior to the relevant decision; ...

...

(5) The public policy and public security requirements of the United Kingdom include restricting rights otherwise conferred by these Regulations in order to protect the fundamental interests of society, and where a relevant decision is taken

on grounds of public policy or public security it must also be taken in accordance with the following principles –

>   (a) the decision must comply with the principle of proportionality;
>
>   (b) the decision must be based exclusively on the personal conduct of the person concerned;
>
>   (c) the personal conduct of the person must represent a genuine, present and sufficiently serious threat affecting one of the fundamental interests of society, taking into account past conduct of the person and that the threat does not need to be imminent;
>
>   (d) matters isolated from the particulars of the case or which relate to considerations of general prevention do not justify the decision;
>
>   (e) a person's previous criminal convictions do not in themselves justify the decision;
>
>   (f) the decision may be taken on preventative grounds, even in the absence of a previous criminal conviction, provided the grounds are specific to the person.
>
> (6) Before taking a relevant decision on the grounds of public policy and public security in relation to a person ('P') who is resident in the United Kingdom, the decision maker must take account of considerations such as the age, state of health, family and economic situation of P, P's length of residence in the United Kingdom, P's social and cultural integration into the United Kingdom and the extent of P's links with P's country of origin."

[17] Regulation 27(5) reflects and expands on Articles 27(1) and (2) of the Citizens' Rights Directive. Regulation 27(6) reflects Article 28(1); Regulation 27(3) corresponds to Article 28(2) (serious grounds protection); and Regulation 27(4) corresponds to Article 28(3) (imperative grounds protection).

[18] In *Restivo (EEA – prisoner transfer)* [2016] UKUT 449 (IAC) the UT considered the right approach to the assessment of whether a person's conduct represents a "genuine, present and sufficiently serious threat" for the purposes of the Regulations.[*] The FtT had held that it was not and could not be established that such a threat was posed by a convicted murderer whom the trial judge had described as "a man capable of inhuman depravity" as he would remain in prison for at least a further 37 years. The UT held that this was an error of law which wrongly conflated the assessment of risk with the question of management of that risk. The UT summarised its conclusions at [34]:

> "Where the personal conduct of a person represents a genuine, present and sufficiently serious threat affecting one of the fundamental interests of society,

---

[*] The issue arose under Regulation 21(5)(c) of the Immigration (EEA) Regulations 2006, but this was in materially identical terms to those of regulation 27(5)(c) of the 2016 Regulations.

the fact that such threat is managed while that person serves his or her prison sentence is not itself material to the assessment of the threat he or she poses. The threat exists, whether or not it cannot generate further offending simply because the person concerned, being imprisoned, has significantly less opportunity to commit further criminal offences."

[19] Regulation 27(8) provides:

"A court or tribunal considering whether the requirements of this regulation are met must (in particular) have regard to the considerations contained in Schedule 1 (considerations of public policy, public security and the fundamental interests of society, etc)"

[20] The considerations contained in Schedule 1 include the following:

"**Considerations of public policy and public security**

1. The EU Treaties do not impose a uniform scale of public policy or public security values: member States enjoy considerable discretion, acting within the parameters set by the EU Treaties, applied where relevant by the EEA agreement, to define their own standards of public policy and public security, for purposes tailored to their individual contexts, from time to time.

Application of paragraph 1 to the United Kingdom

2. An EEA national or the family member of an EEA national having extensive familial and societal links with persons of the same nationality or language does not amount to integration in the United Kingdom; a significant degree of wider cultural and societal integration must be present before a person may be regarded as integrated in the United Kingdom

3. Where an EEA national or the family member of an EEA national has received a custodial sentence, or is a persistent offender, the longer the sentence, or the more numerous the convictions, the greater the likelihood that the individual's continued presence in the United Kingdom represents a genuine, present and sufficiently serious threat affecting one of the fundamental interests of society.

4. Little weight is to be attached to the integration of an EEA national or the family member of an EEA national within the United Kingdom if the alleged integrating links were formed at or around the same time as –

    a) the commission of a criminal offence;

    b) an act otherwise affecting the fundamental interests of society;

    c) the EEA national or family member of an EEA national was in custody.

5. The removal from the United Kingdom of an EEA national or the family member of an EEA national who is able to provide substantive evidence of not demonstrating a threat (for example, through demonstrating that the EEA national or the family member of an EEA national has successfully reformed or rehabilitated) is less likely to be proportionate.

6. ...

7. For the purposes of these Regulations, the fundamental interests of society in the United Kingdom include –

   a) preventing unlawful immigration and abuse of the immigration laws, and maintaining the integrity and effectiveness of the immigration control system (including under these Regulations) and of the Common Travel Area;

   b) maintaining public order;

   c) preventing social harm;

   d) preventing the evasion of taxes and duties;

   e) protecting public services;

   f) excluding or removing an EEA national or family member of an EEA national with a conviction (including where the conduct of that person is likely to cause, or has in fact caused, public offence) and maintaining public confidence in the ability of the relevant authorities to take such action;

   g) tackling offences likely to cause harm to society where an immediate or direct victim may be difficult to identify but where there is wider societal harm (such as offences related to the misuse of drugs or crime with a cross-border dimension as mentioned in Article 83(1) of the Treaty on the Functioning of the European Union);

   h) combating the effects of persistent offending (particularly in relation to offences, which if taken in isolation, may otherwise be unlikely to meet the requirements of regulation 27);

   i) protecting the rights and freedoms of others, particularly from exploitation and trafficking;

   j) protecting the public;

   k) acting in the best interests of a child (including where doing so entails refusing a child admission to the United Kingdom, or otherwise taking an EEA decision against a child);

l)   countering terrorism and extremism and protecting shared values."

[21] Turning to the application of Article 8 of the Convention, deportation is likely to represent an interference with a person's right to respect for private or family life or their home. Where that is so, the question will arise of whether it would be justified under Article 8(2). If deportation would be lawful and pursue a legitimate aim the question will arise of whether it is proportionate to that aim. Part 5A of the Nationality Immigration and Asylum Act 2002 lays down rules for judges to apply when determining that question (referred to as "the public interest question").

[22] Section 117A(2) of the 2002 Act provides that:

"in considering the public interest question the court or tribunal must (in particular) have regard

(a)   in all cases, to the considerations listed in section 117B, and

(b)   in cases concerning the deportation of foreign criminals, to the considerations listed in section 117C"

[23] Section 117B(1) provides that "the maintenance of effective immigration controls is in the public interest". Section 117B(5) provides that "little weight should be given to a private life established by a person at a time when the person's immigration status is precarious". Although this provision does not apply on the facts of this case it is relevant for reasons that will appear.

[24] Section 117C(6) provides that in the case of a foreign criminal (C) who has been sentenced to a period of imprisonment of at least four years (conventionally referred to as a "serious offender") "the public interest requires deportation unless there are very compelling circumstances, over and above those described in exceptions 1 and 2". Those exceptions are set out in s 117C(4) and (5):

"(4)   Exception 1 applies where –

(a)   C has been lawfully resident in the United Kingdom for most of C's life,

(b)   C is socially and culturally integrated in the United Kingdom, and

(c)   there would be very significant obstacles to C's integration into the country to which C is proposed to be deported.

(5)   Exception 2 applies where C has a genuine and subsisting relationship with a qualifying partner, or a genuine and subsisting parental relationship with a qualifying child, and the effect of C's deportation on the partner or child would be unduly harsh."

[25] The purpose of Part 5A of the 2002 Act is to reflect "the Government's and Parliament's view of how, as a matter of public policy, the balance should be struck" and "an assessment of all the factors relevant to the application of article 8 …"; the provisions are designed "to provide clear guidelines to limit the scope for judicial evaluation" and "to narrow rather than to widen the residual area of discretionary

judgement for the court to take account of public interest or other factors not directly reflected in the wording of the statute": *KO (Nigeria) v Secretary of State for the Home Department* [2018] UKSC 53, [2018] 1 WLR 5273 [12]–[15] (Lord Carnwath JSC, with whom the other Justices agreed).

The Decision

[26] The SSHD decided to deport AA pursuant to the 2016 Regulations. The decision letter of December 2020 concluded that he constituted a genuine, present, and sufficiently serious risk to the public to justify his deportation on grounds of public policy and public security, and that it was proportionate to order his removal to Poland on those grounds. The SSHD initially proceeded on the footing that AA had not shown a right of permanent residence but said that the decision would have been the same if he had. In the supplementary decision letter the SSHD accepted that AA did have a right of permanent residence and, further, that he had resided in the UK for a period of at least 10 years between 2006 and 2018. The SSHD did not accept, however, that AA was entitled to "imperative grounds" protection. This was because, applying the "integration" test identified in *Tsakouridis*, AA was insufficiently integrated into the UK community. The SSHD accepted that the case fell within the "serious grounds" category but concluded that this threshold was met because of the real risk of reoffending and the risk of harm if that occurred.

[27] The SSHD rejected AA's human rights claim on the basis that, although the 2002 Act did not apply directly to the case because AA was an EEA national, the provisions of Part 5A were relevant because Article 8 applies equally to everyone regardless of nationality and "it would not be fair to consider Article 8 claims from EEA nationals either more or less generously than claims from non-EEA nationals". The SSHD concluded that AA had not shown that either of the exceptions in s 117C(4) and (5) applied to him or that there were "very compelling circumstances" over and above those exceptions within the meaning of s 117C(6).

The FtT appeal

[28] AA's appeal to the FtT raised four main issues. The first was the level of protection to which AA was entitled (the level of protection issue). The answer turned on whether AA was sufficiently integrated in the UK. The FtT Judge (the FtTJ or the Judge) considered evidence from AA, statements from some character witnesses, and a report on AA prepared by the probation service using the Offender Assessment System known as OASys. The Judge held that the SSHD had erred on this point. He held that AA was entitled to imperative grounds protection because his offending and imprisonment had led to his earlier integration being "weakened but not so broken as to mean that he ceased to be entitled to the highest level of protection".

[29] The Judge's reasons for that conclusion included that AA's offending was "a secret aspect of his life that was not apparent to those around him", his wider life being "productive and faultless": [30]. The Judge went on (at [33]) to say this:

> "The offending that [was] going on in the background had little active effect on the remainder of his public social and cultural life, even though it is by its nature antisocial. While I do not diminish the harm this type of offending causes, in this

appeal it has had a less destructive effect on integration than, for example, would be the case with physically violent conduct in public, gang membership, and so on. It is insidious and conducted behind closed doors, but this also means that normal life continued around it. While at first blush that analysis may seem unpalatable, in my view it is necessary to give effect to the purpose of the present exercise: assessing integration."

[30] The second issue was the level of threat which AA's personal conduct represented (the level of threat issue). The FtTJ addressed this question by reference to the OASys report and the protective measures imposed as part of AA's sentence. The Judge rejected a submission for the SSHD that *Restivo* showed that such measures should be disregarded for this purpose. He distinguished the case as concerned only with the narrow question of whether incarceration should be disregarded when assessing risk at the point of a deportation decision. The Judge said that what was required was "a 'real world' risk assessment" and that he was "entitled to assess the risk posed by the appellant on release in light of the measures to be put in place on release to both manage the risk he poses and facilitate his rehabilitation". Those measures referred to included the SHPO, the notification requirements, and the licence conditions to which AA would be subject upon his release from custody.

[31] The Judge identified the "high watermark" of the SSHD's case as the OASys Assessment that he posed a "medium" risk of serious harm to children when in the community. But he held that this had to be considered "in light of the low risk of reoffending and the protective measures provided by the SHPO", the likelihood that AA would comply with that order, and the existence of "multi-agency protection" against such offending in any event. Applying that approach the Judge held that while AA did pose a genuine and present risk to public security "it cannot be said that this is particularly serious such as to mean that his removal is justified on imperative grounds of public security".

[32] The third issue was whether AA's removal would comply with the principle of proportionality. The FtTJ's decisions on the first two issues made it unnecessary for him to decide that question. He said however that if it had been necessary he would have found that AA's removal would be disproportionate. The Judge explained that AA's gender identity issues had little weight in this calculation; he reached his decision mainly because of the effect that removal would have on AA's "rehabilitation and risk of future offending". He said that AA's social rehabilitation in the state in which he had become generally integrated was in the public interest. A balance was to be struck "between AA's personal conduct and the risk of compromising that rehabilitation". There was no evidence of the support provisions available in Poland, and (the Judge observed) he should not simply assume that they must be worse. Yet it was "vanishingly unlikely" that AA would face "anything like the same scrutiny and access to assistance" in Poland as he would in the UK. Deportation would increase almost all the risk factors identified in the OASys report.

[33] The fourth issue was whether removal would breach AA's human rights (the human rights issue). The FtTJ allowed the appeal against the SSHD's decision on this issue on the basis that the outcome was dictated by the answer to the other grounds of appeal, and no separate analysis was required. At [20] he said that:

"Given that the appellant is a 'serious offender' and not entitled to rely on either statutory exception at s 117C of the 2002 Act, he would be required to demonstrate very compelling circumstances such that his removal would be a disproportionate interference with the right to respect for his private and family life afforded by Article 8(1). The regulations already require a proportionality assessment which takes into account the factors specified at reg 27(5) and (6) and which gives effect to Article 7 of the Charter of Fundamental Rights. If the appeal under the regulations is dismissed then the appellant will already have had his Article 8 ECHR proportionality case considered at its highest within the regulations. If the appeal under the regulations is allowed then, applying s 117B(1) of the 2002 Act, the maintenance of effective immigration controls will require that he be permitted to remain in the UK. That will be positively determinative of his human rights appeal."

At [55] the Judge held that AA's "integrative links to the United Kingdom" as discussed earlier meant that Article 8(1) was "engaged" by the decision to remove and that, removal being contrary to the 2016 Regulations, "applying s 117B(1) the decision is incapable of justification under Article 8(2)". That established "the very compelling circumstances required by s 117C(6)".

The UT decision

[34] The FtT granted the SSHD permission to appeal to the UT on three grounds: that the FtTJ materially misdirected himself in law on the question of AA's integration; failed to give adequate reasons for his finding that the threat posed by AA was not sufficiently serious to provide imperative grounds of public security for deporting AA; and failed to give adequate reasons for his findings on proportionality, both in respect of the 2016 Regulations and Article 8.

[35] The UT accepted that the SSHD's concerns about the case were "unsurprising" given that AA had received a substantial prison sentence for "serious and abhorrent criminal behaviour" and yet the FtTJ had ruled that he would not be deported. As I have said, however, the UT concluded that no error of law had been demonstrated.

[36] On the level of protection issue the UT saw no error in the FtTJ's identification of the relevant legal principles. It said the question for the UT was whether the Judge had failed to apply those principles properly to the facts before him. The Judge had taken account of the relevant factors, conducted the necessary "overall assessment", and reached an evaluative conclusion. His finding that AA was, "*otherwise than with regard to his offending*, strongly integrated" was "well within the range of conclusions open to the judge" [emphasis in original]. The UT said the nub of this aspect of the SSHD's appeal was a challenge to the Judge's handling of the offending itself, and in particular his paragraph [33] (quoted at [29] above). The SSHD's case was, said the UT, that the approach adopted in that paragraph "radically underplays the profoundly counter-social nature of this offending" and that the Judge's "failure to give proper weight to this fundamentally important factor led him into public law error".

[37] The UT rejected these contentions for three main reasons. First, it said the passage in question had to be considered in the context of the judgment as a whole. Secondly, the UT concluded that in that passage "the Judge was making a more limited point about the nature of AA's offending than the SSHD fears". The Judge

had accepted that the offending was "actively repudiatory of the social and cultural norms underpinning integration". In the disputed passage he was making the limited, and fair, point

> "that while some forms of offending are *almost inevitably* inconsistent or incompatible with the development of *other* strong integrative links, some are not, and AA's fell into the second category."

Thirdly, the UT noted that it was inherent in the need for a case-by-case scrutiny of all the relevant factors that "sometimes the overall balance will come down against deportation, even in cases of serious and abhorrent offending marked by substantial prison sentences".

[38] On the level of threat issue, the UT summarised the FtTJ's approach, noting that he had regard to "the measurement of his inherent risk of offending, as set out in the OASys report, and the measures to be put in place on release to facilitate his rehabilitation and manage the continuing risk he did pose". The UT noted that the SSHD's appeal on this issue was based on "insufficiency of reasoning". It rejected that challenge on the basis that the judgment made clear that the Judge had considered the OASys report carefully and in considerable detail and had conducted a legitimate "real world" factual evaluation. The SSHD disagreed with the Judge's assessment of the threat but that was not the test. The UT was satisfied that the Judge's decision was "properly approached, and one to which he was properly entitled, and which he sufficiently explained".

[39] In these circumstances, said the UT, the proportionality issue did not arise. The third ground of appeal became academic since the Decision could not stand in any event.

The appeal to this court

[40] The four grounds of appeal for which permission was granted reflect the issues raised before the FtT.

(1) On the level of protection issue it is said that the FtTJ erred (a) by failing properly or at all to apply paragraph 4 of Schedule 1 to the Regulations when conducting his overall assessment of integrative links; (b) in his paragraph [33], by treating AA's offending as having a less destructive effect on integration than "physically violent conduct in public".

(2) On the level of threat issue it is argued that the Judge erred (a) by taking account of the protective measures and wrongly distinguishing *Restivo*; (b) by discounting the risk identified in the OASys report by reference to matters that had already been taken into account in the OASys assessment.

(3) On the proportionality issue, the SSHD contends that the Judge's reasoning was flawed in two respects: (a) he identified the wrong balancing process: the balance to be struck was between the impact of removal on AA's rights and the imperative public security grounds that supported removal; (b) he assumed, without evidence, that the support available to AA in Poland would be worse than in the UK, despite correctly directing himself that he should not make such an assumption.

(4) On the human rights issue, it is argued that the Judge (a) wrongly treated the issue of proportionality arising under Article 8 as identical to the one arising under the 2016 Regulations, whereas it was incumbent on the FtT to apply the structured analysis mandated by Part 5A of the 2002 Act; (b) failed properly to consider the "very compelling circumstances" test prescribed by s 117C; and (c) erroneously relied on s 117B(1).

[41] These grounds raise some procedural questions. They are all criticisms of the FtTJ. They do not map neatly or precisely onto the issues addressed by the UT in the decision under appeal. AA's Respondent's Notice objected to Ground 4 being relied upon in this court, contending that none of the points now made were advanced before the FtT or on appeal to the UT. AA's Skeleton Argument added that the SSHD's case on Ground 2 was not put to the UT. In her oral submissions, Ms Hirst broadened the objection to encompass Ground 1, contending that this court should not allow the SSHD to rely on any point that was not raised below.

[42] The scope of the appeal is affected in other ways by AA's Respondent's Notice. The main thrust of this is to contend that this is a second appeal from the decision of a specialist fact-finding tribunal which should be respected unless it is quite clear that the tribunal has misdirected itself, which is not the position here. But the Respondent's Notice also seeks to rely on different or additional grounds for upholding the decisions below.

[43] I propose to consider these aspects of the case as I address the four issues in turn.

The level of protection issue

[44] Having scrutinised the written grounds of appeal from the FtT, which the FtT gave permission to argue in the UT, I conclude that both the points now taken by the SSHD were sufficiently covered by the grounds. Ground 1(b) on this appeal was squarely before the UT. That is plain from the reasoning of the UT which I have summarised above. Ground 1(a) was put more broadly in the grounds of appeal to the UT. These alleged that the FtTJ had "failed to have regard to" the relevant provisions of the 2016 Regulations, including Schedule 1. Specific attention was not drawn to paragraph 4 of Schedule 1. As Ms Hirst submitted, this point was "not advanced to the UT in the form it is now". But it was addressed, albeit tangentially, by the UT when it held that the FtTJ had addressed himself correctly to the principles to be applied in conducting the "overall assessment".

[45] In my judgement, the FtTJ did fall into legal error in his approach to this issue in both the ways relied on by the SSHD and the UT erred in law in upholding his decision.

[46] Paragraph 4 of Schedule 1 is in mandatory terms, requiring "little weight … to be attached" to any integrating links formed "at or around the same time as" any offending or imprisonment. Regulation 27(8) of the 2016 Regulations is also in mandatory terms. It is true, as Ms Hirst points out, that what Regulation 27(8) requires the court or tribunal to do is to "have regard to" the matters listed in Schedule 1. But I cannot accept Ms Hirst's submission that these provisions are "not binding" on the FtT which is free to decide how to have regard to the specified matters in any given case. That is too broad a view.

[47] The statutory language is similar to that of s 117B(5) of the 2002 Act, quoted above. In *Rhuppiah v Home Secretary* [2018] UKSC 58, [2018] 1 WLR 5536 [49] Lord Wilson JSC (with whom the other Justices agreed) characterised s 117B(5) as an "instruction" by Parliament to "have regard to the consideration that little weight should be given" to a private life formed by a person when their immigration status was precarious. He concluded that this affords the decision-maker only a small and "limited degree of flexibility"; the statutory provisions provide "generalised normative guidance that may be overridden in an exceptional case by particularly strong features" of the case. I would apply that reasoning to Regulation 27(8) and Schedule 1 paragraph 4 of the 2016 Regulations.

[48] The FtTJ recited those provisions, and this court will always take a benevolent approach to judgments of specialist tribunals, but I think it is clear enough that the Judge did not give effect to these provisions in deciding this issue. That was a material error. In the circumstances of this case the provisions were capable of having real importance. The issue for consideration was the degree of integration achieved by AA in the ten years prior to the Decision in December 2020. For the last 30 months of that period (June 2018 to December 2020) AA was in prison serving a sentence for serious sexual offending. For a period before that he was committing the offences. Although the papers before us do not allow precise identification of that period we do know that it ended with his arrest in February 2016, we know the scale of the offending, we have the sentencing remarks, the OASys report, and the expert evidence provided to the sentencing judge. Having regard to this material I am satisfied that it would be legitimate to infer that AA had a long history of accessing child pornography and that the offending for which he was sentenced in 2018 spanned a period of at least a year before his arrest, that is to say from no later than February 2015. Certainly, it would be fair to conclude that any integrating links formed in the 12-month period from February 2015 onwards were formed "at or around the same time as the commission of a criminal offence".

[49] It has not been suggested that this was an exceptional case involving particularly strong features that would allow the tribunal to depart from the general normative guidance laid down by Regulation 27(8) and paragraph 4 of Schedule 1. On that footing, if AA formed any integrating links with UK society in the 68 months immediately preceding the Decision the FtTJ was duty bound to attribute "little weight" to any such links formed during 42 of those months. In fact, the FtTJ attributed significant weight to integration during the period when AA was offending, as is clear from his paragraph [33]. In that paragraph the Judge placed reliance on outward manifestations of integration at a time when the offending was "going on in the background". In paragraph [34] the Judge also attached real and significant weight to AA's conduct when in prison, saying that he had "engaged as much as he could with the activities on offer". In my judgement this reasoning was inconsistent with Regulation 27(8) and paragraph 4 of Schedule 1.

[50] The reasoning in paragraph [33] of the FtT judgment is also wrong in principle. I am not persuaded by the UT's narrow interpretation of this passage. But I do not think the FtTJ's assessment can withstand scrutiny even on the UT's analysis. The distinction identified by the UT is not a legitimate one. The reason why offending counts against the proposition that a person is integrated into society is that it shows disregard for fellow citizens and the rejection of core values of UK culture. The reasoning of Hamblen LJ in *Binbuga v Secretary of State for the Home Department* [2019] EWCA Civ 551 [56]–[57] is apposite:

"Social integration refers to the extent to which a foreign criminal has become incorporated within the lawful social structure of the UK ... [and] to the acceptance and assumption by the foreign criminal of the culture of the UK, its core values, ideas, customs and social behaviour. That includes acceptance of the principle of the rule of law."

Serious sexual offending such as that committed by AA involves a stark rejection of fundamental societal norms. AA was a large-scale consumer of pornography depicting and involving the abuse of children. He committed contact sexual offending against a vulnerable infant who was his own daughter. Such behaviour involves a repudiation of at least two core values of UK society: the need to protect children and the need to maintain trust between parent and child. The rejection of UK values inherent in offending of this kind is not rendered less significant by the fact that the offending did not involve physical violence, or was conducted in secret. A great deal of serious offending is non-violent and secretive. Nor is it appropriate to draw distinctions based on public activities that give the superficial appearance of integration. Much serious criminality is engaged in by people who lead outwardly decent lives. These are not regarded as mitigating features.

[51] I would add some words about the intermediate period between AA's arrest and sentence (February 2016 to June 2018). In my view it is arguable that the Judge should have attached little weight to any integrative links formed during this 28-month period also. This was a time when AA was no longer offending and was at liberty; but throughout this period he was subject to criminal proceedings and stringent bail conditions. More significantly perhaps, it appears that the delay was largely due to the fact that AA was falsely denying his guilt of the offences involving v His was not a technical, legal defence. AA's case, rejected by the jury, was that the touching of v and the creation of images of her were all innocent and not sexually motivated. It could perhaps be said that this period, or parts of it, fell at "around the same time as" the offending or the imprisonment so that paragraph 4 of Schedule 1 applied directly. Whether or not that is so, it would seem incongruous to attach more than "little weight" to any integrative links formed under those circumstances. The Judge evidently did so, however, finding (at [34]) that during this period AA "threw himself into therapy and addressing his gender identity and the possibility of imprisonment".

The level of threat issue

[52] I can understand why AA objects to pursuit of this ground of appeal. It is certainly fair to say that neither of the points now advanced was directly addressed in the judgment of the UT. I infer that this is because (at the minimum) neither was pressed clearly in oral argument. The mere fact that permission to appeal has been granted does not preclude such an objection: *Mullarkey v Broad* [2009] EWCA Civ 2 [9]. I would however permit the SSHD to pursue this ground, for three reasons. The first is that again, on a careful reading of the grounds of appeal to the UT for which permission was granted by the FtT, Ground 3(a) falls within their scope. Paragraph 12 of those grounds, although somewhat diffuse, does assert that the FtTJ was wrong to have "regard to measures that will be put into place on the appellant's release" as reducing "the seriousness of the threat". Secondly, the UT held that the FtTJ's decision that the threat was not sufficiently serious was "one which was

properly approached, to which he was properly entitled". If the SSHD's Ground 3 is sound that was an error of law.

[53] Thirdly, I would permit reliance on this ground of appeal even if, on a proper analysis, it involved new points not taken below. The applicable criteria are well-known and need no repetition. Thy are summarised in *Singh v Dass* [2019] EWCA Civ 360 and *Notting Hill Finance Ltd v Sheikh* [2019] EWCA Civ 1337, [2019] 4 WLR 146. The points now raised are pure points of law of general importance. They do not turn on any evidence that was not adduced before the FtT, and there is no reason to believe that AA's case would have been conducted differently if the points had been more squarely raised below. It is not unfair to him to allow them to be raised now. He has a fair opportunity to answer them. Any financial impact can be adequately addressed by the court's discretion as to costs.

[54] The passages in *Restivo* which I have cited above are clearly in point. As the FtTJ noted, that case involved a challenge to a deportation order which the SSHD had made with a view to exploring the possibility of transferring the offender to Italy to serve his life sentence there. The offender challenged the order on the footing that there were legal impediments in Italy to effecting such a transfer. The UT addressed that question, holding that such impediments were irrelevant to the validity of the deportation decision. None of this is relevant here. But the passages I have cited from *Restivo* address a separate and distinct question, about the right approach to the assessment of threat. That aspect of the decision is directly material to the present case. In *Restivo* the issue was the relevance of the fact that the person concerned would remain imprisoned for many years after the date of the decision under scrutiny. But that is not a satisfactory ground of distinction. The underlying question of principle is the same: should a sentence or similar measure imposed to prevent or mitigate a threat which an individual's personal conduct poses to the interests of society be taken into account when assessing the seriousness of that threat?

[55] In my view, *Restivo* was rightly decided on this point and the reasoning applies to the present case. Measures such as imprisonment, licence conditions on release, SHPOs, and notification requirements are all put in place *because* a person poses a threat to one of the fundamental interests of society. The existence of such measures is relevant because they involve a recognition of that threat and the need to prevent, manage, or mitigate it. But the preventative or mitigating effects that such measures may have are not themselves material to the question of what level of threat exists. The FtTJ's "real world" approach in this case therefore involved the same error as was perpetrated by the FtT in *Restivo*. The seriousness of the threat that AA's personal conduct represents should have been assessed without regard to the mitigating measures on which the FtTJ placed weight.

[56] The OASys report was clearly a significant item of evidence for this purpose. The FtTJ was justified in placing reliance upon it. He conducted a careful analysis of its content. But I think his reasoning suffered from an error of approach. This was to begin with the OASys assessment that AA posed a "medium" risk of serious harm to children when in the community and then rely on features of the sentencing scheme to which AA was subjected as matters tending to reduce that risk. Mr Pilgerstorfer KC has taken us carefully through the OASys report and persuaded me that this approach did involve the error of "double discounting" alleged by the SSHD and that it fed into the Judge's overall conclusion on this issue, that the risk could not be said to be "particularly serious".

[57] The OASys risk assessment was arrived at "on the basis that [the offender] could be released imminently back into the community" ignoring the length of the sentence left to serve. That is an appropriate starting point for the assessment required for the purposes of the 2016 Regulations. It was also an appropriate starting point on the facts of the case. But the OASys Assessment was not carried out for the purposes of the Regulations nor was its methodology in harmony with the principle I have identified in my discussion of *Restivo* above.

[58] The report makes clear what it means by a "medium risk of serious harm". It means that there are "identifiable indicators of risk of serious harm", and that the offender "has the potential to cause serious harm", but that he is "unlikely to do so unless there is a change in circumstances". The instructions contained within the report make clear that the likelihood of serious harm is assessed by considering a range of items of information logged earlier in the report. These items include factors likely to increase risk and those likely to reduce it. The former include such matters as "unsupervised and unchallenged access" to the internet and to children. The latter include "compliance with Sex Offender Register, [SHPO] and licence conditions". The overall risk identified in the OASys assessment was therefore one that had been discounted to take account of the likelihood of compliance with protective or mitigating measures, and the reduction in risk that this would bring about.

[59] It follows from what I have said about Ground 2(a) that if the OASys risk assessment was to be used as a benchmark for the purposes of assessing "threat" under the 2016 Regulations that discount had to be stripped out or ignored. In the passages cited at [29] above, the FtTJ did the opposite, by applying a discount to the OASys assessment. He did so on the basis of factors that had been taken into account in arriving at the OASys assessment. This was double-counting which must necessarily have led to an under-estimate of the seriousness of the threat that AA posed to the fundamental interests of society. This error further vitiates the Judge's assessment.

[60] For these reasons, I would allow the appeal on this ground.

[61] I add two points, which will merit attention when this case is reconsidered. First, for the reasons given, it may be that the standard against which the seriousness of the threat posed by AA falls to be measured is not the exceptional "imperative grounds" standard applied by the FtTJ but the less demanding "serious grounds" standard. Secondly, it appears to me that the Judge may have misunderstood the OASys report in another respect. The copy which he subjected to analysis was dated 27 January 2020. He said this had been prepared "in anticipation of [AA] being eligible for release into the community" and that it updated an earlier report. I am not sure this is right. We have two copies of the document. They seem to be identical except for the date at the top and bottom of each page. Internal evidence suggests that in each case this is the date on which the document was printed. At all events, each copy records the date of completion and signing as 5 November 2018. The information, or most of it, appears to have been obtained at the time of sentence in June of that year, some 30 months before AA's release and the Decision, both of which took place in December 2020.

The proportionality issue

[62] Neither the FtTJ nor the UT made a dispositive decision on this issue, but the FtTJ expressed a view on the matter and it is (at least) very likely that the issue

will need to be addressed when this case is reconsidered. It is therefore important that we decide whether the SSHD's critique of the FtTJ's reasoning on the point is justified. In my opinion it is.

[63] The first main criticism is that the FtTJ asked and answered the question of whether AA's removal "would be disproportionate" in the abstract, without addressing the question begged by this formulation, namely "disproportionate to what?" The SSHD contends that the Judge's focus was on the risk that removal would pose to AA's prospects of rehabilitation with no, or no proper, regard to the countervailing consideration namely the grounds for removing a person whose conduct posed a serious threat to the fundamental interests of the public here. Secondly, it is said that it is implicit in the Judge's reasoning that he was apportioning weight to the effect on the public in Poland of receiving an offender whose rehabilitation had been compromised, which is clearly wrong in law. Further, it is said, the Judge's assessment of the risk to AA's rehabilitation was arrived at on the basis that his prospects would be worse in Poland than here, which he had rightly recognised as an impermissible line of reasoning.

[64] To some extent the criticism is unfair. The Judge did identify that a balance had to be struck. However, he described it as a balance between "the appellant's personal conduct" and "the risk of compromising [his] rehabilitation". That, in my judgement, is an incomplete and materially inaccurate statement of the true position, and the SSHD's criticisms are otherwise valid.

[65] In EU law the principle of proportionality "involves a consideration of two questions: first, whether the measure in question is suitable or appropriate to achieve the objective pursued; and secondly whether the measure is necessary to achieve that objective, or whether it could be attained by a less onerous method": *R (Lumsdon) v Legal Services Board* [2016] AC 697 [33] (Lords Reed and Toulson JSC). Here, there was no doubt that the measure of removing AA to Poland was apt to achieve at least some of the legitimate UK public interest objectives identified in Schedule 1 to the 2016 Regulations. The real issue was whether removal was necessary or excessive, having regard to the countervailing aim of protecting AA's private life rights under Article 7 of the Charter. (His family life rights were unaffected).

[66] The relevance of AA's "personal conduct" was that it posed a threat to one of the fundamental interests of society in the UK which, *ex hypothesi*, was serious enough to justify his removal to Poland on (at least) "serious grounds". AA's personal interest in rehabilitation was relevant on the other side of the balance, in the context of his private life rights. But the key question in that context was whether and to what extent his rehabilitation would be compromised by deportation. In my opinion the Judge had no adequate basis for concluding that this would be so. There was, as he acknowledged, no evidence of the support provisions that would be available in Poland. The OASys report identified that as an issue but all that it said was that deportation "may impact on [AA's] access to offending behaviour programmes". The report contained no assessment of whether that would in fact be so, still less did it attempt any form of comparison. In my judgement the Judge's conclusion that AA would not receive similar assistance in Poland was essentially speculative. It follows that he had no basis for finding (as implicitly he did) that there was some UK public interest that counted against removing AA and instead ensuring his rehabilitation within the context of UK society.

The human rights issue

[67] The SSHD accepts that the Judge was right to find that removal would represent an interference with AA's Article 8 rights. The Judge considered it followed from his finding that removal was contrary to the 2016 Regulations that the interference was "incapable of justification". In one sense he was right. An interference can only be justified under Article 8(2) if it is "in accordance with the law". If deportation could not be justified under the 2016 Regulations it could not have been justified by reference to s 32 of the 2002 Act either, and it would have had no lawful basis. That would be the end of the human rights argument. But that is not how the Judge approached the matter. It is clear from paragraphs [20] and [55] that he went on to consider the public interest question and concluded that it was answered by the proportionality assessment he had already conducted for the purposes of the 2016 Regulations.

[68] The SSHD's case is that this was an error of law: the proportionality assessment required by the 2016 Regulations is a matter of EU law that is separate and distinct from the public interest question which arises when considering a human rights claim, the latter being governed by Part 5A of the 2002 Act. Mr Pilgerstorfer argues that s 117B(1) is a red herring; it does not detract from the need for an assessment under s 117C(6). He submits that the Judge failed properly to conduct such an assessment, and that a proper application of s 117C(6) would have led inevitably to the dismissal of the human rights appeal.

[69] I can understand AA's objection to this line of argument being raised. It did initially appear to be another new point. It is certainly not addressed in the UT's judgment. The SSHD has however pointed to a contention in paragraph 15 of the Grounds of Appeal to the UT, that the FtTJ erred by failing to follow the approach identified in *Badewa v Secretary of State for the Home Department* [2015] UKUT 329 (IAC). In *Badewa* the UT (Thirlwall J and UTJ Storey) held at [24] that:

"... the correct approach to be applied by tribunal judges in relation to ss 117A–D [of the [2002 Act] in the context of EEA removal decisions ... is: (i) first to decide if a person satisfies [the] requirements of the Immigration (European Community Area) Regulations 2006. In this context ss 117A–D has no application; (ii) second where a person has raised Article 8 as a ground of appeal ss 117A–D applies."

[70] As with Ground 1, it seems to me that Ground 4 is sufficiently covered by the written grounds of appeal to the UT, albeit the point was not presented to the UT in quite the way it has been put in this court. I would in any event allow reliance on Ground 4 because this is a pure point of law, the merits of the case will have to be reconsidered in any event, and it would be (to say the least) highly unsatisfactory for this aspect of the matter to be excluded from consideration.

[71] In my judgement, the correct approach is as indicated in *Badewa*. The application of the 2016 Regulations is a legally distinct exercise from the assessment of a human rights claim. Where both arise, they should be addressed separately and in turn. The 2016 Regulations should be addressed first, including the assessment required by Regulation 27(5)(a) of whether deportation would comply with the EU principle of proportionality. The provisions of Part 5A of the 2002 Act have no part to play at that stage. But they must be addressed as part of the human rights assessment, if the public interest question arises.

[72] The public interest question will not necessarily arise. Although deportation will commonly interfere with Article 8 rights that will not invariably be the case. If it is, the second question arises: whether deportation would be in accordance with the law. That will not be so if deportation would be contrary to the 2016 Regulations. In such a case the human rights analysis need go no further. But if deportation would be consistent with the 2016 Regulations and otherwise lawful the tribunal should address the public interest question in the way that Parliament has prescribed in Part 5A of the 2002 Act. Where, as here, the appellant is a "serious offender" the tribunal will have to apply s 117C(6).

[73] It follows that, given his conclusions on the first two issues, it was unnecessary for the Judge to address the provisions of Part 5A. In doing so, however, he adopted a flawed approach in two respects. First, by placing weight on s 117B(1). On the facts of this case that provision was either neutral or, if relevant, it favoured removal rather than the opposite. Secondly, the Judge erred by treating his conclusion that deportation would breach the EU principle of proportionality as making out the "very compelling circumstances" required by s 117C(6). That was not a legitimate line of reasoning. He should have explicitly asked and answered the question of whether the case featured any and if so what "very compelling" circumstances "over and above" those specified in ss 117C(4) and (5). I would therefore allow the appeal on this ground.

[74] AA is now 40, having come here at the age of 25. He has not spent most of his life here. His wife and child are now in Poland. Against that background, and given what I have said on the issue of rehabilitation, it is easy to see the force of the SSHD's argument that neither of the exceptions referred to in s 117C(4) and (5) could be said to apply in this case and that the desirability of AA's rehabilitation proceeding in the UK could not amount to a very compelling circumstance "beyond" those exceptions. But I do not think it would be appropriate for us to address those issues at this stage. The question of how those issues should now be resolved remains for consideration.

Conclusion and disposal

[75] For the reasons I have given I would allow the appeal on all four grounds. If the other members of the court agree then I would invite submissions on the question of relief. My provisional view is however that we should set aside the order made by the UT and substitute an order that the appeal be allowed and the case be remitted to the FtT for a fresh decision in accordance with the law as set out by this court.

LADY JUSTICE ELISABETH LAING:

[76] I agree.

LORD JUSTICE BAKER:

[77] I also agree.

GEDDES v SECRETARY OF STATE FOR THE HOME DEPARTMENT

ADMINISTRATIVE COURT

Lane J

[2024] EWHC 66 (Admin)
22 January 2024

Procedure and process – deportation – construction of section 104 of the Nationality, Immigration and Asylum Act 2002 – pending permission to appeal before the Supreme Court – impact on a deportation order – meaning of 'finally determined'

The Applicant, a Jamaican national, was convicted of wounding with intent to inflict grievous bodily harm in 2007 and sentenced to six years' detention in a young offenders institution. In April 2014, the Secretary of State for the Home Department decided that his deportation was conducive to the public good under section 3(5)(a) of the Immigration Act 1971. The Applicant's appeals to the First-tier Tribunal and Upper Tribunal ('UT') against that decision were dismissed. The Court of Appeal dismissed a further appeal in October 2016.

In June 2017, following a change of solicitors and an application for extension of time, the Applicant filed a notice of appeal with the Supreme Court. He was then detained in October 2017 to give effect to the deportation order that had been signed against him in September 2017. The decision to detain led to judicial review proceedings, which culminated in a stay on removal until a decision had been made on the outstanding application to the Supreme Court. In February 2022, the Supreme Court refused permission to appeal.

The Applicant then made an application for judicial review of the Secretary of State's deportation order on grounds that, with reference to sections 79 and 104 of the Nationality, Immigration and Asylum Act 2002 ('the 2002 Act'), the order had been unlawful and should not have been made because there was a pending application for permission to appeal to the Supreme Court. The Applicant submitted that the legislature's failure specifically to mention in section 104 appeals to the Supreme Court would represent a serious anomaly, unless the words 'finally determined' in section 104(1)(b) were given their plain and ordinary meaning. He argued that an appeal to the highest court of the land must have been intended to engage the statutory prohibition on removal. He also drew attention to section 14A to 14C of the Tribunals, Courts and Enforcement Act 2007 ('the 2007 Act'), which enabled 'leapfrog' appeals to be made directly to the Supreme Court from the UT. In such a case, he submitted that it would be highly anomalous for there to be no statutory bar on removal, given that there would on any view be such a bar if the appeal had been made to the Court of Appeal.

The question before the Administrative Court was whether the deportation order of September 2017 was rendered unlawful because the Applicant had lodged an application to the Supreme Court.

Held, refusing the application:

(1) There had been a profound change made by Parliament to section 104 of the 2002 Act since the decision in *N (Kenya) v Secretary of State for the Home Department* [2004] EWCA Civ 1141, which held that it was unlawful to remove the claimant while his appeal was pending before the House of Lords. Instead of providing that an appeal was not finally determined while any kind of 'further appeal' was ongoing, section 104(2) of the 2002 Act set out specific circumstances in which certain appeals, or other forms of challenge, would mean that an appeal was not finally determined. Appeals from the Asylum and Immigration Tribunal were covered by section 104, but only insofar as they were to the 'appropriate appellate court', defined in section 103B(5) as the Court of Appeal in England and Wales, the Court of Appeal in Northern Ireland, and the Court of Session in Scotland. No provision was made for appeals from those courts to the House of Lords. Section 104 was consequentially amended when the Asylum and Immigration Tribunal was abolished in 2010. It made no mention of appeals from the Court of Appeal to the Supreme Court, which had been established in 2009 (*paras 7 – 10*).

(2) The Applicant's contention that the words 'finally determined' had to be given what was said to be their plain and ordinary meaning floundered immediately because, if the meaning of those words had been entirely plain, Parliament would not have needed to enact section 104(2) in either of its subsequent forms. It would have been obvious that the Supreme Court was within scope. The interpretative principle *expressio unius est exclusio alterius* became a problem for the Applicant as the legislature had specified a right of appeal to the UT and Court of Appeal, in sections 11 and 13 of the 2007 Act, and must have intended to exclude other appellate situations. The UT observed, in *Niaz (NIAA 2002 s. 104: pending appeal)* [2019] UKUT 399 (IAC), that there was a strong policy reason why Parliament intended for section 104(2) to produce an exhaustive list of situations in which an appeal was not finally determined. There was no place for legislative uncertainty where the legality of something as important as the removal of a person from the United Kingdom was in issue (*paras 13 – 16*).

(3) In any event, the Applicant's categorisation of the position since 2005 as potentially anomalous ignored two matters. First, where a person faced removal and had applied to the Supreme Court it was open to the Secretary of State to decide of his own volition not to remove that person. Secondly, that person could apply to the Court for a stay on removal. Such a 'bespoke' approach was understandable, given that there were far fewer cases of onward challenge to the Supreme Court than those to the UT or Court of Appeal (*para 17*).

(4) Section 14A(6) of the 2007 Act put it beyond doubt that the section 14A process was not an application for permission under section 13 of that Act. However, the fact that those new sections were inserted without any consequential amendment to section 104, or without a provision deeming a section 14A application to be a section 13 application, was as compatible, if not more so, with Parliament having decided in 2005 and 2010 to exclude onward challenges to the highest court, and having seen no reason in 2015 to depart from those decisions. Given the rarity of successful section 14A applications, a bespoke approach was again understandable (*para 18*).

Cases referred to:

KO (Nigeria) v Secretary of State for the Home Department; IT (Jamaica) v Secretary of State for the Home Department; NS (Sri Lanka) and Others v Secretary of State for the Home Department; Pereira v Secretary of State for the Home Department [2018] UKSC 53; [2018] 1 WLR 5273; [2019] 1 All ER 675; [2019] Imm AR 400; [2019] INLR 41

N (Kenya) v Secretary of State for the Home Department [2004] EWCA Civ 1141

Niaz (NIAA 2002 s. 104: pending appeal) [2019] UKUT 399 (IAC); [2020] Imm AR 447

RJG v Secretary of State for the Home Department [2016] EWCA Civ 1042

Legislation judicially considered:

Nationality, Immigration and Asylum Act 2002, sections 103B & 104
Tribunals, Courts and Enforcement Act 2007, sections 11, 13 & 14A

Representation

Dr R Wilcox instructed by Thompson & Co Solicitors, for the Applicant;
Mr J Waite instructed by the Government Legal Department, for the Secretary of State.

Judgment

This judgment was handed down remotely at 10:30am on 22 January 2024 by circulation to the parties or their representatives by e-mail and by release to the National Archives.

MR JUSTICE LANE:

[1] This is an application for judicial review of the defendant's deportation order in respect of the claimant, dated 19 September 2017. The proceedings have a protracted history but are now entirely concerned with the construction of section 104 of the Nationality, Immigration and Asylum Act 2002 ("the 2002 Act"). Permission was granted by Lang J on 7 March 2023 on the single ground that it was arguable the deportation order was unlawful by reason of the claimant's then pending application for permission to appeal to the Supreme Court; and that, if the order were unlawful, the claimant had been illegally detained from 30 October to 15 November 2017, given that his detention was authorised by the defendant so as to give effect to the order.

[2] I am grateful to Dr Wilcox and Mr Waite for their most helpful submissions. Both were of a high order.

Background

[3] The relevant background is as follows. The claimant is a national of Jamaica. On 22 January 2007, at Inner London Crown Court he was convicted of wounding with intent to inflict grievous bodily harm and was subsequently sentenced to six years' detention in a young offenders institution. At the date of conviction and sentence, the claimant was 17 years of age. He also had two warnings against him; for theft in June 2004 and common assault in September 2006.

[4] On 28 April 2014, the defendant decided that the claimant's deportation was conducive to the public good, pursuant to section 3(5)(a) of the Immigration Act 1971. This decision was served on 1 May 2014. The claimant appealed to the First-tier Tribunal under section 82 of the 2002 Act. At that time, an appeal under section 82 was able to be brought directly against such a decision. On 19 November 2014, that Tribunal dismissed his appeal. The claimant appealed to the Upper Tribunal which, on 26 March 2015, dismissed the appeal. The claimant then appealed to the Court of Appeal which, in a judgment handed down on 20 October 2016, dismissed the appeal: *RJG v Secretary of State for the Home Department* [2016] EWCA Civ 1042. The claimant then changed solicitors to Thompson & Co, who were in a position to apply for public funding to pursue an appeal to the Supreme Court. On 24 November 2016, Thompson & Co applied to the Supreme Court for an extension of time for filing an application for permission to appeal, whilst they sought to obtain public funding. On 25 November 2016, the Supreme Court granted an extension of time until 28 days after the final determination of the application for public funding. A copy of that decision was provided to the defendant's solicitors on 29 November 2016. A final determination of the claimant's application for public funding was made on 30 May 2017. On 27 June 2017, the claimant filed his notice of appeal with the Supreme Court.

[5] The claimant was detained on 30 October 2017 in order to give effect to his removal from the United Kingdom pursuant to the deportation order of 19 September 2017. This led to the initiation of the judicial review proceedings. On 13 November 2015, Supperstone J imposed a stay on removal until determination of the claimant's appeal to the Supreme Court. On 2 March 2013, Yipp J stayed the claimant's application for permission to bring judicial review until the Supreme Court had determined his application for permission to appeal. The Supreme Court eventually refused permission to appeal on 15 February 2022, over four years and seven months from the filing of the claimant's notice of appeal with that Court. The order of the Supreme Court said that "permission to appeal was adjourned pending the outcome in *KO (Nigeria)*, but that decision does not make it appropriate to give permission to appeal in this case". The judgment in *KO (Nigeria) v Secretary of State for the Home Department* [2018] UKSC 53 had been handed down on 24 October 2018.

Legislation

[6] I shall set out the relevant legislative provisions. For reasons that will become evident, section 104 of the 2002 Act needs to be set out in its current form (which was the form existing at the time of the deportation order and detention), as well as in its original form and in the form it was from April 2005 to February 2010.

Nationality, Immigration and Asylum Act 2002

"**78 No removal while appeal pending**

(1) While a person's appeal under section 82(1) is pending he may not be –

 (a) removed from the United Kingdom in accordance with a provision of the Immigration Acts, or

 (b) required to leave the United Kingdom in accordance with a provision of the Immigration Acts.

(2) In this section 'pending' has the meaning given by section 104.

(3) Nothing in this section shall prevent any of the following while an appeal is pending –

 (a) the giving of a direction for the appellant's removal from the United Kingdom,

 (b) the making of a deportation order in respect of the appellant (subject to section 79), or

 (c) the taking of any other interim or preparatory action.

(4) This section applies only to an appeal brought while the appellant is in the United Kingdom in accordance with section 92.

79 Deportation order: appeal

(1) A deportation order may not be made in respect of a person while an appeal under section 82(1) that may be brought or continued from within the United Kingdom relating to the decision to make the order –

 (a) could be brought (ignoring any possibility of an appeal out of time with permission), or (b) is pending.

(2) In this section 'pending' has the meaning given by section 104.

…"

The following are the relevant provisions of section 104, as from 15 February 2010 [my emphasis in subsections (1)(b) and (2)]:

"**104 Pending appeal**

(1) An appeal under section 82(1) is pending during the period – (a) beginning when it is instituted, and

(b) ending when it is **finally determined**, withdrawn or abandoned (or when it lapses under section 99).

(2) An appeal under section 82(1) is not finally determined for the purpose of subsection (1)(b) while –

    (a) **an application for permission to appeal under section 11 or 13 of the Tribunals, Courts and Enforcement Act 2007 could be made or is awaiting determination,**

    (b) **permission to appeal under either of those sections has been granted and the appeal is awaiting determination, or**

    (c) **an appeal has been remitted under section 12 or 14 of that Act and is awaiting determination.**"

As mentioned above, it is necessary to set out the relevant provisions of previous versions of section 104. As originally enacted in 2002, they were as follows [my emphasis in subsection (2)]:

"**104 Pending appeal**

(1) An appeal under section 82(1) is pending during the period –

    (a) beginning when it is instituted, and

    (b) ending when it is finally determined, withdrawn or abandoned (or when it lapses under section 99).

(2) An appeal under section 82(1) is not finally determined for the purposes of subsection (1)(b) while **a further appeal** or an application under section 101(2) –

    (a) **has been instituted and is not yet finally determined, withdrawn or abandoned, or**

    (b) **may be brought (ignoring the possibility of an appeal out of time with permission).**

(3) The remittal of an appeal to an adjudicator under section 102(1)(c) is not a final determination for the purposes of subsection (2) above.

…

(5) An appeal under section 82(2)(a), (c), (d), (e) or (f) shall be treated as finally determined if a deportation order is made against the appellant."

As amended on 4 April 2005 by the Asylum and Immigration (Treatment of Claimants, etc.) Act 2004, the relevant provisions of section 104 became as follows [my emphasis in subsection (2)]:

"**104 Pending appeal**

(1) An appeal under section 82(1) is pending during the period –

    (a) beginning when it is instituted, and

    (b) ending when it is finally determined, withdrawn or abandoned (or when it lapses under section 99).

(2) An appeal under section 82(1) is not finally determined for the purposes of subsection (1)(b) while –

    (a) **an application under section 103A(1) (other than an application out of time with permission) could be made or is awaiting determination,**

    (b) **reconsideration of an appeal has been ordered under section 103A(1) and has not been completed,**

    (c) **an appeal has been remitted to the Tribunal and is awaiting determination,**

    (d) **an application under section 103B or 103E for permission to appeal (other than an application out of time with permission) could be made or is awaiting determination,**

    (e) **an appeal under section 103B or 103E is awaiting determination, or**

    (f) **a reference under section 103C is awaiting determination.**

…

(5) An appeal under section 82(2)(a), (c), (d), (e) or (f) shall be treated as finally determined if a deportation order is made against the appellant."

Tribunals, Courts and Enforcement Act 2007

"**11 Right to appeal to Upper Tribunal**

(1) For the purposes of subsection (2), the reference to a right of appeal is to a right to appeal to the Upper Tribunal on any point of law arising from a decision made by the First-tier Tribunal other than an excluded decision.

(2) Any party to a case has a right of appeal, subject to subsection (8).

(3) That right may be exercised only with permission (or, in Northern Ireland, leave).

...

13 Right to appeal to Court of Appeal etc.

(1) For the purposes of subsection (2), the reference to a right of appeal is to a right to appeal to the relevant appellate court on any point of law arising from a decision made by the Upper Tribunal other than an excluded decision.

(2) Any party to a case has a right of appeal, subject to subsection (14).

(3) That right may be exercised only with permission (or, in Northern Ireland, leave).

(4) Permission (or leave) may be given by –

(a) the Upper Tribunal, or

(b) the relevant appellate court, on an application by the party.

(5) An application may be made under subsection (4) to the relevant appellate court only if permission (or leave) has been refused by the Upper Tribunal.

...

(11) Before the Upper Tribunal decides an application made to it under subsection (4), the Upper Tribunal must specify the court that is to be the relevant appellate court as respects the proposed appeal.

(12) The court to be specified under subsection (11) in relation to a proposed appeal is whichever of the following courts appears to the Upper Tribunal to be the most appropriate –

(a) the Court of Appeal in England and Wales;

(b) the Court of Session;

(c) the Court of Appeal in Northern Ireland.

(13) In this section except subsection (11), 'the relevant appellate court', as respects an appeal, means the court specified as respects that appeal by the Upper Tribunal under subsection (11)."

The change to section 104 of the 2002 act

[7] Following the dismissal by the Court of Appeal of the appellant's appeal in *N (Kenya) v Secretary of State for the Home Department* [2004] EWCA Civ 1141, Sedley LJ considered an application by the appellant for a stay on his removal pending either an appeal to the House of Lords, if the Court of Appeal were to grant leave to appeal to that House, or pending a petition for leave to appeal, should the Court of Appeal refuse leave. In the light of section 104, as it then was, Sedley LJ concluded that the appellant did not need a stay, as "it would not be lawful to remove the appellant during the period either of an appeal to the House of Lords if this court gives leave to appeal, or at least the period limited for petitioning the House of Lords if this court refuses it." (paragraph 4)

[8] The change which Parliament made to section 104 in April 2005 was profound. Instead of providing that an appeal was not finally determined while any kind of "further appeal" was ongoing or could be brought, section 104(2) set out the specific circumstances in which particular appeals or other forms of challenge would mean that an appeal was not finally determined. One such challenge involved an application under section 103A for an order requiring the (single-tier) Asylum and Immigration Tribunal to reconsider its decision. Appeals from that Tribunal were covered by section 104; but only insofar as these were to the "appropriate appellate court", defined in section 103B(5) as the Court of Appeal in England and Wales, the Court of Session and the Court of Appeal in Northern Ireland. No provision was made for appeals from those Courts to the House of Lords (the Supreme Court was established in 2009).

[9] When the Asylum and Immigration Tribunal was abolished in 2010, section 104 was consequentially amended, so as to assume what is, for present purposes, its current form. The functions of the Asylum and Immigration Tribunal were taken over by the First-tier Tribunal and the Upper Tribunal, both of which had been established by the Tribunals, Courts and Enforcement Act 2007 ("the 2007 Act"). As can be seen, sections 11 and 13 of that Act, which are mentioned in section 104(2), concern appeals to, respectively, the Upper Tribunal (from the First-tier Tribunal) and the "relevant appellate court" (from the Upper Tribunal). By reason of section 13(12) of the 2007 Act, the "relevant appellate court" can be only the Court of Appeal in England and Wales, the Court of Session and the Court of Appeal in Northern Ireland. No mention is made of appeals from those Courts to the Supreme Court.

[10] In *Niaz (NIAA 2002 s. 104: pending appeal)* [2019] UKUT 00399 (IAC), the Upper Tribunal rejected the "submission that an appeal is not finally determined for the purpose of section 104 of the 2002 Act during the period when a judicial review of the Upper Tribunal's refusal of permission to appeal may be made or whilst an application for such a judicial review is awaiting decision" (paragraph 24). At paragraph 29, the Upper Tribunal held that "[a]lthough section 104(2) is describing situations in which an appeal is not to be regarded as finally determined, the corollary is that, where none of the situations described in subparagraphs (a) to (c) apply (and the appeal has not lapsed or been withdrawn or abandoned), the appeal in question must be treated as having been finally determined". The Upper Tribunal considered that "[a]ny other result would mean the respondent could never safely assume that the removal of an individual would not violate section 78 of the 2002 Act."

The claimant's case

[11] Dr Wilcox submitted that the legislature's failure specifically to mention appeals to (now) the Supreme Court in section 104 would represent a serious anomaly, unless the words "finally determined" in section 104(1)(b) were given what he said was their plain and ordinary meaning. An appeal to the highest Court of the land must have been intended to engage the statutory prohibition on removal. He said that *Niaz* could be distinguished on the basis that it was concerned with what he described as a "horizontal" challenge, by way of judicial review, as opposed to the "vertical" challenge of an upward appeal.

[12] Dr Wilcox also drew attention to sections 14A to 14C of the 2007 Act, which were inserted by the Criminal Justice and Courts Act 2015. These sections enable a "leapfrog" appeal to be made directly to the Supreme Court from the Upper Tribunal. In such a case, Dr Wilcox submitted that it would be highly anomalous for there to be no statutory bar on removal, given that there would on any view be such a bar if the appeal had been made to the Court of Appeal etc.

Discussion

[13] Despite the skill with which the claimant's submissions were advanced, I am in no doubt that they must be rejected. The contention that the words "finally determined" must be given what is said to be their plain and ordinary meaning founders immediately because, if the meaning of the words were entirely plain, there would have been no need for Parliament to enact section 104(2), in either of its subsequent forms. It would have been just as obvious that an appeal to the Court of Appeal etc was covered by the phrase as that an appeal to the Supreme Court was within its scope.

[14] At this point, the interpretative principle, *expressio unius est exclusio alterius* becomes a problem for the claimant. The fact that the legislature has specified sections 11 and 13 of the 2007 Act means it must have intended to exclude other appellate situations. It is also difficult to see how Dr Wilcox's horizontal/vertical distinction is compatible with his "plain and ordinary" argument. A horizontal challenge, such as an application to the court or tribunal concerned to set aside its own judgment, can call the finality of that judgment into question just as much as an onward appeal.

[15] Dr Wilcox drew attention to the explanatory notes to the 2005 and 2010 amendments to the 2002 Act. There is, however, nothing in them which materially advances the claimant's construction of section 104.

[16] As the Upper Tribunal observed in *Niaz*, there is a strong policy reason why Parliament intended section 104(2) to produce an exhaustive list of the situations in which an appeal is not finally determined. There can be no place for legislative uncertainty where the legality of something as important as removal of a person from the United Kingdom is in issue.

[17] In any event, the claimant's categorisation of the position since 2005 as potentially anomalous ignores two matters. First, where a person facing removal has applied for permission to appeal to the Supreme Court, the defendant may decide of his own volition that he will not remove that person, even though there is no statutory bar on the defendant doing so. Secondly, that person can apply to the Court for a stay on removal, as happened in this case and as happened in *N (Kenya)*

(albeit that Sedley LJ found it was unnecessary to grant a stay, in view of section 104 as then in force). Dr Wilcox said that seeking a stay would be equally possible in the case of pending appeals etc to the Court of Appeal, in which case it was difficult to see why such onward challenges are covered. The response to this is that there are far fewer cases of onward challenge to the Supreme Court than there are to the Upper Tribunal and to the Court of Appeal. A "bespoke" approach is, accordingly, understandable at this point.

[18] Dr Wilcox prayed in aid sections 14A to 14C of the 2007 Act as a particularly egregious anomaly, if the defendant's construction of section 104 were correct. Section 14A(6) puts it beyond doubt that the section 14A process is not an application for permission under section 13.* In my view, however, the fact that these new sections were inserted without any consequential amendment to section 104 or without a provision deeming a section 14A application to be a section 13 application, is as compatible, if not more so, with Parliament having decided in 2005 and 2010 to exclude onward challenges to our highest Court and having seen no reason in 2015 to depart from those decisions. Given the rarity of successful section 14A applications, the point made in the last sentence of paragraph 17 above also applies.

Decision

[19] For these reasons, it follows that the deportation order was validly made and there was power to detain the claimant in pursuance of it. The application for judicial review is accordingly dismissed.

---

* "(6) Before the Upper Tribunal decides an application made to it under this section, the Upper Tribunal must specify the court that would be the relevant appellate court if the application were an application for permission (or leave) under section 13."

SECRETARY OF STATE FOR THE HOME DEPARTMENT v OKAFOR

COURT OF APPEAL

Moylan, Stuart-Smith, Snowden LJJ

[2024] EWCA Civ 23
23 January 2024

European Union law – exclusion – public policy grounds – foreign criminals – failure to disclose past conviction – regulation 27 of the Immigration (EEA) Regulations 2016 – BF (Portugal) *[2009] EWCA Civ 923 followed –* Bouchereau *exception not met – cumulative assessment – post-conviction behaviour – low risk of re-offending*

The Claimant, a citizen of Nigeria, was married to a Swedish national who had been granted indefinite leave to remain in the United Kingdom in March 2019. The Claimant was granted entry clearance under the EU Settlement Scheme ('EUSS') in July 2020. He arrived in the United Kingdom in September 2020 with an EUSS family permit, but was refused admission on public policy grounds. His family permit was revoked under regulations 23 and 24 of the Immigration (European Economic Area) Regulations 2016 ('the EEA Regulations') and his leave to enter was cancelled on the same basis under paragraph 321B of the Immigration Rules HC 395 (as amended). That decision was based on a conviction in the USA in 1994 of conspiracy to possess with intent to distribute heroin for which the Claimant was sentenced to 350 months' imprisonment. He had served almost 26 years of that sentence before being released in 2019 and removed to Nigeria. He failed to disclose his conviction or deportation when making his EUSS family permit application in February 2020 and in two earlier visit visa applications. The Claimant appealed the Secretary of State for the Home Department's decision refusing him admission to the United Kingdom and cancelling his leave.

The First-tier Tribunal ('FtT') allowed the Claimant's appeal. The FtT was not satisfied that the Secretary of State had established that the Claimant's conduct represented a genuine, present and sufficiently serious threat affecting one of the fundamental interests of society under regulation 27 of the EEA Regulations. The Secretary of State appealed to the Upper Tribunal ('UT') on the grounds that the Claimant's conduct, arising both from his criminal conviction in the USA and his later conduct in failing to disclose that conviction, justified his exclusion. The UT set aside the FtT's decision on the basis that it had failed to consider the exception established in *R v Bouchereau* (Case 30/77). In remaking the decision, the UT expressly preserved the FtT's finding that the Claimant was unlikely to re-offend based on evidence of his good behaviour while in custody and the qualifications and employment he had obtained during that time. The UT allowed the Claimant's appeal on the grounds that his conduct did not fall within the *Bouchereau* exception which arose only exceptionally when an individual's conduct could be said to engender 'deep public revulsion' and permitted exclusion even in the absence of a propensity to re-offend. Accordingly, his exclusion could not be justified on public policy grounds.

Before the Court of Appeal, the Secretary of State submitted that the UT Judge had erred in law in failing to consider the cumulative effect of the Claimant's behaviour and whether his drug offending, considered in conjunction with the repeated recent deception, fell within the scope of the *Bouchereau* exception.

Held, dismissing the appeal:

(1) The Secretary of State had correctly conceded that the UT Judge's exposition revealed no error of principle. In *BF (Portugal) v Secretary of State for the Home Department* [2009] EWCA Civ 923, Sullivan LJ identified four stages to be followed by the tribunal in applying the EEA Regulations. It had to determine: (i) the individual's relevant personal conduct; (ii) whether that conduct represented a genuine, present and sufficiently serious threat; (iii) whether that threat affected one of the fundamental interests of society; and (iv) whether removal or exclusion would be disproportionate in all the circumstances. There was no doubt that the *Bouchereau* exception formed part of English law. Furthermore, the UT Judge's setting out of the relevant issues and principles had provided a suitable working summary of the established principles that he had to apply in the instant case (*paras 30, 35 and 36*).

(2) The relevant question was whether the UT Judge had erred materially in law in concluding that the *Bouchereau* exception did not apply in the instant case. There might be cases where, on their particular facts, the impact of different aspects of a person's conduct could properly be aggregated when the Secretary of State or the tribunal assessed whether that person represented a genuine, present and sufficiently serious threat affecting one of the fundamental interests of society under regulation 27(5)(c) of the EEA Regulations so as to trigger the application of the exception. The answer to the question of possible aggregation was fact sensitive. In the instant case, the Judge had not impermissibly failed to have regard to the cumulative effect of the different aspects of the Claimant's conduct. To the contrary, the Judge had not only had the correct principles in mind, identified the central issue and asked himself the right question, but had also applied the principles correctly. His appreciation that he was to consider the Claimant's conduct as a whole permeated the judgment. The Judge had also correctly directed himself about the *BF (Portugal)* four-stage test. He made clear that, on his approach, application of the *Bouchereau* exception depended on the Claimant's role, the sentence imposed and his subsequent conduct. The Judge was entitled to find that the deceptive conduct came 'nowhere near' being an exceptional or unusual case where 'deep public revulsion' was engendered. He considered that the deceptive conduct added nothing of substance to the overall assessment he was obliged to undertake. It could have been clearer if the Judge had inserted a single concluding sentence expressly stating that he had reached his conclusion taking all relevant matters into account both singly and cumulatively. It would be perverse, however, to hold that, having consistently and expressly recognised the correct applicable principles and test, his judgment should be struck down. The Judge had taken into account the cumulative effect of all relevant matters and concluded that the deceptive conduct did not tip the balance. His judgment did not disclose any error of law that would justify or permit interference (*paras 37 – 40, 42, 44 and 46 – 49*).

Cases referred to:

BF (Portugal) v Secretary of State for the Home Department [2009] EWCA Civ 923

K v Staatssecretaris van Veiligheid en Justitie; HF v Belgische Staat (Cases C-331/16 and C-366/16); [2019] 1 WLR 1877; [2018] 3 CMLR 26; [2018] INLR 693

KM v Secretary of State for the Home Department [2021] EWCA Civ 693; [2021] Imm AR 1361

R v Bouchereau (Case 30/77); [1978] QB 732; [1978] 2 WLR 250; [1981] 2 All ER 924; [1977] ECR 1999; [1977] 2 CMLR 800

R v Secretary of State for the Home Department ex parte Marchon [1993] 2 CMLR 132; [1993] Imm AR 384

Secretary of State for the Home Department v AH (Sudan) and Others [2007] UKHL 49; [2008] 1 AC 678; [2007] 3 WLR 832; [2008] 4 All ER 190; [2008] Imm AR 289; [2008] INLR 100

Secretary of State for the Home Department v Okafor 14 July 2022 (EA/04590/2020) UTIAC (unreported)

Secretary of State for the Home Department v Robinson (Jamaica) [2018] EWCA Civ 85; [2018] 4 WLR 81; [2018] Imm AR 892

Legislation judicially considered:

Immigration (European Economic Area) Regulations 2016, regulations 23, 27 & 28; paragraph 7 of Schedule 1

Representation

Mr J Lewis instructed by the Government Legal Department, for the Secretary of State;
Mr Z Jafferji and Mr A Rehman instructed by Riverway Law, for the Claimant.

Judgment

This judgment was handed down remotely at 10.30am on 23 January 2023 by circulation to the parties or their representatives by e-mail and by release to the National Archives.

LORD JUSTICE STUART-SMITH:

[1] The Secretary of State for the Home Department ["SSHD"] appeals against the decision of the Upper Tribunal ["UT"] dated 17 June 2022. By that decision, UT Judge Grubb ["the Judge"] allowed Mr Okafor's appeal, which he had brought under the preserved provisions of the Immigration (European Economic Area) Regulations 2016 ["the EEA Regulations"], against the SSHD's decision dated 17 September 2020 refusing him admission to the United Kingdom and cancelling his leave.

[2] There is one permitted ground of appeal, namely that:

"The UT erred in law in failing to consider the cumulative effect of the Respondent's behaviour and whether his drug offending, considered in conjunction with this repeated recent deception, fell within the scope of the *Bouchereau* exception."

It is common ground that the burden of satisfying the Tribunal that Mr Okafor's conduct brings the case within the *Bouchereau* exception (*R v Bouchereau* (Case 30–77) [1978] QB 732 (ECJ)) rested on the SSHD, the standard of proof being the civil standard. The SSHD accepts that the burden on him was "to demonstrate, on the balance of probabilities, that a person represents a genuine, present and sufficiently serious threat affecting one of the fundamental interests of society under regulation 27(5)(c) of the EEA Regulations."

[3] On the hearing of the Appeal, the SSHD was represented by Mr Lewis and Mr Okafor by Mr Jafferji. We are grateful to both counsel for clear and focussed submissions. We are particularly grateful to Mr Lewis, who was instructed at short notice when an emergency prevented his predecessor from attending.

[4] For the reasons set out below, I would dismiss the appeal.

The factual and procedural background

[5] I adopt the background as set out at [3]–[12] of the UT's judgment:

"3. The appellant is a citizen of Nigeria who was born on 1 June 1965. He is married to a Swedish (and therefore EEA) national whom he married in Nigeria on 15 October 2019.

4. The appellant's spouse, … was granted indefinite leave to remain on 11 March 2019.

5. On 30 July 2020, the appellant was granted entry clearance under the EU Settlement Scheme.

6. On 17 September 2020, the appellant arrived at Heathrow Airport with an EUSS family permit. However, he was refused admission on the grounds of public policy and his family permit was revoked under regs 23 and 24 of the Immigration (EEA) Regulations 2016 (SI 1052/2016 as amended) ('the EEA Regulations'). In addition, his leave to enter was cancelled on the same basis under para 321B of the Immigration Rules (HC 395 as amended). Although the decisions were initially taken and served on 17 September 2020, the cancellation of leave, which it was acknowledged had been served on an incorrect form, was reissued on 22 September 2020.

7. The basis of the public policy decision under the EEA Regulations was that in 1994 the appellant had been convicted in the USA of the offence of conspiracy to possess with intent to distribute heroin and had been sentenced to 350 months' imprisonment. He had been imprisoned since his arrest on 12 December 1992 in relation to that offence. He served almost 26 years of the sentence before he was released from prison on 23 January 2019 to the custody of the US Immigration Services. On 5 May 2019, he was removed to Nigeria.

8. The appellant did not disclose his conviction or deportation in his EUSS family permit application made on 15 February 2020, nor in two earlier visit visa applications made on 31 October 2019 and 24 December 2019. Indeed, in all three applications in answer to questions whether he had been convicted of a criminal offence in the United Kingdom or in any other country, the appellant had replied that he had not.

9. The appellant appealed to the First-tier Tribunal. In a decision sent on 27 May 2020, Judge Mailer allowed the appellant's appeal. Judge Mailer was not satisfied that the respondent had established on a balance of probabilities that the appellant's conduct represented a genuine, present and sufficiently serious threat affecting one of the fundamental interests of society. His exclusion from the UK could not, therefore, be justified under EU law.

…

10. The Secretary of State appealed to the Upper Tribunal with permission.

11. In a decision dated 28 February 2022, [the UT, by UTJ Grubb] set aside Judge Mailer's decision on the basis that he had erred in law in allowing the appeal under the EEA Regulations. The reasons are set out in full in [UTJ Grubb's February 2022] decision. In essence, [he] concluded that the judge had failed to consider the so-called '*Bouchereau* exception' in concluding that the appellant did not represent a 'genuine, present and sufficiently serious threat' to a fundamental interest in society based upon his conduct.

12. The appeal was adjourned for a resumed hearing in order for the Upper Tribunal to re-make the decision on that issue."

[6] The UT decision of 28 February 2022 adjourning the appeal included express provision that:

"74. The appeal is adjourned in order to re-make the decision. The judge's finding that it is 'not likely that the appellant will re-offend in the future' in the sense of commit a drugs offence is preserved.

75. The appeal will be relisted in the Upper Tribunal in order to re-make the decision on the basis of the evidence that was before the First-tier Tribunal."

[7] The finding of the First-tier Tribunal ["FtT"] to which the UT was referring had been expressed at [137] of FtT Judge Mailer's decision as follows:

"Having regard to the evidence as a whole, I find that it is not likely that the appellant will re-offend in the future. The appellant has not been shown to have any intention or desire to re-engage in criminal conduct. Nor is there any evidence that he would be likely to lapse so as to breach the United Kingdom laws if he considered it expedient to do so."

The evidence to which the FtT Judge was referring included evidence of good behaviour while in custody and the obtaining of qualifications and employment while in custody, including a BSc in Business Law and becoming a Quality Assurance Clerk.

The UT judgment

[8] Having set out the background, the Judge identified the issue on the appeal to the UT at [14]:

"The scope of the appeal was limited to the issue of whether the appellant's conduct, arising both from his criminal conviction in the USA and his conduct subsequently in failing to disclose his convictions in his UK immigration applications, justified his exclusion on the basis that it represented a 'genuine, present and sufficiently serious threat affecting one of the fundamental interests of society' applying the '*Bouchereau* exception'."

[9] The Judge then addressed the "*Bouchereau* exception", starting with Regulations 27 and 28 of the EEA Regulations, the relevant parts of which I set out below. Having at [20] set out the four stage test established by *BF (Portugal) v SSHD* [2009] EWCA Civ 923 at [3], he returned to the central issue in the appeal at [21]:

"The central issue in this appeal is whether the appellant's conduct falls within reg 27(5)(c). It is not suggested, not (*sic*) sensibly could it be, that his drugs offending does not fall within the rubric of a 'fundamental interest of society' (see e.g., Schedule 1, para 7(g) of the EEA Regulations). The same is equally true of his deceptive conduct in the immigration context (see, e.g. Schedule 1, para 7(a) of the EEA Regulations). The issue is whether the appellant's conduct represents a 'genuine, present and sufficiently serious threat' to one or more of those fundamental interests."

[10] At [22]–[23] the Judge, while recognising that the "usual" case requires the SSHD to establish that the individual has a "propensity" to re-offend or that there is a risk of re-offending, identified (on the authority of *SSHD v Robinson* [2018] EWCA Civ 85) that:

"even in the absence of a propensity to commit further offences, where the individual's conduct can be said to produce a 'deep public revulsion' then the requirement of EU law that the individual should represent a 'genuine, present and sufficiently serious threat' to a fundamental interest of society may still be met. That, as will be clear, unusual case is the so-called '*Bouchereau* exception'."

[11] Amongst other passages, the Judge cited [84]–[86] of *Robinson*, where Singh LJ (with whom Underhill and Lindblom LJJ agreed) declined to attempt an exhaustive definition but (a) identified that what one is looking for is a present threat to the requirements of public policy, (b) accepted that past conduct alone was potentially sufficient if the facts were "very extreme", (c) suggested that "the sort of case" that the ECJ had been thinking of in *Bouchereau* was "where, for example, a person has committed grave offences of sexual abuse or violence against young children", and (d) adopted the phrase "the most heinous of crimes" as giving an indication of the sort of case that the ECJ had in mind when it said that a past offence alone might suffice.

[12] In the light of his review of the authorities, at [27]–[30] the Judge attempted to identify the scope of the *Bouchereau* exception:

"27. First, it is clear from *Bouchereau* itself, and the Court of Appeal's approach subsequently, that a propensity to re-offend or a risk of re-offending is usually a *sine qua non* to establishing that there is a 'genuine, present and sufficiently serious threat' to a fundamental interest of society.

28. Second, the '*Bouchereau* exception' will arise only 'exceptionally' (see the Advocate-General's opinion at [69] of *Robinson* above).

29. Third, the '*Bouchereau* exception' arises when the individual's conduct can be said to engender 'deep public revulsion'. The courts have indicated that conduct which gives rise to 'deep public revulsion' is likely to be in cases which are 'extreme' (see [71] of *Robinson*) and which involve the 'most heinous crimes' and which are 'especially horrifying' and 'repugnant to the public' (see [86] of *Robinson*). In *Robinson*, Singh LJ referred to examples where 'a person has committed grave offences of sexual abuse or violence against young children'.

30. Fourth, without offending the EU law prohibition on applying the public policy exception based upon 'previous criminal convictions' alone (see reg 27(5)(e)), the exceptional or unusual case must be based 'exclusively on the personal conduct of the person concerned' (see reg 27(5)(b)), i.e. an assessment of the seriousness and nature offence and the circumstances of the offending (and the offender) *as a whole*. In *K and HF*, in the context of an individual whose previous offending had excluded him from the Refugee Convention, the CJEU emphasised the need for an overall assessment of the individual's past offending, its circumstances and *his subsequent conduct* (at [66]):

> '66. The finding that there is such a threat must be based on an assessment, by the competent authorities of the host Member State, of the personal conduct of the individual concerned, taking into consideration the findings of fact in the decision to exclude that individual from refugee status and the factors on which that decision is based, particularly the nature and gravity of the crimes or acts that he is alleged to have committed, the degree of his individual involvement in them, whether there are any grounds for excluding criminal liability, and whether or not he has been convicted. *That overall assessment must also take account of the time that has elapsed since the date when the crimes or acts were allegedly committed and the subsequent conduct of that individual, particularly in relation to whether that conduct reveals the persistence in him of a disposition hostile to the fundamental values* enshrined in Articles 2 and 3 TEU, capable of disturbing the peace of mind and physical security of the population. The mere fact that the past conduct of that individual took place in a specific historical and social context in his country of origin, which is not liable to recur in the host Member State, does not preclude such a finding.'" [emphasis added]

[13] In summarising the parties' submissions and arguments, the Judge started by addressing the preserved finding of the FtT at [137] of Judge Mailer's judgment, which I have set out at [7] above. He held that it amounted to a finding that it was not likely that Mr Okafor would re-offend by committing any drug-related offences and that the SSHD had failed to establish on the balance of probabilities that Mr

Okafor is at risk of re-offending or engaging in deceptive conduct of the nature involved in his immigration applications. There is and could be no challenge to those findings.

[14] The Judge then set out the SSHD's submission at [37]:

"Consequently, and Ms Rushforth maintained her argument on both bases, the respondent relies on the '*Bouchereau* exception' both in relation to the appellant's criminal conviction in the USA and also his deceptive conduct in relation to the UK immigration authorities on three occasions in 2019 and 2020."

[15] On behalf of Mr Okafor it was submitted that the SSHD had adduced no evidence about his US criminal conviction apart from the nature of the charge and the length of his sentence. As to that, the Judge referred to evidence adduced on Mr Okafor's behalf from apparently credible independent sources that Mr Okafor's involvement in the drug conspiracy was limited to recruiting and referring a willing drug mule to a Nigerian drug smuggler with whom he had no other relationship, for which he was paid approximately $1,500. His role was described as peripheral and surprise was expressed by the independent sources at the severity of his sentence which, in the view of at least one source, was out of line with the sentences passed on others who were further up the chain. In addition, while in prison, Mr Okafor had, over a course of approximately eight years, recruited numerous inmates of Nigerian origin to provide information on criminal activities in the areas of drug smuggling, money laundering and healthcare fraud.

[16] On the basis of this limited evidence about his offending, as the Judge recorded at [45]–[46], it was submitted on Mr Okafor's behalf that the *Bouchereau* exception was not established either on the basis of his criminal offending or on the basis of his subsequent deceptive conduct in relation to the immigration offences.

[17] The Judge recorded that the SSHD's submissions in reply were to the effect that (a) there were difficulties for the SSHD in obtaining information about Mr Okafor's offending in the USA; (b) in *R v SSHD ex p. Marchon* [1993] Imm AR 384 the conduct of a doctor who was convicted in relation to a conspiracy to import 4½ kg of heroin was described by the court as "especially horrifying" and "repugnant to the public", justifying the application of the *Bouchereau* exception; (c) although sentencing in the USA could not be equated with sentencing in England and Wales, Mr Okafor's sentence was considerably in excess of the norm for involvement in such offences; and (d) the SSHD relied upon Mr Okafor's deceptive conduct with the UK immigration authorities.

[18] The Judge's Discussion section was at [49]–[61] of his judgment. He started by addressing Mr Okafor's criminal conduct in the US, noting at the outset that "there is a paucity of detailed information concerning [Mr Okafor's] offence." Having recorded (a) the conviction for conspiracy to possess with intent to distribute heroin, (b) the 350 month sentence, and (c) that Mr Okafor served nearly 26 years, he noted that the SSHD had adduced no evidence about the circumstances of Mr Okafor's offending and that the only evidence he had was that adduced on behalf of Mr Okafor. Having reviewed the reliability and independence of the sources of evidence, he accepted the evidence of Mr Okafor's limited role, which I have summarised above and which he said would form the basis on which he would proceed.

[19] He then reviewed other information about levels of sentencing in the USA and its disproportionate impact upon African Americans, which he had "not found particularly helpful" because he had no way of knowing how it had impacted upon Mr Okafor in particular. He then said at [53]:

"I prefer, instead, to determine whether the *Bouchereau* exception' applies by looking at the appellant's role, his sentence – bearing in mind the limited information I have about where such a sentence falls upon a spectrum of sentencing for drug related offences – *and his subsequent conduct.*" [emphasis added]

[20] At [54] he summarised Mr Okafor's role in the criminal conspiracy:

"Here, the appellant was involved in a very serious offence – conspiracy to possess with intent to distribute heroin. His role specific role (*sic*) must, however, be taken into account. His involvement was to recruit a courier. For that, he was paid a fee. That role was described by Agent GT, based upon information he received from the FBI agent, to appear to be a 'peripheral role in the conspiracy'. Although it is not entirely clear, it appears that the appellant's role involved recruiting a single courier."

[21] The Judge then addressed the question of "public revulsion" which, he said, needed to take into consideration Mr Okafor's cooperation with the authorities in the United States in providing them with information and the evidence of his positive steps while in prison as found by the FtT Judge. He went on, at [55]:

"The offence took place 30 years ago. The appellant has not been convicted of any offences since his release in 2019, although that is a relatively short time ago, Judge Mailer's finding was that he was not at risk of re-offending. Judge Mailer plainly concluded that the appellant had been rehabilitated."

[22] At [56], the Judge distinguished *Ex p Marchon* on the basis that what made the offending especially horrifying in that case was that the offender was a doctor.

[23] Having reminded himself at [57] that it was for the SSHD to establish the public policy ground, that the SSHD had adduced no evidence concerning the circumstances of Mr Okafor's offending, and that the Tribunal can only reach a decision on whether the SSHD has discharged that burden of proof on the evidence before it, the Judge drew the strands together at [58]–[61] [emphasis added in [58]]:

"58. In assessing whether the appellant's 'personal conduct' gives rise to 'deep public revulsion' *it is, in my judgment, important to take all the factors I have identified above into account.* Here, the appellant's offending though very serious, and his role – like the offence itself – should not be understated, it was not offending (based upon the limited circumstances known in this appeal about the offending) which falls within the exceptional or unusual category that invokes the '*Bouchereau* exception' where the appellant has been found not to have a propensity to offend and is not at risk of re-offending in the future.

59. For the above reasons, the Secretary of State has failed to establish on a balance of probabilities that the appellant's conduct falls within the '*Bouchereau* exception' and therefore amounts to a 'present, genuine and sufficiently serious threat' to a fundamental interest of society.

60. To the extent that [the SSHD] relied upon the appellant's deceptive conduct in relation to the UK immigration authorities, the UT's decision in *Arranz* is no more than a recognition that immigration fraud or abuse can affect a 'fundamental interest of society'. That was, of course, a case where the UT denied, wrongly now given *Robinson*, that the '*Bouchereau* exception' existed and so was only concerned with an individual who had a propensity to commit such offences or was at risk of reoffending. Given that the judge found that there was no risk of the appellant re-offending in the future, whilst his past conduct was such that it affects a 'fundamental interest of society' under Schedule 1 to the EEA Regulations, that conduct comes nowhere near falling within the exceptional or unusual case contemplated by the '*Bouchereau* exception' where 'deep public revulsion' is engendered by that conduct.

61. As it is not established that the appellant's conduct represents a 'genuine, present and sufficiently serious threat' affecting a fundamental interest of society, his exclusion cannot be justified on public policy grounds. The issue of proportionality does not strictly arise given that finding. For these reasons, therefore, the appellant succeeds in his appeal."

The present appeal

[24] I have set out the one permitted ground of appeal at [2] above.

The SSHD's submissions

[25] The SSHD's primary submission, reflecting the permitted ground of appeal, is that the Judge erred in law in failing to consider the cumulative effect of Mr Okafor's behaviour and whether his drug offending, considered in conjunction with his recent deception, fell within the scope of the *Bouchereau* exception. That asserted failure is submitted to have led the Judge to err when considering the time frame of Mr Okafor's reprehensible conduct, which is alleged to have continued to the recent instances of dishonest behaviour. As a result of these alleged errors, the SSHD submits that the Judge reached the wrong conclusion and that "serving a 26 year sentence for the most serious drugs offences and then brazenly lying about that fact in order to secure entry to the UK is precisely the type of behaviour that can be said to cause 'deep public revulsion'."

[26] In addition, by his skeleton argument the SSHD submitted that the Judge failed properly to consider the length of the sentence imposed by the US Authorities when assessing Mr Okafor's drugs offending. As Mr Lewis accepted, this point was not covered by the permission to appeal that had been granted. He proposed a second ground of appeal, namely that "the UT erred in law in failing to take into account Mr Okafor's length of sentence in assessing his behaviour." Mr Jafferji objected on the basis that this was a second appeal and the proposed ground raised no point of principle. We refused permission to add the second proposed ground of

appeal on three grounds. First, it was raised too late. Second, it raised no point of principle. Third, it was simply unarguable. On any fair reading of the UT judgment, it is plain beyond argument that the Judge took fully into account the length of Mr Okafor's sentence. In truth the fact of the conviction and the length of sentence were his starting point; but he then went on to consider the additional evidence which put the bald fact of the length of his sentence into context: see the outline summary at [18] above. In the course of his discussion he said at [52] that

> "... under EU law it is essential to assess not only the seriousness of the offending based upon sentence but to look, in addition, to the circumstances of the offending."

That is what the Judge did, as appears from the passage at [53] of the judgment, which I have set out at [19] above. The fact that he ultimately concluded that there was other material that informed his judgment about how serious the offending had been does not mean, or even suggest, that he did not take the length of the sentence fully into account.

[27] In the course of Mr Lewis' oral submissions he accepted that the Judge's summary of the law disclosed no material error. Specifically, the SSHD did not take issue with the Judge's formulation of the central issue at [21] of the judgment or his summary of the principles, which I have summarised or set out at [9] to [12] above. The substance of the SSHD's concerns and of Mr Lewis' submissions is that the judge applied the law wrongly by failing to aggregate the impact of the criminal conviction and the deceptive conduct when assessing whether the case falls within the *Bouchereau* exception. When Mr Lewis was asked by the Court whether the SSHD accepted that either (a) Mr Okafor's criminal conduct (as found by the Tribunal) on its own or (b) his deceptive conduct in his immigration applications (as found by the Tribunal) on its own would be insufficient to trigger the application of the Bouchereau exception, it emerged that he was without instructions to answer either question.

Mr Okafor's submissions

[28] Mr Okafor rejects the suggestion that the Judge did not have regard to the cumulative effect of the drug offending and the more recent dishonest behaviour. He submits that the Judge made no error of law. Rather, he conducted a thorough review of all relevant features and reached an unassailable conclusion having taken all relevant matters into account. He submits that the SSHD in this appeal is simply trying to re-argue the merits of the Judge's decision and, in doing so, is hamstrung by his failure to adduce any evidence about the circumstances of Mr Okafor's drug offending.

[29] In oral submissions Mr Jafferji submitted that the Judge's approach was unimpeachable and that he had not impermissibly left the conduct leading to his conviction and his deceptive conduct in relation to his immigration applications in segregated silos. He emphasised that each case is fact-specific and the strength of the words that have been used to describe the sort of impact or the seriousness of the conduct that is required to trigger the *Bouchereau* exception: "exceptional", a case whose facts are "very extreme", "especially horrifying", "the most heinous of crimes", and "conduct which has caused deep public revulsion." He cautioned us, moderately but persistently, against interfering lightly with the findings and

assessment of the specialist Tribunals below, relying on well-known passages from *AH (Sudan) v SSHD* [2007] UKHL 49 [2008] 1 AC 678 at [30] and *KM v SSHD* [2021] EWCA Civ 693 at [77].

The legal framework

[30] There is no material distinction between the parties about the principles to be applied. The SSHD's summary of the relevant statutory provisions and the impact of previous decisions is virtually identical to the exposition of principles provided by the Judge. Mr Lewis' concession is properly and correctly made: the Judge's exposition reveals no error of principle. I set out the statutory provisions below for convenience, taken almost entirely from the SSHD's skeleton argument on this appeal; but I could just as well have taken them from the UT judgment. It is not necessary to engage in any detailed exposition of the cases to which we have been referred.

The legislative framework

[31] Regulation 23 of the EEA Regulations deals with the exclusion and removal of individuals from the UK. Regulation 23(1) provides that "a person is not entitled to be admitted to the UK ... if a refusal to admit that person is justified on grounds of public policy ... in accordance with regulation 27".

[32] Regulation 27(5) sets out the public policy requirements as follows:

"(5) The public policy and public security requirements of the United Kingdom include restricting rights otherwise conferred by these Regulations in order to protect the fundamental interests of society, and where a relevant decision is taken on grounds of public policy or public security it must also be taken in accordance with the following principles –

(a) the decision must comply with the principle of proportionality;

(b) the decision must be based exclusively on the personal conduct of the person concerned;

(c) the personal conduct of the person must represent a genuine, present and sufficiently serious threat affecting one of the fundamental interests of society, taking into account past conduct of the person and that the threat does not need to be imminent;

(d) matters isolated from the particulars of the case or which relate to considerations of general prevention do not justify the decision;

(e) a person's previous criminal convictions do not in themselves justify the decision;

(f) the decision may be taken on preventative grounds, even in the absence of a previous criminal conviction, provided the grounds are specific to the person."

[33] Regulation 27(8) states that in deciding whether the requirements of Regulation 27 are met, a court or tribunal must take account of the considerations set out in schedule 1. Schedule 1 provides:

"3. ... Where an EEA national or the family member of an EEA national has received a custodial sentence, or is a persistent offender, the longer the sentence, or the more numerous the convictions, the greater the likelihood that the individual's continued presence in the United Kingdom represents a genuine, present and sufficiently serious threat affecting the fundamental interests of society

...

5. The removal from the United Kingdom of an EEA national or the family member of an EEA national, who is able to provide substantive evidence of not demonstrating a threat (for example, through demonstrating that the EEA national or the family member of an EEA national has successfully reformed or rehabilitated) is less likely to be proportionate."

[34] Paragraph 7 of schedule 1 sets out a number of 'fundamental interests of society' which fall within the ambit of Regulation 27(5)(c). So far as relevant, it provides:

"For the purposes of these Regulations, the fundamental interests of society in the United Kingdom include –

(a) preventing unlawful immigration and abuse of the immigration laws, and maintaining the integrity and effectiveness of the immigration control system (including under these Regulations) and of the Common Travel Area;

...

(c) preventing social harm;

...

(e) protecting public services;

(f) excluding or removing an EEA national or family member of an EEA national with a conviction (including where the conduct of that person is likely to cause, or has in fact caused, public offence) and maintaining public confidence in the ability of the relevant authorities to take such action;

(g) tackling offences likely to cause harm to society where an immediate or direct victim may be difficult to identify but where there is wider societal harm (such as offences related to the misuse of drugs or crime with a cross-border dimension as mentioned in Article 83(1) of the Treaty on the Functioning of the European Union)."

Applicable principles

[35] In *BF (Portugal) v SSHD* at [3] Sullivan LJ identified four stages to be followed by the Tribunal in applying the EEA Regulations. It must determine:

i) what was the relevant personal conduct of the individual?; and

ii) whether that conduct represents a genuine, present and sufficiently serious threat; and if so,

iii) whether that threat affects one of the fundamental interests of society; and if so,

iv) whether the removal or exclusion of the individual would be disproportionate in all the circumstances.

[36] There is now no doubt that the *Bouchereau* exception forms part of English law. Furthermore, in my judgement, the Judge's setting out of the relevant issues and principles at [14], [21], [22]–[23], [27]–[30] of his judgment provided a suitable working summary of the established principles that he had (and intended) to apply: see [8] to [12] above.

Discussion and resolution

[37] The question for us is whether the Judge erred materially in law in reaching his conclusion that the *Bouchereau* exception did not apply in this case.

[38] Both counsel accepted that there may be cases where, on their particular facts, the impact of different aspects of a person's conduct could properly be aggregated when the SSHD or the Tribunal comes to assess whether that person represents a genuine, present and sufficiently serious threat affecting one of the fundamental interests of society under regulation 27(5)(c) of the EEA Regulations so as to trigger the application of the *Bouchereau* exception. I agree. I emphasise that my agreement is on the basis that the answer to the question of possible aggregation will be fact sensitive in every case. I do not consider it necessary to say any more, whether by way of examples or otherwise, since resolution of the question will always depend upon the facts of the given case.

[39] I am, however, quite unable to accept that the Judge in the present case impermissibly failed to have regard to the cumulative effect of the different aspects of Mr Okafor's conduct. To the contrary, a fair reading of the judgment leads to the conclusion that the Judge not only had the correct principles in mind, identified the central issue and asked himself the right question but also that he applied the principles correctly.

[40] The Judge's appreciation that he was to consider Mr Okafor's conduct as a whole permeates the judgment. In formulating the issue at [14] of the judgment, he framed it as being whether Mr Okafor's conduct (by which he expressly meant both the conduct in relation to his criminal conviction and his subsequent failure to disclose his convictions) justified his exclusion: see [8] above. There is nothing to suggest that by "both … and" he meant "either … or". Similarly, when formulating the central issue at [21] of the judgment, he addressed Mr Okafor's conduct as a whole and the issue as being whether his conduct "represent[ed] a 'genuine, present

and sufficiently serious threat' to one or more of those fundamental interests." Once again, there is no suggestion that the question was only to be asked separately in respect of different instances of conduct viewed exclusively on their own: see [9] above.

[41] Any residual doubt about the Judge's meaning in these paragraphs is removed by his reference in [30] of the judgment and the citation from [66] of *K and HF* to "the need for an overall assessment of the individual's past offending, its circumstances and his subsequent conduct"; and that the "overall assessment must also take account of the time that has elapsed since the date when the crimes or acts were allegedly committed and the subsequent conduct of that individual particularly in relation to whether that conduct reveals the persistence in him of a disposition hostile to the fundamental values enshrined in Articles 2 and 3 TEU ....": see [12] above. It is plain from these citations that the Judge considered it necessary to conduct an overall assessment taking into account all relevant conduct.

[42] In between these passages he had at [20] of his judgment correctly directed himself about the *BF (Portugal)* four stage test: see [9] and [35] above.

[43] It is also plain beyond argument that the Judge appreciated the nature of the SSHD's submission, as appears from his summary of the submission at [37] of the judgment, which I have set out at [13] above. Once more, there is no suggestion that the Judge when saying "both ... and" meant "either ... or".

[44] When it came to the section of his judgment where he discussed the competing submissions, analysed the materials before him and resolved the issue he had to decide, the Judge once more indicated his approach at [53], which I have set out at [19] above. Crucially, he made clear that, on his approach, application of the *Bouchereau* exception depended on Mr Okafor's role, the sentence imposed *and* "his subsequent conduct". Just as there is no basis for treating his role and the sentence imposed as separate and mutually exclusive factors, so there is no basis for interpreting the reference to "his subsequent conduct" as meaning or implying anything other than an overall assessment based on all relevant subsequent conduct, his role and the sentence imposed. That approach is repeated in [58] of the judgment (which I have set out at [23] above), where the Judge said that his assessment of whether Mr Okafor's "personal conduct" gave rise to "deep public revulsion" required him "to take all the factors [he had] identified above into account". In the context provided by the judgment as a whole and the passages I have identified in particular, there is no basis for excluding Mr Okafor's deceptive conduct from this entirely general reference to "all factors".

[45] The SSHD is enabled to advance his arguments because the Judge addressed Mr Okafor's offending in [58] of the judgment and his deceptive behaviour in [60] of the judgment having already held in [59] that the SSHD had failed to establish that Mr Okafor's conduct fell within the *Bouchereau* exception. I have set out the concluding paragraphs of his judgment at [23] above. It is not surprising that the Judge addressed the conviction separately from the deceptive conduct in his immigration applications: on the contrary, that was necessary in the interests of clarity. Nor is it surprising that, having stated the need to take all factors into account at the start of [58] he then addressed the criminal conduct first and stated his conclusion that it did not of itself trigger the *Bouchereau* exception. There is and can be no challenge to that conclusion, though Mr Lewis could not and did not concede that it was correct.

[46] Furthermore, the Judge's treatment of the deceptive conduct at [60] reflected the submissions of the SSHD, which had treated the deceptive conduct as something of a makeweight on which he placed "some reliance". The Judge was entitled to find that the deceptive conduct came "nowhere near" being an exceptional or unusual case where "deep public revulsion" is engendered. Once again, there is and can be no challenge to that conclusion, though it was not formally conceded.

[47] Paragraphs [58] to [61] must be read in the context provided by the rest of the judgment. That context, which I have attempted to summarise above, shows that the Judge had the relevant principles, issues and questions in mind at all material times and considered that the deceptive conduct added nothing of substance to the overall assessment he was obliged to undertake. His justifiable use of the dismissive phrase "nowhere near" indicates that the deceptive conduct was not such as to affect the balance as it appeared on consideration of the much more important feature, namely the criminal offending. That led him to his overall conclusion in [61]: see above. That does not indicate that he was failing to consider the cumulative effect of Mr Okafor's behaviour. It merely meant that he concluded that the additive effect of the deceptive conduct, in the circumstances of this case, did not affect the overall balance.

[48] I accept that it could have been clearer if he had inserted a single concluding sentence expressly stating that he had reached his overall conclusion taking all relevant matters into account "both singly and cumulatively" (or some such phrase); or if he had reversed the order of [59] and [60]. However, it would be perverse to hold that, having consistently and expressly recognised the correct principles and test that he had to apply, his judgment should be struck down for what, in a legal sense, was the want of a horseshoe nail.

[49] I would therefore dismiss this appeal on the basis that the Judge took into account the cumulative effect of all relevant matters and concluded that the deceptive conduct did not tip the balance. His judgment does not disclose any error of law that would justify or permit us to interfere.

Lord Justice Snowden:

[50] I agree.

Lord Justice Moylan:

[51] I also agree.

XY v SECRETARY OF STATE FOR THE HOME DEPARTMENT

ADMINISTRATIVE COURT

Lane J

[2024] EWHC 81 (Admin)
23 January 2024

Human rights – Article 8 of the ECHR – private life – substantive and procedural breach – Article 14 of the ECHR – prohibition of discrimination – difference of treatment under unpublished policy not justified – procedure and process – Home Office procedures – pause in decision-making following R (on the application of KTT) *[2021] EWHC 2722 (Admin) – unpublished policy unlawful*

The Applicant was a national of Albania, born in September 2001. He arrived in the United Kingdom in 2018 and claimed asylum on grounds that he had been kidnapped and enslaved by a gang who forced him to sell drugs. In November 2020, he was diagnosed with post-traumatic stress disorder. In July 2021, the Single Competent Authority made a positive conclusive grounds decision which accepted that the Applicant had been a victim of modern slavery. In June 2022, the Applicant's counsellor reported that he was a very vulnerable young man who had been struggling with his mental health over several years. The counsellor concluded that the Applicant's condition was unlikely to improve until such time as he felt safe and stable in the United Kingdom.

Under the Secretary of State for the Home Department's policy 'Discretionary Leave Considerations for Victims of Modern Slavery version 4.0' published on 8 December 2020, discretionary leave could be considered where a person was a confirmed modern slavery victim and leave was necessary owing to their personal circumstances. In October 2021, the Court in *R (on the application of KTT) v Secretary of State for the Home Department* [2021] EWHC 2722 (Admin) declared that the policy required the Secretary of State's decisions to be made in accordance with Article 14(1)(a) of the Council of Europe Convention on Action against Trafficking in Human Beings 2005 ('ECAT'). That provision required the grant of a residence permit to a confirmed victim of modern slavery if their stay in the United Kingdom was necessary owing to their personal situation, which included the fact that they were pursing an asylum claim based on a fear of being re-trafficked.

In November 2021, the Secretary of State informed the Applicant that a provisional decision had been made in his case and that internal checks would be completed in December 2021. Despite repeated requests, a decision was not sent to the Applicant. In July 2022, the Applicant's solicitors issued a pre-action protocol letter and on 1 December 2022 commenced judicial review proceedings. The Applicant challenged the Secretary of State's ongoing refusal to decide whether he was entitled to modern slavery leave since the conclusive grounds decision. He relied on evidence that the ongoing threat of his removal was impeding his psychological recovery and aggravating his mental ill health.

In January 2023, the Secretary of State granted the Applicant 12 months' modern slavery leave and invited him to withdraw his judicial review. The Applicant continued proceedings on the grounds that, in response to the judgment in *KTT*, the Secretary of State was operating a secret policy. He claimed that officials had been instructed to make decisions in cases where confirmed victims of modern slavery were seeking asylum on the grounds of a fear of re-trafficking, but were told not to serve those decisions. He claimed that that approach was unlawful and that he had suffered a substantive and procedural breach of his rights under Article 8 ECHR and of his right not to be discriminated against under Article 14 ECHR. The Secretary of State submitted that staff had merely been instructed to pause all modern slavery leave decisions for confirmed victims of trafficking who had claimed asylum, pending an appeal in *KTT*.

The Administrative Court was asked to determine first, whether the Secretary of State had acted unlawfully in refusing to serve a decision in the Applicant's case; secondly, whether the failure to issue the Applicant leave to remain had resulted in a breach of Article 8 ECHR; and thirdly, whether the Secretary of State's unpublished policy breached Article 14 ECHR.

Held, allowing the application:

(1) The declaration contained in *KTT* represented the law and was an authoritative statement of what the Secretary of State's published policy meant; namely, what was 'necessary' in relation to a victim of modern slavery was the individual's 'stay' in the United Kingdom as understood in Article 14(1)(a) of ECAT. As long as the wording considered in *KTT* formed part of the Secretary of State's published policy, she had to interpret it in accordance with the declaration in *KTT*, unless and until that declaration was disturbed on appeal. It was open to the Secretary of State to publish an amendment to the policy, explaining that until the ultimate stage of the *KTT* litigation was known decisions in respect of those covered by the declaration would not be made. While there might have been political ramifications to the Secretary of State amending her policy to exclude the *KTT* group, or to pause decision-making, such political considerations could not be allowed to dilute the important 'rule of law' principles articulated in *Lumba v Secretary of State for the Home Department* [2011] UKSC 12 and *R v Secretary of State for the Home Department ex parte Anufrijeva* [2003] UKHL 36. Instead, the Secretary of State had adopted a policy or practice in the light of *KTT* which had not been given effect by amending or supplementing the published policy in version 4.0 or a later iteration of the policy in version 5.0. The result was that affected individuals and those advising them had no proper means of knowing what the true position was. The published policy continued to offer those who fell within its ambit discretionary leave. The reality was that Home Office officials had been instructed not to issue decisions to those who sought such leave. The Secretary of State could not deny that what her officials were being told to do, or not do, fell to be treated as a policy. Accordingly, the unpublished policy was unlawful: *Lumba* applied (*paras 53 – 58 and 61 – 63*).

(2) For the purpose of establishing *Lumba* illegality, it did not matter whether decisions were still being made in respect of individuals but not served on them, or whether decisions were paused for reasons that were withheld from the public gaze. The only way the Secretary of State could have avoided the consequences of operating a secret *Lumba*-style policy would have been to characterise the instructions as an exception to the published policy. In the instant case, the Secretary of State had not informed the Applicant of a departure from her policy. Instead, he was given every reason to think his case was being progressed when it was not. As such, the Applicant succeeded in establishing that the Secretary of State had acted unlawfully in refusing to issue her decision *(paras 62 – 65)*.

(3) It was common ground that if the Applicant could demonstrate that Article 8(1) ECHR was engaged then the decision under challenge would not be in accordance with the law for the purposes of Article 8(2): *Malcolm v Secretary of State for Justice* [2011] EWCA Civ 1538 applied. It was the Applicant's evidence that he wanted to be granted discretionary leave as a victim of trafficking whilst his asylum appeal was being determined as it would give him some stability. The Secretary of State submitted that prior medical evidence had demonstrated that the Applicant's anxiety was primarily generated by the uncertainty caused by the wait for an appeal in respect of his asylum claim. That submission did not, however, materially diminish the weight to be placed upon the Applicant's evidence. It was understandable that an individual's main focus might be on their asylum claim, but that did not mean that the individual was indifferent toward the possibility of being granted discretionary leave. As such, Article 8(1) was engaged and there had been a substantive breach from December 2021, when the checks following the provisional decision should have been completed. The effect of the Secretary of State's policy was materially to impair the Applicant's ability to use judicial review to challenge that policy and obtain modern slavery leave. Accordingly, there had also been a procedural breach of Article 8 ECHR *(paras 76 – 97)*.

(4) Under the Secretary of State's unpublished policy, a modern slavery victim who applied for discretionary leave on medical grounds and was refused would have received a decision. A victim who made an application on medical grounds but who also had an outstanding asylum claim would not receive a decision. The opportunity to challenge the negative decision accordingly arose only in the case of those who had not made an asylum claim. That was a difference in treatment in respect of persons in an analogous situation that was not justified. The difference between a victim who claimed asylum and one who did not was that the asylum seeker was subjected to the Secretary of State's unlawful policy and would have to bring a judicial review only by reference to what he considered to be an unlawful delay. The fact such a person, should he bring a claim, was likely to be 'rewarded' with a grant of leave could not justify the difference in treatment. Accordingly, the Article 14 ECHR claim succeeded. The difference in treatment was not justified as it arose directly from the operation of an unlawful policy *(paras 98 – 104)*.

Cases referred to:

Balajigari v Secretary of State for the Home Department; Kawos and Others v Secretary of State for the Home Department; Majumder and Another v Secretary of State for the Home Department; Albert v Secretary of State for the Home Department [2019] EWCA Civ 673; [2019] 1 WLR 4647; [2019] 4 All ER 998; [2019] Imm AR 1152; [2019] INLR 619
EOG v Secretary of State for the Home Department; KTT v Secretary of State for the Home Department [2022] EWCA Civ 307; [2023] QB 351; [2022] 3 WLR 353; [2022] Imm AR 991; [2022] INLR 213, on appeal from *R (on the application of KTT) v Secretary of State for the Home Department* [2021] EWHC 2722 (Admin); [2022] 1 WLR 1312
Malcolm v Secretary of State for Justice [2011] EWCA Civ 1538
Mendizabal v France 2006 ECHR 51431/99; (2010) 50 EHRR 50
Nadarajah v Secretary of State for the Home Department; Amirhanathan v Secretary of State for the Home Department [2003] EWCA Civ 1768; [2004] INLR 139
R v Secretary of State for the Home Department ex parte Anufrijeva [2003] UKHL 36; [2004] 1 AC 604; [2003] 3 WLR 252; [2003] 3 All ER 827; [2003] Imm AR 570; [2003] INLR 521
R (on the application of Gudanaviciene and Others) v Director of Legal Aid Casework and Lord Chancellor [2014] EWCA Civ 1622; [2015] 1 WLR 2247; [2015] 3 All ER 827
R (on the application of IAB and Others) v Secretary of State for the Home Department and Secretary of State for Levelling Up, Housing and Communities [2023] EWHC 2930 (Admin)
R (on the application of JP) v Secretary of State for the Home Department; R (on the application of BS) v Secretary of State for the Home Department [2019] EWHC 3346 (Admin); [2020] 1 WLR 918; [2020] Imm AR 565
R (on the application of PK (Ghana)) v Secretary of State for the Home Department [2018] EWCA Civ 98; [2018] 1 WLR 3955; [2018] Imm AR 961
Stevenson v Secretary of State for Work and Pensions [2017] EWCA Civ 2123
Walumba Lumba (previously referred to as WL (Congo)) v Secretary of State for the Home Department; Kadian Mighty (previously referred to as KM (Jamaica)) v Secretary of State for the Home Department [2011] UKSC 12; [2012] 1 AC 245; [2011] 2 WLR 671; [2011] 4 All ER 1; [2011] UKHRR 437

Legislation and international instruments judicially considered:

Council of Europe Convention on Action against Trafficking in Human Beings 2005, Article 14
European Convention on Human Rights, Articles 8 & 14
Nationality and Borders Act 2022, section 65

Representation

Mr *C Buttler* KC and Ms *Z McCallum* instructed by Asylum Aid, for the Applicant;
Ms *C McGahey* KC and Mr *W Irwin* instructed by the Government Legal Department, for the Secretary of State.

Judgment

This judgment was handed down remotely at 10.30am on 23 January 2024 by circulation to the parties or their representatives by e-mail and by release to the National Archives.

MR JUSTICE LANE:

[1] As a matter of public law, what is a Secretary of State able to do, faced with a judicial declaration on the interpretation of his or her published policy, if he or she does not agree with that interpretation? That important question lies at the heart of the claimant's challenge. The present case also raises issues involving the duty of candour in judicial review and the approach to claims of privilege or irrelevance as reasons for withholding material from the other party.

[2] The policy in question concerns article 14 of the Council of Europe Convention on Action against Trafficking in Human Beings 2005 ("ECAT"). Article 14(1)(a) of ECAT states that each party to the Convention "shall issue a renewable residence permit to victims ... (a) the competent authority considers that their stay is necessary owing to their personal situation".

[3] As is now well known, ECAT has not been incorporated into domestic law. Whether and, if so, how to comply with article 14(1)(a) is, accordingly, a matter for the defendant. The defendant has a published policy, "Discretionary Leave Considerations for Victims of Modern Slavery," which directs the defendant's officials to make decisions regarding leave to remain in the United Kingdom as a victim of modern slavery in accordance with article 14(1)(a) of ECAT. The version with which we are concerned is 4.0, published on 8 December 2020. This provides that discretionary leave may be considered under the policy where the Competent Authority has made a positive conclusive grounds decision that an individual is a victim of modern slavery and they satisfy one of a number of criteria, which for our purposes is that leave is necessary owing to the victim's personal circumstances. After setting out a non-exhaustive list of what might constitute such personal circumstances, the policy provides that, additionally, "a person may provide evidence from a healthcare professional that they need medical treatment. In these cases, consideration should be given to whether it is necessary for the treatment to be provided in the UK".

R (KTT) v Secretary of State for the Home Department [2021] EWHC 2722 (Admin)

[4] In *R (KTT) v the Secretary of State for the Home Department* [2021] EWHC 2722 (Admin), Linden J held that the defendant's policy "overwhelmingly demonstrates a commitment to take decisions as to discretionary leave in accordance with ECAT ..." (paragraph 79). Linden J held that the relevant question under article 14(1)(a) was whether the victim's "stay" was necessary owing to their personal situation, not whether the grant of the residence permit itself was necessary. At paragraph 92, Linden J accepted the claimant's submission that the fact that a victim is pursuing an asylum/protection claim based on fear of re-trafficking may be an aspect of the victim's personal situation for the relevant purposes, given that this interpretation would be in accordance with the aims of ECAT. This was so, notwithstanding that section 77 of the Nationality, Immigration

and Asylum Act 2002 prevents a person from being removed from the United Kingdom while their claim for asylum is pending.

[5] Following the handing down of his judgment in *KTT*, Linden J made an order on 25 October 2021 (sealed on 2 November 2021). The order included a declaration in the following terms:

> "1. On their true construction, versions 2, 3 and 4 of the Defendant's policy 'Discretionary Leave for Victims of Modern Slavery' ('the MSL policy') require the defendant's decisions on the grant of leave to remain to be made in accordance with Article 14(1)(a) ECAT, which requires the grant of a residence permit to a confirmed victim of modern slavery if their stay in the UK is necessary owing to their personal situation.
>
> 2. The statutorily-protected stay in the United Kingdom of a confirmed victim of trafficking pending the resolution of an asylum claim made by them which is based on a fear of being re-trafficked is capable of constituting a stay which is necessary owing to their personal situation within the meaning of Article 14(1)(a) ECAT."

[6] The order also contained a provision whereby the defendant's decision to refuse the claimant leave to remain under the MSL policy was quashed and the defendant required to make a fresh decision on the claimant's application for leave to remain under the MSL policy within 28 days of the order.

[7] The central issue in the present case concerns the defendant's response to the judgment and order in *KTT*. The claimant contends that the defendant's public stance was that the policy contained in the published document Version 4.0 remained in force, with the consequence that the defendant's officials would be assumed to make decisions in accordance with the policy, as interpreted by Linden J and set out in his declaration. Instead, the claimant contends that the defendant operated what he describes as a secret policy, whereby the defendant's officials were instructed to make decisions in cases where confirmed victims of modern slavery were seeking asylum on the grounds of a fear of re-trafficking, but were told not to serve those decisions. This, the claimant asserts, is contrary to the rule of law.

[8] The defendant's position, in essence, is that the defendant merely paused decision-making in respect of those affected by the judgment in *KTT*, until there was no longer any prospect of the defendant challenging Linden J's order. That prospect disappeared when permission to appeal to the Supreme Court was refused by that Court, in respect of the judgment of the Court of Appeal which had upheld Linden J's order. The defendant contends that this was a lawful approach.

[9] If, however, the approach was unlawful, the claimant asserts that he suffered a breach of his Article 8 ECHR rights, both substantively and procedurally. He further asserts that the defendant's actions violated Article 14 ECHR.

[10] It is now necessary to examine the claimant's case in more detail.

The Claimant

[11] The claimant is a national of Albania, born in September 2001. His modern slavery account was that, at the age of 16, he was enslaved in Albania by a gang who kidnapped him and forced him to sell drugs. The resultant trauma has caused the claimant to suffer anxiety and depressive disorder, as well as to exhibit

symptoms of post-traumatic stress disorder. The claimant takes antidepressant medication and sleeping tablets and is in receipt of psychological therapy.

[12] The claimant arrived in the United Kingdom in 2018 and claimed asylum. He had been enabled to flee Albania with the assistance of his uncle. Following his asylum claim, the claimant was placed into foster care, followed by shared accommodation.

[13] The claimant began a long course of therapy in February 2020. In November 2020, he was diagnosed with post-traumatic stress disorder. The claimant continued with his therapy until May 2021, when the service was terminated because of a lack of funding.

[14] On 21 July 2021, the Single Competent Authority promulgated a positive conclusive grounds decision, accepting that the claimant had been subjected to modern slavery. In April 2022, the claimant recommenced psychological therapy. On 21 June 2022, his counsellor reported that the claimant was a very vulnerable young man who had been struggling to manage his mental health over a number of years. The counsellor concluded that it was unlikely that there would be any improvement in the claimant's mental well-being until such time as the claimant felt safe and stable in the United Kingdom.

The Judicial Review

[15] In July 2022, the claimant's solicitors sent a pre-action protocol letter to the defendant, challenging the defendant's delay in determining the claimant's asylum claim.

[16] On 1 December 2022, the claimant commenced the present judicial review proceedings. These sought to challenge what was then the "ongoing refusal since 21 July 2021 (the date of the claimant's conclusive grounds decision) to make a decision on whether the claimant is entitled to leave to remain as a victim of modern slavery ...". It was said that there was evidence that the ongoing threat of removal of the claimant was impeding his psychological recovery and aggravating his mental ill health. At the time, the claimant's appeal against the refusal of his asylum claim was pending before the First-tier Tribunal.

[17] Paragraph 3 of the statement of facts and grounds asserts that the defendant appeared to be operating an unpublished, blanket policy. She would not make a decision on a confirmed victim's entitlement to ECAT leave until the defendant had considered the implications of the judgment in *KTT*. Paragraph 5 asserted that there was some 600 confirmed victims of trafficking in the United Kingdom who had claimed asylum and who would in principle be entitled to ECAT leave in consequence of the judgment in *KTT*. Amongst other matters, a declaration was sought by the claimant that the defendant's unpublished policy was unlawful.

[18] On 23 December 2022, the defendant filed an acknowledgement of service. This contained the statement the defendant had agreed to grant the claimant discretionary leave for a period of 12 months. On that basis, the claimant was invited to withdraw his judicial review. The claimant did not do so. On 18 January 2023, the defendant granted the claimant 12 months' "ECAT leave", on the express basis that it was accepted, in the light of the information supplied by the claimant, that he had a continuing need for counselling.

[19] On 8 March 2023, Lang J granted permission and made an anonymity order in respect of the claimant. On 6 April 2023, the claimant wrote to the defendant, *inter alia*, seeking disclosure of "details of the unpublished policy of suspending or

deferring ECAT leave decisions of confirmed victims of trafficking in light of *KTT* ...". It was stated that the claimant intended to make a CPR Part 18 request if the information was not provided. That included the number of confirmed victims whose decisions had been placed on hold.

[20] As amended, ground 1 challenges the defendant's refusal from 21 July 2021 to 18 January 2023 to consider the claimant's entitlement to ECAT leave as being unlawful, contrary to the claimant's ECAT leave policy and *Wednesbury* unreasonable. Ground 2 asserts that the defendant's refusal from 21 July 2021 until 18 January 2023 to consider the claimant's entitlement to ECAT leave breached his rights under Article 4 and/or Article 8 of the ECHR. I note here that the Article 4 ECHR challenge is not pursued. Ground 3 asserts that the defendant's decision to defer consideration of the claimant's entitlement to ECAT leave breached his rights under Article 14 ECHR, read with Articles 4 and/or 8 and/or Article 1 Protocol 1.

The Defendant's Response to *KTT*

[21] I turn to the evidence concerning the defendant's decision-making in the wake of the judgment and order in *KTT*. At this stage, I am concerned only to set out the evidence in an essentially chronological manner. The latter part of this judgment will examine when and how some of this evidence came to light in the context of the defendant's duty of candour and the related issue of redactions of documents by the defendant on the asserted grounds of lack of relevance and legal professional privilege.

[22] On 29 November 2021, the defendant informed the claimant's solicitors, Asylum Aid, that a provisional decision had been made in the case of the claimant. This decision regarding leave to remain under ECAT was said to be going through internal checks. The deadline for the checking process was 8 December 2021. The defendant refused to disclose the decision letter of 29 November but did so during the course of the hearing (see below).

[23] On 9 December 2021, Asylum Aid pointed out that the deadline for internal checks had passed. They asked to know the position regarding the decision on modern slavery leave. There was no response from the defendant.

[24] On 23 December 2021, the Court of Appeal refused the defendant's application for a stay on that part of the order of Linden J which required the defendant to make a fresh decision on the application for leave made by *KTT*. The fact that the defendant was not seeking a stay on the declaration made by Linden J, which plainly had relevance to others in the same position as *KTT*, was noted by Underhill LJ in his reasons for refusing the stay. Also on 23 December 2021, the defendant granted *KTT* modern slavery leave.

[25] On 19 January 2022, the defendant's Assistant Director to the Trafficking Litigation Lead at the Modern Slavery Unit sought ministerial agreement to a proposed operational handling of discretionary leave decisions, following the judgment in *KTT*. Attached to the Assistant Director's e-mail was a submission entitled "Operational handling of Discretionary Leave decisions post judgment in KTT v SSHD". This noted the refusal by the Court of Appeal of a stay on the mandatory order of Linden J. The submission sought ministerial agreement "for how we proceed in making decisions in similar cases, until such time as our appeal against the judgment reaches conclusion". Express reference was made to the "KTT cohort – that is – cases where an individual has received a positive conclusive grounds decision but is still awaiting the outcome of their asylum claim". The effect

of the judgment in *KTT* was that this cohort was "in scope of a consideration of a grant of leave … where the asylum claim was based on a fear of re-trafficking". Hitherto, decisions on whether to grant modern slavery leave had been deferred, where the person concerned had made an asylum claim. In the light of *KTT*, such decisions should, the document noted, no longer be deferred and a person within the *KTT* cohort should be granted a period of temporary leave, from the date of the conclusive grounds decision to when their asylum claim case had concluded. It was said that data as of mid-January 2022 demonstrated that there were about 800 cases involving individuals awaiting a discretionary leave decision who also had an outstanding asylum claim. To further refine how many of these cases fell within the scope of the *KTT* judgment would require further work. The memo noted that where a decision was made to grant leave, "the individual will have access to mainstream benefits".

[26] The memo referred to "four options for taking decisions set out at paragraph 7". As originally disclosed, the whole of paragraph 7 was redacted. The memo stated that Options A, C and D were not recommended and that the recommendation was to pursue Option B.

[27] A further Part 18 request by the claimant resulted in the defendant providing information on Options A–D, in the GLD's letter of 26 September 2023. The options were:

Option A – decision-making functions continuing as usual, not factoring in the findings of *KTT*.

Option B – decision-making functions continuing as usual but for any victim of modern slavery with an outstanding asylum claim, the modern slavery discretionary leave decision was to be 'held'.

Option C – placing a hold on decisions with outstanding asylum/protection.

Option D – granting discretionary leave in accordance with *KTT*.

[28] The letter of 26 September 2023 explained that the difference between Options B and C was that all individuals with an outstanding asylum/protection claim would have their decision "held" under Option C; whereas Option B would still allow decision-making to take place where an individual could be granted discretionary leave under the existing policy.

[29] On 19 January 2022, an email to the defendant's Private Secretary said that "a decision is required to reduce legal risk and inconsistency in practice". On 26 January 2022, the Assistant Private Secretary to the Minister for Safeguarding raised questions about the litigation risks associated with the options for decision. On 28 January 2022, in an e-mail to "SCA Blue Command – all staff", the defendant appears to have instructed staff to pause all modern slavery leave decisions on the *KTT* basis for confirmed victims of trafficking who had claimed asylum. The instruction was redacted on the grounds of asserted litigation and legal advice privilege. When faced with the claimant's Part 18 request, the defendant explained that the instruction concerned only the service of what, ignoring the right to *KTT* leave, would have been refusals of modern slavery leave. It was these cases that were placed on hold pending the defendant's final position following the *KTT* judgment. Individuals who were entitled to discretionary leave on some other basis,

in accordance with the discretionary leave policy, continued to have decisions made. Decisions were not halted for those who were eligible for a grant of discretionary leave on a non-*KTT* basis or for those who did not have a pending asylum decision.

[30] It is clear from the letter of 26 September 2023 that the instruction was to put the case on hold, irrespective of whether the re-trafficking risk on return was at issue in the asylum claim. Accordingly, the *KTT* cohort comprised a wider category than that contained in Linden J's declaration.

[31] In paragraph 42 of the amended detailed grounds of defence, the defendant accepts that during "this period of pause" the defendant did, in fact, address the position of individuals "who brought or threatened judicial review challenges …. The Defendant contends that this was an entirely reasonable approach; since the time limits for bringing and responding to judicial review challenges are short, the Defendant had no choice but to respond to such challenges or potential challenges within fairly brief time periods, and she did so". This is said, however, not to affect the defendant's entitlement, at a more general level, to take time to consider the implications of *KTT*, both at first instance and on appeal, and to pause, insofar as was possible, the taking of decisions during that period.

[32] On 31 January 2022, the defendant's National Referral Mechanism ("NRM") technical specialist e-mailed the defendant's NRM's team with an instruction "to mitigate further legal challenges". Decision-makers should not serve any Option 1 letter unless advised to do so. If unsure, they should attend a "DL Drop-In or seek advice from the Chief Caseworking Unit". The GLD's letter of 20 September 2023 to Asylum Aid explains that Option 1 was a decision to refuse discretionary leave to an individual who had an extant asylum claim but who did not meet the criteria for discretionary leave because they were not assisting the police/authorities with the investigation; were not pursuing a claim for compensation; and their personal circumstances did not require a grant of discretionary leave. I observe that this last condition ignores the effect of *KTT*.

[33] The message of 31 January 2022 asked for Option 1 decisions to go before what the GLD letter describes as a "second pair of eyes" process for refusal decisions; but with a reminder that these decisions "cannot be served until further notice".

[34] From all this, the claimant contends it is tolerably clear that the defendant's plan was "deliberately not to serve decisions that should have been served under the published policy, so that those who were affected were unable to bring effective legal challenges".

[35] On 3 February 2022, the defendant confirmed her agreement to Option B; namely that "decision making functions [continued] as usual but for any victim of modern slavery with an outstanding asylum claim the modern slavery discretionary leave decision to be 'held'". On 10 March 2022, the defendant responded to Asylum Aid to apologise for the delay in making the claimant's discretionary leave decision. The defendant said that there were certain types of discretionary leave decision that the defendant was "currently unable to serve, causing delays to the process". The letter enclosed a blank personal circumstances questionnaire form, thereby (according to the claimant) generating the impression that the decision was still being progressed.

[36] On 17 March 2022, the Court of Appeal upheld the judgment of Linden J: *R (EOG and KTT) the Secretary of State for the Home Department* [2023] QB 351.

[37] On 13 March 2022, Asylum Aid replied to the defendant, re-appending the questionnaire for a third time and requesting that a decision be made urgently. On 14 April 2022, according to the GLD's letter of 20 September 2023, the claimant's case was assessed and an Option 1 letter drafted. The letter was checked by the second pair of eyes on 31 May 2022 and placed on hold. The defendant refused to disclose a copy of the decision letter of 14 April 2022 but did so during the course of the hearing (see below).

[38] On 18 April 2022, Asylum Aid sent a pre-action letter in respect of the delay and on 26 April 2022 the defendant responded, committing to determine the asylum claim within three months.

[39] On 27 April 2022, the Nationality and Borders Act 2022 received Royal Assent. The effect of section 65(2)(a) is for leave to remain to be granted in accordance with the construction of article 14(1)(a) of ECAT which the defendant had unsuccessfully sought to advance in the *KTT* litigation. Section 65 was not at that stage brought into force.

[40] On 8 July 2022, the Deputy Chief Caseworker at the Single Competent Authority sent an e-mail to staff, stating that all discretionary leave decisions affected by *KTT* remained on hold. On 11 July 2022, the Deputy Chief Caseworker e-mailed staff again, recording the advice that Option 1 letters where there was an open asylum claim should be put on hold. The e-mail said that this guidance "is for internal use only and should not be disclosed to external stakeholders". If anyone was contacted regarding the *KTT* judgment or a decision that was on hold, the matter was to be forwarded to the "Tech Spec inbox for the team to respond". If the case was to be put on hold, "do not draft an Option 1 or full refusal letter".

[41] The defendant has confirmed to the claimant that the reference in the 11 July 2022 email to previous advice was a reference to the instruction not to serve Option 1 letters. The only substantive change to the approach taken since January 2022 was, according to the defendant, to include individuals who had "outstanding further submissions" and not just "first time asylum claims" within the cohort of those whose decisions were being paused.

[42] I have already made reference to the pre-action correspondence in connection with the present proceedings. When Asylum Aid served a further pre-action letter on 27 October 2022, it enclosed the letter of 25 October 2022, confirming that the claimant's therapy remained ongoing and that the claimant's ill health was connected with his fear of removal. A letter from a social worker was also enclosed, explaining that the claimant's inability to work was impeding his psychological recovery.

[43] On 28 October 2022, the Supreme Court refused the defendant permission to appeal against the judgment of the Court of Appeal in *R (EOG and KTT)*.

[44] On 11 January 2023, a further submission was made to Ministers. The defendant's Policy Lead for Victim Support sought approval for a proposal to address the judgment of the Court of Appeal. The proposal was that, from 30 January 2023, there should be a change in policy for permission to stay for victims of human trafficking or slavery, in order to give effect to ECAT 14.1(b) only. "This would mean that the express policy intent was that compliance with article 14(1)(a) is at most an aspiration with expressly no intention to comply in full or at all at present". A second submission, appended to the e-mail but heavily redacted on the asserted grounds of litigation and legal advice privilege, indicated that the change in direction was materially motivated by the litigation risks associated with failing to implement the judgment in *KTT*. This submission noted

that the defendant was receiving challenges from individuals who claimed they were eligible for leave to remain, following *KTT*. It said that generally "we have delayed granting leave to remain to eligible individuals under the KTT judgment until a policy has been published …. We are granting discretionary leave with recourse to public funds …. Without a published policy we risk inefficient and inconsistent decision making …". It was said that further advice would be provided in due course on the approach to be taken to the approximately 1500 individuals who were currently eligible for a consideration of leave to remain as result of *KTT*. Options were "being worked through with a view to mitigating the operational impact whilst reducing policy and legal risks".

[45] The submission explained that there might be adverse political consequences as a result of not complying with article 14(1)(a) of ECAT but that nonetheless this option was preferable to the alternative option of implementing the *KTT* judgment. The reputational impact of changing policy was said to have been carefully considered, including "how this will be viewed by both stakeholders and senior parliamentarians, specifically Rt Hon Sir Iain Duncan Smith and Rt Hon Mrs Theresa May". It was explained that during the passage of the Bill for the Nationality and Borders Act 2022, "we did not expressly state that Section 65 intended to fulfil a maximalist approach to ECAT compliance, however we did say that it was in line with our international obligations … and clarified the policy set out in the Modern Slavery Discretionary Leave Guidance. This may lead to further criticism …" The alternative option of implementing the *KTT* judgment and maintaining a commitment to give full effect to article 14 of ECAT would have "significant operational implications" and would be likely to impact "our ability to clear the asylum legacy backlog by the end of December 2023 and achieve increased removals to Albania due to the resource required to casework these cases".

[46] On 17 January 2023, it was confirmed that the defendant had agreed to the recommendation. On 27 January 2023, a further submission was made to Ministers. This sought agreement to "allow for leave to remain to be granted to individuals with a positive conclusive grounds decision and outstanding asylum claim (or further submissions) on the basis of a risk of re-trafficking as of 30 January 2023 as a result of the KTT judgment". It was said that there were approximately 1500 cases "stayed behind the KTT judgment which need a short-term solution". The recommendation was to grant members of this cohort 12 months leave where the asylum claims or further submissions were based on fear of re-trafficking. This was estimated to be 80% of the cohort of 1500 victims but the data was currently being reviewed. The alternative, which was to determine the entitlement of this cohort in accordance with the process that would be authorised by section 65 of the 2022 Act, was not recommended, on the basis that there would likely be "reputational impact … because we have not processed these cases in a timely manner, and that delay has disadvantaged the cohort, which may be presented negatively externally given the cohort's status as vulnerable due to their confirmed status as victims of modern slavery".

[47] On 30 January 2023, section 65 of the 2022 Act was brought into force. Also on that day, the defendant rescinded the published MSL policy, replacing it with guidance on "Temporary permission to stay considerations for victims of trafficking or slavery," in which the defendant "elected … to no longer give effect to Article 14(1)(a) of ECAT …". On 31 January 2023, decision-making under the new guidance commenced.

[48] On 14 February 2023, an official responded to a question about the submission of 27 January, which had been raised by the defendant's Private Office. The question was whether "doing nothing" was an option. The response was that it was not an option that could be recommended. The official noted that judicial reviews continued to be lodged on grounds linked to the delay in implementing the *KTT* judgment. Locally held data indicated a total of 63 such judicial reviews being launched to date. The official had also seen 96 *KTT*-related pre-action protocols; a number which was said to have risen incrementally.

[49] On 16 March 2023, the defendant published updated guidance on Discretionary Leave (Version 10.0). Under the heading "Modern slavery cases (including human trafficking)" it was said that individuals who before 30 January 2023 had both a positive conclusive grounds decision and had made an asylum claim or further submissions, based in a material part on a claim to a well-founded fear of re-trafficking/real risk of serious harm due to re trafficking, which had not been finally determined, were potentially entitled to discretionary leave, had their applications for leave been determined under the Home Office policies prior to 30 January 2023. Such persons were not to have their applications for discretionary leave determined under the new policy (described above). Instead, where a competent authority had made a positive conclusive grounds decision prior to 30 January 2023 and the individual had prior to that date articulated an asylum claim or further submissions which were trafficking-related and the individual's asylum claim or submission "have at the present date not yet been finally determined (this means that they are still awaiting a decision or still have in-country appeal rights to exercise)", then "you must consider granting DL. DL would normally be granted in these circumstances". I record here that the claimant could not benefit from this policy as he had by then already been granted modern slavery leave in response to these proceedings.

Did the Defendant Act Unlawfully?

[50] For the claimant, Mr Buttler KC relied upon the judgments of the Supreme Court in *R (Lumba) v Secretary of State for the Home Department* [2012] 1 AC 245. At paragraph 20, Lord Dyson held that a policy "if unpublished, ... must not be inconsistent with any published policy". At paragraph 26, Lord Dyson recorded the defendant's acceptance that a decision-maker must follow his published policy and not some different unpublished policy "unless there are good reasons for not doing so". Lord Dyson noted that in *R (Nadarajah) v Secretary of State for the Home Department* [2004] INLR 139, Lord Phillips MR had said "the Secretary of State could not rely on an aspect of his unpublished policy to render lawful that which was at odds with his published policy".

[51] At paragraph 34, Lord Dyson held that the "rule of law calls for a transparent statement by the executive of the circumstances in which the broad statutory criteria will be exercised".

[52] Mr Buttler also relied upon *R (Anufrijeva) v Secretary of State for the Home Department and another* [2004] 1 AC 604. There, the House of Lords identified a constitutional principle which requires an administrative decision which is adverse to an individual to be communicated to that individual before the decision can have the character of a determination with legal effect, thereby enabling the individual to challenge the decision in the courts if they so wish. At paragraph 28 of the judgments, Lord Steyn described this principle as "the antithesis of such a state [as

was described by Kafka, a state where the rights of individuals are overwritten by hole in the corner decisions or knocks on doors in the early hours. That is not our system …" At paragraph 31, Lord Steyn held that it was of importance to an individual to be informed of the decision "so that he or she can decide what to do. Moreover neither cost nor administrative convenience can in such a case conceivably justify a different approach".

[53] The starting point for this aspect of the claimant's case ought to be obvious; but in view of the defendant's actions it nevertheless requires to be clearly and emphatically stated. The declaration contained in the order made by Linden J in *KTT* represented the law. Unless and until disturbed on appeal, it was an authoritative statement of what the defendant's published policy meant. It meant that in the passage of Discretionary Leave Considerations for Victims of Modern Slavery Version 4.0 which stated "Discretionary leave may be considered under the specific policy where the SCA has made a positive conclusive grounds decision that an individual is a victim of modern slavery **and** they satisfy one of the following criteria: leave is necessary owing to personal circumstances …", the reference to leave being "necessary" was not to be read at face value. Rather, as the declaration made plain, what needed to be "necessary" was the individual's "stay" in the United Kingdom, as that expression was understood in article 14 (1)(a) of ECAT. This was the way in which certain individuals could obtain leave to remain because their stay was necessary to pursue an asylum claim based upon a fear of re-trafficking.

[54] So long as the wording set out above formed part of the defendant's published policy, the defendant had to interpret it in accordance with the declaration of Linden J, unless and until that declaration was disturbed on appeal. At no time did the defendant secure a stay on the operation of that declaration. As I have explained, the Court of Appeal was not even asked to impose such a stay.

[55] The defendant was, of course, at liberty to amend the relevant policy. It had been the defendant's decision to create a policy which gave effect to article 14 of ECAT. The defendant could, therefore, have decided that the policy should be abrogated or amended if she did not wish to accept the judgment in *KTT*. Not only did the defendant not do that, however, a new iteration of the policy (Version 5.0) was published on 10 December 2021, almost two months after Linden J gave judgment. In Version 5.0, the passage set out above was reproduced in identical terms to that in Version 4.0.

[56] For the defendant, Ms McGahey KC emphasised that the defendant was entitled to seek to overturn the decision in *KTT*, both in the Court of Appeal and in the Supreme Court. Ms McGahey submitted that until the ultimate fate of the declaration was known, the defendant was entitled to pause decision-making in respect of the *KTT* cohort. It would not, she said, have been appropriate to make decisions during this time on the basis that Linden J was correct in his interpretation of the defendant's policy, only to find that a higher court concluded otherwise.

[57] This is undoubtedly correct. As in the case of any other disappointed litigant, the defendant has the right to pursue all available avenues of appeal, as well as procedural mitigations, such as the imposition of a stay. The problem, however, which was of the defendant's own making, was that, in the meantime, the defendant was saying to the world, through the published policy (as interpreted by the declaration) that individuals falling within the ambit of the declaration could be granted discretionary leave to remain in the United Kingdom when, in reality, the defendant's officials had been instructed not to issue decisions to those who had

sought such leave (and, indeed, others who had claimed asylum on grounds other than a fear of re-trafficking).

[58] It is here that the claimant's complaint about a "secret policy" comes into sharp focus. In the light of what I have said about the defendant's ability to revoke or amend the ECAT policy, it would have been perfectly possible for the defendant to have published an amendment, explaining that until the ultimate stage of the *KTT* litigation was known, the defendant would, as a general matter, not be making decisions in respect of those covered by the declaration or, indeed, in respect of a wider group just described. I accept that there might have been a political price to pay if, in the light of Linden J's judgment, the defendant had at that point decided (without the protective covering of section 65 of the 2022 Act) to take the more extreme step of amending the policy so as to exclude the *KTT* group or some larger category. I also accept that there may even have been political ramifications if the defendant had merely amended the policy in order to pause decision-making, in the way I have described. Political considerations of this kind cannot, however, be allowed to dilute the important "rule of law" principles articulated in *Lumba* and *Anufrijeva*. They may explain the defendant's actions but they can in no way excuse breaking the law.

[59] As Mr Buttler pointed out in reply, there is, in fact, a striking precedent, in the very context with which we are concerned, of the defendant amending the discretionary leave policy for victims of modern slavery in order to pause decision-making in the light of the judgment of a court: namely, that of the Court of Appeal in *R (PK) (Ghana) v the Secretary of State the Home Department* [2018] EWCA Civ 98. In that case, the Court of Appeal held that the defendant's policy, as then in force, failed properly to reflect article 14(1)(a) of ECAT because it imposed a requirement to show "compelling personal circumstances", which was a higher threshold that the concept of necessity articulated in article 14(1)(a).

[60] In the wake of *PK (Ghana)*, the defendant published, on 21 February 2018, "Interim operational guidance: Discretionary leave for victims of modern slavery" (Version 1.0).
In this, the defendant's officials were told as follows:

> "you must **pause decision-making** where you are not minded to grant discretionary leave to remain for any confirmed victim of modern slavery. A confirmed victim of modern slavery is an individual with a positive conclusive grounds decision. **All refusal decisions must be placed on hold.**
>
> The only exception is where the confirmed victim has been granted refugee leave. In these cases, you can issue a refusal of discretionary leave as normal.
>
> In cases where you are issuing a positive conclusive grounds decision and you are not minded to grant discretionary leave you should issue the grant letter template." [original emphasis]

[61] A similar approach could have been taken in the present case. Instead, the defendant adopted a policy or practice in the light of *KTT*, which was not given effect by amending or supplementing the published policy in Version 4.0 or Version 5.0, with the result that affected individuals and those advising them had no proper means of knowing what the true position was. The position is, I find, directly analogous to that in *Lumba*.

[62] Ms McGahey submitted that this crucial aspect of the claimant's challenge, as articulated by Mr Buttler at the hearing, was not to be found in the pleaded grounds. That is, with respect, wrong. In paragraph 3 of the claimant's amended Statement of Facts and Grounds (for which permission to amend was granted by consent on 18 July 2023), it is asserted that the defendant "appeared to be operating an unpublished, blanket policy that she will not make a decision on a confirmed victim's entitlement to ECAT leave until she has considered the implications of that judgment" i.e. *KTT*. Paragraph 5 of the grounds "places at issue a blanket and unpublished policy", as to which "the Court will need to consider its legality. [The claimant] also seeks a declaration that the unpublished policy is unlawful".

[63] The defendant cannot, on the state of the evidence, deny that what the defendant's officials were being told to do (or not to do) falls to be treated as a policy. The instructions were of a generalised nature, bearing upon a particular class of person. However the defendant might wish to categorise them, the instructions were a material departure from the published policy, as it had to be interpreted in the light of the declaration of Linden J. It was a variation or modification of that policy and, thus, itself a policy.

[64] For the purpose of establishing *Lumba* illegality, it matters not whether, as a general matter, decisions were still being made in respect of individuals, but not being served on them, which is what the claimant contends, or whether, as the defendant argues, decision-making was being paused for reasons that were withheld from public gaze. That said, I find that, in the case of the claimant, decisions in the proper sense of the word, refusing leave to remain by reference to his medical needs, were, in fact, made and then placed on file, rather than being communicated to him. I refer particularly to the evidence wherein the claimant was in effect given to understand that his decision was being examined by the second pair of eyes; and the evidence concerning the invitation to complete yet another questionnaire. At the very least, the claimant was being given every reason to think that his case was being progressed when, in reality, it was not. I shall have more to say about this issue later.

[65] The only way in which the defendant could avoid the consequences of operating a secret *Lumba*-style policy would be to seek to characterise the instructions as, in effect, exceptions to the defendant's published policy. As is well known, the owner of a policy may depart from it, where there are good reasons to do so. The problem here, however, is that the person concerned is entitled to be informed that the decision-maker has departed from the policy in their case. As can be seen from the materials, that simply did not happen.

[66] The defendant contends that, in the circumstances of the present case, the principle that a person who is subject to an adverse decision is entitled to be informed of it does not apply because those in the position of the claimant could bring a judicial review on the basis that the defendant's delay in dealing with their case was unlawful. That, after all, was what the claimant eventually did. So too did others similarly affected.

[67] I emphatically reject that submission. Where, in contrast to a decision-maker's publicly articulated stance, she has instructed officials not to make decisions, or to make them and withhold them, it is no answer at all to expect the individuals concerned to suffer the trouble and expense of having to bring legal proceedings in order to discover why the decisions are not being made or communicated.

[68] As can be seen from the preceding account, however, at this point the defendant's position becomes even more problematic. When judicial reviews were brought, the defendant's response was not to explain that decisions were being held back or not made whilst the defendant attempted to challenge the decision in *KTT*. That would have been possible, albeit that, at this stage, it would not have resolved the defendant's *Lumba* problem. Instead, the defendant's reaction, upon being faced with such a judicial review, was to grant discretionary leave to the person who had brought the proceedings.

[69] The defendant contends that this response, when faced with judicial reviews, was appropriate. As Ms McGahey said, a judicial review "needs to be answered" and there are tight time limits within which this needs to be done. To adopt Ms McGahey's metaphor, it was, accordingly, reasonable to move the cases of those who brought judicial review to the top of the queue of those affected by the judgment in *KTT*.

[70] I regret that I find this purported justification entirely inadequate. It would have been possible and, indeed, compatible with the (albeit unpublished) policy of pausing/withholding decisions in the light of *KTT* for the defendant to have said that was what she was doing, when faced with a judicial review. Instead, as the materials reveal, the response was to offer discretionary leave to remain. Not only did that rob the policy of coherence, it strongly supports the claimant's contention that leave to remain was offered in these circumstances precisely in order to keep the policy secret. And so it would have remained, but for the work of Alison Pickup and her colleagues at Asylum Aid who (as her statement and exhibits show) diligently assembled information from others acting for victims of modern slavery, which led to the claimant pursuing this claim, notwithstanding that he had been granted leave, and thus bringing the evidence set out above into the light of day.

[71] There is a further point to make. The defendant's instructions to officials meant that an individual would receive a discretionary grant of leave, notwithstanding *KTT*, if this was considered to be necessary because of the individual's need for medical treatment. The claimant, however, was originally found by the defendant not to be entitled to leave in that regard. This emerges from the materials I described above. It was only when the defendant was supplied with further evidence at the pre-action stage of the present proceedings that the defendant apparently concluded that the claimant was entitled to leave on this ground.

[72] Mr Buttler submitted that the effect of the secret policy was, in the claimant's case, to deny him knowledge of the earlier negative decision on that ground and, thus, the opportunity of challenging that decision at the stage when it would (but for the secret policy) have been communicated to him. I agree that this was the effect of the policy on the claimant. I will return to what this means when examining the issue concerning Article 8 ECHR.

[73] The defendant argues that all of the above is, in effect, immaterial because the claimant and others in his position were not going to be removed from the United Kingdom in any event. They had an extant claim to asylum with the result that, pursuant to section 77 of the 2002 Act, they could not be removed.

[74] I shall return to this issue in the context of Article 8, so far as concerns the claimant's individual circumstances. As a general proposition, however, the submission can in no sense save the day for the defendant on the primary issue of unlawfulness. In *KTT*, Linden J concluded that the fact that the 2002 Act prevented the person from being removed while their claim for asylum (or appeal) was pending did not mean they were unable to put forward a case for leave on the basis

of article 14(1)(a) of ECAT. As he pointed out in paragraph 91 of the judgment, if the position were otherwise, then modern slavery leave would rarely if ever be conferred in respect of a person seeking asylum because such leave would not be necessary to facilitate their stay. As Linden J had earlier noted (paragraph 10), the effect of refusing to grant modern slavery leave was that the person concerned remained "subject to the so-called hostile immigration environment underpinned by the Immigration Act 2014". In normal circumstances, the grant of discretionary leave of this kind carries with it an ability to work, study and claim "mainstream" benefits. It therefore cannot be said that, as a general matter, the defendant's instructions to officials made no difference to the persons within the *KTT* cohort.

[75] The claimant accordingly succeeds on this primary matter. It is therefore necessary to turn to the issue of Article 8 ECHR.

Article 8 ECHR

Substantive breach

[76] In the light of the judgment of the Court of Appeal in *Malcolm v Secretary of State for Justice* [2011] EWCA Civ 1538, it is common ground between the parties that if Article 8(1) can be shown by the claimant to be engaged, then the challenged decision will not be "in accordance with the law" for the purposes of Article 8(2), in the event that I find for the claimant on the primary issue (as I have). This means that the claimant will have suffered an actionable interference with his Article 8 ECHR right to respect for his private and family life and it will be unnecessary to determine whether, in circumstances, that interference was proportionate. This flows from paragraph 32 of *Malcolm*, where the court held (albeit *obiter*) that the principles of public law are part of the relevant domestic law, when deciding whether the "in accordance with the law" principle is satisfied.

[77] In *Mendizabal v France* (Application no. 514314/99), the European Court of Human Rights found that there had been a violation of Article 8 in the case of a Spanish national, lawfully resident in France, who from 1979 to 1989 had been issued with temporary residence permits, each valid for one year. From 1989, she was given a series of grants of leave to remain for three months; a practice which continued until 2003, when she was issued with a ten year residence permit. The applicant complained that the refusal over a 14-year period to issue her with a long term residence permit constituted an interference with her private and family life.

[78] It appears from paragraph 71 of the judgment that the Court concluded that Article 8 was engaged, at least in part because of the uncontradicted fact that "the precariousness of her situation and the uncertainty as to her fate had a significant moral and financial impact on her (casual and unskilled jobs, social and financial difficulties, impossibility, as a result of not having a residence permit, of renting premises and carrying on professional activity which she had undertaken in training)". At paragraph 72, the Court found that, even though the claimant had already been lawfully resident in France for over 14 years, she had suffered "an undeniable interference with her private and family life".

[79] Mr Buttler submitted that, in the present case, the claimant had a right in domestic law to be granted modern slavery leave from either 21 July 2021 or 29 November 2021 to 18 January 2023, which he was unlawfully denied. The consequences were that the claimant could not work or get mainstream benefits.

Nor could he do other things such as become a tenant of property, hold a bank account or obtain a driving licence. The fact that the claimant was not, in the circumstances, destitute was, according to Mr Buttler, immaterial for this purpose. Although Ms Mendizabal had been resident in France for far longer than the claimant had been resident in the United Kingdom, unlike him she had been able to work, albeit not in positions for which she had been trained.

[80] Mr Buttler also relied upon *R (Balajigari) v Secretary of State for the Home Department* [2019] 1 WLR 4647. In that case, a number of claimants contended that decisions to refuse them leave to remain in the United Kingdom under paragraph 322(5) of the Immigration Rules, on the basis that they had dishonestly misrepresented their earnings, engaged their rights under Article 8 ECHR. If Article 8 were engaged, then the claimants would have been able to challenge (by way of appeal) any refusal of their human rights claims. Mr Buttler drew particular attention to what was recorded at paragraph 81 of the judgment of Underhill LJ, where the *Balajigari* claimants pointed to the legal consequences of remaining in the United Kingdom without leave; namely, those stemming from the so-called "hostile environment", which included severe restrictions on the right to work, rent accommodation, have a bank account and hold a driving licence.

[81] Although, at paragraph 91, Underhill LJ did not reach a conclusion on whether those consequences were such as to engage Article 8, he nevertheless observed that it was "not difficult to see that in some cases some of the legal consequences of being present in the UK without leave – for example, the inhibitions on renting accommodation – may engage Article 8; but their impact will vary from case to case …".

[82] Ms McGahey submitted that, in the present case, there is no engagement of Article 8(1). The claimant's anxiety centred on his fear of being returned to Albania. The grant of a temporary period of discretionary leave pursuant to the ECAT policy would not have given the claimant reassurance in that regard. The effect of the discretionary leave would have been merely to have permitted the claimant to remain in the United Kingdom until his asylum claim was resolved. That, however, would have been the position in any event, as a result of section 77 and section 78 (which prohibits removal while an appeal is pending). Although the defendant accepted that being granted discretionary leave would have given the claimant access to mainstream benefits and an entitlement to work, on the facts of his particular case these were not the claimant's concern. The claimant's health was such that he was unable to work. Although the amount of benefits would have been higher, this fact was not such as to reach the minimum level of severity necessary to engage Article 8 ECHR. The claimant was, at the time, being supported by his foster family. He had access to a college course. He could also have lessened any harm by bringing his judicial review at an earlier point in time.

[83] I do not accept the defendant's submissions on this issue. Beginning with the last of these, for the reasons I have given when dealing with the primary issue, the defendant cannot be heard to say that the claimant ought to have accelerated the process of obtaining discretionary leave by bringing the judicial review at an earlier stage.

[84] As for the other submissions, before looking at the claimant's own case, it is necessary to examine the general background, including the rationale in article 14 of ECAT for the grant of residence permit (which, in our jurisdiction, is leave under the 1971 Act). In this regard, I agree with Mr Buttler that it is helpful to note what Murray J recorded at paragraph 81 of his judgment in *R (JP) v Secretary of State*

for the Home Department and another [2020] 1 WLR 918. There, Murray J cited the evidence of Professor Katona, a psychiatrist with undoubted experience in the immigration field, whose evidence was that a delay in granting ECAT leave or some other form of leave to remain to a victim of trafficking makes it much more difficult for the victim to engage fully in, and thereby benefit from, trauma-focused work. The Professor also considered that a prolonged indefinite uncertainty of waiting for a decision was clinically distressing and destabilising; and that an inability to work or study can increase a sense of social isolation, which is further aggravated by difficult financial circumstances.

[85] I fully accept that one cannot simply translate those findings and apply them, without more, to the particular facts of another case. The important point being made by the claimant, however, is that the harmful effects of having been a modern slave and the fear of becoming one again, are generally likely to be adversely affecting the victim and, as a consequence, are likely to play a part in deciding whether a grant of leave is necessary, if the defendant is to comply with what (at the time) was her publicly-stated policy of giving effect to article 14 of ECAT.

[86] With these general observations in mind, I turn to the claimant's witness statement of 25 November 2022. The claimant said that he would like to be granted discretionary leave as a victim of trafficking whilst his asylum appeal was being determined "as at least this could give me some stability in the short term. I do not know how long it will take for my asylum appeal to be finally determined, a hearing date has not yet been set. But discretionary leave to remain would make me feel more secure". The claimant explained that the reason he wanted to be granted leave was "so I can feel safe, and know that I'm not going to be forced to leave the UK and return to Albania. At the moment I feel like I am living on a cliff edge and the support I have around me in the UK might all be taken away". If the claimant's mental health improved, he said he would try to return to college so he could get a qualification, with the aim of being an electrician. If he received additional benefits, as a result of being given discretionary leave, the claimant felt he would be able to buy healthier and better quality food, travel around London and take part in social activities "that would help with my recovery and ongoing emotional difficulties".

[87] Ms McGahey submitted that all this is self-serving. In this regard, she drew particular attention to the letter of 27 October 2022 from Asylum Aid to the defendant. This pre-action protocol letter referred in detail to the opinions of those who had counselled the claimant in respect of his mental health. This medical evidence showed that the claimant was unable to work and, moreover, that his anxiety was primarily generated by the uncertainty caused by having to wait for an appeal in respect of his asylum claim.

[88] Even if this is right, I do not find that it materially diminishes the weight to be placed upon the claimant's witness statement. It is understandable that an individual's main focus may often be on their asylum claim, not least if it involves an appeal to the First-tier Tribunal or the Upper Tribunal. This does not, however, mean that the person should be taken to be indifferent towards the possibility of being granted leave to remain by reason of being a victim of modern slavery. Nor does the fact that the significance of having such leave may need to be explained to the person concerned mean that it falls to be written off, in considering whether the denial of modern slavery leave constitutes a matter that bears upon the engagement of Article 8(1).

[89] I therefore find that Article 8(1) is engaged in the claimant's case. I must, accordingly, consider the period of time that the defendant's unlawful interference with the claimant's Article 8 rights lasted.

[90] The claimant submits that the period should run from 21 July 2021 to 18 January 2023. The first of those dates was when the positive conclusive grounds decision was made by the single competent authority in respect of the claimant. The second date was when the defendant issued a decision granting the claimant modern slavery leave. Alternatively, the claimant submits that the period should run from 29 November 2021. That was when the defendant confirmed to Asylum Aid that a provisional decision had been made "subject to checks". The defendant intimated that those checks would be completed by 8 December 2021 and thereafter the decision would be served.

[91] I do not consider that 21 July 2021 represents the correct starting point for the Article 8 breach. Assuming a lawful decision-making process on the part of the defendant, it would clearly take time for the conclusive grounds decision to translate into the grant of discretionary leave to remain. Nor do I consider that the 29 November 2021 is the correct starting point. The communication on that date referred to a "provisional decision", which was said to be "subject to checks". The defendant was plainly entitled to carry out such checks. I find that the correct starting point is, accordingly, 8 December 2021. That was the date when the officials said that the checks would be completed. In the circumstances, there is no reason to assume that – absent the illegality identified in respect of the primary issue – those checks would have had an adverse consequence for the claimant.

[92] In so concluding, I have had close regard to the witness statement of 30 November 2023 of Mr Scott Evans of the Government Legal Department, together with exhibits. Two of these are draft letters from the defendant to Kate Macpherson of Asylum Aid, in each case refusing the claimant leave under the Modern Slavery Discretionary Leave Policy, on the basis that the claimant's medical situation did not make the grant of leave necessary. They are dated 29 November 2021 and 14 April 2022. They are the letters mentioned in paragraphs 22 and 37 above. The later letter would be relevant for present purposes only if no significance could be attached to the letter of 29 November. The reason there are two letters is because Asylum Aid was continuing to press the defendant for a modern slavery leave decision. These documents had previously been withheld by the defendant in these proceedings. Their belated production is an instance of the procedural shortcomings on the part of the defendant which I address later in this judgment.

[93] Mr Evans categorises the letters as "truly draft decisions that never reached final form and are therefore irrelevant". I do not accept this categorisation. Unlike the letter of 14 April 2022, which has marginal comments from the second pair of eyes, there is nothing on the face of the letter of 29 November to indicate it was scrutinised by the second pair of eyes. What matters, however, is that the defendant expected checks to be completed by 8 December 2021 and, as I have indicated, there is nothing to suggest that these would have resulted in a negative decision if the defendant had applied the published policy as it fell to be construed in the light of Linden J's declaration. The fact that this letter never reached "final form" is immaterial if the only reason it did not do so was because of the operation of the defendant's unlawful policy. I find there is no other discernible reason.

[94] I therefore conclude that there was a substantive breach of Article 8 ECHR from 8 December 2021 to 18 January 2023.

Procedural breach

[95] I turn to the question of whether there was a breach of Article 8 ECHR in its procedural context. Since it adds nothing in terms of remedy, I shall deal with this aspect somewhat briefly.

[96] In *R (Gudanaviciene) v the Director of Legal Aid Casework* [2015] 1 WLR 2247, the Court of Appeal held at paragraph 69 that there was no reason why the procedural requirements inherent in Article 8 ECHR should not apply in immigration cases. Accordingly, the question to be determined is whether the person affected has been involved in the decision-making process, viewed as a whole, to a degree sufficient to provide them with the requisite protection of their interests (paragraph 70). The focus of the procedural aspect of Article 8 is to ensure the effective protection of an individual's Article 8 rights.

[97] Ms McGahey accepted that the success of this aspect of the claim depended upon the court's conclusions on the primary issue. For the reasons I have given above, I find that the effect of the defendant's policy was materially to impair the claimant's ability to use judicial review to challenge that policy and obtain modern slavery leave to remain. Accordingly, this aspect of the claimant's challenge also succeeds.

Article 14 ECHR

[98] I turn to Article 14 ECHR. Here, the claimant places reliance on *JP*. In that case, Murray J held that modern slavery claims fell within the ambit of the rights guaranteed by Articles 4 and 8 of, and Article 1 of the First Protocol to, the ECHR. In the present case, the defendant rightly takes the view that the "ambit" requirement is satisfied by reason of Article 8 ECHR. The question, accordingly, becomes whether the defendant has discharged the burden of proving a proportionate justification for any difference in treatment between two persons in an analogous situation.

[99] In *JP*, Murray J found that there had been a breach of Article 14 ECHR in that the defendant's practice of deferring a decision on whether to grant modern slavery leave until after an asylum claim had been finally determined, disadvantaged those who are seeking modern slavery leave and also claiming asylum. In the present case, in addition to there being no issue regarding the ambit of Article 14 ECHR, there can be no doubt that, just as with *JP*, the claimant has a relevant status within the meaning of that Article. He has the status as an asylum-seeking victim of modern slavery, which is "a personal or an identifiable characteristic assessed in the light of all the circumstances of the case": *Stevenson v Secretary of State for Work and Pensions* [2017] EWCA Civ 213, paragraph 41 (Henderson LJ).

[100] The third requirement is for the claimant to be in an analogous situation to individuals who are treated differently. Here, I accept the claimant's submission that victims of modern slavery who claim asylum have the same need for modern slavery leave, pending the determination of their asylum claim, as does a victim of modern slavery who does not claim asylum. To hold otherwise would be inconsistent with the basic rationale of *KTT*.

[101] Ms McGahey sought to contest the claimant's case in respect of this third matter (difference in treatment/analogous situation), by means of the following argument. She said the claimant's case in this respect was that the defendant ought to have issued a refusal decision in respect of the application for modern slavery leave, based on medical grounds; and that the defendant did not do so because the claimant was an asylum seeker. The inference was that, if the claimant had received a negative decision on medical grounds, he would have challenged that decision. However, since bringing a judicial review requires the claimant to bring at the same time all challenges to the alleged acts or omissions of the defendant, the claimant would in practice have challenged the decision by reference to both the medical issue and the refusal to make a decision on the *KTT* ground.

[102] I do not consider that Ms McGahey's submission can be accepted. A victim of modern slavery *simpliciter* who applied for discretionary leave on medical grounds and was refused received a decision. A victim who made an application on medical grounds but who also had an outstanding asylum claim did not receive a decision. That was a difference in treatment in respect of persons in an analogous situation; namely, those who sought modern slavery leave on medical grounds. The opportunity to challenge the negative decision accordingly arose only in the case of those who had not made an asylum claim. An individual who, as an asylum seeker, did not get a negative decision in respect of their medical grounds case was accordingly treated differently for no reason other than that they had made an asylum claim and were therefore (unbeknown to them) affected by the defendant's unlawful policy. Such a person would not know that they had been the subject of a negative medical grounds decision and would have to bring a judicial review only by reference to what was considered by them to be an unlawful delay in the defendant's reaching a decision in their case. The fact that such a person – if they decided to bring such a judicial review – would likely be "rewarded" with a grant of leave cannot justify the difference in treatment.

[103] Accordingly, I move to the final question under Article 14, which is whether the difference in treatment is justified. Plainly, it was not. For the reasons I have given, the difference in treatment arose directly from the operation of the unlawful policy.

[104] The Article 14 challenge accordingly succeeds.

Duty of Candour, Privilege and Irrelevance

[105] I turn, finally, to the procedural matters foreshadowed in paragraphs 1 and 21 above. The claimant contends that in the defendant's pre-action response letter of 22 November 2022 the defendant breached the duty of candour in failing to disclose the existence of the unpublished policy and the fact that, pursuant to it, the defendant had taken two decisions regarding the claimant's entitlement to modern slavery leave but not served those decisions on the claimant. Instead, the defendant incorrectly asserted that the documents and information were possibly owned by third parties rather than the defendant and that the claimant should file a data subject access request in order to obtain disclosure. I consider that there is force in this criticism. The defendant has not advanced any justification for the assertion.

[106] On 6 April 2023, Asylum Aid wrote to the defendant, explaining the relevance of the alleged secret policy to the claimant's argument in the judicial review that the decision was "not in accordance with the law" for the purposes of Article 8 ECHR. The defendant's detailed grounds of defence, filed on 26 April

2023, contained a limited admission that the defendant had paused the implementation of the published policy. The grounds failed, however, to provide any further details and denied that the defendant was operating an unlawful unpublished policy. The defendant also failed to engage with the claim that the defendant's decision-making was "not in accordance with the law" for the purposes of Article 8.

[107] On 26 April 2023, the defendant filed no evidence and gave no disclosure alongside the detailed grounds of defence. The claimant contends that this was a breach of the duty of candour and, as a result, the claimant still did not know whether all confirmed victims or only a subset thereof were affected by the unpublished policy. Nor did the claimant know when that policy came into force and whether it admitted of any exceptions. It was at this point that Ms Pickup of Asylum Aid began contacting other legal firms and organisations in order to obtain relevant information.

[108] On 24 May 2023, the claimant filed his reply evidence, including witness statements of Ms Pickup and Frances Lipman of Deighton Pierce Glynn Solicitors. Ms Lipman supplied details of modern slavery cases of which she was aware in which, following the initiation of judicial review, the defendant granted, or offered to grant, the person concerned leave to remain. Ms Pickup's witness statement explained that it appeared the defendant was operating a practice of granting periods of leave only in response to a legal challenge or on medical grounds, independently of the individual's right to leave on the basis of the judgment in *KTT*.

[109] I find myself in agreement with the claimant that, if the defendant had earlier complied with the duty of candour and disclosed details of the unpublished policy, it would not have been necessary for the claimant to have gone to the considerable effort of obtaining and analysing the evidence in the witness statements of Ms Pickup and Ms Lipman. It was in the light of this information that the claimant amended his pleadings in order to include a claim for breach of Article 14 ECHR which, as I have found, succeeds.

[110] On 26 May 2023, the claimant made the first of his requests for information under Part 18 of the CPR. The request sought, amongst other things, all records relating to the defendant's decision, policy or practice of suspending or deferring decisions on modern slavery leave in the light of the judgment in *KTT*. On 30 June 2023, the defendant wrote to commit to filing amended detailed grounds of defence within 28 days and providing a "full response" to the Part 18 request. On 3 July 2023, the claimant consented to the 28 day extension.

[111] On 28 July 2023, the defendant filed and served amended detailed grounds of defence, along with certain disclosure. The defendant admitted for the first time that an exception had been made for victims who issued legal proceedings. Paragraph 42 of these grounds contended that it was "entirely reasonable" for the defendant to do so and that "the defendant had no choice but to respond to such a challenges or potential challenges within fairly brief periods, and she did so". This did not, however, affect what was said to be the defendant's entitlement at a more general level to take time to consider the implications of *KTT* "and to pause, insofar as was possible, the taking of decisions during that period". As I have earlier held, that contention of the defendant was wholly unjustified. If the intention was to pause decision-making, that could and should have been explained in response to any judicial review brought on the ground that there had been unlawful delay in reaching a decision in respect of a particular individual. To grant discretionary leave to individuals who were in a position to bring such judicial reviews undermined the

coherence of the defendant's policy and supports the claimant's contention that granting leave in these circumstances can only have been to minimise the risk of the policy becoming public knowledge.

[112] The defendant's response to the Part 18 request at this point was to serve partial disclosure, limited to e-mails to the defendant's caseworkers containing the instructions in January and July 2022. These were heavily redacted but no explanation was provided for the redactions. The covering letter from the defendant asserted that the remaining disclosure required ministerial sign-off and requested an extension until 2 August 2023. The claimant agreed to this.

[113] On 1 August 2023, the defendant disclosed three submissions for ministerial approval. These were the submissions of 19 January 2022 and 11 and 27 January 2023. The claimant contends that the disclosure was so heavily redacted as to be largely unintelligible. No explanation was offered for the redactions.

[114] In response to a letter from the claimant of 18 August 2023, the defendant replied on 1 September 2023, asserting that the redactions were made to protect "legal professional privilege" and to "remove e-mail addresses or other information not for entry into the public domain". The defendant stated that no further response to the first Part 18 request would be made. This was said to be on the basis that the amendments made to the defendant's detailed grounds of defence were sufficient. However, as the claimant points out, those amended grounds failed to state the date on which the unpublished policy began or ended; to identify the cohort to whom the policy had applied; and to confirm whether the defendant had applied it to the claimant. Furthermore, the defendant had still not pleaded to the claimant's "not in accordance with the law" argument.

[115] On 6 September 2023, the claimant made a second Part 18 request which, amongst other matters, pointed out that much of the disclosure was unintelligible owing to redactions and that the defendant had not adequately explained the basis for them. An explanation was also sought of the four options for implementing the *KTT* judgment, which were the subject of the first ministerial submission seeking approval for the unpublished policy but which had been completely redacted.

[116] On 20 September 2023, the defendant said that decision-making for the cohort affected by the "pause" restarted on 26 April 2023. The response then purported to provide a "summary" of the four redacted options. The claimant regarded the summary as unintelligible.

[117] On 21 September 2023, the claimant served a third Part 18 request. This was done in order to try to make sense of the unintelligible disclosure. The claimant explained that it was impossible for him fully to assess the relevance of the defendant's disclosure and whether the duty of candour had been discharged. On 26 September 2023, re-amended grounds of defence were filed and served by the defendant. These now pleaded to the "not in accordance with the law" argument. On 26 September 2023, the defendant responded to the third Part 18 request. This purported to correct the earlier summary of Options A-D, and offered an explanation for the differences between them. The defendant stated the date when the unpublished policy was first applied; described the cohorts affected; admitted that the unpublished policy had been applied to the claimant; and gave disclosure of an incomplete e-mail chain relating to one of the two unserved decisions in respect of the claimant. On 28th September 2023, the defendant wrote to the claimant to say that the defendant was "satisfied that the redactions are privileged and that she is not obliged to/neither will she go through the procedure that led her to the redactions".

[118] On 4 October 2023, the claimant filed a fourth Part 18 request. So far as the redactions were concerned, the claimant pointed out that the defendant maintained the earlier refusal to identify the categories of privilege on which the defendant was relying and refused to confirm whether lawyers subject to professional duties to the court were involved in the process of redacting the documents.

[119] The letter continued as follows:

"It is a matter of particular concern that, when pressed for a summary of redacted Options A–D presented to the Defendant for interim implementation in consequence of the judgment in KTT, the Defendant changed her description of redacted Option B. In her Part 18 response dated 20 September, she summarised (redacted) Option B as *'for decisions which may be impacted by an appeal of KTT v SSHD to be "held"'*. However, when pressed for the distinction between this and redacted Option C ('placing a hold on decisions with an outstanding asylum/protection claim') in her Part 18 response dated 26 September, she redefined the summary of Option B ... as *'decision making functions continuing as usual but for any victim of modern slavery with an outstanding asylum claim the [MSL] decision to be "held"'*.

There is a big difference between *'holding'* decision-making and for *'decision making functions to continue as usual'*. It appears that the Defendant has glossed the description of the options and, at the same time, deprived the Claimant of the opportunity to check the accuracy of the description. Again, we reserve the right to draw the Court's attention to this conduct."

[120] On 12 October 2023, the defendant responded to the fourth Part 18 request. The defendant filed and served corrected re-amended detailed grounds of defence and explained that the defendant refused to provide disclosure of the two unserved decisions on the grounds that they were "draft decisions never relied on or served by my client". By a separate letter, the defendant confirmed that reliance was placed on both legal advice privilege and litigation privilege in respect of the redactions and confirmed that they "were reviewed by both the GLD and counsel prior to disclosure and were properly made".

[121] On 16 October 2023, Asylum Aid wrote to explain in detail the relevance of the two unserved decisions to the claims under Article 8 and Article 14 ECHR and gave the defendant a further opportunity to disclose the two unserved decisions. On 24 October 2023, the defendant replied, refusing to disclose the two unserved decisions. The defendant dismissed the claimant's letter of 16 October as "simply conjecture about why you believe the documents are relevant and how your client would have sought to challenge any decision if it were served". It was said that the decisions were not relevant to the claim.

[122] I have earlier referred to the witness statement of Mr Evans, so far as it addresses the decision letters of 29 November 2021 and 14 April 2022. Mr Evans also deals with the duty of candour and the rationale for the redactions. In this regard, he first addresses the e-mail of 28 January 2022. This was the e-mail in which officials in the Single Competent Authority were reminded of the judgment in *KTT* and that the defendant had been successful in seeking permission to appeal against it. The litigation in *KTT* accordingly remained live. There was then a redacted passage, before the sentence "Decision Makers will be informed of the outcome of the KTT appeal". A final sentence in that paragraph was also redacted.

[123] Mr Evans states that during the course of the reconsideration which followed the claimant's application of 24 November 2023 for (amongst other things) a further explanation of, and justification for, redactions in the light of the judgment of Swift J in *IAB and others v Secretary of State for the Home Department and Secretary of State for Levelling up, Housing and Communities* [2023] EWHC 2930 (Admin), Mr Evans undertook a reconsideration of the documents disclosed by the defendant in the present proceedings. In the course of that reconsideration, he determined that the redactions just described were made in error. Accordingly, Mr Evans has exhibited the e-mail in a form which "un-redacts" the passages in question. They read as follows:

"To mitigate further legal challenges, Decision Makers should *not* serve any *option 1* letters unless advised to do so by the Chief Caseworking Unit. If Decision Makers are unsure what to do with the case, they should attend a DL Drop In or seek advice from the Chief Caseworking Unit.

...

Until that appeal is concluded, the above will remain in place." [original emphasis]

[124] The fact that officials were being told not to serve Option 1 letters in order to "mitigate further legal challenges" was, in fact, known to the claimant before receipt of the witness statement of Mr Evans. As I have earlier recorded, the defendant had previously disclosed an e-mail of 31 January 2022, from an official in the Single Competent Authority to other officials there, in which it was said "as per Beccy's e-mail dated 28/01/2022, to mitigate further legal challenges this option 1 decision should *not* be served until further notice." [original emphasis]

[125] At the hearing, Ms McGahey was adamant that she should take responsibility for the error in redacting the passages in the e-mail of 28 January 2022. She also pointed out the passage in the e-mail of 31 January 2022, to which I have just referred. Mr Buttler submitted that Ms McGahey's taking of responsibility did not absolve the defendant from blame; and that it was pure happenstance that the claimant already knew, from the e-mail of 31 January 2022, what the motivation had been for not serving the Option 1 letters. Mr Buttler submitted that the breach of the duty of candour was, as a result, serious.

[126] Mr Evans' statement then deals with Options A, B, C & D in the ministerial submission of 19 January 2022. Mr Evans says that the options set out in paragraph 7 of the submission (which was redacted in its entirety) were "set out in the context of, and by reference to, legal advice. For that reason, the whole of paragraph 7 was redacted". Mr Evans says that, in his response of 26 September 2023 to the claimant, he stated that the options were:

"Option A – decision-making functions continuing as usual not factoring in the findings of KTT v SSHD.

Option B – decision-making functions continuing as usual but for any victim of modern slavery with an outstanding asylum claim the MSDL decision to be 'held'.

Option C – placing a hold on decisions with an outstanding asylum/protection claim.

Option D – grant discretionary leave in accordance with KTT v SSHD."

[127] Mr Evans says that the wording he used in his letter of 26 September 2023 was "not my own interpretation of the options but a close representation of the options as set out in the submission of 19 January 2022". For what he describes as "the utmost clarity," Mr Evans reproduces in his witness statement the "exact words used in the submission" as follows:

"Option A – decision-making functions should continue as normal, as set out in paragraph 4, but not factor in the findings of *KTT v SSHD*.

Option B – decision-making functions should continue as normal as set out in paragraph 4 but, for any victim of modern slavery with an outstanding asylum claim, the MSDL decision should be 'held' 'pending the conclusion of the *KTT* appeal or asylum claim (including appeal, whichever is first)'

Option C – all decisions on Modern Slavery Discretionary Leave, where there is an outstanding asylum/protection claim should be automatically placed on hold pending the *KTT* appeal.

Option D – Grant a period of Discretionary Leave in accordance with the *KTT* judgment – that is, until the conclusion of the individual's asylum claim."

[128] Exhibited to the witness statement of Mr Evans is a copy of the submission of 19 January 2020. In paragraph 7, for the first time, the wording of each of the Options A to D is now unredacted, together with text stating that Option A, Option C and Option D are "not recommended" that that Option B "is recommended".

[129] Mr Evans then turns to the judgment of Swift J in *IAB*. Mr Evans says he understands that the documents in *IAB* were very different from those being considered in the present case. In *IAB*, Swift J observed that the reasons for redactions were not obvious from the context of the redactions within specific documents. In the present case, by contrast, the documents in question were, Mr Evans says, all generated by the defendant as she grappled with the adverse decisions in *KTT*, the implications of those decisions and the options arising from them. It was, accordingly, obvious that documents created in this context would contain significant quantities of information in respect of which legal professional privilege could properly be claimed. There was even express reference in the submission of 19 January 2022 to the fact that counsel's advice had been incorporated in the body of the submission. Nevertheless, Mr Evans confirms that, apart from the exceptions described in his statement, the redactions were properly made under either or both litigation privilege and legal advice privilege.

[130] The witness statement then addresses the issue of the names of civil servants. Mr Evans confirms that no names of civil servants had been redacted. The relevant redactions instead removed e-mail addresses, telephone numbers and other contact details. This was explained by the defendant to the claimant on 1 September 2023. A single redaction to an e-mail of 8 July 2022 concerned General Data Protection Regulation matters.

[131] It is necessary for me to address the candour and redaction matters raised in the statement of Mr Evans. The first concerns the error in redacting passages from the email 28 January 2022. There can be no doubt that this involves a breach of the duty of candour. Its effect on the litigation is, however, ameliorated by the fact that the relevant information (i.e. mitigating the risk of legal challenge) has been disclosed to the claimant, albeit that Mr Buttler attributes this merely to good fortune.

[132] Ms McGahey sought to take sole responsibility for the error. The court's concern to ensure compliance by parties with the duty of candour is not, however, to be equated with a desire to seek out and name any individual, whether they be an official, solicitor or counsel, and lay the blame at their door. The duty is one owed by the parties themselves. In the present case, the most important breach of the duty of candour occurred far earlier. As the above chronology shows, all the information which the claimant has had laboriously to drag out of the defendant should have been disclosed by, at latest, the stage when the defendant first filed detailed grounds of defence. I consider that the honest mistake which occurred in respect of the e-mail of 28 January 2022 (for such it plainly was) is attributable to what, at least on the facts of the present case, appears to be an approach by the defendant to the duty of candour which I regret to say is misconceived. It is an approach which, at almost every stage, involved revealing as little as possible, and only then in response to specific requests from the other party. The defendant's approach in the present case is about as far from the requirement of "laying one's cards face up on the table" as could be imagined. It is an approach which risks committing the sort of error seen with respect to the email of 28 January 2022.

[133] A graphic instance of this apparent mindset can be seen in the defendant's stance to the disclosing of information regarding the exact nature of Options A-D. Instead of taking a proper approach to what constitutes legal professional privilege, whereby only that which is truly privileged can be withheld, vast amounts of the ministerial submission of 19 January 2022 were redacted, including the whole of paragraph 7, seemingly on the basis that the whole of any passage that had a privileged element within it should be redacted in its entirety. If the correct course had been taken at the outset, with the passages containing the actual text of the options being unredacted (as they finally have been only in the course of the hearing), a considerable amount of effort and expense on the part of the claimant would have been avoided.

[134] The present case also discloses a serious misunderstanding on the part of the defendant as to what might qualify for redaction on the ground of irrelevance. In the context of the duty of candour, particular care needs to be taken before material is withheld on this ground. Unless disclosure would be positively harmful (e.g. to a third party) or would involve a wholly disproportionate amount of disclosure, material should not, in general, be withheld on the claimed ground of irrelevance. Otherwise, there is a risk that the duty of candour will be breached or, at the very least, that the other party may be led to assume something untoward lies behind the refusal to disclose.

[135] Again, a notable instance of these dangers can be seen in relation to the draft decisions made in respect of the claimant. Mr Evans is, with respect, wrong to contend that because the draft decisions never reached "final form" they must be "therefore irrelevant." They were, on any view, documents that specifically concerned decision-making in respect of the claimant. It seems that the defendant's thinking on this issue is that because in the defendant's view the claimant would not be able to succeed in persuading the court that the "draft decisions" had a material bearing on his case, the claimant and his legal team were not entitled to see them. That, however, was a matter for submission to the court. It was emphatically not a reason to prevent the claimant from seeing the documents.

[136] I also do not understand how Mr Evans can say that the claimant's wish to see the decisions in question went substantially beyond the claimant's pleaded case. The documents were, on the contrary, relevant to the pleaded contention that the defendant was operating a secret policy of making, but not serving, decisions; and that the effect of this in the claimant's case was to breach his Article 8 ECHR rights. Even if there might be room for argument on this matter (which there is not), it lies ill with the defendant to take such a belated point, given the procedural failures on his part.

[137] I need now to turn to the judgment of Swift J in *IAB*. The judge held that the defendant was not entitled, as a matter of course, to redact the names of junior civil servants from documentation disclosed in judicial review proceedings. I understand that this aspect of the judgment is under appeal. Towards the end of his judgment, however, Swift J had this to say on the issue of procedure (which I am told is not the subject of appeal):

"41. The parties made submissions on the procedure to be adopted by a party who wishes to disclose redacted documents in judicial review proceedings. The principal point in issue is whether there is any obligation on the disclosing party to explain a redaction at the point of disclosure or, whether redacted documents may be disclosed without explanation, so that the onus is on the receiving party to make an application for specific disclosure to see the part redacted, and the disclosing party's obligation to explain the redaction would only arise if and when an application for specific disclosure is made.

42. Both parties submitted that any guidance given ought to favour a process that is as simple and efficient as possible. I entirely agree.

43. A party disclosing a redacted document ought to explain the reason for the redaction at the point of disclosure. The explanation need not be elaborate; the simpler and shorter it can be the better. The explanation ought to be such that it affords the receiving party a sensible opportunity to decide whether to apply for disclosure of the document, unredacted. The approach taken by the Secretaries of State in this case, the provision of single word explanations, 'relevance', 'privilege' and so on, will rarely be sufficient. All will depend on context. I do not consider the approach I suggest will be unduly onerous for the disclosing party. Before deciding to provide a disclosable document in redacted form at all, the disclosing party will have given careful thought to the reason for redaction. It is neither unreasonable nor onerous to expect the disclosing party to reduce that reason, succinctly, to writing. A requirement to explain at the point when the documents are served reflects in part the provision made in CPR 79.24. That Rule

has no application either to these proceedings or to the general run of judicial review claims, but is certainly a model for an efficient and pragmatic approach.

44. When redacted documents are exhibited to a witness statement it may be appropriate for the reason for redaction to be given in that statement. All will depend on the reason for the redaction and the identity of the person making the witness statement. If the redaction is made on LPP grounds it will usually be better for the explanation to be given in a witness statement made by the solicitor with conduct of the case. If the redaction is made for some other reason, it will be for the disclosing party to decide who is best placed to provide the explanation. Whoever provides the explanation should do so in a witness statement. Experience shows that the process of reducing an explanation into a signed statement produces decisions that are better considered. A party receiving a redacted document can decide, taking account of the explanation provided, whether to apply for disclosure of an unredacted version of the document.

45. I consider that the steps sketched above will ensure matters are addressed fairly and proportionately."

[138] I have set out above what Mr Evans says about the redactions in the present case based on legal professional privilege. I accept what he says on this issue, albeit that I do not accept the existence of privileged passages entitled the defendant to redact to the extent he did.

[139] Ms McGahey took issue with the sentence in paragraph 44 of *IAB*, where Swift J said that experience shows that the process of reducing an explanation into a signed statement produces decisions that are better considered. Ms McGahey said that neither she nor her junior, Mr Irwin, had ever come across a case where a witness statement had been said to be necessary in order to explain redactions on the ground of legal advice privilege. Mr Buttler concurred.

[140] I do not consider that Swift J was, in fact, suggesting that there has hitherto been a practice of using a witness statement to explain redactions on the ground of legal advice privilege or litigation privilege. His point is that a witness statement is likely to focus minds on the extent, if any, to which privilege exists and so prevent or at least minimise instances of "knee-jerk" or otherwise ill-considered invocations of privilege. As the present proceedings graphically demonstrate, whatever may or may not have happened hitherto, explaining the reasons for redactions by means of a witness statement is likely to avoid many of the problems that have arisen in this case. What Mr Evans says at paragraphs 12 to 18 of his statement about legal professional privilege could and (with hindsight) should have been articulated earlier, in the form of a witness statement. The fact that a matter of privilege might be "obvious" to a party does not mean it will necessarily be obvious to the other party and the court. The same is true of redactions made on the ground of relevance. In the present case, a timely witness statement explaining the defendant's thinking about the "draft decisions" would plainly have been beneficial.

[141] The point made by Swift J in the penultimate sentence of paragraph 44 of *IAB*, that reducing an explanation into a signed statement produces decisions that are better considered, must, therefore, with respect, be right, regardless of whether this has routinely happened hitherto in the contexts with which we are concerned. Producing a witness statement, with its statement of truth, is an important action. The person making it will be concerned to get it right. That is, of course, particularly

so where the maker of the statement is someone with legal professional duties. Had the redactions originally made by the defendant in the present case been subjected to the discipline of a witness statement, it is likely that, amongst other things, the error in the redaction of the e-mail of 28 January 2022 would not have been made.

Decision

[142] The judicial review succeeds, to the extent set out above. I invite the parties to agree, if possible, an order that gives effect to my judgment and any consequential matters.

MD AND OTHERS ('JOINING' – APPENDIX EU FAMILY PERMIT) GHANA

UPPER TRIBUNAL (IMMIGRATION AND ASYLUM CHAMBER)

Mandalia UTJ

[2024] UKUT 64 (IAC)
26 January 2024

European Union law – family members – paragraph FP6.(1)(c) & FP6.(1)(d) of Appendix EU (Family Permit) to the Immigration Rules – 'joining them in the UK' – cancellation of leave to enter – change of circumstances – proportionality

The Claimants, citizens of Ghana, were three siblings. They were the children of Mr D and Ms P. In April 2014, Mr D came to the United Kingdom. The Claimants remained in Ghana with their mother. In March 2017, Mr D married Ms O, a citizen of the Netherlands. He was issued with an EEA residence card as the family member of an EEA national exercising treaty rights in the United Kingdom. In August 2020, Ms O was granted settled status under the EU Settlement Scheme ('EUSS'). In December 2020, the Claimants applied for entry clearance to the United Kingdom under Appendix EU (Family Permit) to the Immigration Rules HC 395 (as amended) as family members of a relevant EEA citizen. They were issued with an EUSS family permit. They arrived in the United Kingdom in December 2021. On their arrival, the Secretary of State for the Home Department cancelled their leave to enter as she was satisfied that there had been a change in the Claimants' circumstances which was relevant to their eligibility for entry clearance. Ms O had informed the Secretary of State that she had not sponsored the Claimants' applications for an EUSS family permit and that Mr D had named her as the sponsor without her knowledge or consent. Furthermore, Ms O confirmed that she was unwilling to sponsor the applications.

The First-tier Tribunal ('FtT') allowed the Claimants' appeal against the Secretary of State's decision. The FtT held that paragraph FP6.(1)(c) and FP6.(1)(d) of Appendix EU (Family Permit) only required the EEA citizen to be resident in the United Kingdom before the Claimants' arrival, and did not require her consent. It found that Ms O was resident in the United Kingdom when the children arrived in December 2021 and, on balance, the Claimants satisfied the requirement that they travelled to the United Kingdom to join the relevant EEA citizen and their father in the United Kingdom.

The Upper Tribunal granted the Secretary of State permission to appeal on the ground that the use of the word 'joining' in paragraph FP6.(1)(d) of Appendix EU (Family Permit) should properly be construed to require the applicant to reside together with the sponsor in the United Kingdom and that the paragraph was not satisfied simply by the applicant and sponsor both being in the United Kingdom at the same time but otherwise not associating.

Held, substituting a fresh decision dismissing the appeal:

(1) The eligibility requirements in paragraph FP6. had to be satisfied at the date of application, not at the date of any decision or the date of arrival in the United Kingdom. Where entry clearance in the form of an EUSS family permit had been granted, the question whether the Secretary of State or an Immigration Officer was satisfied that it was proportionate to cancel any leave granted fell to be considered by reference to the position at the date of that subsequent decision. To meet the eligibility requirements for entry clearance under Appendix EU (Family Permit), paragraph FP6.(1)(c) required that the relevant EEA citizen was either resident in the United Kingdom, or would be travelling to the United Kingdom with the applicant within six months of the date of application. Paragraph FP6.(1)(d) imposed an additional requirement, namely that, the applicant would be accompanying the relevant EEA citizen to the United Kingdom ('or joining them in the UK') within six months of the date of application. The reference to 'them' in 'joining them in the UK' could only sensibly be read as a reference to the applicant joining the relevant EEA citizen. If, as the Claimants submitted, all that was required was that the EEA citizen in question be resident in the United Kingdom, at the date of application, paragraph FP6.(1)(d) would be *otiose*. Paragraph FP6.(1)(c) on its own dealt with that requirement. On the Claimants' construction, FP6.(1)(d) would add nothing (*paras 19 – 23*).

(2) The focus of paragraph FP6.(1)(d) was upon keeping the applicant and EEA citizen together, or uniting or reuniting them. If the EEA citizen was resident in the United Kingdom at the date of application for the purposes of FP6.(1)(c), the applicant would not be accompanying the EEA citizen to the United Kingdom, because the EEA citizen was already resident in the United Kingdom. The applicant therefore had to establish that he or she was 'joining' the EEA citizen in the United Kingdom. That had to mean that the applicant was being united or reunited with the EEA citizen. The purpose of Appendix EU (Family Permit) was to provide a basis, consistent with the EU-UK Withdrawal Agreement and Directive 2004/38/EC, for EEA citizens resident in the United Kingdom by the end of the transition period, and their family members, to apply for the required leave to remain or enter. The primary objective of Directive 2004/38/EC was to promote the right of free movement of EEA nationals. Family reunification was a corollary to the exercise of that right. An EEA national would not be free to exercise that right without consideration of his or her family circumstances. The focus of paragraph FP6.(1)(d) was upon keeping the applicant and the EEA citizen together, uniting or reuniting them, and that was consistent with the Directive (*paras 27 – 31*).

(3) The FtT had erred in concluding that paragraph FP6.(1)(c) and (d) only required the EEA citizen to be resident in the United Kingdom before the Claimants' arrival, and not her consent. To remain eligible for entry clearance, it had been for the Claimants to establish that they were 'joining' the relevant EEA citizen in the United Kingdom. The definition of a 'relevant EEA citizen' did not extend to the spouse of an EEA citizen. It was therefore not sufficient that the Claimants had come to the United Kingdom to join their father. The FtT did not engage with Ms O's assertion that she had not sponsored the Claimants' applications for an EUSS family permit, that their father had named her as the sponsor without her knowledge or consent, and that she was unwilling to sponsor the applications. The FtT's assessment of the evidence was infected by its misinterpretation of the requirements

of paragraph FP6.(1)(d), and its understanding that the 'consent' of Ms O was not required. Accordingly, the decision had to be set aside *(paras 36 – 41)*.

(4) The evidence demonstrated that Ms O did not support the applications for entry clearance by the time the Claimants arrived in the United Kingdom and the Claimants had not been joining her in the United Kingdom. Therefore, they could not satisfy the eligibility requirement in paragraph FP6.(1)(d). There had therefore been a change in circumstances that was relevant to their eligibility for entry clearance. Although the Claimants might wish to live in the United Kingdom with their father and benefit from an education here, that did not equate to a right to do so. It would not be disproportionate to cancel their leave *(paras 42 – 49)*.

Legislation and international instruments judicially considered:

Directive 2004/38/EC ('the Citizens Directive'), Recital 1
Immigration Rules HC 395 (as amended), Annex 1(d)&(e) and paragraphs A.3.4(c) & FP6.(1)(c)&(d) of Appendix EU (Family Permit)

Representation

Mr P Lawson, Senior Home Office Presenting Officer, for the Secretary of State;
Mr M Marziano, Westkin Associates, for the Claimants.

Decision and Reasons

UPPER TRIBUNAL JUDGE MANDALIA:

[1] The appellant in the appeal before me is the Secretary of State for the Home Department ("SSHD") and the respondents to this appeal are; (1) MD, (2) MSD, and (3) JD. However, for ease of reference, in the course of this decision I now adopt the parties' status as it was before the FtT. Hereafter, I refer to the three respondents as the appellants, and the Secretary of State as the respondent.

Background

[2] The three appellants are siblings. They are the children of Mr Dah ("Mr Duah") and Ms Felicia Pokuaa. Following the appellants' birth, in April 2014, their father came to the UK, and he has remained here since. The appellants' continued to live in Ghana with their mother. Mr Duah was married to Lydia Afua Opoku ("Ms Opoku"), a national of the Netherlands, by way of a customary marriage on 11 March 2017. In July 2019 Mr Duah was issued with an EEA Residence Card as the family member of an EEA national exercising treaty rights in the UK. On 22 August 2020 Ms Opoku was granted settled status under the EU Settlement Scheme.

[3] On 8 December 2020, the appellants applied for entry clearance to the UK under Appendix EU (Family Permit) as family members of a relevant EEA Citizen. On 5 November 2021 they had each been issued with an EU Settlement Scheme family permit, which is a form of entry clearance granted under Appendix EU (Family Permit) of the Immigration Rules. They arrived in the United Kingdom on 2 December 2021.

[4] Following enquiries made upon the appellants arrival in the UK, the respondent issued and served a 'Notice of Cancellation of Leave to Enter'. The Immigration Officer was satisfied that there had been a change in the appellants' circumstances that was, or would have been, relevant to their eligibility for entry clearance. The Notice served on each of the appellants is for all intents and purposes in similar terms. The respondent said:

> "You were eligible for that entry clearance on the basis that Lydia Afua Opoku is resident in the UK or would be travelling to the UK within six months of the date of your application, and you would be accompanying them to the UK or joining them in the UK. As Lydia Opoku is not present in the UK nor accompanying you today, I am satisfied that there has been a change of circumstances which would have been directly relevant to your eligibility for entry clearance under FP6.(1)(d) of Appendix EU (Family Permit).
>
> When you arrived in the United Kingdom on 2nd December 2021 accompanied by your two siblings ... you claimed to be joining your father Fred Kwaku Duah ... (who holds limited leave to remain until 20 August 2024) and your stepmother Lydia Afua Opoku who holds EU Settled Status. Numerous attempts were made on the date of your arrival to contact your stepmother (your sponsor) without success. An appointment was scheduled for 17 December 2021 for your father and stepmother to attend for further interview together. On 17 December 2021 your stepmother Lydia Afua Opoku attended at Terminal 5 with an unknown male. During the interview she stated that she had not sponsored yours or your siblings' applications for a EUSS Family Permit and that your father had done so without her knowledge or consent. Furthermore, she confirmed that she was unwilling to sponsor your applications."

The Decision of the First-tier Tribunal

[5] The appellants' appeals were allowed by First-tier Tribunal Judge Phull for reasons set out in a decision promulgated on 5 September 2020. The appellants and their father attended the hearing. In summary, Judge Phull found that Ms Opoku was resident in the UK when the children arrived in the UK on 2 December 2021 and on balance, the appellants satisfy the requirement that they travelled to the UK to join the relevant EEA citizen and their father in the UK.

The Appeal to the Upper Tribunal

[6] The respondent claims Judge Phull erred in finding, at [24], that the respondent's guidance dated 6 April 2022 concerning FP6.(1)(c) and FP6.(1)(d) of Appendix EU (Family Permit), only requires the EEA citizen to be resident in the UK before the appellants arrival, and does not require her consent. The respondent claims the guidance clearly identifies that *"the applicant will be accompanying the relevant EEA citizen (or, as the case may be, the qualifying British citizen) to the UK (or joining them in the UK) within 6 months of the date of application"*. [my emphasis]

[7] The respondent claims the decision of Judge Phull is vitiated by a material error of law. In particular, the evidence of the appellant's father was that he is no

longer in a relationship with Ms Opoku and they no longer live together. The respondent claims there had clearly been a change in circumstances, and Judge Phull erred in concluding the appellants will be "joining" their step mother when she did not know of or support the applications, does not wish to sponsor the appellants, and she has neither resided with them in the past nor will she do so in the future.

[8] Permission to appeal was granted by Upper Tribunal Judge Lane on 12 January 2023. He said:

"It is arguable that the use of the word *'joining'* in paragraph FP(6)(1)(d) of Appendix EU (Family Permit) should properly be construed to require the applicant to reside together with the sponsor in the United Kingdom and that the paragraph is not satisfied simply by the applicant and sponsor both being in the United Kingdom at the same time but otherwise not associating."

[9] The appellants have filed a Rule 24 response. It is accepted by the appellants that they had not lived with, or had any significant relationship with the EU Citizen sponsor, Ms Opoku. Rather, they are the biological children of the spouse of the EU Citizen sponsor. The appellants submit Judge Phull was right to say at paragraph [24] of her decision that that Home Office guidance, dated 6 April 2022, is to be read as meaning that the EEA Citizen's presence in the UK on the date of arrival is required, but nothing more. There is, the appellants claim, nothing in that guidance which interprets FP6.(1)(c) or (d) as requiring cohabitation or further association.

[10] Before me, Mr Lawson submits that here, the appellants must establish that, at the date of application, the relevant EEA citizen (Ms Opoku) is in the UK (FP6.(1)(c)) and the appellants would be joining her in the UK (FP6.(1)(d)). He accepts the word "joining" is not defined in Appendix EU (Family Permit) and submits the ordinary "Oxford Dictionary" definition of that word as a verb is "to put (things) together, so that they become physically united or continuous". It involves, Mr Lawson submits, "two things either connecting or being united". Here, Mr Lawson submits Ms Opoku had said when she was interviewed on 17 December 2021 that her husband (Mr Duah) had made the applications for entry clearance without speaking to her, and, that she had not seen the appellants. She claimed she had not "sponsored" the appellants and did not want to do so.

[11] In reply, Mr Marziano adopted the appellants' skeleton argument that was prepared for the hearing before the FtT. He submits the word "joining" referred to in FP6.(1)(d) of Appendix EU (Family Permit) is not defined, and the "continued consent of Ms Opoku" is not required. He submits the respondent's guidance; EU Settlement Scheme Family Permit and Travel Permit, published on 6 April 2022 states:

"Under rule FP6.(1)(c) and (d) or, as the case may be, rule FP6.(2)(c) and (d) of Appendix EU (Family Permit), in an application for an EUSS family permit (and where rule FP8A does not apply), you must be satisfied, including in light of any relevant information or evidence provided by the applicant, at the date of application both that:

- the relevant EEA citizen (or, as the case may be, the qualifying British citizen) is resident in the UK or will be travelling to the UK with the applicant within 6 months of the date of application

- the applicant will be accompanying the relevant EEA citizen (or, as the case may be, the qualifying British citizen) to the UK (or joining them in the UK) within 6 months of the date of application

This means that the relevant EEA citizen (or, as the case may be, the qualifying British citizen) must either:

- *be travelling with the applicant, at the same time, from the same country*
- *be resident in the UK before the applicant arrives"* [emphasis added]

[12] Mr Marziano submits that all that is required therefore, is that the relevant EEA citizen is in the UK at the date of the application, unless they are overseas, in which case there must be evidence that they will be accompanying the applicant to the UK within six months of the date of the application. Here, the respondent does not deny that Ms Opoku was in the UK at the date of the application or the date of the decision to grant the appellants an EU Settlement Scheme family permit.

[13] Mr Marziano submits that whilst it is unfortunate that Ms Opoku made negative comments about the appellants and Mr Duah in her interview, and appeared to withdraw her consent to the appellants living in the UK with Mr Duah, that is not to say that she was not in the UK or not resident in the UK at the material time. She had attended an interview in the UK, which of itself, is proof of her presence in the UK.

[14] Mr Marziano submits the definition of "joining" in this context is much wider than that contended for by the respondent. "Joining" includes the place, or junction, at which two parts are joined. Here, the "junction" or conduit is the United Kingdom. The appellants were "joining" in the sense that they were coming to the UK. Appendix EU (Family Permit) does not require there to be a subsisting relationship between the appellants and the relevant EEA citizen. Ms Opoku remains married to the appellant's father and the appellants continue to be a "family member of a relevant EEA citizen" as defined in Appendix 1. Where the applicant is the child of the spouse or civil partner of a relevant EEA citizen that relationship is required to have existed before the specified date (save as set out), and all the family relationships must continue to exist at the date of application. Here, Ms Opoku remained married to the appellant's father and the relationship between the appellants and their father plainly continued to exist.

[15] In the circumstances, Mr Marziano submits it was open to the judge to allow the appeal for the reasons she gave.

The Relevant Legal Framework

[16] Appendix EU (Family Permit) sets out the basis on which a person will, if they apply under it, be granted an entry clearance:

"FP6.(1) The applicant meets the eligibility requirements for an entry clearance to be granted under this Appendix in the form of an EU Settlement Scheme Family Permit, where the entry clearance officer is satisfied that at the date of application:

(a) The applicant is not a British citizen;

(b) The applicant is a family member of a relevant EEA citizen;

(c) The relevant EEA citizen is resident in the UK or will be travelling to the UK with the applicant within six months of the date of application;

(d) The applicant will be accompanying the relevant EEA citizen to the UK (or joining them in the UK) within six months of the date of application; and

(e) The applicant ('A') is not the spouse, civil partner or durable partner of a relevant EEA citizen ('B') where a spouse, civil partner or durable partner of A or B has been granted an entry clearance under this Appendix, immediately before or since the specified date held a valid document in that capacity issued under the EEA Regulations or has been granted leave to enter or remain in the UK in that capacity under or outside the Immigration Rules."

[17] Insofar as is relevant, the words "family member of a relevant EEA citizen" are defined in Annex 1 as follows:

"a person who has satisfied the entry clearance officer, including by the required evidence of family relationship, that they are:

…

(d) the child or dependent parent of a relevant EEA citizen, and the family relationship:

(i) existed before the specified date (unless, in the case of a child, the person was born after that date, was adopted after that date in accordance with a relevant adoption decision or after that date became a child within the meaning of that entry in this table on the basis of one of sub-paragraphs (a)(iii) to (a)(xi) of that entry); and

(ii) continues to exist at the date of application; or

(e) the child or dependent parent of the spouse or civil partner of a relevant EEA citizen, as described in subparagraph (a) above, and:

(i) the family relationship of the child or dependent parent to the spouse or civil partner existed before the specified date (unless, in the case of a child, the person was born after that date, was adopted after that date in accordance with a relevant adoption decision or after that date became a child within the meaning of that entry in this table on the basis of one of sub-paragraphs (a)(iii) to (a)(xi) of that entry); and

(ii) all the family relationships continue to exist at the date of application; or

..."

[18] Finally, insofar as cancellation, curtailment and revocation of leave to enter is concerned, the relevant provision of Appendix EU (Family Permit) here is paragraph A.3.4 (c):

"A3.4. A person's leave to enter granted by virtue of having arrived in the UK with an entry clearance that was granted under this Appendix may be cancelled where the Secretary of State or an Immigration Officer is satisfied that it is proportionate to cancel that leave where:

...

(c) Since the entry clearance under this Appendix was granted, there has been a change in circumstances that is, or would have been, relevant to that person's eligibility for that entry clearance, such that their leave to enter ought to be cancelled"

Decision

The proper construction of paragraph FP6.(1)(d) of Appendix EU (Family Permit)

[19] In his skeleton argument and the rule 24 response Mr Marziano makes repeated reference to the "date of decision" or the appellants "date of arrival in the UK". To begin with, it is worth highlighting that the eligibility requirements set out in paragraph FP6. of Appendix EU (Family Permit) must be satisfied at the date of application.

[20] Where entry clearance in the form of an EUSS Family permit has been granted, the question whether the Secretary of State or an Immigration Officer is satisfied that it is proportionate to cancel any leave granted, falls to be considered by reference to the position at the date of that subsequent decision.

[21] In order to meet the eligibility requirements for entry clearance under Appendix EU (Family Permit), paragraph FP6.(1)(c) requires that the relevant EEA citizen is either resident in the UK, or will be travelling to the UK with the applicant within six months of the date of application. The focus of FP6.(1)(c) is upon the relevant EEA citizen. They must either already be in the UK (*i.e. resident in the UK*) or they will be travelling to the UK with the applicant.

[22] Paragraph FP6.1(d) imposes an additional requirement and is directed to the applicant. That is, the applicant will be accompanying the relevant EEA citizen to the UK (or joining them in the UK) within six months of the date of application. The reference to "them" in "joining them in the UK" can only sensibly be read as a reference to the applicant joining the relevant EEA citizen.

[23] I do not accept that the definition of "joining" in this context is much wider than that contended for by the respondent. The difficulty with the construction of the word "*joining*" contended for by Mr Marziano, is that paragraph FP6.1(d) is not concerned with "the junction at which two parts are joined", so that all that is required is that at the date of application the EEA citizen is resident in the UK and

the applicant will be coming to the UK. That is to entirely misread and misconstrue the provisions. It involves either importing words into the provision that are not there, or to disregard the wording of the provision. If, as Mr Marziano submits, all that is required is that the EEA citizen in question be resident in the UK, unless they are overseas at the date of application, paragraph FP6.(1)(d) would be *otiose*. Paragraph FP6.(1)(c) on its own deals with the requirement that the relevant EEA citizen is in the UK, or will be travelling to the UK with the applicant within six months of the date of the application. On Mr Marziano's construction, FP6.1(d) would add nothing.

[24] The published guidance that Mr Marziano relies upon is simply guidance. It cannot be construed in the same way as primary or secondary legislation. The guidance refers to FP6.(1)(c) and (d) and states:

"This means that the relevant EEA citizen (or the qualifying British citizen) must either:

- be travelling with the applicant, at the same time, from the same country
- be resident in the UK before the applicant arrives"

[25] As far as it goes, that is undoubtedly correct but that guidance is not in any way exhaustive. It assumes that the applicant is either travelling to the UK with the relevant EEA citizen or joining a relevant EEA citizen who is resident in the UK before the applicant arrives. There is no concession within that guidance that, as Mr Marziano submits, all that is required is that at the date of application, the relevant EEA citizen is resident in the UK, unless they are overseas, in which case there must be evidence of them travelling to the UK with the applicant.

[26] If there were any doubt about that, one only has to turn to what is said in the guidance immediately preceding the passage that is emphasised by Mr Marziano, that I have cited at paragraph [11] above. The published guidance is absolutely clear that paragraphs FP6.(1)(c) and (d) must both be satisfied at the date of application.

[27] In my judgement, the focus of paragraph FP6.(1)(d) is upon keeping the applicant and EEA citizen together (*the applicant will be accompanying the relevant EEA citizen*), or uniting or reuniting with them (*joining them in the UK*). If the relevant EEA citizen is resident in the UK at the date of application for the purposes of paragraph FP6.1(c), the applicant will not be accompanying the relevant EEA citizen to the UK because the EEA citizen is already resident in the UK. The applicant must therefore establish that they are "joining" the relevant EEA citizen in the UK.

[28] I accept, as Mr Lawson submits that the word "joining" in this context must, applying the ordinary meaning of the word in the English language, mean that the applicant is being united or reunited with the relevant EEA citizen.

[29] Mr Lawson and Mr Marziano both agree that the purpose of Appendix EU (Family Permit) is to provide, *inter alia*, a basis, consistent with the Withdrawal Agreement with the European Union reached on 17 October 2019, and with the citizens' rights agreements reached with the other EEA countries and Switzerland, for EEA and Swiss citizens resident in the UK by the end of the transition period at 2300 GMT on 31 December 2020, and their family members, to apply for the required leave to remain or enter.

[30] Directive 2004/38/EC of the European Parliament and of the Council of 29 April 2004 on the right of citizens of the Union and their family members to move and reside freely within the territory of the Member States was concerned with the right of the family members, and other dependents of the Union citizen, also to exercise those rights. In summary, the primary objective of the Directive was to promote the right of free movement of EEA nationals. Having to live apart from family members or members of the family in the wider sense may be a powerful deterrent to the exercise of that freedom. An EEA national would not be "free" to exercise the right of free movement under the underlying Directive absent consideration of their family circumstances and domestic responsibilities.

[31] The primary objective of the underlying Directive is to promote the right of free movement of EEA nationals subject to limitations and conditions of public policy, public health, and public security. (See Recital 1). Family reunification is a corollary to the exercise of that right. It is axiomatic that an EEA national would not be "free" to exercise the right of free movement absent consideration of their family circumstances. In my judgement, the focus of paragraph FP6.(1)(d) of Appendix EU (Family Permit) is upon keeping the applicant and EEA citizen together, uniting or reuniting them, and that is entirely consistent with the Directive.

The Decision of the FtT

[32] In summary, the FtT judge recorded the undisputed facts at paragraphs [10] to [13] of her decision. She noted the appellants are the children of Mr Duah and that he is married to Ms Opoku, an EEA national resident in the UK with leave under Appendix EU. She noted that Mr Duah had been granted settled status on 7 July 2022 and that both he and Ms Opoku were employed in the UK when the appellants arrived on 2 December 2021.

[33] The judge went on to refer to the applications made by the appellants and the reasons provided by the respondent for cancelling the entry clearance to the appellants following their arrival in the UK. She noted the claim made by the respondent that as at 29 December 2021 (*the date of the decision to cancel the entry clearance granted*) there has been a change of circumstances that is, or would have been, relevant to the appellants' eligibility for entry clearance.

[34] The judge found that Mr Duah and Ms Opoku remain married, and that the appellants are 'family members of a relevant EEA citizen' as defined in Appendix EU (Family Permit). That is, they are the children of the spouse or a relevant EEA citizen, and that all the family relationships continued to exist at the date of application.

[35] At paragraphs [23] and [24] the judge said:

"23. I find on balance the above evidence satisfies that Lydia was resident in the UK when the children arrived on the 02 December 2021. I therefore find on balance the Appellants satisfy the requirement that they travelled to the UK to join the relevant EEA citizen and their father in the UK.

24. As regards the change in circumstances, I find on balance, Mr Duah's evidence satisfies that Lydia gave her documents to be submitted with the Appellants applications to join them in the UK. I find the Home Office Guidance dated 06/04/2022 on FP6.(1)(c) and FP6.(1)(d) of Appendix EU (Family Permit), only requires the EEA citizen to be resident in the UK before the Appellants

arrival and not her consent (page 53. I find on balance the unchallenged evidence satisfies, that Lydia has been resident in the UK, since the 01 January 2015. She was at work in the UK when the Appellants arrived on the 02 December 2021 to join her and their father."

Error of Law

[36] The appeal before the FtT was against the respondent's decision dated 29 December 2021 to cancel/revoke the appellants' EUSS Family Permits, and refuse leave to enter the UK under Appendix EU (Family Permit). The issue at the heart of the appeal was whether it is proportionate to cancel that leave because since the entry clearance was granted, there has been a change in circumstances that is, or would have been, relevant to the appellants' eligibility for that entry clearance such that their leave to enter ought to be cancelled.

[37] The issue is dealt with in paragraph [24] of the judge's decision. The reasons given are brief. I accept the reasons do not need to be lengthy, but reading the decision as a whole I am satisfied that the judge erred when she concluded at [24], relying upon the published guidance she had been referred to, that paragraphs FP6.(1)(c) and (d) *"only requires the EEA citizen to be resident in the UK before the Appellants arrival and not her consent"*. That, for the reasons I have set out in my analysis of the proper construction of paragraph FP6.(1)(d), is wrong in law.

[38] To remain eligible for entry clearance, it was for the appellants to establish that they are *"joining"* the relevant EEA citizen in the UK. That is, they were being united or reunited with the relevant EEA citizen. I add that paragraph FP6.1(d) is not concerned with the applicant travelling to the UK to join the relevant EEA citizen *or their spouse* [my emphasis]. The words used in the provision expressly require that the applicant is accompanying *the relevant EEA citizen* or joining them [my emphasis]. A "relevant EEA citizen", is defined in Annex 1 and the focus is upon the EEA citizen. Neither party suggests the definition of a "relevant EEA citizen" extends to include the spouse or civil partner of an EEA citizen. It was not therefore sufficient that the appellants had come to the UK to join their father.

[39] Although the judge referred to the interview of Ms Opoku conducted by an Immigration Officer on 17 December 2021, the judge did not engage with the record of the claim made by her during that interview that she had not sponsored the appellants' applications for a EUSS Family Permit, that their father had done so without her knowledge or consent, and her claim that she was unwilling to sponsor the applications. The appeal was heard in July 2022 and in her decision the judge accepted the evidence of Mr Duah that Ms Opoku had provided the documents that were required to be submitted with the appellants' applications to join them in the UK.

[40] The judge failed to engage with the information provided by Ms Opoku when she was interviewed and it was obvious from the evidence of Mr Duah himself that he and his partner had been separated for several months by the time the appeal was heard. The judge made no findings as to whether the appellants had in fact ever met Ms Opoku. Although the judge said she found the appellants had arrived on 2 December 2021 "to join [Ms Opoku] and their father", by the 29th December 2021 and certainly by the time the appeal was heard, the relationship between Ms Okolu and Mr Duah had broken down and Ms Opoku did not support the appellants' application and they were not joining her in the UK. In my judgement, the judge's assessment of the evidence was infected by the judge's misinterpretation of the

requirements of paragraph FP6.(1)(d), and her understanding that the "consent" of Ms Opoku, as the judge put it, was not required.

[41] Standing back and reading the decision of the FtT as a whole, I am satisfied that the decision of the judge is infected by material errors of law and must be set aside.

Remaking the decision

[42] Having found that the decision of the FtT involved the making of an error on a point of law, together with the FtT's findings of fact, I have before me the evidence which was before the FtT on which I can re-make the decision in relation to the appellants' appeals pursuant to section 12(2)(b)(ii) of the Tribunals, Courts and Enforcement Act 2007. By virtue of section 12(4) of that Act, I may make any decision which the FtT could make if it were re-making the decision and may make such findings of fact as I consider appropriate.

[43] I have already referred to the findings that were made by the Judge. The judge found Mr Duah to be a credible witness.

[44] There is no evidence that the appellants have ever lived with Ms Opoku either before, or after their arrival in the UK. As the judge found previously, Ms Opoku was resident in the UK at the date of the applications for entry clearance. The judge accepted Ms Opoku had provided Mr Duah with the documents necessary to support the appellants applications to join them in the UK. I am prepared to accept that at the date of the applications the appellants were to be joining Ms Opoku (*the relevant EEA citizen*) in the UK within six months of the date of the application. That much is uncontroversial because the appellants were granted entry clearance and the relevant EUSS Family Permits were issued to them by the respondent.

[45] The question is whether it is proportionate to cancel that leave because since the entry clearance was granted, there has been a change in circumstances that is, or would have been, relevant to the appellants' eligibility for that entry clearance, such that their leave to enter ought to be cancelled.

[46] The record of the discussions between an Immigration Officer and the appellants upon their arrival in the UK [RB/C2/page 36] records that the appellants claimed they had been in regular contact with their father but "*did not really know or had met their step mother Lydia*". When Ms Opoku was interviewed on 17 December 2021 [RB/D2/pages 38–41], she said that she had not seen the appellants, she only knew the name of one of the appellants and she did not wish to sponsor the appellants.

[47] The evidence of Mr Duah as set out in his witness statement dated 30 June 2022 was that after the appellants' applications had been submitted Ms Opoku's behaviour towards him changed, and when she was told the applications were granted "*... her behaviour was awful and I could sense danger for my children because when Lydia is angry, she could do bad and worsen things ...*". His evidence was that when he bought the tickets and confirmed the date the appellants would be coming to the UK, her answer was awkward, unwelcome and she told him that she could not go with him to welcome them at the airport. He explains the difficulties that were encountered establishing contact with Ms Opoku when the appellants arrived in the UK and the events leading to their respective interviews. He states that on 21 December 2021, Ms Opoku met the appellants for the last time. There is no reference in the statement to her having ever met the children previously. He claims that on 22 December 2021, Ms Opoku left London for Amsterdam to

celebrate Christmas with her own children. It was hoped she would return after Christmas but it appears she did not do so. Mr Duah confirms that he is no longer in a relationship with Opoku, albeit they remain married. He states he cannot trust her to give a truthful account of her actions.

[48] The account set out in the statement of Mr Duah regarding the reservations Ms Opoku demonstrated about the appellants coming to the UK, is consistent with the claim made by Ms Opoku when she was interviewed, that she does not support the applications. Even if she supported the applications for entry clearance when they were first made, it is clear she did not support the applications by the time of the appellants arrival in the UK. I find that by the date of the appellants arrival in the UK, 2 December 2021, the appellants application was no longer supported by Ms Opoku and on the evidence before me, I find that the appellants were not joining her in the UK. By 29 December 2021, on the evidence before me, I find that the appellants could not and cannot satisfy the eligibility requirement in paragraph FP6.(1)(d) that they were joining Ms Opoku in the UK.

[49] I find that since the entry clearance was granted to the appellants, there has clearly been a change in the appellants' circumstances that is, or would have been relevant to the appellants' eligibility for that entry clearance such that by 29 December 2021, it was open to the Immigration Officer to conclude that it is proportionate to cancel that leave. As to proportionality, the appellants had for a number of years lived in Ghana and were cared for by their mother. There is no evidence that they were not adequately cared for. When the appellants spoke to the Immigration Officer on 2 December 2021, the appellants confirmed they lived with their biological mother in Ghana and that the whole family had dropped them off at the airport. Their mother was pleased to see them go, because she thought they would have a better life in the UK. They said they have no other family here in the UK. In his witness statement, Mr Duah states they hope to remain in the UK to have a family life which they have been missing for many years and to have a good quality education. I have no doubt that the appellants would wish to live in the UK with their father, but that does not equate to a right to do so. The benefit they gain of living with their father is to the detriment of the stability they enjoyed in Ghana, and the relationships and attachments they have to their mother and wider family in Ghana. The appellants may wish to benefit from an education in the UK, but again, that does not equate to a right to be educated in the UK, in circumstances where they are unable to meet the rules, and in particular the eligibility requirements as set out in Appendix EU (Family Permit).

[50] It follows that I remake the decision and dismiss the appeal.

Notice of Decision

[51] The decision of First-tier Tribunal Judge Phull is set aside.
[52] I remake the decision and dismiss the appeal.

YALCIN v SECRETARY OF STATE FOR THE HOME DEPARTMENT

COURT OF APPEAL

Underhill (Vice-President of the Court of Appeal (Civil Division)), King and Warby LJJ

[2024] EWCA Civ 74
6 February 2024

Human rights – Article 8 of the ECHR – family and private life – proportionality – best interests of the child – loss of financial support – procedure and process – deportation – foreign criminal – exceptions in section 117C(4) & (5) of the Nationality, Immigration and Asylum Act 2002 – proportionality assessment – section 117C(6) – NA (Pakistan) [2016] EWCA Civ 662 applied

The Claimant was a Turkish national of Kurdish ethnicity. He first arrived in the United Kingdom in 2003, but was eventually removed in 2010 after a failed asylum claim. Later in 2010 he married a British national in Turkey before returning to the United Kingdom on a spouse visa in 2011. He was granted indefinite leave to remain in 2013. The Claimant had two sons, K and D, born in 2013 and 2014 respectively; both were British citizens. The Claimant separated from his wife in 2015. In March 2016 he pleaded guilty to possession of a prohibited weapon and possessing that firearm without a certificate. He was sentenced to a total of five years and four months in prison. In December 2016 the Secretary of State for the Home Department notified the Claimant of her intention to deport him pursuant to section 32 of the UK Borders Act 2007 because of his conviction and sentence. The Claimant's human rights claim resisting deportation was refused in a decision dated August 2017.

In October 2021 the First-tier Tribunal ('FtT') allowed the Claimant's appeal against the refusal of his human rights claim. In finding the Claimant's deportation to be disproportionate in all the circumstances, the FtT noted in particular the best interests of his children and his close relationship with D who had significant learning and behavioural issues. The Secretary of State appealed that decision.

The Upper Tribunal ('UT') held that the FtT's decision should be set aside for error of law because the Judge had failed to approach his reasoning expressly pursuant to the statutory framework established by section 117C of the Nationality, Immigration and Asylum Act 2002 ('the 2002 Act'). That had led to the Judge taking into account immaterial considerations and impermissibly downgrading the public interest in the Claimant's deportation. The UT Judge directed that the decision be re-made at a further hearing of the UT with no retained findings of fact. That hearing took place in November 2022. By a decision promulgated in February 2023, the UT allowed the Secretary of State's appeal. The Claimant appealed against that decision.

Held, allowing the appeal:

(1) When considering whether the FtT had made an error of law, it was well established that a cautious approach should be taken to interfering with a decision of a specialist fact-finding tribunal: *HA (Iraq) v Secretary of State for the Home Department* [2022] UKSC 22 and *AA (Nigeria) v Secretary of State for the Home Department* [2020] EWCA Civ 1296 considered. The situation was not comparable in relation to the Court of Appeal interfering with a decision of the UT. It was for the Court of Appeal to reach its own conclusion on whether the FtT had made an error of law, which was of its nature a question to which there could be only one right answer. Careful consideration was, however, given to the reasons given by the experienced UT Judge (*paras 50 – 52*).

(2) Section 117C(6) of the 2002 Act provided that the public interest required deportation unless there were very compelling circumstances over and above the two exceptions described in section 117C(4) and (5). Those exceptions applied only to medium offenders where the public interest question was answered in favour of the foreign criminal without the need for a full proportionality assessment. In cases where the two exceptions did not apply, namely a serious offender or a medium offender who could not satisfy their requirements, a full proportionality assessment was required: *HA (Iraq)* applied. In *NA (Pakistan) v Secretary of State for the Home Department* [2016] EWCA Civ 662, Jackson LJ rejected a submission that the effect of the 'over and above' requirement was that circumstances of the kind mentioned in the two exceptions had to be excluded from any proportionality assessment under section 117C(6). *NA (Pakistan)* established that the effect of the 'over and above' requirement was that, where the 'very compelling circumstances' on which a claimant relied under section 117C(6) included an exception-specified circumstance, there had to be something substantially more than the minimum necessary to qualify for the relevant exception under section 117C(4) or (5). The Article 8 ECHR case had to be especially strong. That higher threshold could be reached either because the circumstance in question was present to a degree 'well beyond' what was sufficient to establish a 'bare case', or because it was complemented by other relevant circumstances, or because of a combination of both. Even if the 'over and above' requirement were not explicit, it was inherent in the structure of section 117C that a serious offender would need to meet a higher threshold than a medium offender in order to satisfy the test in subsection (6) (*paras 53 – 58*).

(3) The UT held that it followed from *NA (Pakistan)* that the FtT was obliged to consider 'expressly' first, whether the impact of the Claimant's deportation on his family was unduly harsh, and secondly, if it was, to identify what was the 'something more' which meant that the higher threshold under subsection (6) was met; and that it had failed to do so. That was not correct. It was not necessary as a matter of law for a tribunal in a serious offender case to make explicit findings in the claimant's favour on the two questions enumerated by the UT. A tribunal had to identify the factors to which it had given significant weight in reaching its overall conclusion. It should also indicate the relative importance of those factors, but there were limits to the extent to which that was practically possible: the factors in play were of their nature incommensurable, and calibrating their relative weights would often be an artificial exercise. It would place an unrealistic burden on tribunals for them to have to decide and specify in every case whether the 'something more' consisted of the exception-specific circumstance being present to an elevated

degree, or of some other circumstance or circumstances, or a combination of the two. It might be necessary in some cases, but there was no universal rule. That approach was not inconsistent with *NA (Pakistan)*. Tribunals were encouraged to follow the course suggested by Jackson LJ in *NA (Pakistan)*, which was likely to help focus on the key considerations. The instant case, however, was only concerned with whether there was a rule that a tribunal must in all cases explicitly address the two points identified by the UT so that any failure to do so was necessarily an error of law. The FtT's decision could have been better expressed and structured; however, it was not clear that it had misdirected itself. The FtT had not erred in law in the first respect identified by the UT (*paras 59, 60, 62, 63, 65, 67 and 68*).

(4) The loss to the children, and particularly D, of the financial support that the Claimant had been providing was clearly an admissible consideration in the proportionality assessment: it would interfere, directly or indirectly, with their Article 8 rights and affect their best interests. The FtT was wrong to classify it as a consideration going to the public interest, but that by itself was no more than a misclassification. It did not mean that the effect on the children of being deprived of the Claimant's financial support should not have gone into the balance at all, and there was no reason to suppose that the FtT Judge had given it additional weight because of the wrong label he had attached to it. The problem, however, was the explicit reference to a 'saving to the public purse'. That went further than saying simply that it was in the public interest for the children to receive financial support from the Claimant: it was of its nature a consideration going specifically to the public interest. It could not to that extent be defended on the basis that it was an admissible consideration which had simply been given the wrong label. That aspect did not, however, appear to be a material part of the Judge's reasoning. It was no more than an ill-judged rhetorical embellishment of his real point, made in the previous sentence, that it was important not to deprive the children of the Claimant's financial support. Accordingly, that part of the FtT's apparent reasoning did not vitiate its overall conclusion (*paras 71 – 73*).

(5) The FtT's decision was restored. Its reasons could be criticised in various respects, but the shortcomings in question did not justify the conclusion that the FtT had erred in law in finding that the Claimant's deportation would be disproportionate (*para 74*).

Cases referred to:

Beoku-Betts v Secretary of State for the Home Department [2008] UKHL 39; [2009] 1 AC 115; [2008] 3 WLR 166; [2008] 4 All ER 1146; [2008] Imm AR 688; [2008] INLR 489

Ghising (family life – adults – Gurkha policy) [2012] UKUT 160 (IAC)

HA (Iraq) v Secretary of State for the Home Department; RA (Iraq) v Secretary of State for the Home Department; AA (Nigeria) v Secretary of State for the Home Department [2022] UKSC 22; [2022] 1 WLR 3784; [2023] 1 All ER 365; [2022] INLR 425; [2022] Imm AR 1516, on appeals from *HA (Iraq) v Secretary of State for the Home Department; RA (Iraq) v Secretary of State for the Home Department* [2020] EWCA Civ 1176; [2021] 1 WLR 1327; [2021] 2 All ER 898; [2021] Imm AR 59; [2020] INLR 639 and *AA (Nigeria) v Secretary of State for the Home Department* [2020] EWCA Civ 1296; [2020] 4 WLR 145; [2021] Imm AR 114; [2020] INLR 599

Hesham Ali (Iraq) v Secretary of State for the Home Department [2016] UKSC 60; [2016] 1 WLR 4799; [2017] 3 All ER 20; [2017] Imm AR 484; [2017] INLR 109
KO (Nigeria) v Secretary of State for the Home Department; IT (Jamaica) v Secretary of State for the Home Department; NS (Sri Lanka) and Others v Secretary of State for the Home Department; Pereira v Secretary of State for the Home Department [2018] UKSC 53; [2018] 1 WLR 5273; [2019] 1 All ER 675; [2019] Imm AR 400; [2019] INLR 41
LC (China) v Secretary of State for the Home Department [2014] EWCA Civ 1310; [2015] Imm AR 227; [2015] INLR 302
MK (section 55 – Tribunal options) Sierra Leone [2015] UKUT 223 (IAC); [2015] INLR 563
NA (Pakistan) v Secretary of State for the Home Department; Secretary of State for the Home Department v KJ (Angola), WM (Afghanistan) and MY (Kenya) [2016] EWCA Civ 662; [2017] 1 WLR 207; [2017] Imm AR 1; [2016] INLR 587
R v Secretary of State for the Home Department ex parte Razgar [2004] UKHL 27; [2004] 2 AC 368; [2004] 3 WLR 58; [2004] 3 All ER 821; [2004] Imm AR 381; [2004] INLR 349
R (on the application of Kiarie) v Secretary of State for the Home Department; R (on the application of Byndloss) v Secretary of State for the Home Department [2017] UKSC 42; [2017] 1 WLR 2380; [2017] 4 All ER 811; [2017] Imm AR 1299; [2017] INLR 909
Secretary of State for the Home Department v MA (Somalia) [2015] EWCA Civ 48
Unuane v United Kingdom 2020 ECHR 80343/17; (2021) 72 EHRR 24; [2021] Imm AR 534; [2021] INLR 152

Legislation and international instruments judicially considered:

Borders, Citizenship and Immigration Act 2009, section 55
European Convention on Human Rights, Article 8
Immigration Rules HC 395 (as amended), paragraphs 398, 399 & 399A
Nationality, Immigration and Asylum Act 2002, sections 117A, 117C & 117D
UK Borders Act 2007, sections 32 & 33

Representation

Mr Z Malik KC and Mr A Rehman instructed by Acharyas Solicitors, for the Claimant;
Ms A Mannion instructed by the Government Legal Department, for the Secretary of State.

Judgment

This judgment was handed down remotely at 10.30am on 6 February 2024 by circulation to the parties or their representatives by e-mail and by release to the National Archives.

Lord Justice Underhill:

INTRODUCTION

[1] The Appellant is a Turkish national, of Kurdish ethnicity, born on 15 January 1988. He first came to the UK in 2003 as an asylum seeker but his claim was refused and he was eventually removed in 2010. Later in 2010 he married a British national in Turkey, and in 2011 he returned to the UK on a spouse visa. He was granted indefinite leave to remain in 2013 and has two sons – K, born in February 2013, and D, born in February 2014: both are British citizens.

[2] On 4 March 2016 the Appellant pleaded guilty to possessing a prohibited weapon, namely a Glock 17 semi-automatic pistol, and possessing that firearm without a certificate. He was sentenced to a total of five years and four months in prison.

[3] On the basis of that conviction and sentence, on 19 December 2016 the Secretary of State notified the Appellant of her intention to deport him pursuant to section 32 of the UK Borders Act 2007. He made a human rights claim resisting deportation, which was refused by a decision dated 9 August 2017. He appealed to the First-tier Tribunal ("FtT"). That appeal was not heard until March 2021. The reason for the delay is not clear, but it may be that it was thought necessary to await the result of a further asylum claim which the Appellant made in June 2018 and which was refused only in January 2021.

[4] The Appellant's appeal, together with an appeal against the refusal of his asylum claim, was heard by First-tier Tribunal Judge Cohen on 17 March 2021. By a decision promulgated on 19 October 2021 he dismissed the appeal as regards the asylum claim but allowed it as regards the human rights claim. It is surprising that seven months elapsed between the hearing and the decision, but counsel were not aware of any explanation for the delay and no point was taken about it.

[5] The Secretary of State appealed against the decision of the FtT. On 23 August 2022 Upper Tribunal Judge Stephen Smith held that the decision should be set aside for error of law. He directed that it be re-made at a further hearing of the Upper Tribunal ("UT"), with no retained findings of fact. That hearing took place on 2 November 2022. By a decision promulgated on 1 February 2023 the Secretary of State's appeal was allowed.

[6] The Appellant sought permission to appeal against both the original decision of the UT setting aside the decision of the FtT and, if that appeal were unsuccessful, its decision to re-make the decision rather than remit to the FtT. (There was no challenge to the UT's substantive decision if those challenges were unsuccessful.) Andrews LJ gave permission only as regards the first challenge. That means that the only issue for us is whether the FtT did indeed err in law in the respects found by the UT.

[7] The Appellant has been represented before us by Mr Zane Malik KC leading Mr Arif Rehman, and the Secretary of State by Ms Amy Mannion, none of whom appeared below. The case was very well argued on both sides.

THE BACKGROUND LAW

[8] Section 32 (4) of the 2007 Act provides that "the deportation of a foreign criminal is conducive to the public good". Subsection (5) requires the Secretary of State to make a deportation order in respect of a "foreign criminal", defined (so far as relevant for our purposes) as a person who is not a British citizen and who is convicted in the UK of a criminal offence for which they are sentenced to a period of imprisonment of at least twelve months. That obligation is subject to various exceptions set out in section 33. We are concerned only with the exception in section 33 (2)(a), which applies "where removal of the foreign criminal in pursuance of the deportation order would breach ... a person's Convention rights". The Convention rights in question are of course rights under the European Convention on Human Rights ("ECHR"): the relevant right in most cases is the right to respect for private and family life accorded by article 8.

[9] In a case where the removal of a person from the UK, including by way of deportation, would interfere with their article 8 rights, article 8 (2) requires the Secretary of State to show that that interference is justified. That entails a proportionality assessment in which the effect of the interference is weighed against the public interest in removal. There is a good deal of Strasbourg case-law about the proper approach to such an assessment, which is authoritatively reviewed in the judgment of Lord Reed in *Hesham Ali v Secretary of State for the Home Department* [2016] UKSC 60, [2016] 1 WLR 4799, at paras 24–35.

[10] Part 5A of the Nationality, Immigration and Asylum Act 2002 was introduced by the Immigration Act 2014. It is headed "Article 8 of the ECHR: public interest considerations". Its purpose, in general terms, is "to promote consistency, predictability and transparency in decision making and to reflect ... Parliament's view of how as a matter of public policy, [the proportionality balance] should be struck", and more particularly "to produce a straightforward set of rules, and in particular to narrow rather than widen the residual area of discretionary judgment for the court to take account of public interest or other factors not directly reflected in the wording of the statute": see the judgment of Lord Carnwath in *KO (Nigeria) v Secretary of State for the Home Department* [2018] UKSC 53, [2018] 1 WLR 5273, at paras. 12 and 15. Unfortunately, Part 5A is not very well drafted, and its provisions have required a good deal of judicial exposition.

[11] Part 5A comprises four sections, 117A-117D. I need only set out sections 117A and 117C.

[12] Section 117A provides, so far as material for our purposes, that in considering whether the interference with a potential deportee's right to respect for their private and family life is justified (defined as "the public interest question")

"the court or tribunal must (in particular) have regard –

(a) in all cases, to the considerations listed in section 117B, and

(b) in cases concerning the deportation of foreign criminals to the considerations listed in section 117C."

[2024] Imm AR 2

[13] Section 117C reads, so far as material:

"(1) The deportation of foreign criminals is in the public interest.

(2) The more serious the offence committed by a foreign criminal, the greater is the public interest in deportation of the criminal.

(3) In the case of a foreign criminal ('C') who has not been sentenced to a period of imprisonment of four years or more, the public interest requires C's deportation unless Exception 1 or Exception 2 applies.

(4) Exception 1 applies where –

(a) C has been lawfully resident in the United Kingdom for most of C's life,

(b) C is socially and culturally integrated in the United Kingdom, and

(c) there would be very significant obstacles to C's integration into the country to which C is proposed to be deported.

(5) Exception 2 applies where C has a genuine and subsisting relationship with a qualifying partner, or a genuine and subsisting parental relationship with a qualifying child, and the effect of C's deportation on the partner or child would be unduly harsh.

(6) In the case of a foreign criminal who has been sentenced to a period of imprisonment of at least four years, the public interest requires deportation unless there are very compelling circumstances, over and above those described in Exceptions 1 and 2.

(7) …"

The term "qualifying child" is defined in section 117D (1) in terms that include a child who is a British citizen.

[14] At the risk of spelling out the obvious, the effect of section 117C is to prescribe different approaches to the public interest question by reference to the length of the sentence imposed. Specifically:

(1) In the case of those sentenced to imprisonment for at least twelve months but less than four years (described in the case-law as "medium offenders"), the effect of subsection (3) is that deportation will not be justified if either of the two Exceptions identified in subsections (4) and (5) applies – Exception 1 being concerned with private life and Exception 2 with family life with a partner and/or with children.

(2) Where the potential deportee, to whom I will refer as "the claimant", has been sentenced to more than four years' imprisonment (a "serious offender"), those Exceptions are not available and subsection (6) provides that in considering the public interest question deportation will be justified

unless there are "very compelling circumstances, *over and above those described in Exceptions 1 and 2*". The italicised words ("the over-and-above requirement") are central to the main issue on this appeal: I will come back to them later.

(There is a rather fuller summary at para. 53 below.) I will sometimes for convenience refer to the proportionality assessment in cases where the Exceptions do not apply as being "required by", or "under", subsection (6), although that is not strictly accurate since the assessment is required by article 8 itself.

[15] It should be noted that, although the circumstances described in Exceptions 1 and 2 represent common circumstances in which a claimant's private or family life may be engaged, they do not cover all circumstances on which a medium offender might wish to rely. For example, he or she may well have a private life that would be interfered with by deportation even if they have lived in the UK for less than half their life; or they may enjoy a family life in the UK with parents or siblings rather than (or as well as) a partner or children.

[16] The provisions of Part 5A were at the material time reproduced in substantially identical terms (so far as material for present purposes) in Part 13 of the Immigration Rules, at paragraphs 398–399D. The equivalent to section 117C (6) formed part of paragraph 398 and the equivalents to Exceptions 1 and 2 appear under paragraphs 399 and 399A respectively.[*]

[17] In taking any immigration decision the best interests of any child affected by it must be treated as a primary consideration: see section 55 of the Borders, Citizenship and Immigration Act 2009.

[18] At the time of the argument and decision in the FtT the most recent authorities on the effect of the provisions summarised above were the decisions of this Court in *HA (Iraq) v Secretary of State for the Home Department* and *RA (Iraq) v Secretary of State for the Home Department*, [2020] EWCA Civ 1176, [2021] 1 WLR 1327, which were heard together and to which I will refer as *HA (Iraq)*; and *AA (Nigeria) v Secretary of State for the Home Department* [2020] EWCA Civ 1296, [2020] 4 WLR 145. The two *HA (Iraq)* cases concerned medium offenders, but *AA (Nigeria)* concerned a serious offender. All three decisions were subsequently upheld, and (so far as relevant to the issues on this appeal) their reasoning approved, by the Supreme Court under the name of *HA (Iraq)* [2022] UKSC 22, [2022] 1 WLR 3784: the only judgment was given by Lord Hamblen. The analysis in both *HA (Iraq)* and *AA (Nigeria)* was to a considerable extent based on the important judgment of this Court, given by Jackson LJ, in *NA (Pakistan) v Secretary of State for the Home Department* [2016] EWCA Civ 662, [2017] 1 WLR 207.

[19] I will return in due course to the particular points established by those authorities which are material to the issues on this appeal. It is sufficient at this stage to quote Lord Hamblen's summary, at para. 51 of his judgment in *HA*, of the correct approach to the proportionality assessment in a case to which the Exceptions do not apply:

---

[*] Part 13 has been recast with effect from 12 April 2023, but it contains provisions which appear to be to substantially the same effect.

"When considering whether there are very compelling circumstances over and above Exceptions 1 and 2, all the relevant circumstances of the case will be considered and weighed against the very strong public interest in deportation. As explained by Lord Reed in *Hesham Ali* at paras 24 to 35, relevant factors will include those identified by the European Court of Human Rights ('ECtHR') as being relevant to the article 8 proportionality assessment."

He goes on to reproduce the lengthy summary of potentially relevant factors given by the ECtHR in *Unuane v United Kingdom* (2021) 72 EHRR 24, but I need not quote that here: the important point is that what is involved is a broad holistic assessment. Lord Hamblen's description of the public interest in the deportation of foreign criminals as "very strong" derives from a long line of authorities which, again, it is unnecessary to cite here. It is of course because the public interest is so strong that very compelling circumstances are required to outweigh it; and at para. 33 of his judgment Lord Hamblen quotes with approval an observation in *NA (Pakistan)* that such cases would be rare.

THE FACTS

[20] Given the limited nature of the issue before this Court, there is no need to set out the facts in any detail. I have already given the essentials of the Appellant's immigration history. I need only say a little more about the offence for which he was imprisoned and about his family circumstances.

[21] As to the offence, the essential facts are as follows. The Appellant had arranged to purchase the firearm online. In fact, the sale had been conducted pursuant to an undercover police operation, and when he arrived at the pre-arranged meeting point he was arrested as soon as he had taken possession of the gun. It does not appear to have been established what particular purpose he had in mind in obtaining it, but the sentencing judge found that his intention had been that it would be used for criminal purposes of some kind by himself or others.

[22] As to his family circumstances, the Appellant separated from his wife in 2015. He was in prison or detained, initially on remand and then following his conviction and until the grant of immigration bail, between 21 December 2015 and 9 September 2018. During that time his wife, who is estranged from her own family, had to bring up K and D on her own, although she received some support from the Appellant's brother. Following his release the Appellant returned to live near his wife, although not with her, and continued to be involved in the upbringing of the children: the depth of the relationship is a matter about which the FtT made findings to which I will come later. He has two hairdressing businesses. His wife does not work and receives universal credit.

THE FTT'S REASONS

INTRODUCTION AND THE FACTS

[23] Paras. 1–13 of the FtT's Reasons set out the procedural background, including a summary of the Secretary of State's reasons for refusing the Appellant's human rights claim.

[24] At paras. 14–20 the FtT summarises the Appellant's case on the appeal and the contents of his witness statements. I need not set out those paragraphs in full. His broad case was that his deportation would be disproportionate in view of his long residence in this country and his family life with his wife and in particular his children, one of whom, D, had serious difficulties. He expressed deep remorse for the offence which he had committed. He exhibited prison reports showing that he had a good record in prison and was at low risk of reoffending. He had his own business and was able to and did provide significant financial support to his wife and children. He was well integrated in the community and supplied character references from friends and family. As regards the children, his wife did not have a partner and was, as I have said, estranged from her own family. She was said to be dependent on the Appellant's involvement in the care of the children at weekends and in school holidays and on financial support from him supplementing her benefit income.

[25] For the purpose of this appeal the FtT's summary of what is said in the witness statements about D, the younger child, is particularly important. Specifically:

(1)   Para. 15 begins:

"Amongst further evidence supporting the appellant's appeal was a witness statement from the appellant together with a witness statement from the appellant's ex-partner (sponsor)*; evidence in respect of [D] indicating that he has speech and language and behavioural disabilities and that an EHCP [Education Health and Care Plan]† is in place for him and that he is in receipt of DLA [Disability Living Allowance]. There is evidence indicating that there is a very strong bond between the appellant and his children, particularly [D] who amongst other things he has taken to Euro Disney in the past. [D] struggled during COVID restrictions."

(2)   Para. 17 includes the following passage:

"[D] has significant learning difficulties and [the Appellant] has a strong bond with him. He had been particularly involved in the children's lives during lockdown. The sponsor relies on him significantly .... If he is deported from the UK they will suffer enormously as will their health."

(3)   Para. 20 records evidence that while the Appellant was in prison D had been physically aggressive towards his brother K and that he has been referred to the local Child and Adolescent Mental Health Services ("CAMHS") team.

[26] At paras. 21–28 of the Reasons the FtT summarises the evidence at the hearing. The Appellant, his wife and his brother all gave oral evidence consistent with and amplifying the evidence in their witness statements. Again, I need not

---

* Although the FtT uses this language, it was common ground before us that the Appellant and his wife were legally married (and have not been divorced).
† An EHCP is defined on the gov.uk webpage *Children with special educational needs and disabilities* as being "for children and young people aged up to 25 who need more support than is available through special educational needs support".

quote these paragraphs in full. However, I should note two points relating to D. The Appellant gave evidence that D has "1-2-1 support" at school (para. 25). His wife gave evidence that D's relationship with the Appellant was "very close", that D "struggled greatly and his behaviour deteriorated significantly whilst the appellant was in prison", and that if the Appellant were deported it would have an enormous detrimental emotional effect on him (para. 27).

"DECISION"

[27] Paras. 31–47 of the Reasons are headed "Decision". I need to analyse these in some detail. The exercise is not entirely straightforward: apart from some particular problems which I will have to address, it is unhelpful that there are no headings, or equivalent signposts, identifying the structure of the reasoning. I will in the course of my analysis refer to some secondary criticisms made by the UT, but I will deal separately later with the principal points which were held to constitute errors of law.

[28] Paras. 31–32 of the Reasons are introductory. Paras. 33–36 appear to be intended as the judge's self-direction on the applicable law. They read as follows:

> "33. I have regard to paragraphs A362 and 398 to 399D in respect of the appellant's human rights claim.
>
> 34. I have also considered whether the appellant's removal from the United Kingdom would breach his human rights. In so doing, I note the questions that must be addressed as outlined in *Razgar*.
>
> 35. The appellant has been convicted of a particularly serious offence in respect of seeking to obtain a firearm. He was sentenced to 5 years and four months imprisonment. There is a presumption towards deportation. The appellant's deportation is conducive to the public good and in the public interest because he has been convicted of an offence for which he has been sentenced to a period of imprisonment of at least 4 years or more. The public interest requires the appellant's deportation unless there are very compelling circumstances over and above those described in the exceptions to deportation set out in paragraphs 399 and 399A of the Immigration Rules.
>
> 36. The exceptions to deportation do not apply to the appellant. He has been convicted of serious offences and sentenced to a term of 5+ years imprisonment in the UK including for firearms."

[29] I have the following observations about that self-direction:

(1) The judge does not refer to the provisions of Part 5A of the 2002 Act but only to the corresponding provisions of the Immigration Rules. This omission is criticised by the UT, though it accepts that it did not amount to an error of law. I agree with the UT that it is good practice for tribunals to refer to the statutory provisions, since that entails a specific recognition that the principles stated in the Rules are not merely a matter of policy but are mandated by Parliament. But I also agree that since the Rules are to identical effect it is not an error of law to refer only to them.

(2) It is surprising to see no reference to the extensive case-law referred to above specifically concerned with the deportation of foreign criminals – most obviously *Hesham Ali* and the decisions of this Court in *NA (Pakistan)*, *HA (Iraq)* and *AA (Nigeria)*. (*R (Razgar) v Secretary of State for the Home Department* [2004] UKHL 27, [2004] 2 AC 368, which is the only authority referred to, is not entirely irrelevant but it is not concerned with deportation.) However, at a later point in the Reasons the judge does refer to *AA (Nigeria)* and to other authorities which cover the main principles – see para. 37 below.

(3) The final sentence of para. 35 accurately states the approach required by section 117C (6) (albeit by reference to the corresponding Rule) – that is, that the public interest required the Appellant's deportation unless there were very compelling circumstances over and above those described in the Exceptions under subsections (4) and (5).

(4) Para. 36 correctly states that the Exceptions do not apply, because the Appellant is a serious offender; and no further reference is made to them. That might seem unexceptionable; but, as will appear, there is an issue about whether the FtT was in fact obliged to consider them expressly because of the over-and-above requirement in subsection (6).

[30] At paras. 37–43 and 45–47 of the Reasons the FtT conducts the proportionality assessment under subsection (6). Those two groups of paragraphs are separated by para. 44 (which considers and rejects the asylum appeal and with which we are not concerned on his appeal), and the intended relationship between them is not immediately apparent. I take them in turn.

Paras. 37–43

[31] Paras. 37–39 are apparently intended to identify the aspects of the Appellant's private and family life which engage article 8. Para. 37 reads:

"The appellant has not lived in the UK for 20 years or more. He has lived in the UK for 18+ years. He is not a child. The appellant does not have a partner but does have children in the UK."

Para. 38 starts by rejecting a contention by the Secretary of State that the Appellant was not the father of D and K. It continues:

"38. ... I accept that the appellant has joint responsibility for raising his children. His son, D, has speech and language and behavioural issues and I accept that he is particularly close to the appellant who provides a calming and guiding influence to him. I note that D has been referred to CAMHS in respect of his identified issues.

39. I must consider the best interests of the appellant's children and the effect of the appellant's removal on his remaining family members in the UK. I note that D's issues are significant and that he has been awarded DLA and provided with one-to-one teaching support at school. I have received evidence that his behaviour deteriorated whilst the appellant was in prison and this evidence is confirmed by his school. I accept that the appellant's relationship with D is

particularly strong in [*sic*: this must be a slip for 'and']* extends beyond normal familial ties."

[32] I have the following observations on those paragraphs:

(1) The first three sentences of para. 37 are puzzling. They appear to be directed to establishing that the Appellant does not satisfy two particular criteria relating to his private life – that is, that he has not lived in the UK for twenty years and he is not a child – but the criteria in question are not those in Exception 1 (I think they derive from paragraph 276 ADE of the Rules). Fortunately, however, the question why the FtT referred to them does not need to be resolved.

(2) The rest of the passage is concerned with the family life of the Appellant and his children. The focus is clearly on the interference with the article 8 rights of D, and the judge rightly reminds himself of the obligation under section 55 of the 2009 Act. Paras. 38 and 39 identify D's problems, and his dependence on the Appellant, only in summary terms, but it is clear that the judge accepted the evidence set out more fully in the earlier part of the Reasons (see paras. 25–26 above).

(3) The UT points out that the phrase "normal familial ties" is typically deployed in the case-law about relationships between adult family members: see para. 44 below. However, it is in my view clear that in this context the judge is intending to make the point that the extent of D's emotional dependence on the Appellant is exceptional. To put it another way, he is finding that the relationship went beyond what Jackson LJ in *NA (Pakistan)* (see paras. 34 and 35) referred to as "the natural love between parents and children" and "the desirability of children being with both parents" and which he said would not constitute sufficiently compelling circumstances for the purpose of section 117C (6).

[33] Paras. 40–43 contain what appears to be the core of the FtT's reasoning. They read as follows:

"40. The appellant was convicted of a particularly serious offence. However, this was apparently a one-off offence and the appellant has had no other interaction with the police, no other arrests or convictions. He has spent 2+ years out of prison and during that time has had no further convictions. The appellant is industrious and has established two businesses in the UK. He creates employment. I have received consistent evidence that there are no other family members remaining in the UK who may assist the sponsor in raising her children. The appellant's brother stepped in whilst the appellant was in prison, but he has now relocated outside of London and is no longer in a position to help. He has responsibilities with his own family. The sponsor is estranged from her own

---

* I have only resorted to "*sic*" where the passage in question is significant: other typographical errors in the Reasons I have silently corrected.

family members. This evidence was consistently given to me by all three witnesses. I accept the same.

41. I acknowledge the public interest in deporting the appellant. However, there is also a public interest in keeping the appellant in the UK in order to provide extremely valuable support both financially and emotionally in raising his children, particularly in respect of D noting his significant issues. If the appellant was deported from the UK, there would be a considerable additional drain on the public purse. In considering the appellant's strong relationship with his family members, I have regard to appropriate case law including *Ghising* and *Beoku-Betts*.

42. Another issue in respect of the appellant's case is that there has been a delay on the part of the respondent in considering the appellant's human rights and Refugee Convention applications. The application was made on 26 June 2018 but not decided until 14 January 2021. I find this to be indicative of the fact that the appellant's removal from the UK was not a priority for the respondent. His parole documentation and reports indicate that he poses a low risk of reoffending. He has been in the community for almost 3 years since his discharge from prison and during that time has cemented his family and private life in this country.

43. I accept that the appellant has a strong family life with his children in the UK. In considering the strength of the appellant's family life in the UK and noting the particular significant circumstances arising out of his relationship with D and noting D's significant learning and behavioural issues, and noting the best interests of the appellant's children, I find that the appellant's removal from the UK would be disproportionate in all the circumstances."

(Although the judge does not say for what purpose he refers in para. 41 to the cases of *Ghising* ([2012] UKUT 160 (IAC)) and *Beoku-Betts* ([2008] UKHL 39, [2009] 1 AC 115), both are authorities which make clear that it is necessary to take into account not simply the impact on the claimant of losing his or her family life with the relevant family members but also the impact on the family members themselves.)

[34] In these paragraphs the FtT is engaged in weighing the public interest in the Appellant's deportation against the interference with his family life which it would entail. The judge explicitly acknowledges the seriousness of the Appellant's offending and the public interest in his deportation – see the beginnings of both para. 40 and para. 41 – but he sets out various factors that weigh against it. In reaching the conclusion at para. 43 that the Appellant's deportation would be disproportionate it is clear that the factor to which he attaches decisive weight is its impact on D. Other factors are referred to – in summary, his rehabilitation (in the broad sense) (first part of para. 40); financial considerations (para. 41); and delay (para. 42) – but these are plainly secondary.

Paras. 45–47

[35] This second group of paragraphs reads as follows:

"45. In respect of the appellant's private life, I acknowledge that the appellant had spent a significant period of time in the UK. He arrived in the UK aged 15 years old. He has lived here since that time being approximately 18 years. The appellant has settled well in the UK, he has established two hairdressing businesses. The appellant submitted a substantial amount of character references and witness statements from friends in support of his appeal. They will attest to his good character other than his one issue of offending behaviour. I do not find that the appellant's removal would be disproportionate on the basis of his private life alone.

46. I note the public interest criteria. I have regard to appropriate case law in this respect, including *Binloss* [sic], *AA Nigeria, LC China (CA)* and *MA (Somalia)*. The appellant in this case, as in those, has a particularly strong family life in the UK. I note the strong public interest in maintaining law and order and public protection, but in the light of the fact that the appellant has been convicted of one serious offence, is assessed as posing a low risk of reoffending and noting the significant length of time that he has spent in the UK and strong links [sic] he has a particularly the family life with his children and noting [D's] significant issues, I find that the appellant's deportation is neither justified nor proportionate in all the circumstances. The appellant has demonstrated a family life in the UK meeting the threshold for deeming his deportation disproportionate.

47. In the light of my findings above, I find that the appellant's appeal succeeds on human rights grounds."

[36] The intended role of these paragraphs needs to be identified. The FtT had already in para. 43 concluded that the Appellant's deportation would be disproportionate, essentially because of the impact on D; and it might be thought that no more needed to be said. However, the position of para. 46 at the end of the Reasons suggests that it is intended to provide a definitive summary of the reasons for the finding (in the following paragraph) that the appeal succeeded. Although, like para. 43, it focuses primarily on the impact of the Appellant's deportation on D, it goes beyond the previous reasoning, both because it identifies what is said to be relevant case-law and because it refers to "the significant length of time that he has spent in the UK", which is a factor going to his private life rather than his family life.* I should say something more about both points.

---

* It seems that the judge in fact intended to refer to some further aspect of the Appellant's private life since some words appear to be missing after "strong links". I suspect that the intended reference was to links with the local community, which would be supported by the findings in para. 45; but it is impossible to be sure.

[37] As to the authorities, those referred to in para. 46 are: *AA (Nigeria)*, to which I have already referred; *R (Kiarie and Byndloss) v Secretary of State for the Home Department* [2017] UKSC 42, [2017] 1 WLR 2380; *LC (China) v Secretary of State for the Home Department* [2014] EWCA Civ 1310; and *Secretary of State for the Home Department v MA (Somalia)* [2015] EWCA Civ 48.* It is unsatisfactory that the judge does not identify specifically what guidance he draws from these cases, beyond noting that in all of them the claimant had "a particularly strong family life in the UK". However, each does in fact contain substantial guidance as to the correct approach to the proportionality assessment. In particular, paras. 9–14 of Popplewell LJ's judgment in *AA (Nigeria)*, which was the most recent authority in this area at the time of the decision, contain a clear summary of the applicable law. That summary includes (at para. 13) two extracts from the judgment of Lord Wilson in *Byndloss* about the meaning of "very compelling circumstances": this is itself based partly on Lord Reed's seminal judgment in *Hesham Ali* and emphasises the strength of the public interest in deportation of foreign criminals and the consequent height of the threshold required to satisfy section 117C (6). Popplewell LJ also quotes (at para. 14) most of paras. 29–38 of the judgment of the Court in *NA (Pakistan)*, to which I will have to refer in detail below.

[38] As to the reference to the Appellant's private life, although what is said in para. 46 itself is very summary it has to be read with para. 45, which sets out a number of points about the depth and value of his private life in the UK. Although the judge concludes that the Appellant's deportation would not be disproportionate "on the basis of his private life *alone* [my italics]", that way of putting it suggests, consistently with the reference in para. 46, that he had taken his private life into account as part of the overall proportionality assessment.

Overview

[39] The circumstances on which the FtT relied in concluding that the Appellant's deportation would be disproportionate have to be gleaned both from paras. 37–43 and from paras. 45–47, but with particular reference to para. 46 as the final summary. It is clear from that paragraph that the predominant circumstance was the impact that being deprived of his father's support would have on D because of his particular problems. However, the judge also took into account some other circumstances as part of the overall assessment. These include the Appellant's rehabilitation (referred to in paras. 40 and 46) and his long private life in the UK (referred to in paras. 45 and 46). In making the proportionality assessment the judge quoted the correct statutory test (albeit by reference to paragraph 398 of the Immigration Rules rather than section 117C (6)). He also referred in para. 46 to authorities which contained the relevant guidance as to the application of that test, although he did not quote from them or attempt to summarise their effect.

---

* I should say that it was bad practice not to give full citations for these authorities, and also those referred to in para. 41. In the cases of *AA (Nigeria)*, *MA (Somalia)* and *Ghising* an online search comes up with more than one authority with those names; and *Binloss* would come up with nothing because it is mis-spelt. Although it was not difficult for the Court, with the assistance of counsel, to identify the correct cases, that would not be so for all readers.

[40] The UT, as we know, reached a different conclusion about proportionality when it came to re-make the decision, and it might be thought that the way that the FtT struck the balance in this case was generous to the Appellant. However, that in itself cannot constitute an error of law unless its conclusion can be characterised as perverse, which neither the UT nor the Secretary of State has suggested: this point is made in several authorities – for a recent summary see para. 36 of Popplewell LJ's judgment in *AA (Nigeria)*. It is inevitable that decision-takers will sometimes differ in their assessment of the same facts – see, again, *AA (Nigeria)*, at para. 41. I would add that it is in any event not possible to form a reliable view of the strength or otherwise of the Appellant's article 8 case without sight of the underlying evidence. We have not ourselves seen that evidence – perfectly properly, since there is no perversity challenge. It can at least be said that the facts that D has an EHCP (including a requirement for one-to-one teaching), qualifies for DLA and has been referred to the CAMHS suggest that his problems are substantial.

THE DECISION OF THE UT

[41] The UT's finding that the FtT had erred in law is at paras. 31–42 of the Reasons. Para. 33 makes the preliminary observation that the judge "did not expressly conduct his analysis pursuant to the structure and statutory considerations established by Part 5A of the 2002 Act". The UT judge acknowledges that, since the FtT did nevertheless explicitly state the correct statutory test, that might be thought to be a criticism of form rather than substance. But he continues, at para. 34:

> "However, in this case, I consider that the judge's failure to approach his reasoning expressly pursuant to the statutory framework established by section 117C meant that he omitted key considerations and failed to address material considerations. In turn, that led to the judge taking into account immaterial considerations, and impermissibly downgrading the public interest in the claimant's deportation, for the reasons set out below."

There appear to be two "reasons set out below", the first being expounded in paras. 35–39 and the second in para. 40. I take them in turn.

[42] As to the first, paras. 35 and 36 and the first part of para. 37 read as follows:

> "35. First, since the claimant had been sentenced to a term of imprisonment that exceeded four years, section 117C(6) of the 2002 Act was engaged, requiring the judge to determine whether there were any 'very compelling circumstances' over and above the statutory Exceptions to deportation. What amounts to 'very compelling circumstances' is an assessment that must be informed by the extent to which the claimed very compelling circumstances exceed the factors set out in the statutory Exceptions to deportation. The judge did not address the substance of either statutory Exception. He simply stated at paragraph 36 that:
>
>> 'The exceptions to deportation do not apply to the [claimant]. He has been convicted of serious offences and sentenced to a term of 5+ years imprisonment in the UK including for firearms.'

36. Since any assessment of 'very compelling circumstances' must be conducted by reference to the extent to which the appellant meets the substance of Exception 1 or 2, even if neither exception was capable of being engaged on account of the seriousness of the foreign criminal's offending, it was incumbent upon the judge expressly to consider those exceptions in any event, to address the extent to which they could be met. So much is clear from *NA (Pakistan)* at [37]:

> [The judge quotes para. 37 of the judgment in *NA (Pakistan)*, but I omit it since I set it out at para. 56 below.]

37. It follows that it was incumbent upon the judge to address the substance of the relevant Exception, namely Exception 2 (see section 117C(5)) and to determine whether the appellant's deportation would be 'unduly harsh' on K and D. In turn, that assessment would inform the 'very compelling circumstances' assessment, consistent with *NA.*"

The judge then sets out the well-known gloss on the term "unduly harsh" from para. 46 of the decision of the Upper Tribunal in *MK (Sierra Leone) v Secretary of State for the Home Department* [2015] UKUT 223 (IAC), and notes that it was endorsed by the Supreme Court in *HA (Iraq)*.

[43] At para. 38 the UT judge finds that the FtT did not follow the approach so identified. He says:

> "While the judge recorded the Secretary of State's case in relation to the unduly harsh test at paragraphs 8 and 10 of his decision, he did not in terms address it during his operative reasoning. The judge observed at paragraph 38 that the claimant had a calming and guiding influence on D. At paragraph 39 he observed that D had a number of behavioural and other conditions that had resulted in the family being awarded the Disability Living Allowance, and that D's relationship with the claimant 'is particularly strong in [sic] extends beyond normal familial ties'. However, what the judge did not do as part of this analysis was consider (i) whether those factors were 'unduly harsh' and (ii) if they were, what the factors were of particular significance in that assessment that meant that they took the case into the territory of 'very compelling circumstances', since this claimant was a serious offender."

[44] Para. 39 says that the FtT's use of the phrase "extends beyond normal familial ties" does not remedy the deficiency. He notes that the language derives from the case-law about dependency between adults and continues:

> "If the judge meant that the ties between the claimant and D were stronger than those ordinarily found between a father and a son, that would have meant, presumably, that the judge had in mind some form of notional father/son comparator, by which to calibrate such an assessment. The test the judge should have applied was the unduly harsh test, which he failed to do."

[45] As to the second reason, para. 40 reads as follows:

"Secondly, while the judge correctly noted that the claimant's deportation was in the public interest at paragraphs 35 and 46, at paragraph 41 he impermissibly held that there was 'a public interest in keeping the [claimant] in the UK' due to the impact on public funds that the judge thought there would be if the claimant were deported. The public interest factors to which the judge should have had regard are those set out in Part 5A of the 2002 Act, in particular, section 117C. Section 117C(1) provides that '[t]he deportation of foreign criminals is in the public interest'. Since the claimant had been sentenced to a term of imprisonment greater than four years, 'the public interest requires deportation' unless there are very compelling circumstances over and above the exceptions to deportation (section 117C(6)). The potential burden on public funds through an individual being deported is not a factor to which Parliament has ascribed any significance. It was an error for the judge to seek to redefine the public interest in that way."

[46] Those two reasons are followed by para. 41, which reads:

"As I conclude, it is necessary to address the judge's remarks that claimant's 'removal from the UK was not a priority' for the Secretary of State, at paragraph 42. I consider this criticism to be inappropriate, especially in light of the timing of the asylum claim and the time taken to process such claims.".

Ms Mannion submitted that in that paragraph the judge was intending to identify a further and distinct error of law by the FtT, beyond the two which I have set out above. I can see that the introductory words might suggest that, but I do not believe that it is correct. Although the original (very diffusely pleaded) application for permission to appeal to the UT did contain a criticism of what the FtT said about delay, it is far from clear that this was intended as a distinct ground of appeal, and it is not identified in the Reasons given by UTJ Pickup when he granted permission. The judge's reference at para. 34 to the FtT "taking into account immaterial considerations, and impermissibly downgrading the public interest in the claimant's deportation" suggests two reasons, which would correspond to his use of "First" and "Secondly" when beginning paras. 35 and 40. If the judge was treating what the FtT said about delay as a distinct error of law, I do not believe that he would have described it as no more than "inappropriate", and he would certainly have explained his reasoning more fully. The paragraph reads to me as simply, as King LJ observed in the course of the argument, a "postscript".[*]

[47] That being so, I need not consider para. 41 further. But for what it is worth I would agree with the UT that such delays as occurred in deciding the Appellant's human rights and asylum claims cannot be treated as evidence that the Secretary of State regarded his deportation as low-priority: delay is alas endemic in the system. Having said that, I do not think that the FtT judge's observation to that effect played a significant part in his reasoning. His main point, rather, appears to have been the conventional one that the delay tended to "cement" the relationships that were the basis of the Appellant's family life case.

---

[*] It did indeed occur to me that "necessary" might have been a slip for "unnecessary", which would make the first sentence read rather more naturally; but I do not base my reasoning on that.

[48] The UT concludes, at para. 42:

"These errors are such that it is necessary for the judge's decision to be set aside; they go to the heart of the assessment of the proportionality of the claimant's deportation."

THE ISSUES ON THIS APPEAL

[49] The question in this appeal is whether the two reasons given by the UT for finding that the FtT erred in law are well-founded. There is no Respondent's Notice from the Secretary of State seeking to uphold the UT's decision on other grounds: in particular, as already noted, it is not contended that the decision of the FtT was perverse.

[50] I consider the UT's two reasons in turn. But before doing so I should recapitulate the approach that should be taken in considering whether the FtT made an error of law. At para. 72 of his judgment in *HA (Iraq)* (but with reference to the appeal in *AA (Nigeria)*) Lord Hamblen said:

"It is well established that judicial caution and restraint is required when considering whether to set aside a decision of a specialist fact finding tribunal. In particular:

(i) They alone are the judges of the facts. Their decisions should be respected unless it is quite clear that they have misdirected themselves in law. It is probable that in understanding and applying the law in their specialised field the tribunal will have got it right. Appellate courts should not rush to find misdirections simply because they might have reached a different conclusion on the facts or expressed themselves differently – see *AH (Sudan) v Secretary of State for the Home Department* [2007] UKHL 49; [2008] AC 678 *per* Baroness Hale of Richmond at para 30.

(ii) Where a relevant point is not expressly mentioned by the tribunal, the court should be slow to infer that it has not been taken into account – see *MA (Somalia) v Secretary of State for the Home Department* [2010] UKSC 49; [2011] 2 All ER 65 at para 45 *per* Sir John Dyson.

(iii) When it comes to the reasons given by the tribunal, the court should exercise judicial restraint and should not assume that the tribunal misdirected itself just because not every step in its reasoning is fully set out – see *R (Jones) v First-tier Tribunal (Social Entitlement Chamber)* [2013] UKSC 19; [2013] 2 AC 48 at para 25 *per* Lord Hope."

[51] Mr Malik relied on that passage but added some further points by way of amplification. The only one that I need mention is that in *AA (Nigeria)* in this Court Popplewell LJ said, at para. 34:

"Experienced judges in this specialised tribunal are to be taken to be aware of the relevant authorities and to be seeking to apply them without needing to refer to them specifically, unless it is clear from their language that they have failed to do so."

[52] There was some discussion before us about whether this Court should take the same cautious approach to interfering with a decision of the UT, which is itself a specialist tribunal. In my view it is clear that that the two situations are not comparable – see *per* Popplewell LJ in para. 41 of his judgment in *AA (Nigeria)* – and that it is for this Court to reach its own conclusion on whether the FtT made an error of law, which is of its nature a question to which there can be only one right answer. Having said that, it is of course right that we give careful consideration to the reasons for finding that it did so given by an experienced UT judge.

Failure to apply "unduly harsh" test

[53] The starting-point is to identify the basic structure of the law in this area. At para. 47 of his judgment in *HA (Iraq)* Lord Hamblen approved the summary which I gave at para. 29 of my judgment in this Court:

> "(A) In the cases covered by the two Exceptions in subsections (4)-(5), which apply only to medium offenders, the public interest question is answered in favour of the foreign criminal, without the need for a full proportionality assessment. Parliament has pre-determined that in the circumstances there specified the public interest in the deportation of medium offenders does *not* outweigh the article 8 interests of the foreign criminal or his family: they are, given, so to speak, a short cut. The consideration of whether those Exceptions apply is a self-contained exercise governed by their particular terms.
>
> (B) In cases where the two Exceptions do not apply – that is, in the case of a serious offender or in the case of a medium offender who cannot satisfy their requirements – a full proportionality assessment is required, weighing the interference with the article 8 rights of the potential deportee and his family against the public interest in his deportation. In conducting that assessment the decision-maker is required by section 117C (6) (and paragraph 398 of the Rules) to proceed on the basis that 'the public interest requires deportation unless there are very compelling circumstances over and above those described in Exceptions 1 and 2'."

[54] It might be thought to follow from the fact that the Exceptions are a "self-contained" short-cut they have no role to play where a full proportionality assessment is required, and that accordingly in the present case the FtT was right to make no reference to them. But the complicating factor is the requirement in section 117C (6) that the public interest requires deportation unless "there are very compelling circumstances *over and above those described in Exceptions 1 and 2*". The effect of those words was considered in *NA (Pakistan)*. I need to consider with some care what the Court said in that case.

[55] The most relevant part of Jackson LJ's judgment is at paras. 28–32, though it is also necessary to consider para. 37. He was considering in particular a submission that the effect of the over-and-above requirement was that circumstances of the kind mentioned in the two Exceptions – which I will call "Exception-specified circumstances"* – had to be excluded from any proportionality assessment under section 117C (6). That submission was rejected, but his reasoning involved explaining more generally the effect of the requirement. At para. 29 he said:

"... [A] foreign criminal is entitled to rely upon such matters, but he would need to be able to point to features of his case of a kind mentioned in Exceptions 1 and 2 ..., *or features falling outside the circumstances described in those Exceptions* [my italics] ..., which made his claim based on Article 8 especially strong."

He went on at para. 30 to illustrate what that meant in the case of a serious offender. He said:

"In the case of a serious offender who could point to circumstances in his own case which could be said to correspond to the circumstances described in Exceptions 1 and 2, but where he could only just succeed in such an argument, it would not be possible to describe his situation as involving very compelling circumstances, over and above those described in Exceptions 1 and 2. One might describe that as a bare case of the kind described in Exceptions 1 or 2. On the other hand, if he could point to factors identified in the descriptions of Exceptions 1 and 2 of an especially compelling kind in support of an Article 8 claim, going well beyond what would be necessary to make out a bare case of the kind described in Exceptions 1 and 2, they could in principle constitute 'very compelling circumstances, over and above those described in Exceptions 1 and 2', whether taken by themselves *or in conjunction with other factors relevant to application of Article 8* [my italics]."

That passage was quoted with approval by Lord Hamblen in *HA (Iraq)* – see para. 50 of his judgment.

[56] Jackson LJ goes on to amplify the point, and deal with some other aspects of the test, at paras. 31–34. At para. 35 he says, on the basis of the previous paragraphs, that the scheme of the Act provided "the following structure for deciding whether a foreign criminal can resist deportation on article 8 grounds". Para. 37 (which is the paragraph quoted at para. 36 of the UT's Reasons) reads:

"In relation to a serious offender, it will often be sensible first to see whether his case involves circumstances of the kind described in Exceptions 1 and 2 both because the circumstances so described set out particularly significant factors bearing upon respect for private life (Exception 1) and respect for family life (Exception 2) and because that may provide a helpful basis on which an assessment can be made whether there are 'very compelling circumstances, over and above those described in Exceptions 1 and 2' as is required under section 117C(6). It will then be necessary to look to see whether any of the factors falling

---

* I apologise for this ugly piece of jargon, but it saves a great deal of wordage.

within Exceptions 1 and 2 are of such force, whether by themselves or taken in conjunction with any other relevant factors not covered by the circumstances described in Exceptions 1 and 2, as to satisfy the test in section 117C(6)."

[57] *NA (Pakistan)* thus establishes that the effect of the over-and-above requirement is that, in a case where the "very compelling circumstances" on which a claimant relies under section 117C (6) include an Exception-specified circumstance ("an Exception-overlap case"),[*] it is necessary that there be something substantially more than the minimum that would be necessary to qualify for the relevant Exception under subsection (4) or (5): as Jackson LJ puts it at para. 29, the article 8 case must be "especially strong". That higher threshold may be reached *either* because the circumstance in question is present to a degree which is "well beyond" what would be sufficient to establish a "bare case", *or* – as shown by the phrases which I have italicised in paras. 29 and 30 – because it is complemented by other relevant circumstances, *or* because of a combination of both. I will refer to those considerations, of whichever kind, as "something more". To take a concrete example, if the Exception-related circumstance is the impact of the claimant's deportation on a child (Exception 2) the something more will have to be either that the undue harshness would be of an elevated degree ("unduly unduly harsh"?) or that it was complemented by another factor or factors – perhaps very long residence in this country (even if Exception 1 is not satisfied) – to a sufficient extent to meet the higher threshold; or, as I have said, a combination of the two.

[58] There is nothing at all surprising about this, at least in the case of a serious offender. Even if the over-and-above requirement were not explicit, it is in my view inherent in the structure of section 117C that a serious offender will need to meet a higher threshold than a medium offender in order to satisfy the test in subsection (6).

[59] The UT held that it followed from the judgment in *NA (Pakistan)* that the FtT was obliged, apparently as a matter of law, to consider "expressly" (i) whether the impact of the Appellant's deportation on his family – in practice on D – was unduly harsh, and (ii), if it was, to identify what was the something more which meant that the higher threshold under subsection (6) was met; and that he failed to do so. That appears from para. 36 of its Reasons, but more particularly from para. 38, which, as Ms Mannion correctly observed, encapsulates the essence of the error of law which the UT found.

[60] Ms Mannion argued cogently in support of the UT's conclusion, but after careful consideration I do not believe it is correct. That is, I do not believe that it is necessary as a matter of law for a tribunal in a serious offender case to make explicit findings in the claimant's favour on the questions enumerated by the UT as (i) and (ii). I take them in turn.

---

[*] At the risk of repetition, not every case under subsection (6) will be an Exception-overlap case: see para. 15 above. On the face of it, it is hard to see that the words "over and above those described in Exceptions 1 and 2" have any function in a case where the claimant is not relying on circumstances falling within either Exception. But, as I have already observed, these provisions are not well-drafted.

[61] As for (i), if in an Exception-overlap case – say, a case where the circumstance in question is impact on family members – a tribunal finds explicitly that subsection (6) is satisfied, and has fully identified the particular facts relied on, it adds nothing for it to spell out that that means that the impact in question is unduly harsh, since that is logically inherent in the overall finding. There is no need for additional reasoning or fact-finding, because the facts about that impact will have been found and assessed in any event as part of the reasoning on the subsection (6) issue.

[62] As for (ii), it is also logically inherent in such a case that the tribunal will have found the "something more" which is necessary to satisfy the higher threshold under subsection (6): see para. 57 above. I agree that it would in principle conduce to transparent decision-making if the tribunal identified with precision in every case what the something more consisted of; but that will not always be straightforward. The proportionality assessment is generally multi-factorial and requires a holistic approach. A tribunal must of course in its reasons identify the factors to which it has given significant weight in reaching its overall conclusion. It is no doubt also desirable that it should indicate the relative importance of those factors, but there are limits to the extent to which that is practically possible: the factors in play are of their nature incommensurable, and calibrating their relative weights will often be an artificial exercise. It would in my view place an unrealistic burden on tribunals for them to have to decide, and specify, in every case whether the something more consists of the Exception-specific circumstance being present to an elevated degree, or of some other circumstance or circumstances, or a combination of the two. There may be cases where for some reason peculiar to the case this degree of specificity is necessary; but I do not believe that there is any universal rule. We should not make decision-making in this area more complicated than it regrettably already is.

[63] I do not believe that that approach is inconsistent with para. 37 of the judgment in *NA (Pakistan)*, on which the UT particularly relied. Ms Mannion submitted that that paragraph operated as a "funnel": the effect of the first sentence was that a tribunal should start by identifying whether an Exception-specific circumstance was being relied on, and, if it was, the effect of the second sentence was that it was "necessary" for it to decide whether the required something more was present. As a matter simply of language, there are difficulties about this submission. The first sentence says only that it will "often be sensible" to consider whether the claimant's case involves an Exception-specific circumstance; and the reason that it gives is that such consideration may encourage a focus on "particularly significant factors" bearing on private or family life and thus provide "a helpful basis" for the application of the test under section 117C (6). None of that is the language of legal obligation. Although the word "necessary" appears in the second sentence, that applies only if the tribunal has chosen to take the course suggested in the first. But I do not in fact think that the answer needs to depend on this kind of detailed verbal analysis. It is important to focus on the substance of the point that Jackson LJ was making – namely, as he says in the second sentence of para. 37 (consistently with paras. 29 and 30) that in an Exception-overlap case subsection (6) requires something more over and above the minimum required to satisfy the Exception in question. It does not follow, and he does not say, that a tribunal is in every case obliged to make an explicit and particularised finding as to how that something more is made up.

[64] Mr Malik referred us to para. 60 of my judgment in *HA (Iraq)*, where I said (in the context of a medium-offender case):

"There may be cases where a tribunal is satisfied that there is a combination of circumstances, including but not limited to the harsh effect of the appellant's deportation on his family, which together constitute very compelling reasons sufficient to outweigh the strong public interest in deportation, but where it may be debatable whether the effect on the family *taken on its own* (as section 117C (5) requires) is unduly harsh. ... In such a case, although the tribunal will inevitably have considered whether the relevant Exception has been satisfied, it is unnecessary for it to cudgel its brains into making a definitive finding. The Exceptions are, as I have said, designed to provide a shortcut for appellants in particular cases, and it is not compulsory to take that shortcut if proceeding directly to the proportionality assessment required by article 8 produces a clear answer in the appellant's favour."

The effect of the over-and-above requirement was not the subject of argument in *HA (Iraq)*, and in any event the point being made in this passage is not exactly the same as the point which I have just been considering. But the spirit of it does seem to me to be to the same effect, namely that the focus must be on the conclusion under subsection (6), and that explicit findings on particular matters feeding into that conclusion are not in all cases required as a matter of law.

[65] I should emphasise that I do not disagree in any way with what Jackson LJ says in para. 37 of the judgment in *NA (Pakistan)*. On the contrary, I would encourage tribunals to follow the course he suggests, which is likely to help focus the mind on the key considerations. But I am at this stage only concerned with whether there is a rule that a tribunal must in all cases explicitly address points (i) and (ii) identified by the UT, so that any failure to do so is necessarily an error of law.

[66] That disposes of the UT's reasoning as expressed. But I do not think that it would be right to treat the judge's criticism of the FtT as being limited to that specific point. It is clear that his underlying concern was that, given the absence of any real exposition by the FtT, based on the authorities, of what the test under subsection (6) entails and of any clear structure to the Reasons, the judge did not in truth appreciate the height of the necessary threshold or apply it to the facts of this case. I believe I should address that concern.

[67] I am bound to say that I have not found this question entirely easy. The FtT's decision could certainly have been better expressed and structured. However, it is important to bear in mind the principles summarised at paras. 50–51 above: the focus should be on the way the judge performed the essence of the task required. As to that, he considered the factors that would have been relevant to an assessment of undue harshness under section 117C (5), and it is in my view obvious that he did regard the effect on D of the Appellant's deportation as unduly harsh, although he did not use that actual phrase. It is also, I think, adequately clear that he understood that the threshold required by subsection (6), whose terms he had correctly set out in para. 35 of the Reasons, was substantially higher than that required by subsection (5). As I have observed, that is in truth self-evident in the case of a serious offender, even apart from the language of the over-and-above requirement; and the height of the applicable threshold is repeatedly emphasised in the well-known authorities with which it should be assumed, in the absence of evidence to the contrary, that he

was familiar (and to some of which he referred, albeit only by their names). It is clear from para. 46 of the Reasons that he took into account other factors, relating to the Appellant's private life, over and above the impact of his deportation on D. He does not say whether it was those, or a sufficiently elevated degree of undue harshness, or (as seems most likely) a combination of the two, which lifted the case to the level required by subsection (6); but for the reasons that I have given above I do not believe that he was obliged to do so. Taking all that into account, I do not feel able to say – using the language of point (i) in Lord Hamblen's guidance quoted at para. 50 above – that it is quite clear that the FtT misdirected itself.

[68] For those reasons I do not believe that the FtT erred in law in the first respect identified by the UT.

Unjustified redefinition of the public interest

[69] The UT held that it was wrong for the FtT in para. 41 of its Reasons to refer to a "public interest in keeping the appellant in the UK" so that he could provide financial and emotional support to his children, thereby preventing a "considerable additional drain on the public purse". His point, as supported before us by Ms Mannion, is that for the purpose of Part 5A of the 2002 Act the public interest is comprehensively stated as being that foreign criminals should be deported (see not only section 117C but also section 32 (4) of the 2007 Act); and that that precludes the FtT from bringing into the proportionality balance a supposed countervailing public interest of any kind.

[70] I am prepared to accept – though, as will appear, I need not definitively decide – that the FtT did indeed err in law in this respect. It may be debatable whether the statutory statement of the public interest is intended to be wholly comprehensive: some factors which would appear to go to the public interest are commonly included in the proportionality assessment, such as particular benefits that the claimant confers on the community. But it is hard to think that a public benefit of the highly general nature referred to, which would apply in every case where deportation deprived a family of its breadwinner, should be treated as diminishing the public interest in deportation declared by the statute.

[71] The question then is whether that error of law was material to the FtT's conclusion. I do not believe that it was. The starting-point is that the loss to the Appellant's children, and particularly D, of the financial support that he had been providing was clearly an admissible consideration in the proportionality assessment: it would interfere, directly or indirectly, with their article 8 rights and affect their best interests. The FtT was wrong to classify it as a consideration as going to the *public* interest, but that by itself is no more than a mis-classification. It does not mean that the effect on the children of being deprived of the Appellant's financial support should not have gone into the balance at all, and there is no reason to suppose that the judge gave it additional weight because of the wrong label he attached to it.

[72] The problem, however, is the explicit reference to a "saving to the public purse". That goes further than saying simply that it was in the public interest for the children to receive financial support from the Appellant: it is of its nature a consideration going specifically to the public interest. It cannot to that extent be defended on the basis that it was an admissible consideration which had simply been given the wrong label. However, this aspect of what the judge said does not appear, on a fair reading, to be a material part of his reasoning: I note in particular that he does not mention it in para. 46, which is the authoritative summary of his reasons

for finding that the Appellant's deportation would be disproportionate. In my view, it is no more than an (ill-judged) rhetorical embellishment of his real point, made in the previous sentence, that it was important not to deprive the children of the Appellant's financial support.

[73] I accordingly do not accept that this part of the FtT's apparent reasoning vitiated its overall conclusion.

CONCLUSION

[74] For those reasons I would allow this appeal and restore the decision of the FtT. The FtT's Reasons can indeed be criticised in various respects, and I can understand why the UT came to the conclusion that it did. But in the end I do not believe that the shortcomings in question justify the conclusion that the FtT erred in law in finding that the Appellant's deportation would be disproportionate.

LORD JUSTICE KING:

[75] I agree.

LORD JUSTICE WARBY:

[76] I also agree.

R (ON THE APPLICATION OF ZHOU, FEI AND ZHOU) v SECRETARY OF STATE FOR THE HOME DEPARTMENT

COURT OF APPEAL

King, Whipple LJJ and Cobb J

[2024] EWCA Civ 81
7 February 2024

Human rights – Article 8 of the ECHR – family and private life – overstayers – 'hostile environment' – no unlawful interference with rights – immigration – leave to remain – deferral of substantive decision on application – pending criminal investigation – delay lawful and rational – paragraph 34BB(1) of the Immigration Rules – variation of first application – appeal academic

The Claimants were a family of Chinese nationals. The first Claimant, Z, arrived in the United Kingdom in 2005. He had permission to remain until April 2018. His wife, the second Claimant, joined him in 2010. Their daughter, the third Claimant, was born in China but had lived in the United Kingdom for most of her life. Z unsuccessfully applied for indefinite leave to remain in March 2018. The Claimants became overstayers thereafter and were on immigration bail from June 2019.

In March 2021, Z was arrested on suspicion of money laundering and interviewed by the police. He denied any wrongdoing and was released pending further investigation and a charging decision. In June 2021 he applied for leave to remain as a Tier 2 Skilled Worker. His wife and daughter simultaneously applied for leave to remain as his dependants. In July 2021 the Home Office responded that consideration of the application would be deferred because Z had an outstanding criminal prosecution. It was accepted that that statement was wrong as no charging decision had been made. The Claimants served a pre-action letter of claim in February 2022. The Secretary of State for the Home Department replied that, as the application raised 'exceptionally complex issues', a decision would not be possible within the usual eight-week timeframe and was expected by 5 April 2022. The Claimants issued judicial review proceedings on 4 April 2022 in the absence of a decision on their pending immigration applications. In May 2022 the National Crime Agency ('NCA') informed the Home Office that a charging decision was expected in late August 2022.

The Upper Tribunal ('UT') refused the Claimants' application for permission to apply for judicial review, first on the papers and then at an oral hearing in July 2022. The UT Judge followed *R (on the application of X and Others) v Secretary of State for the Home Department* [2021] EWCA Civ 1480 and held that the Secretary of State had an implied power under the Immigration Act 1971 to defer, or delay, taking a decision on an application for leave to remain. The delay in the instant case was not considered arguably unlawful or irrational. The Judge noted that there was evidence that the money laundering investigation was ongoing and that the case file had been submitted to a Senior Crown Prosecutor for a charging decision. The Claimants appealed the UT's decision. They argued, *inter alia*, that the Judge had failed to take proper account of the ongoing restrictions they faced being subject to the 'hostile environment' and the best interests of the daughter. The Claimants were granted permission to appeal against the UT's decision, however they issued a further application for leave to remain in August 2023 under Article 8 ECHR. That application was expressed as an application to vary their outstanding application with Z's wife as lead applicant and Z and their daughter as her dependants.

On appeal, the two issues to be decided by the Court of Appeal were first, whether the Claimants' application in August 2023 had effectively rendered their appeal academic; and secondly, whether the Secretary of State's deferral of a substantive decision was lawful.

Held, dismissing the appeal:

(1) Paragraph 34BB(1) of the Immigration Rules HC 395 (as amended) provided that where an applicant had an outstanding application for entry clearance or permission to stay which had not been decided, any further application for entry clearance or permission to stay would be treated as an application to vary the previous application and only the most recent application would be considered. That paragraph was buttressed by version 7.0 of Home Office guidance titled 'Validation, Variation, Voiding and Withdrawal of Applications'. The Claimants accepted that their application for leave to remain would be considered on their August 2023 application, which post-dated the decision under appeal. The August 2023 application had materially varied the June 2021 application and the grounds on which the Claimants' application for leave to remain was based were now completely different. The clock had effectively stopped on the challenge to the deferment of the decision on the earlier application and associated delay on 9 August 2023. The Secretary of State was now required to make his substantive decision on the Claimants' application for leave to remain in the United Kingdom on the basis of the 'family route' rather than the 'skilled worker route'. The decisions on the June 2021 application, which were the focus of the earlier application for permission to apply for judicial review in the UT, were now likely to be largely irrelevant. The appeal was, therefore, rendered academic. However, as the point was taken within, and as part of, the appeal hearing itself, the arguments on the merits were addressed (*paras 19, 20, 32 and 33*).

(2) The UT Judge was right to found her refusal of permission to pursue judicial review on the basis of the decision in *X*, despite the different factual context. In almost every sense, the judgments in that case answered the Claimants' arguments. There was no material difference on the facts of the instant case between an implied statutory duty on the Secretary of State to make a decision in a reasonable time or a duty to act reasonably in a *Wednesbury* sense. The real question was whether on the facts of a particular case the exercise of a power to defer taking a decision on an application (whether pending the outcome of a criminal investigation or some other reason) was a lawful exercise of that power: *X* followed. What was lawful would be fact-sensitive, and what was a 'reasonable time' would inevitably involve a degree of elasticity or 'flexibility': *Secretary of State for the Home Department v R (S)* [2007] EWCA Civ 546 followed. On the instant facts, and given the apparent seriousness of the matters in respect of which Z had been arrested, the UT Judge was entitled to view the decision to defer as lawful. At the time of the UT Judge's decision, the delay had not become unlawful, irrational or unreasonable. The fact that a charging decision was still awaited, nearly three years after Z's arrest, was no doubt a particular frustration for the Claimants and the Secretary of State. The UT

Judge could not, however, be criticised for relying in July 2022 on the information provided by the NCA. She was entitled to expect that a charging decision would be made later that summer. The Judge correctly reflected in her decision that the June 2021 application was made out of time. She determined that any prejudice or detriment suffered by Z's wife and daughter had not been caused by the Secretary of State's delay in deciding their leave to remain application. The Claimants had been overstayers for well over a year by the time they made their June 2021 application. They had conceded that the Article 8 ECHR point was essentially a corollary of their submissions about the 'hostile environment' in which they had lived for some time. The fact that the situation had continued for much longer than they expected did not entitle them to assert any unlawful interference with their Article 8 rights as a consequence of the Secretary of State's decision-making: *Balajigari v Secretary of State for the Home Department* [2019] EWCA Civ 673 considered. Although not specifically referred to by the UT Judge, sections 117A, 117B(4) and 117B(5) of the Nationality, Immigration and Asylum Act 2002 were applicable in the circumstances. While the Judge's conclusion that Article 8 was 'not engaged' on the instant facts was vulnerable to challenge, had those matters been considered she would have reached the same conclusion as to the Secretary of State's lawful and rational decision-making (*paras 34 and 36 – 42*).

Cases referred to:

Asiansky Television Plc and Asiansky Properties Limited v Bayer-Rosin [2001] EWCA Civ 1792; [2010] 1 WLR 1082

Associated Provincial Picture Houses, Limited v Wednesbury Corporation [1947] EWCA Civ 1; [1948] 1 KB 223; [1947] 2 All ER 680

Audergon v La Baguette Ltd and Others [2002] EWCA Civ 10

Balajigari v Secretary of State for the Home Department; Kawos and Others v Secretary of State for the Home Department; Majumder and Another v Secretary of State for the Home Department; Albert v Secretary of State for the Home Department [2019] EWCA Civ 673; [2019] 1 WLR 4647; [2019] 4 All ER 998; [2019] Imm AR 1152; [2019] INLR 619

Denisov v Ukraine 2018 ECHR 76639/11

Gillberg v Sweden 2012 ECHR 41723/06

R v Secretary of State for the Home Office ex parte Salem [1999] UKHL 8; [1999] 1 AC 450; [1999] 2 WLR 483; [1999] 2 All ER 42

R (on the application of (1) Crowter and (2) Aidan Lea-Wilson (by his mother and litigation friend Maire Lea-Wilson) v Secretary of State for Health and Social Care [2022] EWCA Civ 1559; [2023] 1 WLR 989; [2023] 4 All ER 963

R (on the application of MA) v Secretary of State for the Home Department 8 November 2023 (JR-2022-LON-001664) UTIAC (unreported)

R (on the application of New London College Ltd) v Secretary of State for the Home Department; R (on the application of West London Vocational Training College) v Secretary of State for the Home Department [2013] UKSC 51; [2013] 1 WLR 2358; [2013] 4 All ER 195; [2014] Imm AR 151; [2014] INLR 66

R (on the application of TS) v Secretary of State for the Home Department [2010] EWHC 2614 (Admin); [2011] Imm AR 164

R (on the application of X and Others) v Secretary of State for the Home Department [2021] EWCA Civ 1480; [2021] 4 WLR 137

Secretary of State for the Home Department v R (S) [2007] EWCA Civ 546; [2007] ACD 94; [2007] Imm AR 781; [2007] INLR 450

Legislation and international instruments judicially considered:

Borders, Citizenship and Immigration Act 2009, section 55
European Convention on Human Rights, Article 8
Immigration Rules HC 395 (as amended), paragraph 34BB
Nationality, Immigration and Asylum Act 2002, sections 117A & 117B

Representation

Mr M Biggs instructed by Eldwick Law, for the Claimants;
Mr T Tabori instructed by the Government Legal Department, for the Secretary of State.

Judgment

This judgment was handed down remotely at 10.30am on 7 February 2024 by circulation to the parties or their representatives by e-mail and by release to the National Archives.

MR JUSTICE COBB:

Introduction

[1] This is an appeal against the decision of Upper Tribunal ('UT') Judge Frances, dated 22 July 2022, by which she refused the Appellants permission to apply for judicial review. By their application before the UT, the Appellants had sought to challenge decisions of the Respondent dated 28 July 2021 and/or 22 February 2022 deferring a substantive decision on their applications (dated 3 June 2021) for leave to remain in the United Kingdom. The First and Second Appellants are husband and wife; the Third Appellant is their daughter. They are all Chinese nationals. The appeal is brought with permission of Males LJ dated 24 July 2023.

The factual background

[2] The First Appellant arrived in the United Kingdom from China in August 2005, with leave to enter until 2006. He was permitted to remain in this country under a sequence of subsequent permissions until April 2018. The Second Appellant joined him in 2010. The Third Appellant was born in China but has in fact lived in this country for most of her life. In March 2018, the First Appellant applied for indefinite leave to remain as a Tier 1 General (Migrant) Worker under the points based system; this application was refused. He applied for administrative review of that decision which was also refused. In 2019 he applied for judicial review of the decision, but this application was withdrawn by him in March 2020.

[3] On the 24 March 2021, the First Appellant was arrested with others on suspicion of money laundering over an 18 month period; he was interviewed by the police. He was released pending further investigation and charging decision. He denies involvement in any wrongdoing.

[4] On 3 June 2021, the First Appellant applied for leave to remain in the United Kingdom as a Tier 2 Skilled Worker (a financial analyst). I shall refer to this as the 'June 2021 application'. He was sponsored by a financial services company which wished to employ him; the Second and Third Appellants simultaneously applied for leave to remain as the First Appellant's dependants. By this time, all the Appellants had been overstayers under the Immigration Act 1971 for many months; from June 2019 they were on immigration bail.

[5] In response to that application, on 28 July 2021 the Home Office (Work Sponsored Routes Team) sent a communication to the First Appellant in these terms:

"Although we would normally decide your application within eight weeks from the date it was submitted, unfortunately this is not going to be possible in your case.

This is because records show that you have an *outstanding criminal prosecution*. No decision will be taken on your application until this matter has been concluded …." [emphasis added]

[6] It is now accepted by the Respondent that the Home Office team was wrong then to rely on an 'outstanding criminal prosecution' as a reason for deferring the decision; no charging decision had then (or indeed even now) been made in relation to the matters in respect of which the First Appellant had been arrested, and there was no outstanding or pending criminal prosecution. It is also clear (and rightly conceded on behalf of the Respondent in the UT) that the First Appellant's situation did not fall within the Home Office's 'Impending Prosecutions' Guidance (2016) (then in force). That guidance was supplemented by the Home Office's guidance 'General Grounds for Refusal – Criminality' of November 2021, and replaced in August 2022 by the Home Office's guidance 'Pending Prosecutions'. In the response to the judicial review before the UT in 2022 the Respondent referred to this explanation for her decision as a "technical breach", given that, irrespective of the import of the 2016 Guidance, there was and is in fact an outstanding criminal investigation, which she maintained gave her an implied power to defer determination of the application for leave to remain. I return to this later.

[7] On 15 February 2022, the Appellants served on the Respondent a pre-application letter of claim. This provoked a reply on 22 February 2022 in these terms:

"… Although we would normally decide your application within eight weeks from the date it was submitted, unfortunately this is not going to be possible in your case. This is because your *application raises exceptionally complex issues* and we require further time to consider your case thoroughly and reach a decision.

I am sorry for the delay in dealing with your application and for the inconvenience this is causing. Please be assured that we are doing all we can to make a decision on your case as quickly as possible.

We expect to make a decision on your application by 5th April 2022, but we will write to you again if this is not going to be possible." [emphasis added]

[8] On 4 April 2022, the Appellants issued proceedings for judicial review seeking to challenge the decisions of 28 July 2021 and 22 February 2022 "in the absence of a decision on their pending immigration applications". The Respondent filed an acknowledgement of service and set out her grounds for contesting the claim.

[9] On 10 May 2022, the National Crime Agency ('NCA') e-mailed the Respondent as follows:

"I can confirm that on the 10/05/2022 a case file … was submitted to [a] Senior Crown Prosecutor … for a decision to charge. This is regarding money laundering offences believed to have been committed by [the First Appellant] and others. After consultation with the Crown Prosecution Service ('CPS'), a provisional date of late August 2022 was given for a decision to be made by the lawyer. Obviously this is subject to change and is dependent upon further consultations with the CPS and lawyers etc. A Released Under Investigation (RIU) letter will be sent in due course to [the First Appellant] and others …. I am aware that this matter has taken some considerable time to reach this stage, but I am confident of a positive response from the CPS. Thank you for your patience in this matter and I will update as and when I am able."

[10] On 7 June 2022, UT Judge Sheridan considered the Appellants' application for permission to apply for judicial review on the papers. He refused it. The Appellants renewed their application for an oral hearing.

The Upper Tribunal's decision

[11] Following an oral hearing on 22 July 2022, UT Judge Frances refused the Appellants' renewed application for judicial review. The order reads as follows:

"(1) The applicants challenge the respondent's ongoing failure to decide their applications for further leave to remain as a skilled worked [*sic*] and dependants made on 3 June 2021. The respondent wrote to the applicants on 28 July 2021 stating the applications would not be decided within the standard processing time of eight weeks owing to 'an outstanding criminal prosecution'.

(2) It is not in dispute the applicants' leave to remain expired on 8 October 2018 and they have remained in the UK without leave since then. On 24 March 2021, the first applicant was arrested on suspicion of money laundering and released under investigation pending a Crown Prosecution Service charging decision.

(3) The alleged mistake of fact is not material given the respondent's guidance: 'grounds for refusal criminality' (the guidance) is not relied on by the respondent.

(4) Following *R (on the application of X and others) v SSHD* [2021] EWCA Civ 1480, the respondent has an implied power under the Immigration Act 1971 to defer, or delay, taking a decision on an application for leave to remain. The issue is whether that power had been exercised lawfully. I am not persuaded that this decision can be distinguished on its facts or on the basis the court did not consider the guidance.

(5) The investigation into money laundering offences is relevant to the first applicant's character and conduct. There is evidence that the investigation is ongoing and the case file has been submitted to the Senior Crown Prosecutor for a decision to charge.

(6) The application for further leave was made out of time. Any prejudice or detriment suffered by the second and third applicants as a result of being subjected to the 'hostile environment' was not caused by the respondent's delay. On the facts asserted, Article 8 is not engaged.

(7) The respondent's delay in taking a decision on the applications for leave to remain was not arguably unlawful or irrational."

[12] It is against this decision that the Appellants now appeal.

[13] The application for permission to appeal was placed before Males LJ on 23 June 2023. Doubtless he was mindful of the indication from the NCA in May 2022 (see § 9 above), so he directed the Respondent to file a statement in accordance with CPR PD52C.19 within 21 days, to advise whether the First Appellant had indeed been charged with any (and if so what) offence. On 17 July 2023, the Government Legal Department on behalf of the Respondent replied by letter:

"… the CID records, updated on 10 July 2023 states: – 'Impending Prosecution'. Please do not casework, place case on hold new checks 6 weeks."

The letter contained a request for more time to provide the key information, but in fact no further information was provided.

[14] Males LJ gave permission to appeal on 24 July 2023; he was of the view that "it is arguable that there has been more than enough time for the prosecuting authorities to decide whether to charge the [First Appellant] and that a decision on the application should now be made".

[15] On 9 August 2023, the Appellants issued a further application for leave to remain in the United Kingdom (the 'August 2023 application'). This is expressed in the accompanying letter as an application "to vary their outstanding application for [Leave to Remain]". In this application, the Second Appellant is the lead applicant; the First and Third Appellants apply as her dependants. The application is made under Article 8 ECHR (the 'family route'). Mr Tabori told us that this application will therefore be processed by a different team from the team who determined the June 2021 application.

[16] In respect of the August 2023 application, Mr Tabori advised us that it is likely that the Respondent will again defer a decision in relation to the First Appellant's application (in which he now applies as a dependant) given the ongoing police investigation and the absence of a charging decision. In this regard, he added that on 18 January 2024 (i.e., four working days before the appeal hearing) the NCA

apparently provided further evidence to the CPS in relation to its criminal investigation concerning the First Appellant, and (once again) it is said that a decision on charge is soon to be expected. Mr Tabori could not say how the Respondent would be likely to respond to the new application by the Second and Third Appellant.

Review or Re-Hearing

[17] Mr Biggs invited us to consider dealing with this appeal by way of a rehearing of the application for permission to apply for judicial review, rather than a review of the decision of UT Judge Frances (per CPR rule 52.21(1)(a)/(b)). He relied on the case of *Audergon v La Baguette Ltd & Others* [2002] EWCA Civ 10 at [83](3) ("the decision to hold a rehearing must inevitably rest on the circumstances of the particular appeal"). Insofar as any assistance in deciding that question is available, some is to be found in *Asiansky Television plc & Anor v Bayer-Rosin* [2001] EWCA civ 1792 (cited extensively in *Audergon*) wherein at [82] Dyson LJ, as he then was, commented that a rehearing may be appropriate:

"... if the judgment of the lower court is so inadequately reasoned that it is not possible for the appeal court to determine the appeal justly without a rehearing; or if there was a serious procedural irregularity in the court below so that, for example, the appellant was prevented from developing his case properly."

[18] The request for a re-hearing in this case was plainly driven by the Appellants' contention that it would be in the "interests of justice" for this court to consider the continuing deferment of the substantive decision by the Respondent on the Appellants' application for leave to remain, while awaiting a charging decision in respect of the First Appellant. However, the submission failed, in my judgement, to take proper account of the fact that any re-hearing of the application for permission to apply for judicial review by this court would need also to consider the impact of the August 2023 application, as to which, crucially, the Respondent has not yet made any decision. A re-hearing in this case would in the circumstances be largely, if not entirely, futile. I was therefore unpersuaded that it is in the interests of justice to proceed in the way proposed by Mr Biggs. I am of the view that the appeal should be determined, conventionally, by way of review of the decision of the UT.

The August 2023 application and this appeal

[19] Mr Tabori raised the preliminary point that the August 2023 application had effectively rendered the appeal academic. The appeal before us concerns the Respondent's decisions to defer determination of an application which will, in light of more recent events, in fact no longer be considered. He suggested that this short point should summarily dispose of this appeal. He relied on rule 34BB of the Immigration Rules which provides that:

"(1) Where an applicant has an outstanding application for entry clearance or permission to stay which has not been decided ("the previous application"), any further application for entry clearance or permission to stay will be treated as an application to vary the previous application *and only the most recent application will be considered.*" [emphasis added]

[20] Rule 34BB is buttressed by the Home office Guidance on "Validation, Variation, Voiding and Withdrawal of Applications" (Version 7.0) ('the Variation Guidance') which provides that:

"Where a person submits an application under the Immigration Rules and has a previous application that has not yet been decided, *the latest application varies the previous application and only the new application will be considered.*" [emphasis added]

[21] The rules make clear that a second or subsequent application will trigger a notification from the Respondent to an applicant to the effect that "the application is being treated as an application to vary and that any previous application will have been varied" (rule 34BB(4)). It will also generate a refund of the fee of the first application (page 23 of the Variation Guidance). We were told that these steps have not in fact yet been taken in this case because of an apparent ongoing digital technology issue at the Home Office.

[22] Mr Biggs accepts that his clients' application for leave to remain will now be considered on their August 2023 application, which of course post-dates the decision under appeal. He argues that it is still relevant for this court to consider the decision of the UT to refuse the application for permission to bring judicial review against the Respondent's decisions on the June 2021 application; he contends that the earlier decisions will be relevant to (and may possibly be re-stated in respect of) the August 2023 application, and ought therefore to be considered on this appeal.

[23] Although raised as a preliminary point, Mr Tabori did not seek to persuade us to rule on this discretely before considering the merits of the appeal. We therefore heard the arguments on the appeal. I set out my conclusions on this preliminary point at § 32 below.

The arguments

[24] It is the Appellants' case that UT Judge Frances was wrong to conclude that there was not a properly arguable case when she refused their applications for permission to apply for judicial review of the Respondent's decision(s) to *defer* determining their applications (June 2021) for leave to remain in the United Kingdom.

[25] While the Appellants accept that the Respondent has an incidental power to defer decision-making (acknowledging the import of the Court of Appeal's decision in *Regina (X and others) v Secretary of State for the Home Department* [2021] EWCA Civ 1480) ("*R (X) v SSHD*"), they nonetheless asserted that in order to be lawful, the decision to defer must take full account of the individual facts of the case, and the delay caused by the deferment must not be unreasonable in all the circumstances. In this case, the Appellants contended that the UT Judge failed to take proper account, when rejecting their application, of the fact that they are currently subject to the so-called "hostile environment" which includes severe restrictions on the right to work, rent accommodation, access to the National Health Service, and/or the ability to have a bank account; reliance was placed in this regard on *Balajigari v Secretary of State for the Home Department* [2019] EWCA Civ 673

at [81] and [91] ("*Balajigari*"). They also contended that the UT Judge was wrong to reject the Article 8 rights of the Appellants; Mr Biggs accepted that although not specifically pleaded, the Article 8 rights fell to be considered "as a corollary" of his arguments about the "hostile environment". They further asserted that the UT Judge failed to consider the absence of any reference by the Respondent in her decision to the best interests of the Third Appellant (in this regard, relying on section 55 Borders, Citizenship and Immigration Act 2009).

[26] Mr Biggs further argued that the UT Judge was wrong to reject as unarguable the Appellants' case that the Respondent's *delay* in making the substantive decision on these facts was unlawful (in the sense that it was in breach of an implied statutory obligation to make a decision within a reasonable time) or unreasonable (in the *Wednesbury* sense). The point on delay was not front and centre of the pleaded grounds before us, but I accept that it was incorporated into the Grounds of Appeal by way of cross-reference to the Grounds of Claim before the UT. He emphasised passages from Andrews LJ's judgment in *R (X) v SSHD* (notably at [52]) and the judgment of Carnwath LJ, as he then was, in *R (S) v SSHD* [2007] EWCA Civ 546 at [51] ("*R (S) v SSHD*"). It is right to note that the decisions of both UT Judge Sheridan and UT Judge Frances referred to the "*ongoing* failure" of the Respondent to decide the Appellants' applications for leave to remain. Indeed such a finding (i.e., of *ongoing* failure) was essential in the court below (albeit not now) given that the Appellants would otherwise have been significantly out of time in launching their application for judicial review against the Respondent's first (28 July 2021) decision (CPR rule 54.5).

[27] The Grounds of Appeal further included complaint that the Respondent had initially allegedly unlawfully deferred the decision because the First Appellant was the subject of an "outstanding criminal prosecution"; it was said that she had misapplied the 2016 Guidance. The Appellants now accept that the Respondent was entitled to take into account the arrest of the First Appellant, and the ongoing police investigation into alleged criminal activity, irrespective of the precise terms of the 2016 Guidance. In any event, the Respondent's second decision (22 February 2022) made no reference at all to any alleged "prosecution" of the First Appellant.

[28] Mr Biggs finally submitted that if as a consequence of the judicial review leave to remain had been granted, it could later be curtailed under Part 9 of the Immigration Rules; this was rightly not pursued with any vigour.

[29] On behalf of the Respondent, Mr Tabori argued that the Respondent possesses a number of implied ancillary and incidental administrative powers to facilitate the effective administration of the system of immigration control; these are not expressly spelt out in the Immigration Acts: *R (New London College Ltd) v SSHD* [2013] 1 WLR 2358 at § 28–29 (Lord Sumption). He argued that those implied powers include a power to decide when and how applications for leave to remain are to be dealt with, including a power in appropriate circumstances to defer taking a decision on an application: see also *R (X) v SSHD*, § 31 (Lewis LJ). Exercise of that power is subject to judicial review on established public law grounds (*ibid.*).

[30] He observed that the claim based on Article 8 ECHR was not heralded in the Grounds of Appeal. Insofar as the Appellant purports to rely on this now, he argued that reliance on Article 8 in this case is misplaced because the claimed interference is self-induced; before their June 2021 application for leave to remain, the Appellants had already put themselves in a position of being unable to return to the United Kingdom following any trip to China. They had already been refused

indefinite leave to remain. They were subject of notices of liability to removal. He referenced the *Gillberg* principle (cf. *Gillberg v Sweden*, application no 41723/06, decision dated 3 April 2012 [GC]), namely, that Article 8 cannot be relied on in order to complain of personal, social, psychological and economic suffering which is a foreseeable consequence of one's own actions, such as the commission of a criminal offence or similar misconduct: *Denisov v Ukraine* (Application no. 76639/11) [GC], §§ 98 and 121. Moreover, he argued, the claimed interference is *de minimis* in the case of the Third Appellant given that at its height, the evidence of the First Appellant is that she has "become rather withdrawn and anxious due to these ongoing issues".

[31] Mr Tabori further contended that any alleged "error of fact" which may be deduced from the 28 July 2021 decision was immaterial because, as the UT Judge held, a power to defer a decision exists behind the investigations of third party agencies; this was identified by the Court of Appeal in *R (X) v SSHD* § 31 and was held to have been rationally exercised on the very similar facts of that case.

Discussion and conclusion

[32] I turn, first, to the Respondent's preliminary submission that the appeal is now academic in light of the August 2023 application (see § 19–23 above). Counsel agree, and the position is indeed clear, that the August 2023 application has materially varied the June 2021 application; indeed, the grounds on which the Appellants' application for leave to remain is based are now completely different. I agree with Mr Tabori that the "clock effectively stopped" on the challenge to the deferment of the decision on the earlier application (and associated delay) on 9 August 2023. Both counsel agree that the Respondent will now be required to make his substantive decision on the Appellants' application for leave to remain in the United Kingdom on the basis the "family route" rather than the "skilled worker route". It seems to me that the decision(s) on the June 2021 application, which were the focus of the earlier application for permission to apply for judicial review in the UT, are now likely to be irrelevant, or largely so. For these reasons, I found myself persuaded to Mr Tabori's submission that the August 2023 application has rendered the appeal academic.

[33] Had this preliminary point been taken discretely, and had it required a separate and immediate determination, it follows that this court may well not have gone on (had we followed the direction of Lord Slynn in his speech in *R v Secretary of State for the Home Office ex parte Salem* [1991] 1AC 450 (HL) at pp.456–457) to hear, let alone determine, the merits of the arguments on the appeal. However, the point was taken within, and as part of, the appeal hearing itself, and I therefore address the arguments on the merits which were ably presented on both sides.

[34] In my judgement, UT Judge Frances was not just entitled, she was indeed right, to found her refusal to give permission to the Appellants to pursue judicial review on the basis of this court's judgment in *R (X) v SSHD* (see § 11(4) above). In almost every sense, the judgments in that case answered the Appellants' arguments notwithstanding the somewhat different factual context. Lewis LJ recognised and articulated (at [31]) the Respondent's power to act in ways expressly authorised by the Immigration Act 1971, and/or to act in ways which are ancillary or incidental to the exercise of the functions conferred by the Act. At [32] he added:

"The function of regulating immigration in this way necessarily involves the Secretary of State having power to establish a system for receiving, considering and deciding on such applications. It includes *a power to decide when and how such applications are to be dealt with including a power in appropriate circumstances to defer taking a decision on an application.* That power is ancillary or incidental to the exercise of the functions relating to the administration and control of immigration conferred by the Act. The exercise of that power will be subject to review in accordance with the established rules of public law to ensure that the decision is not irrational and does not run counter to the purposes of the Act. *A power to defer a decision pending the outcome of a criminal investigation is, therefore, incidental and ancillary to the Secretary of State's functions under the Act.* There is no rational basis for interpreting the scope of the power to defer a decision as excluding deferrals pending the outcome of a criminal investigation. Rather, the question is whether, on the facts of a particular case, the exercise of a power to defer taking a decision on an application (whether pending the outcome of a criminal investigation or some other reason) is a lawful exercise of that power." [emphasis added]

[35] On the facts of this case, as on the facts in *R (X) v SSHD*, it is relevant to note further what Lewis LJ said at [45]:

"… there is a rational link between the reasons for deferring a decision on the applications for leave and the grounds upon which leave may be granted or refused. Rule 245DD(1) provides that the application for leave to remain must not fall for refusal under the general grounds. These include the ground in paragraph 322(5) of the Rules, namely the undesirability of permitting the person concerned to remain in the United Kingdom in the light of "his conduct … character or associations". The information emerging in the criminal investigation into an alleged conspiracy to commit fraud or alleged money laundering was, potentially, relevant to the first claimant's conduct, character or associations. *The respondent is entitled to make further enquiries or seek further information if she considers that that information is potentially relevant to the decision to be taken.*" [emphasis added]

[36] I was unpersuaded by Mr Biggs' argument that there is any material difference on the facts of this case between an implied statutory duty on the Respondent to make a decision in a reasonable time or a duty to act reasonably in a *Wednesbury* sense. Insofar as he based his argument on Andrew LJ's judgment in *R (X) v SSHD*, I was not convinced that her judgment bore out his interpretation. In any event, as Lewis LJ (with whom Moylan LJ agreed) said in *R (X) v SSHD* at [32], the real question is whether on the facts of a particular case:

"… the exercise of a power to defer taking a decision on an application (whether pending the outcome of a criminal investigation or some other reason) is a lawful exercise of that power."

[37] What is lawful will be "fact-sensitive", and what is a "reasonable time" will inevitably involve a degree of elasticity or "flexibility" (*per* Carnwath LJ at [51] in *R (S) v SSHD)*. On the facts of this case, and given the apparent seriousness of the matters in respect of which the First Appellant has been arrested and questioned,

the UT Judge was entitled in my judgement to the view that the Respondent's decision to defer was lawful.

[38] In my judgement, at the time of the UT Judge's decision, and on the facts of this particular case, the delay had not – as she rightly found – become either "unlawful or irrational" or unreasonable (see § 11(7) above). It is notable that in the case of *R (X) v SSHD*, there was an ongoing delay in the decision-making (as a result of the Respondent awaiting a decision of the CPS) which stood at 4½ years at the time of the appeal. In this context, we were also referred to the recently delivered judgment in *R (MA) v SSHD* UT(IAC) (November 2023) (JR-2022-LON-001664: unreported); this was a case, similar in material respects to the instant case, in which an applicant challenged the SSHD's ongoing delay in deciding an application for leave to remain against the background of a criminal investigation into money laundering involving the applicant's husband. In that case, the head of the Home Office Migrant Criminality Policy Unit had given evidence to UT Judge Canavan (in the same vein as his evidence in *R (X) v SSHD* before the UT) to this effect:

"… it would be reasonable and proportionate to await the outcome of the HMRC investigation and/or any criminal proceedings relating to the applicant's husband before deciding the application given the seriousness and scale of the HMRC investigation. It would not be proportionate for the respondent to review the large amount of material involved in the investigation for herself." (Judgment [12]).

The Judge agreed with this approach and, having considered *R (X) v SSHD* at length, observed that:

"While acknowledging that the delay of *over three years* is significant, and no doubt frustrating for the applicant, I conclude that the respondent's decision to await the outcome of any charging decision is not unlawful at the current time." [emphasis added]

[39] I am conscious that a charging decision is still awaited in this case, nearly three years after the First Appellant's arrest; this is no doubt a particular frustration to the Appellants, but I suspect also a frustration to the Respondent. In my judgement the UT Judge cannot be criticised for relying in July 2022 on information provided to her by the NCA that the case file had recently been sent to the Senior Crown Prosecutor for a decision as to charge. She was entitled to expect, on information provided to her, that a charging decision would be made later in the summer, albeit "dependent upon further consultations with the CPS and lawyers" (see § 11(5) above).

[40] The UT Judge rightly reflected in her decision that the June 2021 application was made out of time; she determined that any prejudice or detriment suffered by the Second and Third Appellants as a result of being subjected to the "hostile environment" was not caused by the Respondent's delay in deciding on their application for leave to remain. It is right to point out that the Appellants had been overstayers and subject to that "hostile environment" for well over a year by the time they made their June 2021 application. They were subject to notices of liability to removal. Having withdrawn their challenge to the refusal of their previous application for leave to remain, they then chose to remain in the United Kingdom unlawfully, and to endure the so-called "hostile environment".

[41] The Appellants did not specifically plead reliance on Article 8 ECHR as a freestanding point in this appeal; Mr Biggs concedes that the Article 8 point is essentially a "corollary" of his submission about the "hostile environment" in which the Appellants have now lived for some time (see § 40 above). While the Article 8 rights of the Appellants were impacted when they were refused indefinite leave to remain in October 2018, they did not in the end challenge that decision. In June 2019 they became subject to notices of liability to removal. This was the situation when the June 2021 application was made; that this situation has continued for much longer than the Appellants had expected does not in my judgement entitle them to assert any unlawful interference with their Article 8 rights as a consequence of the Respondent's decision-making. The decision in *Balajigari* supports them only to a limited extent; the court there merely contemplated at [91] (and not as the basis for the court's decision) that the legal consequences of being in the United Kingdom without leave "may" engage Article 8:

"… but their impact will vary from case to case and, further, in the generality of cases *if the refusal of leave is itself justified the interference caused by the legal consequences of such refusal are very likely to be justified too*." [emphasis added]

Although not specifically referred to by UT Judge Frances, sections 117A/117B(4)/117B(5) of the Nationality Immigration and Asylum Act 2002 apply in these circumstances, and in my judgement bear materially upon this point.

[42] Thus, while the UT Judge's conclusion that Article 8 was "not engaged" on these facts (see § 11(6)) is at least vulnerable to challenge, I am satisfied that had the UT Judge explicitly taken into consideration the points discussed above, she would have reached the same conclusion as to the Respondent's lawful and rational decision-making.

[43] For completeness, I add that I am unpersuaded by Mr Biggs' further submission that the Respondent had failed to comply with her duty to ensure that her functions are discharged "having regard to the need to safeguard and promote the welfare of children who are in the United Kingdom" (section 55 of the Borders, Citizenship and Immigration Act 2009, as usefully interpreted by Wyn Williams J in *R (TS) v SSHD* [2010] EWHC 2614 (Admin) at [32]: "at least an important consideration"). At the time when the Respondent discharged her functions, the Third Appellant was in the care of her parents, and attending school; that she was an overstayer was essentially a decision of her parents, exercising (as they are entitled to do) their parental responsibility for her. The Third Appellant's "anxiety" (see § 30 above) at the uncertainty of her current situation (however understandable) was not said to have impacted significantly on her welfare, any more than it reached the threshold of seriousness which is necessary to engage Article 8(1): see *R (Crowter) v SSHSC* [2023] 1 W.L.R. 989, § 129 (Peter Jackson LJ).

[44] For the reasons set out herein, I would dismiss the appeal.

LADY JUSTICE WHIPPLE:

[45] I agree.

LADY JUSTICE KING:

[46] I also agree.

R (ON THE APPLICATION OF VLT (VIETNAM)) v SECRETARY OF STATE FOR THE HOME DEPARTMENT (TRAFFICKING, DL POLICY, TRANSITIONAL PROVISIONS, DEPORTATION)

UPPER TRIBUNAL (IMMIGRATION AND ASYLUM CHAMBER)

Frances UTJ

[2024] UKUT 67 (IAC)
8 February 2024

Immigration – Home Office policies and concessions – victims of trafficking – discretionary leave policy – transitional provisions – deportation exception

The Applicant, a citizen of Vietnam, had travelled to the United Kingdom on a number of occasions and had previously undergone deportation. He had been trafficked to the United Kingdom and forced to cultivate cannabis to repay a debt he owed. He was convicted of conspiracy to produce cannabis and sentenced to eight months' imprisonment in June 2012. The Secretary of State for the Home Department made a deportation order in January 2013. The Applicant claimed asylum in June 2018 based on a well-founded fear of being re-trafficked on return to Vietnam. In May 2018, he was referred to the National Referral Mechanism. The Single Competent Authority concluded that he was a victim of trafficking and issued a positive conclusive grounds decision in September 2022. In October 2022, the Applicant made further submissions in respect of his deportation. The Secretary of State refused his protection and human rights claim in August 2023. The Applicant had a pending appeal against the refusal to revoke his deportation order on asylum, humanitarian protection and human rights grounds.

In November 2022, the Applicant requested discretionary leave to remain ('DL'). Those representations were supported by a psychological report. In June 2023, the Secretary of State refused temporary permission to stay ('VTS') under the policy guidance: 'Temporary Permission to Stay considerations for Victims of Human Trafficking or Slavery', version 3.0, published on 8 June 2023 ('VTSP'). She considered that it was not necessary for the Applicant to receive VTS for a medical reason. She went on to state that consideration had been given to part 9 of the Immigration Rules HC 395 (as amended) and VTS must be refused because 'previous behaviour [was] deemed not conducive to the public good'.

On judicial review, the Applicant challenged the Secretary of State's decision on the grounds that she had considered the wrong policy and/or failed to grant limited leave to remain under version 10 of the policy guidance on Discretionary Leave published on 16 March 2023 ('DLP'). The Applicant raised three grounds. First, the refusal to grant DL/decision to exclude the Applicant from consideration for a grant of leave under the DLP was in breach of Article 14(1)(a) of the Council of Europe Convention on Action against Trafficking in Human Beings ('ECAT') which was implemented at the relevant time by the DLP. Secondly, the DLP breached Article 14(1)(a) ECAT and Article 4 ECHR. Thirdly, the decision to refuse VTS was unlawful owing to the Secretary of State's failure to take into account material expert evidence and/or her erroneous approach to the evidence.

Held, granting the application:

(1) The VTSP clearly demonstrated a shift in policy intention as regards how the Secretary of State complied with the obligations under ECAT. In particular, the VTSP did not intend to apply Article 14(1)(a) ECAT which stated that a renewable residence permit should be granted to victims of trafficking if the competent authority considered that their stay was necessary owing to their personal situation. The DLP expressed no such intention. The DLP identified two categories of modern slavery cases. Post-30 January 2023 modern slavery cases would be considered under the VTSP based on the criteria in section 65 of the Nationality and Borders Act 2022 ('NABA 2022'). Pre-30 January 2023 modern slavery cases would be considered under the DLP. The DLP made transitional provisions in respect of victims of trafficking who had received a positive conclusive grounds decision and had an outstanding asylum claim before 30 January 2023. Those transitional provisions were intended to give effect to Article 14(1)(a) ECAT and *EOG and KTT v Secretary of State for the Home Department* [2022] EWCA Civ 307 in respect of victims of trafficking who received a positive conclusive grounds decision and had an outstanding asylum claim, based in a material part on a well-founded fear of being re-trafficked, before 30 January 2023 ('DLMS Cases') (*paras 38 – 45*).

(2) Having committed to giving effect to Article 14(1)(a) in respect of pre-30 January 2023 cases, the DLP carved out an exception for those DLMS Cases that were subject to deportation proceedings ('the deportation carve out'). There was no public order exception in Article 14(1)(a). The deportation carve out in the DLP made no reference to the definition of a foreign criminal or whether an individual posed a threat to public order. Imposing a blanket requirement not to be subject to a deportation order failed to give effect to the obligation in Article 14(1)(a) to consider whether the applicant's stay was necessary owing to their personal situation and was contrary to the transitional provisions in respect of DLMS Cases implementing *EOG and KTT*. Accordingly, the deportation carve out was unlawful in so far as it excluded individuals who were not a threat to public order or foreign criminals within the meaning given by section 32(1) of the UK Borders Act 2007 ('the 2007 Act') from benefiting from the transitional provisions. The deportation carve out was incompatible with the obligations in Article 14(1)(a) ECAT and contrary to the requirements of sections 63 and 65 of NABA 2022 currently in force (*paras 46 – 57*).

(3) The conclusive grounds decision found that the Applicant was subject to forced criminality which resulted in a single conviction for which he was sentenced to eight months' imprisonment. The Applicant was not a threat to public order. Under section 63 NABA 2022, the Applicant was not a foreign national offender and section 32 of the 2007 Act did not apply. He would not be excluded from a grant of leave to remain under the VTSP or Appendix: Temporary Permission to Stay for Victims of Human Trafficking or Slavery to the Immigration Rules ('IR-VTS') on suitability grounds notwithstanding his deportation order. There was no lawful basis to exclude the Applicant from the benefit of the transitional provisions in the DLP on the basis of his extant deportation order which did not meet the current threshold for public order disqualification. His personal situation brought

him within the transitional provisions of the DLP and the decision to refuse DL and/or refuse to consider DL under the DLP was unlawful. Accordingly, the first ground succeeded (*paras 58 – 63*).

(4) The obligations under Article 4 ECHR and the obligations under the transitional provisions in the DLP, which intended to comply with the obligations in Article 14(1)(a), had to be analysed separately. The application of the DLP was not a mechanism by which the United Kingdom satisfied its procedural obligations under Article 4: *Secretary of State for the Home Department v Hoang Anh Minh* [2016] EWCA Civ 565 applied. Article 4 did not have the effect of incorporating Article 14(1)(a) ECAT adopted by *EOG and KTT* into domestic law via the Human Rights Act 1998. Accordingly, the second ground failed (*paras 64 – 72*).

(5) The refusal of VTS was unlawful because the Secretary of State had applied the wrong policy. The reference in the Secretary of State's refusal letter to part 9 of the Immigration Rules was misconceived. A grant of VTS was made under the criteria in IR-VTS. The refusal on the basis that VTS must be refused because 'previous behaviour [was] deemed not conducive to the public good' was clearly wrong and demonstrated the decision-maker's misunderstanding of the relevant applicable rules and policy. Accordingly, the third ground succeeded (*paras 73 – 75*).

Cases referred to:

EOG v Secretary of State for the Home Department; KTT v Secretary of State for the Home Department [2022] EWCA Civ 307; [2023] QB 351; [2022] 3 WLR 353; [2022] Imm AR 991; [2022] INLR 213, on appeal from *R (on the application of KTT) v Secretary of State for the Home Department* [2021] EWHC 2722 (Admin); [2022] 1 WLR 1312

R (on the application of AB) v Secretary of State for the Home Department [2021] UKSC 28; [2022] AC 487; [2021] 3 WLR 494; [2021] 4 All ER 777

R (on the application of TDT, by his Litigation Friend Tara Topteagarden) v Secretary of State for the Home Department [2018] EWCA Civ 1395; [2018] 1 WLR 4922

Rantsev v Cyprus and Russia 2010 ECHR 25965/04; (2010) 51 EHRR 1

SM v Croatia 2020 ECHR 60561/14; (2021) 72 EHRR 1

Secretary of State for the Home Department v Hoang Anh Minh [2016] EWCA Civ 565; [2016] Imm AR 1272; [2017] INLR 267

VCL and AN v United Kingdom 2021 ECHR 77587/12 & 74603/12; (2021) 73 EHRR 9

XY v Secretary of State for the Home Department [2024] EWHC 81 (Admin)

Legislation and international instruments judicially considered:

Council of Europe Convention on Action against Trafficking in Human Beings, Articles 13 & 14(1)

European Convention on Human Rights, Article 4

Human Rights Act 1998, section 6

Immigration Rules HC 395 (as amended), paragraphs VTS 2.1 & VTS 3.1 – 3.4 of Appendix: Temporary Permission to Stay for Victims of Human Trafficking or Slavery

[2024] Imm AR 2

Nationality and Borders Act 2022, sections 63 & 65
UK Borders Act 2007, section 32

Representation

Ms G Mellon and Ms E Doerr instructed by Turpin Miller, for the Applicant;
Mr M Biggs instructed by the Government Legal Department, for the Secretary of State.

Judgment

UPPER TRIBUNAL JUDGE FRANCES:

Introduction

[1] The applicant is an asylum seeker and confirmed victim of trafficking. Having considered the Presidential Guidance on Anonymity Orders, I make an order under Rule 14 of the Procedure Rules.

[2] This application for judicial review is concerned with the interpretation of policy guidance in respect of victims of trafficking who received a positive conclusive grounds decision and had an outstanding asylum claim before 30 January 2023. The applicant in this case was also subject to a deportation order.

[3] The central issue is the interpretation of the policy guidance on Discretionary Leave, version 10, published on 16 March 2023 (DLP). Reference to the DLP is to this version of the policy guidance.

Decision under challenge

[4] The applicant challenges the respondent's decision of 12 June 2023 refusing temporary permission to stay under the policy guidance: Temporary Permission to Stay considerations for Victims of Human Trafficking or Slavery, version 3.0, published on 8 June 2023 (VTSP). Reference to the VTSP is to this version of the policy.

[5] The respondent considered the psychological report by Lisa Davies, the country information on Vietnam and the current circumstances questionnaire (CCQ) and concluded the applicant was not taking medication or receiving counselling and he could obtain treatment in Vietnam. The respondent refused temporary permission to stay (VTS) because it was not necessary for the applicant to receive VTS for a medical reason. The respondent went on to state that consideration had been given to part 9 of the Immigration Rules and VTS must be refused because "previous behaviour is deemed not conducive to the public good".

[6] The applicant also seeks to challenge the respondent's response to the pre-action protocol letter dated 4 August 2023. I find this is not a challengeable decision. It explains why the applicant's case was considered under the VTSP and not the DLP. I am satisfied the applicant challenges the decision of 12 June 2023 on the grounds the respondent considered the wrong policy and/or failed to grant limited leave to remain under the DLP.

R (ON THE APPLICATION OF VLT (VIETNAM)) (Frances UTJ)

Grounds

[7] The applicant challenges the decision of 12 June 2023 on 3 grounds (the applicant no longer relies on ground 2 alleging breach of a legitimate expectation):

a) *Ground 1*: The refusal to grant DL/decision to exclude the applicant from consideration for a grant of leave under the DLP was in breach of Article 14(1)(a) of the Council of Europe Convention on Action against Trafficking in Human Beings (ECAT) which was implemented at the relevant time by the DLP;

b) *Ground 3*: The DLP breaches Article 14(1)(a) of ECAT and Article 4 of the European Convention on Human Rights (ECHR); and

c) *Ground 4*: The decision to refuse VTS was unlawful owing to the respondent's failure to take into account material expert evidence and/or her erroneous approach to the evidence.

Agreed facts

[8] The applicant's immigration history is complex and is set out in the chronology at pages 101 to 104 of the Trial Bundle. The following relevant facts were agreed at the hearing at which the applicant relied on the respondent's decision dated 23 September 2022 referred to below.

[9] The applicant is a national of Vietnam and is 57 years old. He was trafficked to the UK on three occasions, in 2009, 2015 and 2018, and forced to cultivate cannabis to repay a debt he owed. He was convicted of conspiracy to produce cannabis and sentenced to 8 months' imprisonment on 26 June 2012. A deportation order was signed on 16 January 2013. The applicant claimed asylum on 1 June 2018 on the basis of a well-founded fear of being re-trafficked on return to Vietnam.

[10] On 29 May 2018, the applicant was referred to the National Referral Mechanism (NRM) and he received a positive reasonable grounds decision on 27 June 2018. The Single Competent Authority (SCA) concluded the applicant had given a consistent and plausible account corroborated by objective evidence. The SCA decided the applicant was a victim of trafficking, in Vietnam, Laos, Thailand and the UK and issued a positive conclusive grounds decision (CGD) dated 23 September 2022.

[11] On 26 October 2022, the applicant made further submissions in respect of his deportation and the respondent refused his protection and human rights claim on 15 August 2023. The applicant has a pending appeal against the refusal to revoke his deportation order on asylum, humanitarian protection and human rights grounds. He fears being re-trafficked on return to Vietnam. The applicant is not removable whilst his appeal is pending. He does not have permission to work and is accommodated and supported by the Vietnamese community in the UK.

[12] The applicant, through his solicitors, requested discretionary leave to remain (DL) by email on 10 November 2022. These representations were supported by a psychological report by Lisa Davies dated 21 July 2021. It is not in dispute that the applicant was not assisting a public authority with their enquiries or claiming compensation.

Relevant procedural history

[13] The applicant applied for permission to apply for judicial review on 15 September 2023. Expedition was granted and time was extended on the same date. Upper Tribunal Judge Norton-Taylor granted permission on 16 October 2023. The respondent raised the issue of jurisdiction in the summary grounds of defence (SGD). Judge Norton-Taylor was of the view that there was no challenge to the Immigration Rules or legislation and therefore the Upper Tribunal had jurisdiction. The respondent did not rely on this issue in his skeleton argument or at the hearing before me.

Chapter III ECAT

[14] Article 14 (1) of the ECAT provides:

"1. Each Party shall issue a renewable residence permit to victims, in one or other of the two following situations or in both:

(a) the competent authority considers that their stay is necessary owing to their personal situation;

(b) the competent authority considers that their stay is necessary for the purpose of their co-operation with the competent authorities in investigation or criminal proceedings."

[15] Article 13 of the ECAT provides for a 'recovery and reflection period' of at least 30 days when there are reasonable grounds to believe that the person concerned is a victim of trafficking. Article 13(3) provides an exception to the duty to provide the relevant recovery period where "grounds of public order prevent it." Article 14(1)(a) contains no exception on grounds of public order equivalent to that set out in Art 13(3).

Relevant authority

[16] In *EOG and KTT v SSHD* [2022] EWCA Civ 307 (*KTT*), Underhill LJ (with whom Dingemans LJ and Sir Geoffrey Vos MR agreed) considered justiciability as a preliminary issue and reviewed a number of cases in which the respondent's guidance about the treatment of victims of modern slavery and trafficking had been challenged on the basis they did not give proper effect to the requirements of chapter III of ECAT. It was recognised in all these cases that ECAT was not incorporated into UK law and did not have 'direct effect'. However, insofar as guidance intended to, and purported to, give effect to ECAT and failed to do so, that would be a justiciable error of law and a decision based on that error would be unlawful ([25]-[30]).

[17] Underhill LJ found that Linden J's analysis of this issue at [15]-[59] of his judgment (*R (KTT) v SSHD* [2021] EWHC 2722 (Admin)) was convincing and made two points in clarification. Firstly, many of the obligations imposed by ECAT were in general terms and it was a matter for the Government (subject to public law constraints) in what manner it chooses to implement them. It was always open to

the Government, since ECAT was unincorporated, to make it clear that it has chosen not to give effect to it. As a matter of constitutional principle such a decision could not be challenged in the domestic courts. Secondly, the conclusion that the guidance was unlawful was not the only possible outcome. Where the guidance was ambiguous it may be enough for the court to hold that a construction which complies with ECAT should be preferred to one which did not ([32]-[34]).

[18] Underhill LJ at [37] concluded that in principle there were two questions in cases of this kind: "(1) whether the guidance is in the relevant respects intended by the Secretary of State to give effect to the requirements of ECAT and (2) whether it in fact does so."

[19] In considering the first question, Underhill LJ noted there were a large number of revised versions of the original guidance. The version relevant in KTT's case included a statement that this guidance is based on ECAT and the sections dealing with the grant of DL on grounds of personal circumstances plainly corresponded to Article 14(1)(a) of ECAT. Underhill LJ found that it was plain that the intention was to give effect to Article 14 (1)(a) ([68]-[77]).

[20] Underhill LJ again endorsed the reasoning of Linden J when considering whether the guidance, as applied in KTT's case, did give effect to Article 14(1)(a) and concluded that it did not do so. In summary, Article 14(1)(a) of ECAT required a grant of leave to remain to allow an established victim of trafficking to pursue an asylum claim which is related to the claimant's situation as a victim of trafficking. The relevant guidance in force at the time did not provide for this situation.

[21] The Court of Appeal upheld the order of Linden J:

"1. On their true construction, versions 2, 3 and 4 of the Defendant's policy 'Discretionary Leave for Victims of Modern Slavery' ('the MSL policy') require the defendant's decisions on the grant of leave to remain to be made in accordance with Article 14(1)(a) ECAT, which requires the grant of a residence permit to a confirmed victim of modern slavery if their stay in the UK is necessary owing to their personal situation.

2. The statutorily-protected stay in the United Kingdom of a confirmed victim of trafficking pending the resolution of an asylum claim made by them which is based on a fear of being re-trafficked is capable of constituting a stay which is necessary owing to their personal situation within the meaning of Article 14(1)(a) ECAT."

Nationality and Borders Act 2022 (NABA)

[22] Section 65 of the provides:

"**Leave to remain for victims of slavery or human trafficking**

(1) This section applies if a positive conclusive grounds decision is made in respect of a person –

　　(a) who is not a British citizen, and

　　(b) who does not have leave to remain in the United Kingdom.

(2) The Secretary of State must grant the person limited leave to remain in the United Kingdom if the Secretary of State considers it is necessary for the purpose of –

    (a) assisting the person in their recovery from any physical or psychological harm arising from the relevant exploitation,

    (b) enabling the person to seek compensation in respect of the relevant exploitation, or

    (c) enabling the person to co-operate with a public authority in connection with an investigation or criminal proceedings in respect of the relevant exploitation.

(3) Subsection (2) is subject to section 63(2).

…

(6) Subsection (7) applies if the Secretary of State is satisfied that –

    (a) the person is a threat to public order, or

    (b) the person has claimed to be a victim of slavery or human trafficking in bad faith.

(7) Where this subsection applies –

    (a) the Secretary of State is not required to grant the person leave under subsection (2), and

    (b) if such leave has already been granted to the person, it may be revoked.

(8) Leave granted to a person under subsection (2) may be revoked in such other circumstances as may be prescribed in immigration rules.

(9) Subsections (3) to (7) of section 63 apply for the purposes of this section as they apply for the purposes of that section."

[23] Section 63 provides in material part:

"Identified potential victims etc: disqualification from protection

(1) A competent authority may determine that subsection (2) is to apply to a person in relation to whom a positive reasonable grounds decision has been made if the authority is satisfied that the person –

    (a) is a threat to public order, or

(b) has claimed to be a victim of slavery or human trafficking in bad faith.

(2) Where this subsection applies to a person the following cease to apply –

(a) any prohibition on removing the person from, or requiring them to leave, the United Kingdom arising under section 61 or 62, and

(b) any requirement under section 65 to grant the person limited leave to remain in the United Kingdom.

(3) For the purposes of this section, the circumstances in which a person is a threat to public order include, in particular, where –

…

(f) the person is a foreign criminal within the meaning given by section 32(1) of the UK Borders Act 2007 (automatic deportation for foreign criminals); …"

Immigration Rules

[24] Appendix: Temporary Permission to Stay for Victims of Human Trafficking or Slavery (IR-VTS) commenced on 30 January 2023. The suitability requirements for temporary permission to stay as a victim of modern slavery or human trafficking are that:

"VTS 2.1. The applicant must not fall for refusal as a threat to public order (as defined in Section 63 of the Nationality and Borders Act 2022), or as a person who has claimed to be a victim of Human Trafficking or Slavery in bad faith (as per Section 63 of the Nationality and Borders Act 2022)."

[25] The eligibility requirements for temporary permission to stay provide that:

"VTS 3.1. The requirements to be met by a person for permission to stay on the grounds of being a confirmed victim of Human Trafficking or Slavery are (as set out in Section 65 (2) (a) to (c) of the Nationality and Borders Act 2022), that the grant of permission to stay is necessary for the purpose of: –

(a) assisting the person in their recovery from any physical or psychological harm arising from the relevant exploitation; or

(b) enabling the person to seek compensation in respect of the relevant exploitation, or

(c) enabling the person to co-operate with a public authority in connection with an investigation or criminal proceedings in respect of the relevant exploitation.

VTS 3.2. For the purpose of VTS 3.1 the following apply:

(a) 'physical or psychological harm' means harm of a type that results in physical trauma to the person; or psychological harm that causes mental or emotional trauma or that causes behavioural change or physical symptoms that require psychological or psychiatric care and where the physical or psychological harm arises from the 'relevant exploitation'; and

(b) 'assisting the person in their recovery' for psychological or physical harm means that the applicant requires support either through the National Referral Mechanism or other services to assist in their recovery from their exploitation (this support does not need to accomplish recovery); and

(c) 'seeking compensation' means that the person must have made an application for compensation in respect of the relevant exploitation; and

(d) 'an investigation or criminal proceedings' means an investigation by the public authorities or criminal proceedings within the UK which has been confirmed by the relevant public authority or by the Criminal Prosecution Service; and

(e) 'relevant exploitation' means the conduct resulting in the positive conclusive grounds decision.

VTS 3.3. Permission to stay is not necessary for the purpose of VTS 3.1(a), as set out in Section 65 (4) (a) of the Nationality and Borders Act 2022:

(a) if the Secretary of State considers that the applicant's need for assistance is capable of being met in a country or territory of which they are a national or citizen; or one to which they may be removed in accordance with an agreement between that country or territory and the UK (which may be, but does not need to be, an agreement contemplated by Article 40(2) of the Trafficking Convention).

VTS 3.4. Permission to stay is not necessary for the purpose of VTS 3.1(b) as set out in Section 65 (4) (b) of the Nationality and Borders Act 2022, if the applicant is capable of seeking compensation from outside the UK, and it would be reasonable for them to do so in the circumstances."

Policy Guidance

[26] The policy guidance on DL was published in June 2013 and has been updated on numerous occasions since then. The DLP version 10 was published on 16 March 2023 and the section on modern slavery and human trafficking cases was updated to implement caselaw (*KTT*).

[27] The policy guidance on VTS was first published on 30 January 2023 and VTSP version 3 was published on 8 June 2023. The relevant versions of both policies, DLP and VTSP, post-date the coming into force of sections 63 and 65 of NABA 2022 on 30 January 2023.

DLP

[28] The DLP provides that it must be read in conjunction with other key guidance, in particular and including the VTSP. It states (at page 6 of 30):

"Individuals with a positive conclusive grounds decision whose outstanding asylum claim or further submissions (which is based in a material part on a claim to a well-founded fear of re-trafficking/real risk of serious harm due to re-trafficking) has not been finally determined before 30 January 2023 should be considered for DL. DL will normally be granted in these circumstances on the grounds that their 'stay in the UK is necessary' to pursue their asylum claim or further submissions. Cases on or after 30 January 2023 – this includes individuals who received a positive conclusive grounds decision before 30 January 2023 but did not claim asylum or lodge further submissions until after 30 January 2023 (or vice versa) – will be considered under the Temporary Permission to Stay considerations for Victims of Human Trafficking or Slavery policy."

[29] The section on modern slavery and human trafficking cases states that from 30 January 2023 those with a CGD may be eligible for VTS based on the criteria in section 65 NABA 2022. The DLP then goes on the consider pre-30 January 2023 cases and states:

"Individuals who before 30 January 2023, had both a positive conclusive grounds decision and had made an asylum claim or further submissions, based in a material part on a claim to a well-founded fear of re-trafficking/real risk of serious harm due to re-trafficking, which had not been finally determined, were potentially entitled to DL had their applications for leave been determined under the Home Office policies prior to 30 January 2023.

...

Individuals who meet the requirements above may be entitled to DL because the Home Office policies in force at the time implemented Article 14 (1)(a) of the Council of Europe Convention on Action against Trafficking in Human Beings 2005 (ECAT).

The Court of Appeal in the case of *EOG & KTT v Secretary of State for the Home Department* [2022] EWCA Civ 307 (17 March 2022), referred to as 'KTT', determined that the Home Office approach to applications for Modern Slavery Discretionary Leave was not in accordance with Article 14 (1)(a) of ECAT (which the policy was found to commit to implementing). Article 14 (1)(a) of ECAT leads states to consider whether the victim's 'stay is necessary owing to their personal situation'. The Court found that a confirmed victim of trafficking, who has an outstanding asylum claim which is trafficking-related, requires a consideration of leave to remain in the UK because their 'stay in the UK is necessary', owing to their personal situation as a victim of trafficking, in order to pursue that asylum claim."

[30] In considering when to grant DL, the DLP states:

"Under this policy, those individuals who were eligible for consideration of leave to remain under the KTT judgement prior to 30 January 2023, will not have their applications for DL determined under Temporary Permission to Stay considerations for Victims of Human Trafficking or Slavery. Instead, where:

- a competent authority made a positive conclusive grounds decision prior to 30 January 2023; and

- the individual had prior to 30 January 2023 articulated an asylum claim or further submissions which were trafficking-related as set out above; and

- the individual's asylum claim or further submissions have at the present date not yet been finally determined (this means that they are still awaiting a decision or still have in-country appeal rights to exercise)

you must consider granting DL. DL will normally be granted in these circumstances.

This leave will either be curtailed or varied once the asylum or further submissions decision has been finally determined. Any future application for an extension of leave will be determined under Temporary Permission to Stay considerations for Victims of Human Trafficking or Slavery."

[31] The DLP states that DL does not need to be considered where the individual falls to be refused under part 9 of the immigration rules (general grounds of refusal) or is subject to deportation proceedings. In respect of deportation cases the DLP states (at page 14 of 30):

"Where the individual is currently subject to deportation proceedings, either by way of an extant deportation order or where a deportation decision has been made and deportation continues to be pursued, they must not be considered under the DL policy for modern slavery (including human trafficking) cases pre-30 January 2023. Instead they will be considered under Temporary Permission to Stay considerations for Victims of Human Trafficking or Slavery upon application." ('the deportation carve out')

VTSP

[32] The VTSP clearly states under the section on "policy intention" that it represents a shift in policy intention as regards how the Secretary of State complies with its obligations under ECAT. It states:

"As discussed in the section below on The Council of Europe Convention on Action against Trafficking in Human Beings (ECAT) this guidance represents a shift in our policy intention as regards how the Secretary of State complies with obligations regarding grants of renewable residence permits to victims of modern slavery under ECAT.

As set out below, ECAT is clear that under Article 14 signatory states can elect whether to grant a residence permit in the circumstances described in 14(1)(a) or 14(1)(b) or in both.

From the date of this guidance the Secretary of State will grant VTS in the circumstances described in Article 14(1)(b) as mirrored in s65(2)(c) of the Nationality and Borders Act 2022 (NAB Act). The Secretary of State will also grant VTS in compliance with section 65 of the NAB Act. This is not because she considers that, other than s65(2)(c) as discussed above, this is required by ECAT (or any other international obligations), but because she has been bound to do so by Parliament as a matter of domestic law."

[33] In the section dealing with International Obligations: ECAT it states:

"Historically the Secretary of State's policy intention was to grant leave in both situations (14(1)(a) and 14(1)(b)). However, the Secretary of State has decided to change the policy approach as follows with effect from the date of this Guidance. From this date the UK will fulfil its obligations regarding grants of renewable residence permits to victims of modern slavery through the grant of temporary permission to stay (VTS) as follows:

- the Secretary of State will grant VTS in the circumstances described in Article 14(1)(b) and accordingly s65(2)(c) of the Nationality and Borders Act (NAB Act) mirrors ECAT Article 14(1)(b)

- the Secretary of State will also grant VTS in compliance with section 65 of the NAB Act – this is not because she considers that, other than s65(2)(c) as discussed above, this is required by ECAT [or any other international obligations], but because she has been bound to do so by Parliament as a matter of domestic law.

References in this guidance to when VTS leave may be granted for reasons beyond those in 65(2)(c) of the NAB Act are not intended to fulfil A14(1)(a) but is a matter of domestic policy only as set out in s65 of the NAB Act."

Conclusions on the interpretation of policy

[34] In *KTT*, the Court of Appeal considered the statutory guidance on modern slavery and the guidance entitled "Discretionary leave considerations for victims of modern slavery" referred to as the MSL policy. The court upheld the order of Linden J that versions 2, 3 and 4 of the MSL policy require decisions on a grant a leave to be made in accordance with Article 14(1)(a) ECAT.

[35] The situation has moved on since then and the legal landscape has changed with the coming into force of section 65 NABA 2022 on 30 January 2023. The criteria for granting permission to stay in relation to confirmed victims of modern slavery and trafficking are set out in the IR-VTS and the VTSP. It is not in dispute that the VTSP expresses a clear intention not to implement the obligations in Article 14(1)(a) of the ECAT from 30 January 2023.

[36] The applicant challenges the refusal of VTS on the grounds that the VTSP does not apply and he should have been considered and granted DL under the DLP.

The DLP version 10 published on 16 March 2023 post-dates the coming into force of section 65 NABA 2022 and the first publication of the VTSP. I am not persuaded that the VTSP, in light of section 65 NABA 2022, is the starting point because both policies remain in force and the DLP states it must be read in conjunction with other key guidance including the VTSP.

[37] The principles at [37] of *KTT* apply and I first have to consider whether the DLP evinces an intention to give effect to the requirements of ECAT and secondly whether it in fact does so.

Does the DLP intend to give effect to Article 14(1)(a) ECAT?

[38] The VTSP demonstrates a distinct shift in policy intention whereas the DLP expresses no such intention notwithstanding it was published after section 65 NABA 2023 came into force.

[39] In addition, the DLP identifies two categories of modern slavery cases. Post-30 January 2023 modern slavery cases will be considered under the VTSP (VTS Cases) based on the criteria in section 65 NABA 2022. Pre-30 January 2023 modern slavery cases will be considered under the DLP (DLMS Cases).

[40] The DLP makes specific provision for individuals who have received a positive CGD and made an asylum claim, based in material part on a well-founded fear of re-trafficking, before 30 January 2023 which has not been finally determined (DLMS Cases). The DLP states at the outset (page 6) that DL will normally be granted in these circumstances on the grounds that their "stay in the UK is necessary" to pursue their asylum claim.

[41] The respondent accepts these are transitional provisions, but submits there was no clear commitment to Article 14(1)(a) ECAT in the DLP and no basis for that inference. To do so would be inconsistent with the VTSP which expressly takes the position that the respondent does not intend to apply Article 14(1)(a) as in *KTT*.

[42] The DLP states that DLMS Cases were potentially entitled to DL had their applications for leave to remain been determined under Home Office policies prior to 30 January 2023 and that they may be entitled to DL because those policies implement Article 14(1)(a) ECAT. The DLP then sets out the decision in *KTT* confirming that DLMS Cases required consideration for a grant of leave because their stay in the UK was necessary, owing to their personal situation as a victim of trafficking, in order to pursue their asylum claim.

[43] I do not accept that the use of the words "potentially entitled" or "may be entitled" merely acknowledges that DLMS Cases could have qualified for DL but did not because their applications were not decided before 30 January 2023. I am not persuaded that these are benevolent transitional provisions that might have resulted in a grant of leave under *KTT*, had they been decided sooner. The DLP was updated on 16 March 2023 to implement case law in relation to the section on modern slavery and human trafficking cases. There is no reason for these transitional provisions if they do not apply to decisions made on DLMS Cases after 30 January 2023.

[44] Nor am I persuaded that these words indicate that the respondent did not intend to apply ECAT or *KTT*. The DLP makes clear on page 6 that DL will be granted in line with the judgment in *KTT*. Under the heading "when to consider DL" the DLP states that those individuals who were eligible for consideration of leave under the *KTT* judgment prior to 30 January 2023 will not have their applications determined under the VTSP. The DLP specifically states that DL must be

R (ON THE APPLICATION OF VLT (VIETNAM)) (Frances UTJ)

considered and will normally be granted to individuals in DLMS Cases. Therefore, section 65 NABA 2022 does not prevent DLMS Cases from benefitting from the judgment in *KTT*.

[45] I am of the view that properly interpreted the DLP provides that DLMS cases should be decided in accordance with Article 14(1)(a) given the lack of an express intention to the contrary and the clear and explicit reference to ECAT and *KTT*. I find the DLP was intended to give effect to Article 14(1)(a) ECAT in respect of pre-30 January 2023 modern slavery and human trafficking cases.

Does the DLP give effect to Article 14(1)(a)?

[46] Having committed to giving effect to Article 14(1)(a) in respect of pre-30 January 2023 cases, the DLP "carves out" an exception for those DLMS Cases who are subject to deportation proceedings (the deportation carve out).

[47] Mr Biggs submits, on a correct interpretation of the DLP, the transitional provisions do not evince a commitment to apply ECAT and *KTT* on the facts of this case because the respondent's current approach is explicitly contrary to *KTT*. The respondent had to follow Parliament's decision to adopt a particular interpretation of the ECAT provisions and the point is only justiciable if the policies, properly interpreted, require Article 14(1)(a) to be applied. Even if the deportation carve out was unlawful under ECAT, ECAT was not part of domestic law and the DLP did not evince a commitment to apply Article 14(1)(a). The applicant cannot benefit from the transitional provisions because of the deportation carve out.

[48] Ms Mellon submits the transitional provisions demonstrated a commitment by the respondent to comply with Article 14(1)(a) in respect of those who had a positive CGD and an outstanding asylum claim before 30 January 2023. Accordingly, following *KTT*, the respondent was not entitled to exclude the applicant because he was subject to deportation proceedings. She submits the policy in force before the DLP did not exclude those subject to deportation proceedings and section 65 NABA 2022 did not fetter the respondent's ability to grant leave in trafficking cases on a broader basis than section 65 requires.

[49] Ms Mellon submits the policy prior to 30 January 2023 demonstrated a commitment to comply with Article 14(1)(a) ECAT and it was clear that the intention of the DLP, when viewed objectively, was to honour Article 14(1)(a). It was for the Tribunal to review whether the respondent correctly implemented Article 14(1)(a) and to conclude that the deportation carve out was unlawful because it had no basis in ECAT. It was not the respondent's case that he had made a policy decision to comply with ECAT save for deportation cases nor does he argue ECAT allows for a public order exemption.

[50] The respondent accepts in the response to the pre-action protocol letter dated 4 August 2023 that under the modern slavery DL guidance which was in place prior to 30 January 2023, Foreign National Offenders (FNOs) should not normally benefit from DL because it is a Home Office Policy to remove foreign criminals from the UK as soon as possible. Leave was to be considered on a case by case basis. The respondent goes on to state that:

"Therefore, the current discretionary leave policy sets out that those who are subject to deportation proceedings should have their entitlement to leave considered under the new Temporary Permission to Stay policy post 30 January in line with current legislation, section 65 of the Nationality and Borders Act and

Appendix: Temporary Permission to Stay for Victims of Human Trafficking or Slavery (VTS) in the Immigration Rules."

[51] This letter makes clear that FNOs will be considered under section 65 of NABA 2022 and the Immigration Rules introduced on 30 January 2023 which allows for leave to remain not to be granted where the public order disqualification applies.

[52] There is no public order exception in Article 14(1)(a) as in Article 13 ECAT which provides for a recovery and reflection period after a reasonable grounds decision. This is recognised in the explanatory note to section 63 of NABA 2022. Section 63(3)(f) provides that a threat to public order includes where a person is a foreign criminal within the meaning of section 32(1) of the UK Borders Act 2007. A foreign criminal includes a person who is convicted of an offence and sentenced to a period of imprisonment of at least 12 months.

[53] The public order disqualification in the VTSP states that the respondent is not required to grant permission to stay where the person is a threat to public order and refers to the specific criteria in section 63(3) to (7) NABA 2022.

[54] The deportation carve out in the DLP makes no reference to the definition of a foreign criminal or whether an individual poses a threat to public order. It makes no reference to the public order disqualification in respect of NRM support and is inconsistent with the Modern Slavery Statutory Guidance on Public Order Disqualification (referenced at page 13 of the VTSP).

[55] The DLP provides for a grant of DL to DLMS Cases where the victim's stay is "necessary owing to their personal situation". Imposing a blanket requirement not to be subject to a deportation order fails to give effect to the obligation in Article 14(1)(a) to consider whether the applicant's stay is necessary owing to their personal situation and is contrary to the transitional provisions in respect of DLMS Cases implementing *KTT*.

[56] The deportation carve out excludes those who would benefit from the transitional provisions in the DLP even though they are not foreign criminals or a threat to public order as defined under the policy in force prior to 30 January 2023, the VTSP (post-30 January 2023), the UK Borders Act 2007 or NABA 2022. The deportation carve out excludes DLMS Cases on suitability grounds which have no foundation in the IR-VTS or the VTSP.

[57] I conclude that the deportation carve out in the DLP goes beyond the scope of the public order disqualification and is unlawful because it is incompatible with the obligations in Article 14(1)(a) ECAT and the requirements in sections 63 and 65 NABA 2022 currently in force.

Conclusions on the grounds of application

Ground 1

[58] The DLP intends to comply with Article 14(1)(a) ECAT in respect of DLMS Cases and the decision to exclude the applicant from consideration under the DLP was contrary to Article 14(1)(a) ECAT and unlawful. The transitional provisions in the DLP clearly intend to implement the judgment of *KTT* and there is no lawful basis for exclusion from those provisions on the grounds the applicant is subject to deportation proceedings.

[59] It is not in dispute the applicant had a positive CGD and a pending asylum claim based on a well-founded fear of being re-trafficked before the 30 January 2023. His application for leave to remain was made in November 2022.

[60] On the agreed facts the applicant comes within the cohort of DLMS Cases and would qualify for consideration for DL under the DLP and a grant of DL following *KTT*. The respondent refused to consider and/or grant leave under the DLP because of the applicant's deportation order. However, the CGD finds that the applicant was subject to forced criminality which resulted in a single conviction for which he was sentenced to 8 months' imprisonment. The applicant is not a threat to public order.

[61] The respondent submits that the applicant does not fall within the cohort of DLMS Cases because he is subject to deportation and therefore the VTSP and IR-VTS apply. However, the applicant would not be refused on grounds of suitability under these provisions.

[62] Under section 63 NABA 2022, the applicant is not a foreign national offender and section 32 of the UK Borders Act 2007 does not apply. The applicant would not be excluded from a grant of leave to remain under the VTSP or IR-VTS on suitability grounds notwithstanding his deportation order dated 16 January 2013.

[63] Therefore, there is no lawful basis to exclude the applicant from the benefit of the transitional provisions in the DLP on the basis of his extant deportation order which does not meet the current threshold for public order disqualification. I find the applicant's personal situation brings him within the transitional provisions of the DLP and the decision to refuse DL and/or refuse to consider DL under the DLP was unlawful.

Ground 3

[64] The applicant also succeeds under ground 3 in so far as the transitional provisions in the DLP evince an intention to comply with the obligations in Article 14(1)(a) ECAT and the deportation carve out in respect of the cohort of DLMS Cases fails to do so. However, notwithstanding the DLP fails to give effect to ECAT and the decision refusing to consider or grant leave under the DLP was unlawful, this did not involve the direct enforcement of an unincorporated treaty because ECAT was not the source of the obligation: [32] *KTT*.

[65] The applicant seeks a declaration that the DLP is contrary to Article 4 and unlawful under section 6 of the Human Rights Act 1998 (HRA). I am of the view such a declaration is not necessary for the reasons given above.

[66] With both of these points in mind, I go on to consider whether the decision to refuse the applicant a residence permit on account of the deportation order breaches Article 4 ECHR. I can therefore deal with the remainder of ground 3 briefly.

[67] Article 4 of the European Convention of Human Rights (ECHR) materially provides that:

"1. No one shall be held in slavery or servitude.

2. No one shall be required to perform forced or compulsory labour."

[68] It is settled law that the positive obligations under Article 4 ECHR include the duty in certain circumstances to take operational measures to protect victims or

potential victims of trafficking: *Rantsev v Cyprus and Russia* (2010) 51 EHRR 1 and *SM v Croatia* (2021) 72 EHRR 1. The Article 4 positive obligations must be construed in light of ECAT and protection measures include assisting victims with their physical, psychological and social recovery *VCL and AN v UK* (2021) 73 EHRR 9.

[69] Ms Mellon submits the operational duty under Article 4 includes the duty to assist recovery. There is a risk of re-trafficking for those who have been trafficked in the past and who remain in the UK without leave seeking asylum which is an inherently insecure position. Article 14(1)(a) as interpreted in *KTT*, requires that recognised victims of trafficking whose asylum claims are pending must be granted a period of leave. She submits that Article 4 interpreted in the light of ECAT, imposes the same obligation.

[70] Ms Mellon refers to *R (TDT (Vietnam)) v SSHD* [2018] EWCA Civ 1395 in her skeleton argument and accepts there is no automatic read across, but in her submission that is exactly what she is asking the Tribunal to do. Applying the *dicta* at [31], the obligations under Article 4 ECHR and the obligations under the transitional provisions in the DLP, which intend to comply with the obligations in Article 14(1)(a), have to be analysed separately. In my view, the application of the DLP was not a mechanism by which the UK satisfied its procedural obligations under Article 4: *SSHD v Minh* [2016] EWCA Civ 565.

[71] Having reviewed the Strasbourg case law and considered [54] of *R (AB) v SSHD* [2021] UKSC 28, I am not persuaded that the obligation imposed by Article 14(1)(a), as interpreted by *KTT*, can be derived from the operational duty recognised in *Rantsev*, *TDT* and *VCL*.

[72] I am persuaded by the respondent's submission that Article 4 does not have the effect of incorporating Article 14(1)(a) ECAT adopted by *KTT* into domestic law via the HRA 1998.

Ground 4

[73] The refusal of VTS was unlawful because the respondent applied the wrong policy for the reasons given above.

[74] I am fortified in this view by the letter from the SCA dated 7 March 2023 (page 155 of the trial bundle) that a decision would be made on applicant's application for limited leave to remain once policies had been reviewed in the light of *KTT*. If the VTSP first published on 30 January 2023 was applicable there was no need to await further review of the DLP.

[75] I note that the decision of 12 June 2023 makes reference to part 9 of the immigration rules. This is misconceived. The VTSP on page 9 makes clear that this is relevant to the cancellation of permission to stay. A grant of VTS is made under the criteria in IR-VTS. The refusal on the basis that VTS must be refused because "previous behaviour is deemed not conducive to the public good" is clearly wrong and demonstrates the decision maker's misunderstanding of the relevant applicable rules and policy.

Summary

[76] The transitional provisions in the DLP applicable to DLMS Cases were intended to commit the respondent to making decisions on DL in accordance with

Article 14(1)(a) ECAT and *KTT*. The respondent has failed to do so. The decision of 12 June 2023 is therefore in breach of the DLP and unlawful.

[77] The case of *XY v SSHD* [2024] EWHC 81 (Admin) was handed down on 23 January 2024. It was concerned with the policy guidance on Discretionary Leave Considerations for Victims of Modern Slavery, version 4 published on 8 December 2020 and raised different issues to those argued in the applicant's case.

Permission to appeal

[78] The respondent applied for permission to appeal on the following grounds:

"The Upper Tribunal erred in its interpretation of the transitional provisions within the policy guidance on discretionary leave, version 10, published on 16 March 2023 (the 'DLP'). Whether or not the transitional provisions within the DLP, properly construed, apply article 14(1)(a) of ECAT as interpreted in (*EOG and KTT v SSHD* [2022] EWCA Civ 307 ('KTT')) in cases to which the transitional provisions apply, the DLP is clear that article 14(1)(a) of ECAT as interpreted in KTT does not to apply in cases covered by the deportation 'carve out'. In other words, such cases simply fall outside the scope of the relevant transitional provisions, on their correct construction. Properly interpreted as a whole the DLP transitional provisions therefore do not and cannot provide that the KTT interpretation of article 14(1)(a) of ECAT must be applied in the applicant's case, given that he falls within the deportation 'carve out', and therefore falls outside the scope of the relevant transitional provisions. There is no principle of interpretation that could allow the Tribunal to construe the DLP transitional provisions without regard to, or so as to override, that clear limitation of their scope."

[79] The respondent does not challenge my conclusion that the transitional provisions under the DLP intended to give effect to Article 14(1)(a) ECAT and the judgment in *KTT*. The respondent submits that Article 14 (1)(a) ECAT as interpreted in *KTT* does not apply in deportation cases and the applicant falls within the deportation carve out.

[80] This argument has no merit because the deportation carve out is unlawful for the following reasons. The respondent is seeking to exclude the applicant from the benefit of the transitional provisions in the DLP (which implements Article 14(1)(a) and *KTT*) and decide his application under the less favourable provisions in the VTSP (which does not implement Article 14(1)(a) and *KTT*) for reasons which are not sustainable under the VTSP or indeed NABA 2022 and the IR-VTS.

[81] I refuse permission to appeal because there is no arguable case that I have erred in law or there is some other reason that requires consideration by the Court of Appeal.

ABDULLAH & ORS (EEA; DEPORTATION APPEALS; PROCEDURE)

UPPER TRIBUNAL (IMMIGRATION AND ASYLUM CHAMBER)

Kebede and Rintoul UTJJ

[2024] UKUT 66 (IAC)
28 February 2024

Procedure and process – deportation – EEA nationals – scope of protection under the Withdrawal Agreement – scope of protection under domestic law – rights of appeal

These three appeals were listed together in order to permit the Upper Tribunal ('UT') to resolve a number of issues of law concerning the power of the Secretary of State for the Home Department to deport EEA nationals who had resided in the United Kingdom since before the United Kingdom left the European Union on 31 December 2020 and the rights of appeal against deportation decisions. The Claimants had each been convicted of criminal offences. The Secretary of State had decided to deport them.

The first Claimant, ZA, a citizen of the Netherlands, submitted that he had acquired the right of permanent residence under EU law prior to his criminal conviction in July 2021. The Secretary of State refused his human rights claim and his application under the EU Settlement Scheme ('EUSS'). The First-tier Tribunal ('FtT') allowed ZA's appeal on human rights grounds but dismissed the appeal under the EUSS on the basis that ZA had not acquired permanent residence. The UT set aside that decision in its entirety.

The second Claimant, AS, a citizen of Poland, made a human rights claim in response to the decision to deport him. He also claimed that he had made an application under the EUSS in February 2020. The Secretary of State did not accept that AS had made the EUSS application and refused his human rights claim. AS appealed against that decision under section 82 of the Nationality, Immigration and Asylum Act 2002 ('the 2002 Act'). The FtT allowed the appeal, having concluded that the Immigration (European Economic Area) Regulations 2016 ('EEA Regulations') applied. The Secretary of State was granted permission to appeal on the grounds that the FtT had wrongly considered the appeal under the EEA Regulations and had failed to give adequate reasons for finding that AS had made an application under the EUSS in February 2020.

The third Claimant, RR, a citizen of Lithuania, was granted settled status under the EUSS in January 2020. RR appealed against the Secretary of State's decision to deport him on the grounds that it breached his Article 8 ECHR rights and that his deportation was not conducive to the public good. The FtT allowed RR's appeal on human rights grounds. The Secretary of State was granted permission to appeal against that decision on the grounds that the FtT had misdirected itself as to the law and had given inadequate reasons for its decision.

The UT first considered the scope of the protection against deportation provided by the EU-UK Withdrawal Agreement ('WA') to those EEA citizens who had resided in the United Kingdom prior to 31 December 2020 and the scope of protection afforded to such individuals by other domestic legislation. The UT then considered the mechanism of how decisions to deport EEA nationals could be appealed and on what grounds.

Held, allowing the appeals and directing that the decisions be remade:

(1) In an appeal where conduct prior to 11pm on 31 December 2020 gave rise to a decision to deport an EEA citizen, it was necessary to determine the following questions, as at 31 December 2020 (and at the point a decision was taken): (i) was the EEA citizen resident in the United Kingdom; (ii) if so, for what continuous period (as defined in regulation 3 of the EEA Regulations) before that; (iii) was the residence lawful in accordance with the EEA Regulations; (iv) had the individual acquired permanent residence under the EEA Regulations; (v) had the individual applied under the EUSS before the end of the Grace Period, that was 30 June 2021; and (vi) if so, was it pending. The answers to those questions would determine whether the EEA citizen came within the scope of the WA, the Citizens' Rights (Application Deadline and Temporary Protection) (EU Exit) Regulations 2020 ('the Grace Period Regulations') or the EUSS. They would also determine whether that individual was a 'relevant person' for the purposes of section 3(5A) and (10) of the Immigration Act 1971 and section 33(6B and 6C) of the UK Borders Act 2007 ('the 2007 Act'), as expanded by regulations 3(4) and 12(1)(b) of the Grace Period Regulations (*para 105(A)–(B)*).

(2) In respect of conduct carried out prior to 31 December 2020, the EEA Regulations only applied directly to an individual (and thus gave rise to an appeal under those Regulations) if: first, the decision had been taken under the EEA Regulations prior to 31 December 2020 or in connection with an application pending under the Regulations; or, secondly, the individual was an EEA citizen (or a family member of such a person) lawfully resident under the EEA Regulations (including those who had acquired permanent residence under regulation 3 of the EEA Regulations) and either: (i) the decision had been taken by 30 June 2021; or (ii) had been taken after that date but when a valid application under the EUSS had been made before 30 June 2021 and was still pending (but not if they had been granted leave under the EUSS); or, thirdly, was a person who fell within the scope of the Citizens' Rights (Restrictions of Rights of Entry and Residence) (EU Exit) Regulations 2020 (*para 105(C)*).

(3) With the passage of time, the class of individuals falling under the EEA Regulations and entitled to a right of appeal under those provisions would diminish to very small numbers. If a decision to deport was not made under the EEA Regulations, then there was no right of appeal under those Regulations. In an appeal under the Immigration (Citizens' Rights Appeals) (EU Exit) Regulations 2020 ('CRA Regulations'), it would be necessary to consider the application under regulation 27 of the EEA Regulations. That could arise under either ground of appeal as: (i) if the EEA citizen was within the scope of the WA, then Articles 20 and 21 of the WA applied; (ii) if not in the scope of the WA, the definition of deportation order was such that only one which was justified by reference to regulation 27 of the EEA Regulations made the EEA citizen ineligible for a grant of status under the EUSS. There was a distinction between (i) and (ii) because under the definition of a deportation order under the EUSS, only five years' continuous

residence (as opposed to lawful residence under the EEA Regulations) was needed to acquire enhanced protection (*para 105(D)–(G)*).

(4) The effect of a finding that the deportation was not justified by reference to regulation 27 of the EEA Regulations was that Exception 7 under section 33 of the 2007 Act was met, and the Secretary of State's policy was then to revoke any deportation order, at which point leave to remain under the EUSS could be granted. If the deportation decision against an EEA citizen arose in a human rights appeal under section 82 of the 2002 Act, then that appeal should be stayed pending resolution of any outstanding application under the EUSS to allow an appeal against a negative decision to be determined at the same time as a human rights appeal. Where an appeal had been allowed under the EEA Regulations; or, in an appeal under the CRA Regulations on the basis that the deportation decision was not justified by reference to regulation 27 of the EEA Regulations, it followed that any linked appeal against the same decision under section 82 of the 2002 Act would be allowed on the basis that the decision under appeal was not in accordance with the law (*para 105(H)–(J)*).

(5) ZA had a right of appeal under the CRA Regulations on both available grounds and a right of appeal under section 82 of the 2002 Act. He did not have a right of appeal under the EEA Regulations as there was no decision made under those Regulations. That would have been the case had he fallen within the scope of the WA at the relevant time, due to exercise of Treaty Rights as at 31 December 2020, a matter that needed to be resolved. In any event, the issue on appeal under the CRA Regulations was whether the test in regulation 27 of the EEA Regulations was met, and thus the result was the same. It remained to be determined whether ZA had acquired permanent residence prior to 31 December 2020 or alternatively whether he was exercising Treaty Rights as at that date. The appeal would be remade in the UT (*paras 107 – 116*).

(6) The scope of AS's appeal was confined to section 82 of the 2002 Act, a human rights appeal. The FtT had made a material error of law in applying the EEA Regulations as they were not directly applicable, there being no decision under those Regulations. The FtT had also erred in concluding that AS had made an application under the EUSS in February 2020 and had given inadequate reasons for that conclusion. The FtT was entitled to consider the EEA Regulations but only indirectly in considering Appendix EU of the Immigration Rules HC 395 (as amended), given how the deportation order was defined under that by reference to regulation 27 of the EEA Regulations. Whether AS fell within the scope of the WA depended on whether he had made an EUSS application before 30 June 2021, an issue to be determined. The appeal would be remade in the UT (*paras 118 – 138*).

(7) RR's right of appeal was under the CRA Regulations, the grounds being set out in regulation 8, subject to regulation 9. The FtT did not have jurisdiction to decide the appeal by reference to the EEA Regulations, as they did not apply. There being no human rights decision, the permissible grounds of appeal did not allow the FtT to reach a decision on Article 8 ECHR grounds. The appeal was remitted to the FtT for remaking (*paras 140 – 159*).

Cases referred to:

Celik v Secretary of State for the Home Department [2023] EWCA Civ 921; [2023] Imm AR 1599
Charles (human rights appeal: scope) [2018] UKUT 89 (IAC); [2018] Imm AR 911

Dano v Jobcentre Leipzig (Case C-333/13); [2015] 1 WLR 2519; [2015] 1 CMLR 48
Goralczyk v Upper Tribunal (Immigration and Asylum Chamber) [2018] CSIH 60; 2019 SC 66; 2018 SLT 1183
Hesham Ali (Iraq) v Secretary of State for the Home Department [2016] UKSC 60; [2016] 1 WLR 4799; [2017] 3 All ER 20; [2017] Imm AR 484; [2017] INLR 109
R v Kansal [2001] UKHL 62; [2002] 2 AC 69; [2001] 3 WLR 1562; [2002] 1 All ER 257
R v Secretary of State for the Home Department ex parte Razgar [2004] UKHL 27; [2004] 2 AC 368; [2004] 3 WLR 58; [2004] 3 All ER 821; [2004] Imm AR 381; [2004] INLR 349
R (on the application of A) v B [2009] UKSC 12; [2010] 2 AC 1; [2010] 2 WLR 1; [2010] 1 All ER 1149
R (on the application of Bridges) v Chief Constable of South Wales [2020] EWCA Civ 1058; [2020] 1 WLR 5037; [2021] 2 All ER 1121
R (on the application of Independent Monitoring Authority for the Citizens' Rights Agreements) v Secretary of State for the Home Department [2022] EWHC 3274 (Admin); [2023] 1 WLR 817; [2023] 2 CMLR 14; [2023] Imm AR 476
Secretary of State for the Home Department v AA (Poland) [2024] EWCA Civ 18; [2024] Imm AR 298
Secretary of State for the Home Department v Straszewski; Secretary of State for the Home Department v Kersys [2015] EWCA Civ 1245; [2016] 1 WLR 1173; [2016] 2 CMLR 3; [2016] Imm AR 482; [2016] INLR 531
TZ (Pakistan) v Secretary of State for the Home Department; PG (India) v Secretary of State for the Home Department [2018] EWCA Civ 1109; [2018] Imm AR 1301
Zambrano v Office national de l'emploi (Case C-34/09); [2012] QB 265; [2012] 2 WLR 886; [2011] All ER (EC) 491; [2011] 2 CMLR 46; [2011] Imm AR 521; [2011] INLR 481

Legislation and international instruments judicially considered:

Agreement on the withdrawal of the United Kingdom of Great Britain and Northern Ireland from the European Union and the European Atomic Energy Community ('Withdrawal Agreement'), Articles 1(a), 10, 13, 18, 20 & 21
Citizens' Rights (Application Deadline and Temporary Protection) (EU Exit) Regulations 2020, regulations 3, 4 & 12(1)(b)
Citizens' Rights (Restrictions of Rights of Entry and Residence) (EU Exit) Regulations 2020, regulations 2 & 8
Directive 2004/38/EC ('the Citizens Directive'), Articles 7(1), 14, 15(1) & 31(4)
European Convention on Human Rights, Article 8
European Union (Withdrawal) Act 2018, section 7A
Human Rights Act 1998, sections 6 & 7
Immigration Act 1971, sections 3 & 5
Immigration and Social Security Co-ordination (EU Withdrawal) Act 2020, section 1; Schedule 1; paragraphs 4, 5 & 6 of Schedule 3
Immigration (Citizens' Rights Appeals) (EU Exit) Regulations 2020, regulations 6, 8 & 9
Immigration (European Economic Area) Regulations 2016, regulations 3, 27 & 36
Immigration Rules HC 395 (as amended), paragraphs EU11, EU14, EU15 & Annex 1 of Appendix EU; Appendix EUSS

Nationality, Immigration and Asylum Act 2002, sections 82, 84, 113, 117C & 120
Treaty on the Functioning of the European Union, Articles 20, 21, 45 & 49
UK Borders Act 2007, sections 32 & 33

Representation

Ms J Smyth and *Ms K Elliot* instructed by the Government Legal Department, for the Secretary of State;
Ms I Sabic KC and *Ms E Doerr* instructed via Direct Access, for ZA;
Ms G Patel instructed by A & M Solicitors, for AS;
RR did not appear;
Mr T Buley KC, *Ms B Asanovic* and *Mr A Shattock*, for the AIRE Centre, as Intervenor.

Judgment

UPPER TRIBUNAL JUDGE RINTOUL:

Preliminary matters

Abbreviations

1971 Act	Immigration Act 1971
2002 Act	Nationality, Immigration and Asylum Act 2002
2007 Act	UK Borders Act 2007
AS	Adrian Andrzej Szuba, the respondent in the Second Appeal UI-2023-000505
Citizens' Rights Directive	Directive 2004/38/EC
CRA Regulations	Immigration (Citizens' Rights Appeals) (EU Exit) Regulations 2020
CRRE Regulations	Citizens' Rights (Restrictions of Rights of Entry and Residence) (EU Exit) Regulations 2020
EEA Regulations	Immigration (European Economic Area) Regulations 2016
EUSS	EU Settlement Scheme
EUWA 2018	European Union (Withdrawal) Act 2018
EUWA 2020	European Union (Withdrawal Agreement) Act 2020
FtT	First-tier Tribunal
Grace Period Regulations	Citizens' Rights (Application Deadline and Temporary Protection) (EU Exit) Regulations 2020
ISSCA 2020	Immigration and Social Security Co-ordination (EU Withdrawal) Act 2020

RR	Rukas Rudokas, the respondent in the Third Appeal UI-2023-001538.
SSHD	Secretary of State for the Home Department
TFEU	Treaty on the Functioning of the European Union
Transitional Provisions Regulations	Immigration and Social Security Co-ordination (EU Withdrawal) Act 2020 (Consequential, Saving, Transitional and Transitory Provisions) (EU Exit) Regulations 2020
WA	Withdrawal Agreement
ZA	Zain-al-Abidin Abdullah, the respondent in the First appeal UI-2022-006321

Introduction

[1] These three appeals were listed together in order to permit the Upper Tribunal to resolve a number of issues of law concerning the SSHD's power to deport EEA nationals who had resided in the United Kingdom and have done so since before the United Kingdom left the European Union and the rights of appeal against such decisions.

[2] We are in these appeals concerned only with EU nationals, rather than Swiss nationals or nationals of other EEA states. There are different Withdrawal Agreements relating to those states but they mirror broadly the WA with the EU, as do the domestic legal provisions.

The appeals

ZA (Abdullah)

[3] Mr ZA is a citizen of the Netherlands. He has resided in the United Kingdom since 2008 when he was 15/16 years of age. His case is that he had acquired the right of permanent residence under EU law (which the SSHD does not accept) prior to his conviction on 30 July 2021 for Grievous Bodily Harm in an incident which took place on 28 November 2019. On 30 June 2021 he made an application under the EUSS and on 11 October 2021 was notified by the SSHD of her intention to make a deportation order against him. He made representations as to why he should not be deported; and made a human rights claim. On 3 May 2022, the SSHD made two decisions: to refuse his human rights claim and to make a deportation order pursuant to s 32(5) of the 2007 Act; and, to refuse his EUSS application.

[4] ZA's appeal to the FtT was allowed on human rights grounds but was dismissed under the EUSS on the basis that ZA had not acquired permanent residence. The SSHD was granted permission to appeal and on 3 May 2023, UTJ Kebede set aside the decision in its entirety.

AS (Szuba)

[5] AS is a national of Poland. He has resided in the United Kingdom since 2007 when he was 11. He has been convicted of multiple offences between 2013 and 2020, the most serious being a conviction on 14 October 2020 for possession with intent to supply drugs for which he was sentenced to five years' and three months' imprisonment. On 24 October 2021, the SSHD served a notice of intention to deport him on the basis that s 32 of the 2007 Act applied. On 9 November 2021, AS' solicitors made representations, making a human rights claim, and asserting that he had made an application under the EUSS in February 2020. On 7 March 2022 he was asked to provide details of that application. The SSHD was not satisfied by what was provided that he had made an application under the EUSS in February 2020.

[6] On 23 May 2022 the SSHD refused AS's human rights claim and made a deportation order against him. He was, however, satisfied that he had been lawfully resident in the United Kingdom at the end of the transition period. On 30 May 2022, AS appealed against that decision under section 82 of the 2002 Act and on 30 June 2022 made an application under the EUSS which is still pending.

[7] On 20 January 2023, having concluded that this was an appeal to which the EEA Regulations applied and that the relevant test was whether imperative grounds were met, FtTJ Dixon allowed the appeal. The SSHD was granted permission to appeal on the grounds that the FtT had wrongly considered the appeal under the EEA Regulations and had failed to give adequate reasons for finding that AS had made an application under the EUSS in February 2020.

RR (Rudokas)

[8] RR is a national of Lithuania. He came to the United Kingdom in about 2005. On 21 January 2020 he was granted settled status under the EUSS. On 13 July 2022 he was convicted of several offences which had started on 12 October 2021 and for which he was sentenced to two years' imprisonment. On 9 August 2022, the SSHD notified him that she intended to deport him pursuant to s 32 of the 2007 Act; that he had a right of appeal under reg. 6 of the CRA Regulations; and that consideration would be given to any representations and whether those would give rise to an appeal under s82 of the 2002 Act. A one-stop notice under section 120 of that Act was attached to that notification.

[9] On 23 August 2022, RR appealed against the decision on the grounds that it breached his article 8 rights and that his deportation was not conducive to the public good. On 18 December 2022, the SSHD made a deportation order against him.

[10] On 12 February 2023, the FtT allowed RR's appeal on human rights grounds. The SSHD was granted permission to appeal against that decision on the grounds that the judge had misdirected himself as to the law and had given inadequate reasons for his decision.

Procedural history

[11] There have been two case management hearings in these appeals with a view to identifying the issues. These were to a substantial extent agreed. The AIRE centre was also granted permission to intervene.

[12] The issues as identified in each of the appeals are set out in the form settled by the Upper Tribunal in the annex to this decision.

[13] Subsequent to the hearing, and before an embargoed draft was circulated to the parties, the Court of Appeal handed down *SSHD v AA (Poland)* [2024] EWCA Civ 18. The SSHD drew attention to that decision in the response to the draft, and the panel then gave directions for written submissions on that case to be served. We have taken them into account in reaching our decision.

Broad outline of the issues

[14] In these appeals we are concerned with the scope of the protection against deportation provided by the WA to those EEA citizens who had resided in the United Kingdom prior to 31 December 2020 and with the scope of protection afforded to such individuals by other domestic legislation. We are concerned also with the mechanism of how decisions to deport EEA nationals can be appealed and on what grounds.

[15] The first issue we must consider is the scope of the WA: does it, as ZA and AS and the Aire Centre submit, apply regardless of whether ZA and AS were exercising Treaty Rights at the end of the implementation period so that they qualify for protection under Article 20 of the WA? Second, if so, should a decision to deport such a person be made under the EEA Regulations? Or, as the SSHD submits, is the correct position that for an individual to benefit from the WA, he or she must have been exercising Treaty Rights and so a decision to deport a person who had not done so should proceed under domestic law? Further, what are the relevant rights of appeal and grounds of appeal? And, does it make a difference if, as the SSHD submits, the test applied under either route is the same?

The Law

[16] We have endeavoured to set out the law as it applies to EEA nationals and we are grateful to counsel, in particular Ms Smyth in her skeleton argument setting out the legal framework, for their assistance. We are also grateful to counsel for their further submissions which the panel considered necessary in the light of the Court of Appeal's decision in *AA (Poland)*.

Background

[17] The United Kingdom has left the EU. The transition period during which EU law had continued to apply came to an end at 11pm on 31 December 2020. At that point, EU Free Movement rights ceased to be effective or enforceable – see section 1 and schedule 1 of the ISSCA – and the EEA Regulations were revoked. Two discrete bodies of law, however, remained – retained EU law which is not relevant to these appeals, and the WA which has direct effect by operation of section 7A of EUWA 2018.

[18] The rights of EU nationals under EU law to enter and reside in the United Kingdom are described in detail in *Celik v SSHD* [2023] EWCA Civ 921 at [10]–[18]. Prior to the United Kingdom's exit from the EU, by operation of section 7 of the Immigration Act 1988, those having a right to enter or reside under European

Law did not (absent any exclusion or deportation order) require leave to enter or remain that would otherwise have been imposed by section 3 of the 1971 Act. Those rights to enter and reside were primarily set out, for domestic purposes, in the EEA Regulations, although those relied on the machinery of the 1971 Act to effect deportation.

[19] Although these rights came to an end, one of the purposes of the WA was to provide reciprocal protection for United Kingdom and EU nationals who had exercised free movement rights, and to ensure that their rights under the WA were enforceable as part of the United Kingdom's withdrawal from the EU. Article 18 of the WA permits states to require applications for a new residence status to be made. The United Kingdom chose to require such applications to be made, setting up a residence scheme, the EUSS which enables EU, other EEA and Swiss citizens resident in the United Kingdom prior to 31 December 2020, and their family members, to obtain the necessary immigration status – a grant of leave pursuant to the Immigration Rules.

[20] Despite being revoked by ISSCA, certain provisions of the EEA Regulations were preserved by the Grace Period Regulations and the Transitional Provisions Regulations.

The Grace Period Regulations

[21] The purpose of the Grace Period Regulations was to preserve the residence rights enjoyed under the EEA Regulations at the end of the transition period, that is, 31 December 2020 until 30 June 2021, the date on which the "grace period" ended. In the case of those who made applications under the EUSS which remained undecided as at that date, the residence rights are preserved until a decision is made and any appeal rights are exhausted. Although the Grace Period Regulations do not make provision for late applications to be made, this can be done under the Immigration Rules as set out in Appendix EU in certain circumstances.

[22] It is, however, important to note that (a) only some of the EEA Regulations continue to apply* and (b) they continue to apply only to a "relevant person" as defined in reg. 3(6).

[23] To meet the "relevant person" test the person in question must have been lawfully resident (or had a right of permanent residence), in accordance with the EEA Regulations, immediately before 23:00 GMT on 31 December 2020 and does not yet have leave to enter or remain under the EUSS. Whether a person was "residing" in the United Kingdom at a time when it would be taken into account for purposes of calculating continuous residence under reg. 3 of the EEA Regulations – see reg. 3(5)(b).

[24] Reg. 4 of the Grace Period Regulations also protects "an applicant", that is, a person who has made an in-time application under the EUSS and who was lawfully resident in the United Kingdom, or had a right of permanent residence, under the EEA Regulations at the end of the transition period until that application is finally decided.

---

* Grace Period Regulations regs. 3(2) and 3(3).

[25] It must, however, be noted in the context of deportation, that in order to come within reg. 3 or 4 of the Grace Period Regulations "residence" immediately before 31 December 2020 requires falling within the meaning of continuous residence as set out in reg.3 of the EEA Regulations which provided:

"3. (1) This regulation applies for the purpose of calculating periods of continuous residence in the United Kingdom under these Regulations.

(2) Continuity of residence is not affected by –

(a) periods of absence from the United Kingdom which do not exceed six months in total in any year;

(b) periods of absence from the United Kingdom on compulsory military service; or

(c) one absence from the United Kingdom not exceeding twelve months for an important reason such as pregnancy and childbirth, serious illness, study or vocational training or an overseas posting.

(3) Continuity of residence is broken when –

(a) a person serves a sentence of imprisonment;

(b) a deportation or exclusion order is made in relation to a person; or

(c) a person is removed from the United Kingdom under these Regulations.

(4) Paragraph (3)(a) applies, in principle, to an EEA national who has resided in the United Kingdom for at least ten years, but it does not apply where the Secretary of State considers that –

(a) prior to serving a sentence of imprisonment, the EEA national had forged integrating links with the United Kingdom;

(b) the effect of the sentence of imprisonment was not such as to break those integrating links; and

(c) taking into account an overall assessment of the EEA national's situation, it would not be appropriate to apply paragraph (3)(a) to the assessment of that EEA national's continuity of residence."

Withdrawal Agreement

[26] The relevant provisions of the WA are set out in detail in *Celik* at [19] to [29]. Part Two of the WA makes provision in relation to citizens' rights. The scope of Part Two, and the rights and obligations arising under it are matters we will address in due course.

Citizens' Rights (Restrictions of Rights of Entry and Residence) (EU Exit) Regulations ("CRRE Regulations")

[27] Although these regulations are not directly applicable to any of these cases, they do form part of the framework whereby some rights conferred by EU law are preserved by the WA. In brief, these regulations preserve the EEA Regulations (as amended by the CRRE regulations) for a person who is "protected by the citizens' rights provisions" (reg. 2(2)):

"(2) For the purposes of paragraph (1), a person is protected by the citizens' rights provisions if that person –

(a) has leave to enter or remain in the United Kingdom granted by virtue of residence scheme immigration rules;

(b) is in the United Kingdom (whether or not they have entered within the meaning of section 11(1) of the Immigration Act 1971) having arrived with entry clearance granted by virtue of relevant entry clearance immigration rules; [i.e under Appendix EUSS or EU-FP]

(c) is in the United Kingdom (whether or not they have entered within the meaning of section 11(1) of the Immigration Act 1971) having arrived with entry clearance granted by virtue of Article 23 of the Swiss citizens' rights agreement; or

(d) may be granted leave to enter or remain in the United Kingdom as a person who has a right to enter the United Kingdom by virtue of –

(i) Article 32(1)(b) of the withdrawal agreement;

(ii) Article 31(1)(b) of the EEA EFTA separation agreement; or

(iii) Article 26a(1)(b) of the Swiss citizens' rights agreement, whether or not the person has been granted such leave.

(3) For the purposes of these Regulations, a person is also protected by the citizens' rights provisions if that person was protected by the citizens' rights provisions at the time that they became subject to a decision to remove them under regulation 23(6)(b) of the EEA Regulations 2016, including as those Regulations continue to have effect by virtue of these Regulations."

[28] The rights under the EEA Regulations which are preserved are limited by these regulations, as the "EEA decision" against which an appeal under reg. 36 can lie is limited to a decision to remove a person from the United Kingdom. Reg. 27 is preserved, subject to amendments the more important of which (para 4 of the Schedule) are to preserve the enhanced protection for those with permanent residence and ten years residence but with the change that "permanent residence" is amended to cover those eligible for, indefinite leave to enter or remain in the United Kingdom granted under Appendix EUSS or EU-FP. That mirrors the definition of "deportation order" within Appendix EUSS (see [50] below)

[29] The appeal rights against an EEA decision in reg. 36 of the EEA Regulations are preserved, albeit with the omission of regs 36(3) to (6) and (12) which imposed the requirement to provide certain documents in order for an appeal to be effective.

Criminality and deportation

[30] We turn next to the specific provisions relating to the power to deport EU and EEA nationals.

[31] As is well-established, prior to the United Kingdom's exit from the EU, there were in effect two deportation regimes: one applicable to EU (and EEA) nationals and their family members; one applicable to other foreign nationals (see e.g. *Straszewski v SSHD* [2015] EWCA Civ 1245 at [12] ff and *Goralczyk v Upper Tribunal* [2018] CSIH 60 at [21] to [22]) but both regimes were subject to the requirement that deportation be deemed conducive to the public good but EEA nationals were subject to the regime under the 2007 Act, but subject to the exception set out in section 33.

Deportation under the EEA Regulations

[32] Under the EEA Regulations, the deportation of an EEA national was a decision taken on grounds of public policy, public security or public health and so subject to the provisions of reg. 27 which in turn gave effect to Chapter VI of the Citizens' Rights Directive.

Domestic law on deportation

[33] Under section 5 of the 1971 Act, the SSHD may make a deportation order against a person whose deportation is deemed to be conducive to the public good, by operation of section 3(5)(a), or is a member of the family of such a person; or whose deportation has been recommended by a court (section 3(6)). We are concerned here only with the first category of persons.

[34] Section 32(4) of the 2007 Act deems the deportation of foreign criminals (as defined) to be conducive to the public good for the purposes of section 3(5)(a) of the 1971 Act and requires the SSHD to deport such persons unless an exception set out in section 33 of the 2007 Act applies.

[35] Prior to 31 December 2020, if the removal of the foreign criminal would breach his rights under the EU Treaties, an exception applied with the result that it was assumed neither that deportation was conducive to the public good, or that it

was not conducive to the public good; the application of an exception did not however prevent the making of a deportation order.

[36] The EUWA 2020 introduced s 3(5A) of the 1971 Act which provides:

"(5A) The Secretary of State may not deem a **relevant person** [our emphasis]'s deportation to be conducive to the public good under subsection (5) if the person's deportation –

(a) would be in breach of the obligations of the United Kingdom under Article 20 of the EU withdrawal agreement, Article 19 of the EEA EFTA separation agreement or Article 17 or 20(3) of the Swiss citizens' rights agreement, or

(b) would be in breach of those obligations if the provision in question mentioned in paragraph (a) applied in relation to the person."

[37] A relevant person is defined in section 3(10) of the 1971 Act which, so far as is relevant, provides:

"(10) For the purposes of this section, a person is a "relevant person" –

(a) if the person is in the United Kingdom (whether or not they have entered within the meaning of section 11(1)) having arrived with entry clearance granted by virtue of relevant entry clearance immigration rules,

(b) if the person has leave to enter or remain in the United Kingdom granted by virtue of residence scheme immigration rules [*i.e. under EUSS*]"

[38] This definition must also, as the SSHD submits, be read subject to regs 3(4) and 12(1)(b) of the Grace Period Regulations which provide that "relevant person" within s 3(10) of the 1971 Act also includes a person who is a "relevant person" for the purposes of those Regulations. In effect, it expands s 3(10) to include those who had resided here under the EEA Regulations prior to 31 December 2020 (a) until 30 June 2021, and (b) beyond that, if they had made an application under the EUSS before that date which is still pending or under appeal.

Automatic Deportation

[39] As noted above at [34] the 2007 Act requires the SSHD to make a deportation order against a foreign criminal unless an exception applies. If no exception applies, then there is no need to assess whether deportation is conducive to the public good.*

---

* See *Hesham Ali v SSHD* [2016] UKSC 60 at [10].

[40] Section 33 of the 2007 Act provides:

"(2)   Exception 1 is where removal of the foreign criminal in pursuance of the deportation order would breach –

  (a)   a person's Convention rights

...

(6B)   Exception 7 is where –

  (a)   the foreign criminal is a relevant person, and

  (b)   the offence for which the foreign criminal was convicted as mentioned in section 32(1)(b) consisted of or included conduct that took place before IP completion day.

(6C)   For the purposes of subsection (6B), a foreign criminal is a "relevant person" –

  (a)   if the foreign criminal is in the United Kingdom (whether or not they have entered within the meaning of section 11(1) of the Immigration Act 1971) having arrived with entry clearance granted by virtue of relevant entry clearance immigration rules

  (b)   if the foreign criminal has leave to enter or remain in the United Kingdom granted by virtue of residence scheme immigration rule [i.e. EUSS]

...

(7)   The application of an exception –

  (a)   does not prevent the making of a deportation order;

  (b)   results in it being assumed neither that deportation of the person concerned is conducive to the public good nor that it is not conducive to the public good;

but section 32(4) applies despite the application of Exception 1 or 4."

The WA in detail

[41] Article 10 provides, in full, as follows:

"Personal scope

1. Without prejudice to Title III, this Part shall apply to the following persons:

    (a) Union citizens who exercised their right to reside in the United Kingdom in accordance with Union law before the end of the transition period and continue to reside there thereafter;

    (b) United Kingdom nationals who exercised their right to reside in a Member State in accordance with Union law before the end of the transition period and continue to reside there thereafter;

    (c) Union citizens who exercised their right as frontier workers in the United Kingdom in accordance with Union law before the end of the transition period and continue to do so thereafter;

    (d) United Kingdom nationals who exercised their right as frontier workers in one or more Member States in accordance with Union law before the end of the transition period and continue to do so thereafter;

    (e) family members of the persons referred to in points (a) to (d), provided that they fulfil one of the following conditions:

        (i) they resided in the host State in accordance with Union law before the end of the transition period and continue to reside there thereafter;

        (ii) they were directly related to a person referred to in points (a) to (d) and resided outside the host State before the end of the transition period, provided that they fulfil the conditions set out in point (2) of Article 2 of Directive 2004/38/EC at the time they seek residence under this Part in order to join the person referred to in points (a) to (d) of this paragraph;

        (iii) they were born to, or legally adopted by, persons referred to in points (a) to (d) after the end of the transition period, whether inside or outside the host State, and fulfil the conditions set out in point (2)(c) of Article 2 of Directive 2004/38/EC at the time they seek residence under this Part in order to join the person referred to in points (a) to (d) of this paragraph and fulfil one of the following conditions:

- both parents are persons referred to in points (a) to (d);

- one parent is a person referred to in points (a) to (d) and the other is a national of the host State; or

- one parent is a person referred to in points (a) to (d) and has sole or joint rights of custody of the child, in accordance with the applicable rules of family law of a Member State or of the United Kingdom, including applicable rules of private international law under which rights of custody established under the law of a third State are recognised in the Member State or in the United Kingdom, in particular as regards the best interests of the child, and without prejudice to the normal operation of such applicable rules of private international law;

(f) family members who resided in the host State in accordance with Articles 12 and 13, Article 16(2) and Articles 17 and 18 of Directive 2004/38/EC before the end of the transition period and continue to reside there thereafter.

2. Persons falling under points (a) and (b) of Article 3(2) of Directive 2004/38/EC whose residence was facilitated by the host State in accordance with its national legislation before the end of the transition period in accordance with Article 3(2) of that Directive shall retain their right of residence in the host State in accordance with this Part, provided that they continue to reside in the host State thereafter.

3. Paragraph 2 shall also apply to persons falling under points (a) and (b) of Article 3(2) of Directive 2004/38/EC who have applied for facilitation of entry and residence before the end of the transition period, and whose residence is being facilitated by the host State in accordance with its national legislation thereafter.

4. Without prejudice to any right to residence which the persons concerned may have in their own right, the host State shall, in accordance with its national legislation and in accordance with point (b) of Article 3(2) of Directive 2004/38/EC, facilitate entry and residence for the partner with whom the person referred to in points (a) to (d) of paragraph 1 of this Article has a durable relationship, duly attested, where that partner resided outside the host State before the end of the transition period, provided that the relationship was durable before the end of the transition period and continues at the time the partner seeks residence under this Part.

5. In the cases referred to in paragraphs 3 and 4, the host State shall undertake an extensive examination of the personal circumstances of the persons concerned and shall justify any denial of entry or residence to such persons."

[42] Article 13 of the WA provides that those within scope of Article 10 are entitled to reside in the host State (in this case the United Kingdom), subjection to various limitations, and at Article 13(4) provides:

"13.4. The host State may not impose any limitations or conditions for obtaining, retaining or losing residence rights on the persons referred to in paragraphs 1, 2 and 3, other than those provided for in this Title. There shall be no discretion in applying the limitations and conditions provided for in this Title, other than in favour of the person concerned."

[43] Article 18.1 and Article 18.3 of the WA provide:

"1. The host State may require Union citizens or United Kingdom nationals, their respective family members and other persons, who reside in its territory in accordance with the conditions set out in this Title, to apply for a new residence status which confers the rights under this Title and a document evidencing such status which may be in a digital form.

…

3. Pending a final decision by the competent authorities on any application referred to in paragraph 1, and pending a final judgment handed down in case of judicial redress sought against any rejection of such application by the competent administrative authorities, all rights provided for in this Part shall be deemed to apply to the applicant, including Article 21 on safeguards and right of appeal, subject to the conditions set out in Article 20(4)."

[44] Articles 20 and 21 of the WA provide:

"Article 20

1. The conduct of Union citizens or United Kingdom nationals, their family members, and other persons, who exercise rights under this Title, where that conduct occurred before the end of the transition period, shall be considered in accordance with Chapter VI of Directive 2004/38/EC.

2. The conduct of Union citizens or United Kingdom nationals, their family members, and other persons, who exercise rights under this Title, where that conduct occurred after the end of the transition period, may constitute grounds for restricting the right of residence by the host State or the right of entry in the State of work in accordance with national legislation.

3. The host State or the State of work may adopt the necessary measures to refuse, terminate or withdraw any right conferred by this Title in the case of the abuse of those rights or fraud, as set out in Article 35 of Directive 2004/38/EC. Such measures shall be subject to the procedural safeguards provided for in Article 21 of this Agreement.

4. The host State or the State of work may remove applicants who submitted fraudulent or abusive applications from its territory under the conditions set out in Directive 2004/38/EC, in particular Articles 31 and 35 thereof, even before a final judgment has been handed down in the case of judicial redress sought against any rejection of such an application.

Article 21

The safeguards set out in Article 15 and Chapter VI of Directive 2004/38/EC shall apply in respect of any decision by the host State that restricts residence rights of the persons referred to in Article 10 of this Agreement."

Appendix EU of the Immigration Rules

[45] Appendix EU gives effect to Title II of Part 2 of the WA, setting out the rules for applications under the EUSS. There are three broad requirements: the applicant must make a valid application, must meet the suitability requirements and must meet the eligibility requirements. Rules EU14 and EU11 set out the eligibility requirements for pre-settled and settled status.

[46] Rule EU11 provides, so far as it is material:

"EU11. The applicant meets the eligibility requirements for indefinite leave to enter or remain as a relevant EEA citizen ... where the Secretary of State is satisfied ... that, at the date of application, one of conditions 1 to 7 set out in the following table is met:

...

Condition 3:

(a) The applicant:

(i) is a relevant EEA citizen ... and

(b) The applicant has completed a **continuous qualifying period** of five years in any (or any combination) of those categories; and

(c) Since then, no **supervening event** has occurred in respect of the applicant." [emphasis added]

[47] "Continuous qualifying period" is defined in Annex 1, so far as is relevant to these appeals, as

"a period of residence in the UK and Islands ... (a) which began before the specified date ... and (b)[(i)] during which none of the following occurred [absences from the United Kingdom] and (b)

- (ii) any period of absence due directly to an order or decision to which sub-paragraph (b)(iii) below refers, where that order or decision has been set aside or revoked; or
- (ii) the person served or is serving a sentence of imprisonment of any length in the UK and Islands, unless the conviction which led to it has been overturned; or
- (iii) any of the following in respect of the person, unless it has been set aside or revoked"

[note: the numbering is taken from the bundle and appears to be incorrect there being two sub-paragraphs (ii)]

[48] "Supervening event" is defined in Annex 1 as occurring when:

"(a) a person has been absent from the UK and islands for (a) more than five consecutive years or

(b) any of the following events has occurred in respect of the person, unless it has been set aside or revoked:

- (i) any decision or order to exclude or remove under regulation 23 or 32 of the EEA Regulations (or under the equivalent provisions of the Immigration (European Economic Area) Regulations of the Isle of Man); or
- (ii) a decision to which regulation 15(4) of the EEA Regulations otherwise refers, unless that decision arose from a previous decision under regulation 24(1) of the EEA Regulations (or the equivalent decision, subject to the equivalent qualification, under the Immigration (European Economic Area) Regulations of the Isle of Man); or
- (iii) an exclusion decision; or
- (iv) a deportation order, other than by virtue of the EEA Regulations; or
- (v) an Islands deportation order; or
- (vi) an Islands exclusion decision"

[49] With regard to suitability, we note that rule EU15 provides:

"EU15.(1) An application made under this Appendix will be refused on grounds of suitability where any of the following apply at the date of decision:

(a) The applicant is subject to a **deportation order** or to a decision to make a deportation order; or

(b) The applicant is subject to an **exclusion order** or **exclusion decision**."

[50] A deportation order is defined in Annex 1 as follows:

as the case may be:

"(a) an order made under section 5(1) of the Immigration Act 1971 by virtue of regulation 32(3) of the EEA Regulations; or

(b) an order made under section 5(1) of the Immigration Act 1971 by virtue of section 3(5) or section 3(6) of that Act in respect of:

   (i) conduct committed after the specified date; or

   (ii) conduct committed before the specified date, where the Secretary of State has decided that the deportation order is justified on the grounds of public policy, public security or public health in accordance with regulation 27 of the EEA Regulations, irrespective of whether the EEA Regulations apply to the person (except that in regulation 27 for 'with a right of permanent residence under regulation 15' and 'has a right of permanent residence under regulation 15' read 'who meets the requirements of paragraph EU11 or EU12 of Appendix EU to the Immigration Rules'; and for 'an EEA decision' read 'a deportation decision')

in addition, for the avoidance of doubt, (b) includes a deportation order made under the Immigration Act 1971 in accordance with section 32 of the UK Borders Act 2007."

[51] We pause here to note that, as Ms Smyth submitted, the effect of the amendment of reg. 27 of the EEA Regulations is that the enhanced right of protection granted by reg. 27(3) to those who had acquired permanent residence through five years' residence in accordance with the EEA Regulations is extended by the EUSS to those who had simply resided in the United Kingdom for that period.

[52] In addition to the legislative provisions set out above, we note also that the SSHD has provided guidance on conducive deportation which sets out under which power a deportation decision should be made.

Grounds of appeal

[53] Although the EEA Regulations have been revoked, as noted above [20], in a case where the Grace Period Regulations do not apply, the appeal rights under those regulations have been preserved by paragraphs 4 and 5 to Schedule 3 of the Transitional Provisions Regulations. Paragraph 5(1) of those regulations draws a distinction between appeals and decisions taken prior to 31 December 2020 on the one hand (1(a) to 1(c)) and those taken after that date (1(d)). That distinction is maintained in paragraph 6(1)(cc) which sets out the rights of appeal in each of these different categories.

[54] Thus, in an appeal against a decision taken under the EEA Regulations after 31 December 2020, the ground of appeal is whether the decision under challenge breached the appellant's rights under the EEA Regulations as they are continued in effect by the Transitional Provisions Regulations or the CRA Regulations, not whether they breached Treaty Rights.

[55] Under the CRA Regulations a right of appeal is granted to those refused leave under Appendix EU. The permissible grounds of appeal are set out in reg. 8 and provide, so far as is relevant:

"**Reg. 8 – Grounds of appeal**

(1)   An appeal under these Regulations must be brought on one or both of the following two grounds.

(2)   The first ground of appeal is that the decision breaches any right which the appellant has by virtue of –

   (a)   [Chapter 1, or Article 24(2), 24(3), 25(2) or 25(3) of Chapter 2], of Title II [, or Article 32(1)(b) of Title III,] of Part 2 of the withdrawal Agreement,

(3)   The second ground of appeal is that –

   (a)   where the decision is mentioned in regulation 3(1)(a) or (b) or 5, it is not in accordance with the provision of the immigration rules by virtue of which it was made; …"

[56] Finally, a decision refusing a human rights claim can be appealed under sections 82(1)(b) and 84(2) of the 2002 Act on the ground that the decision is unlawful under section 6 of the Human Rights Act 1998.

Discussion

The position prior to 31 December 2020

[57] Prior to the United Kingdom leaving the EU, citizens of the member states (and their families as defined) were entitled to move to and reside in the United Kingdom under article 20 of the TFEU, so long as they did so within the limitations provided for in articles 21, 45 and 49 TFEU. Those rights were set out primarily in the Citizens' Rights Directive.*

[58] We observe that the right of free movement was not absolute; it is tied primarily to economic activity, that is, the exercise of Treaty Rights. That can be seen from *Dano v Jobcentre Leipzig* [2014] EUECJ C-333/13 at [71] and in article 7(1) of the Citizens' Rights Directive. It is also evident from article 14 of that Directive that those who cease to meet the requirements can be removed, although not automatically. The position is different for those who had acquired the permanent right of residence.

[59] A distinction is drawn in the Citizens' Rights Directive between expulsion *per se* and an exclusion order (or ban on entry – see article 15(1) of the Citizens' Rights Directive); on an analogy, in domestic law terms, that is the distinction between removing an individual and the imposition of a deportation order.

[60] It follows from this that EU nationals may have been living in the United Kingdom prior to 31 December 2020 but may not have had a right of residence under EU law. That was the situation in *Dano* where Ms Dano, a Romanian national, had no right of residence in Germany.

[61] We pause at this point to note that, as Ms Smyth explained, EU nationals who had simply resided in the United Kingdom, without not necessarily exercising Treaty rights, are entitled to status under the EUSS.

The Withdrawal Agreement

[62] We accept that, as Ms Sabic and Mr Buley submitted, the WA has effect in domestic law by operation of section 7A(2) of EUWA 2018.

[63] The SSHD submits that the WA in terms of personal scope is confined to those who had resided "in accordance with Union Law". As a result, and consistent with the sixth recital, not all EU nationals fall within the scope of the Withdrawal Agreement and the rights it confers, in particular the protection conferred by Article 20.

[64] Ms Sabic for Mr Abdullah and Mr Buley for the AIRE centre submitted that it was not necessary for an individual to have been exercising Treaty Rights in order to qualify for the protection given by Article 20.

[65] We are not persuaded that the creation of the EUSS, a scheme that covers those not within the scope of article 10 of the WA, alters the provisions of the WA. We do not accept that is the effect of article 13(4), following *Celik*.

---

* But not "derivative rights" based on interpretation of the TFEU by the ECJ in cases such as Zambrano [2011] EUECJ C- 34/09.

[66] We do not accept either Mr Buley's submission that article 10 can be construed such that "exercised their right to reside in the United Kingdom in accordance with Union Law…" includes a person who had an enforceable right not to be removed. That is simply inconsistent with the Union law as set out above.

[67] We are not persuaded either that the safeguards set out in articles 20 and 21 of the WA are applicable to those not within the scope of article 10. That submission is contrary to the express wording of article 10.1, the limitation in article 20.1 and the express reference to article 10 in article 21.

[68] It is sufficiently clear from the structure of the WA that it continues the rights of those who fall within scope prior to them acquiring status pursuant to article 18, pending a decision on a timely application. We acknowledge that the Secretary of State takes the view that the protections flowing from article 18.3 apply to those who have made applications, even late. That is, we accept, a reasonable interpretation; the alternative – that those who made late applications did not have the rights conferred – would be contrary to the reference to "any application" within 18.1 which is not qualified by any reference to time. But, we do not accept that this interpretation or the Secretary of State's practice and guidance means that those who do not come within the scope of article 10 are, if they make an application, brought within scope of the WA. To do so would be to ignore the purpose of the procedure as set out in article 1(a) which is to verify an entitlement to the residence rights set out in Title II which, as we have seen, is limited to those who had residence rights immediately before 31 December 2020.

[69] Despite the submissions made, we do not consider that article 18.3 has the effect of applying articles 20 and 21 to all those who have made an application for a new residence status. First, this article comes within the ambit of article 10.1. Second, it is permissive; it allows a member state to require those who reside in accordance with the conditions set out in that title to apply. It does not state that any scheme put in place must apply only to those meeting the scope of article 10 (and the EUSS is wider). Further, it would make no sense for those out of scope of article 10 due to a lack of prior exercise of Treaty Rights to be granted rights in those states which do have a constitutive scheme like the EUSS but not in those states which do not have such a scheme. That it is open to a member state to operate a scheme more generous than that provided for in the Withdrawal Agreement does not operate to alter the wording of that agreement, whatever the position may be in domestic law. As was noted in *R (Independent Monitoring Authority) v SSHD* [2022] EWHC 3274 ("*IMA*") at [134]:

> "134. I have mentioned that the defendant, in framing the EUSS, has adopted a policy which is more generous than what is required by the WA, in that leave may be granted under the EUSS by reference to 'mere' residence in the United Kingdom at the relevant point in time, rather than residence in accordance with EU free movement rights. This policy, however, sheds no light on the interpretative task for this court."

[70] Thus, the rights conferred by article 20 and 21 of the WA apply only to those within the scope of article 10 and those to whom article 18 extends those rights. In any event, we are not persuaded that any practice of the Secretary of State or the Immigration Rules is capable of altering the effect of the WA.

Domestic law

[71] We turn next to the position under domestic law. At the outset, we observe that the EUSS is a constitutive scheme; the rights under it flow from the grant of status, unlike EU law rights of free movement where the documents issued only confirmed rights conferred by operation of law. That being so, it was necessary to provide protection of those free movement rights for those moving from EU free movement rights which ended on 31 December 2020 to rights granted under EUSS, hence the Grace Period Regulations which are necessary to comply with article 18 of the WA.

[72] It follows also, as a matter of logic, that in the context of deportations, convictions in respect of conduct up until 31 December 2020 may not occur until well after that date, and in respect of persons who either had or did not have rights under the WA, and who may have been granted leave under the EUSS prior to conviction, or have a pending application at that point; or, may simply not have applied at that point.

[73] We accept that, as Ms Smyth submitted, the effect of the EUSS as it is structured is that reg. 27 of the EEA Regulations is applied by operation of the definition of "deportation order" as set out in Annex 1 to Appendix EU. We accept also that whether that test is met is a matter to be considered on appeal.

When do the EEA Regulations apply?

[74] As noted above at [21] to [25] the EEA Regulations continued to apply, subject to modifications, to a "relevant person" during the "grace period", the latter being from 31 December 2020 to 30 June 2021. That is by operation of reg.3 of the Grace Period Regulations. They also apply (reg. 4) to a person who made an application within the grace period and apply while that application is pending, that period extending until a final decision on appeal is made.

[75] It is thus necessary to consider whether the residence relied upon, be that residence immediately before 31 December 2020, or the residence necessary to acquire permanent residence, falls within these provisions. If that is not the case, then the individual is not a "relevant person" for the purposes of the Grace Period Regulations, or possibly section 3(5A) of the 1971 Act. In doing so, attention must be paid to the definition of continuous residence – see [25] above.

[76] In addition, as noted above at [27] to [29], the EEA Regulations may apply by operation of the CRRE.

The domestic deportation regime

[77] Ms Sabic and Mr Buley submitted that the Secretary of State was wrong to apply the automatic deportation regime to ZA, given the effect of article 18.3 and section 3(5A) of the 1971 Act.

[78] Ms Sabic submitted that s 3(5A)(b) applies article 18.3 to all those who have made applications, and that this supports her argument as to the scope of article 18, given that it is part of domestic law. In interpreting the effect of section 3(5A)(a), it is necessary to step back and consider what article 20 says. It sets out broad principles, but it is article 21 that applies those principles to an individual and it is that structure which is replicated in section 3(5A)(a) and (b). Section (5A)(b) cannot

be interpreted as covering those who are not relevant persons either within section 3(10) or by operation of the Grace Period Regulations, relevant persons being those who were lawfully resident and who made timely applications. In effect, section 3(5A)(a) gives force to article 20 and section 3(5A)(b) gives force to article 21.

[79] There is an apparent tension between the automatic deportation regime under the 2007 Act and the provisions of the 1971 Act. Under section 3(5)(a) of the 1971 Act the SSHD has a discretion to deport someone if he considers it conducive to the public good. That requires an evaluation of that issue first. Section 3(5A) of that Act prevents the SSHD from deeming a deportation to be conducive to the public good if it would be contrary to articles 20 and 21 of the WA, that is, the EU deportation provisions.

[80] In contrast, the regime under the 2007 Act imposes a duty on the SSHD to deport foreign criminals (see [34] above). Section 32(4) of the 2007 Act deems the deportation of a foreign criminal to be conducive to the public good. Not all EU nationals convicted of offences would meet the definition of foreign criminal, although in practice it is unlikely that the Secretary of State would seek to deport such persons. Section 32(4) is, however disapplied if Exception 7 applies. But, the application of that exception does not prevent the making of a deportation order.

[81] The effect of this scheme is that once the Secretary of State has considered whether an exception applies, and concludes that it does not, he does not need to consider whether deportation is conducive to the public good and is then under a duty to make a deportation order.

[82] In the cases of ZA and AS, a two-stage process was operated. A decision to make a deportation order was made, and submissions invited as to why a deportation order should not be made. The SSHD then made an order, having concluded that none of the exceptions were met. Implicit in that is a finding that deportation was justified by reference to the EU deportation regime as set out in the EEA Regulations as preserved and as provided for in article 20 and 21 of the WA.

[83] We do not accept the argument that the making of a deportation order against an EEA national is contrary to the WA or for that matter the Citizens' Rights Directive. It is evident from the scheme enacted in Chapter VI of the Directive (and in particular article 31.4) that an expulsion decision can be taken before an appeal. If the appeal is successful, then the deportation order is revoked whereas if the decision under appeal was simply a decision to make a deportation order, then the order is not made.

[84] In our experience, it was formerly the SSHD's practice to make a decision to deport an EEA national giving rise to a right of appeal but more recently, the SSHD has followed the process under the 2007 Act whereby a deportation order is issued and then the appeal follows.

[85] Further, where there is no deportation decision taken under the EEA Regulations as preserved, and there is consideration under the EUSS rules, the means by which "deportation order" as defined in the EUSS has the effect of requiring the SSHD to consider whether the deportation is justified by reference to reg. 27 of the EEA Regulations has to be applied in respect of pre-31 December 2020 conduct of EEA nationals. That applies also to those not within the scope of the WA but within scope of the EUSS. We are satisfied also, that the ground of appeal under the CRA Regulations permits that issue to be considered by a Tribunal and a finding reached as to whether an appellant's deportation is justified by reference to reg. 27 of the EEA Regulations.

[86] We do not accept Mr Buley's submission that there is in substance, any breach of the principle of equality in how the Secretary of State has dealt with cases either under the EEA Regulations or under the EUSS; in both cases the relevant tests under the EEA Regulations were applied.

[87] The arguments he advances come down to sequencing. We accept that there will be cases where an application under EUSS is made late and after a deportation order was made. But, if such a person was at the time of the deportation decision out of scope of the WA, that cannot be faulted. The making of an application under the EUSS cannot retroactively make such a decision unlawful, and the EUSS as properly understood requires an evaluation of the deportation order in question by reference to the Chapter VI of the Citizens' Rights Directive.

Scope of the rights of appeal

[88] As stated above at [53], paragraph 6(1)(cc) sets out the rights of appeal applicable to different categories. Thus, in an appeal against a decision taken under the EEA Regulations after 31 December 2020, the ground of appeal under section 84 of the Nationality, Immigration and Asylum Act 2002 (as inserted by the EEA Regulations) is whether an appellant's rights under the EEA Regulations as continued in force either by the Transitional Provisions Regulations or by the WA are breached.

[89] As noted above at [55] a decision under the EUSS can be appealed on two grounds: that the decision is not in accordance with the EUSS rules or is contrary to the WA.

Appeals where human rights grounds apply

[90] The ground of appeal in the case of a human rights decision is as set out in section 84 of the 2002 Act.

[91] It is not in dispute that in an appeal raising article 8 of the Human Rights Convention a judge must adopt the five-step approach set out in *Razgar* [2004] UKHL 27. The focus of the submissions we heard was on the fourth question: is the decision in accordance with the law? As noted above at [9] this is an issue on which we received further submissions.

[92] In her skeleton argument and in oral submissions before us, Ms Smyth for the Secretary of State submitted that whether a decision was "in accordance with the law" is to be decided in line with *R (Bridges) v Chief Constable of South Wales* [2020] EWCA Civ 1058 where the Court of Appeal set out [55] a statement of the principles:

> "55. The Divisional Court set out the general principles on this issue at [80]:
>
> > The general principles applicable to the 'in accordance with the law' standard are well-established: see generally *per* Lord Sumption in *Catt*, above, [11]–[14]; and in *Re Gallagher* [2019] 2 WLR 509 at [16]–[31]. In summary, the following points apply.

(1) The measure in question (a) must have 'some basis in domestic law' and (b) must be 'compatible with the rule of law', which means that it should comply with the twin requirements of 'accessibility' and 'foreseeability' (*Sunday Times v United Kingdom* (1979) 2 EHRR 245; *Sliver v United Kingdom* (1983) 5 EHRR 347; and *Malone v United Kingdom* (1985) 7 EHRR 14).

(2) The legal basis must be 'accessible' to the person concerned, meaning that it must be published and comprehensible, and it must be possible to discover what its provisions are. The measure must also be 'foreseeable' meaning that it must be possible for a person to foresee its consequences for them and it should not 'confer a discretion so broad that its scope is in practice dependent on the will of those who apply it, rather than on the law itself' (Lord Sumption in *Re Gallagher, ibid*, at [17]).

(3) Related to (2), the law must 'afford adequate legal protection against arbitrariness and accordingly indicate with sufficient clarity the scope of discretion conferred on the competent authorities and the manner of its exercise' (*S v United Kingdom*, above, at [95] and [99]).

(4) Where the impugned measure is a discretionary power, (a) what is not required is 'an over-rigid regime which does not contain the flexibility which is needed to avoid an unjustified interference with a fundamental right' and (b) what is required is that 'safeguards should be present in order to guard against overbroad discretion resulting in arbitrary, and thus disproportionate, interference with Convention rights' (*per* Lord Hughes in *Beghal v Director of Public Prosecutions* [2016] AC 88 at [31] and [32]). Any exercise of power that is unrestrained by law is not 'in accordance with the law'.

(5) The rules governing the scope and application of measures need not be statutory, provided that they operate within a framework of law and that there are effective means of enforcing them (*per* Lord Sumption in *Catt* at [11]).

(6) The requirement for reasonable predictability does not mean that the law has to codify answers to every possible issue (*per* Lord Sumption in *Catt* at [11])."

[93] We pause here to note that it does not appear from the judgment in *AA (Poland)* that this case or indeed any others on this issue were cited, nor does there appear to have been argument on the point.

[94] In her oral submissions to us, Ms Smyth submitted that, applying those principles, and as *Charles (Human Rights Appeal; scope)* [2018] UKUT 00089 confirmed that the principles of United Kingdom deportation law met the relevant test, on no proper view could it be argued that the deportation decisions in the cases of either ZA or AS were not in accordance with the law.

[95] In her initial submissions, Ms Sabic submitted that the question of whether the decision to deport him was "in accordance with the law" required consideration not just of whether there is adequately accessible and sufficiently precise domestic law but that the test encompasses the requirement for a public authority to act in compliance with domestic law.

[96] Mr Buley submitted that the WA is part of domestic law by operation of section 7A EUWA 2018, and that a deportation order will only be in accordance with the law if it does not breach the rights granted by the WA.

[97] Since we heard these submissions the Court of Appeal has handed down *AA (Poland)* where Warby LJ held [67]:

"67. The SSHD accepts that the Judge was right to find that removal would represent an interference with AA's Article 8 rights. The Judge considered it followed from his finding that removal was contrary to the 2016 Regulations that the interference was 'incapable of justification'. In one sense he was right. An interference can only be justified under Article 8(2) if it is 'in accordance with the law'. If deportation could not be justified under the 2016 Regulations it could not have been justified by reference to s 32 of the 2002 Act either, and it would have had no lawful basis. That would be the end of the human rights argument. But that is not how the Judge approached the matter. It is clear from paragraphs [20] and [55] that he went on to consider the public interest question and concluded that it was answered by the proportionality assessment he had already conducted for the purposes of the 2016 Regulations."

[98] And, at [71] to [72]:

"71. In my judgement, the correct approach is as indicated in *Badewa*. The application of the 2016 Regulations is a legally distinct exercise from the assessment of a human rights claim. Where both arise, they should be addressed separately and in turn. The 2016 Regulations should be addressed first, including the assessment required by Regulation 27(5)(a) of whether deportation would comply with the EU principle of proportionality. The provisions of Part 5A of the 2002 Act have no part to play at that stage. But they must be addressed as part of the human rights assessment, if the public interest question arises.

72. The public interest question will not necessarily arise. Although deportation will commonly interfere with Article 8 rights that will not invariably be the case. If it is, the second question arises: whether deportation would be in accordance with the law. That will not be so if deportation would be contrary to the 2016 Regulations. In such a case the human rights analysis need go no further. But if deportation would be consistent with the 2016 Regulations and otherwise lawful the tribunal should address the public interest question in the way that Parliament has prescribed in Part 5A of the 2002 Act. Where, as here, the appellant is a 'serious offender' the tribunal will have to apply s 117C(6)."

[99] It is submitted by ZA, AS and the AIRE centre, that a finding that a deportation decision is contrary to the EEA Regulations, and by extension the WA, will result in a finding that it is "not accordance with the law" and thus any article 8 appeal will succeed on that basis, it being unnecessary to consider proportionality within article 8. It is further submitted that this will also be the case where there is a finding in an appeal under the CRA Regulations that the decision was not in accordance with the relevant Immigration Rules.

[100] While the Court of Appeal in *AA (Poland)* did not make express reference to the principles set out in *Bridges* we have no hesitation in concluding that they must have borne them in mind. We accept, also that the Court of Appeal did not consider the position where there is no appeal under the EEA Regulations. It does not decide what the position would be if there had been an appeal under the CRA Regulations.

[101] In that context, we pause here to remind ourselves of the consequences of the finding that a decision to deport is contrary to the EEA Regulations, the WA or the EUSS. In doing so, we note Ms Smyth's acceptance before us that the consequence for the person who was successful in such an appeal would be that the deportation order against them would be revoked, and leave granted under the EUSS. At that point the person in question would be a relevant person for the purposes of Exception 7 under section 33 of the 2007 Act and section 3(5A) of the 1971 Act. The effect of Exception 7 differs significantly from Exception 1[*] in the effect it has on section 3(5)(a) of the 1971 Act and whether a deportation is conducive.

[102] We remind ourselves also of the difficulty posed by sections 117A to 117D, and in particular, 117C of the 2002 Act, as identified in *AA (Poland)*. Unlike the situation in *TZ (Pakistan) and PG (India) v The Secretary of State for the Home Department* [2018] EWCA Civ 1109, where a foreign criminal is involved, the policy as set out in the statute, is that they should be deported. Even were that overcome, an anomalous situation arises whereby, if the appeal is allowed on EEA Regulations Grounds (or under the CRA Regulations when leave is granted) Exception 7 would apply and all that flows from that, but if Exception 1 applies, as a result of allowing the appeal on human rights grounds, with a different result as to the conduciveness of deportation. This situation would be all the more anomalous were the EEA Regulations test to be considered as part of an assessment of proportionality in considering the fifth *Razgar* question that it is necessary to consider whether the requirements of the immigration rules are met.

[103] Taking all of these factors into account and applying the principles set out in *Bridges*, we consider that because of the particular nature of the two deportation regimes, that it flows from a finding that a deportation decision is contrary to the EUSS rules because it is not justified by reference to reg. 27 will result in a finding that it is "not in accordance with the law" and thus any article 8 appeal would succeed on that basis. This should not, however, be understood as applying to those situations where other provisions of the Immigration Rules are met; that still requires an assessment of proportionality in line with *TZ (Pakistan)*.

[104] In the light of this, there is all the more reason why any appeal under section 82 should be stayed pending a decision on any EUSS claim then under consideration.

---

[*] See section 33(1) of the 2007 Act.

[105] Pausing there to take stock, we consider that the following principles apply:

(A) In an appeal where conduct prior to 11pm on 31 December 2020 give rise to a decision to deport an EEA citizen is in issue, it is necessary to determine whether, as at 31 December 2020 (and at the point a decision is taken):

  (1) Was the EEA citizen resident in the United Kingdom?

  (2) If so, for what continuous period (as defined in reg. 3 of the EEA Regulations) before that?

  (3) Was the EEA citizen's residence lawful, that is, in accordance with the EEA Regulations?

  (4) Had the EEA citizen acquired permanent residence under the EEA Regulations?

  (5) Had the EEA citizen made an application under the EUSS before the end of the Grace Period, that is 30 June 2021, and

  (6) If so, is it pending?

(B) The answers to these questions will determine whether the EEA citizen came within the scope of the Withdrawal Agreement, the Grace Period Regulations or the EUSS. They will also determine whether that individual is a "relevant person" for the purposes of section 3(5A) and (10) of the Immigration Act 1971 and section 33(6B) and (6C) of the UK Borders Act 2007, as expanded by regs 3(4) and 12(1)(b) of the Grace Period Regulations.

(C) In respect of conduct carried out prior to 31 December 2020, the EEA Regulations only apply directly to an individual (and thus gave rise to an appeal under those regulations) if:

  (1) The decision was taken under the EEA Regulations prior to 31 December 2020 or in connection with an application pending under the regulations; or,

  (2) The individual was an EEA citizen (or a family member of such a person) lawfully resident under the EEA Regs (including those who had acquired permanent residence under reg. 3 the EEA Regulations) and either:

    (i) The decision was taken by 30 June 2021; or

    (ii) Was taken after that date but when a valid application under the EUSS had been made before 30 June 2021 and was still pending (but not if they had been granted leave under the EUSS); or

  (3) Is a person who falls within the scope of the CRRE Regulations

(D) With the passage of time, the class of individuals falling under the EEA Regulations and entitled to a right of appeal under those provisions will diminish to very small numbers.

(E) If a decision to deport was not made under the EEA Regulations, then there is no right of appeal under those regulations.

(F) In an appeal under the CRA Regulations, it will be necessary to consider the application of reg. 27 of the EEA Regulations. This can arise under either ground of appeal as:

   (1) if the EEA citizen is within the scope of the WA, then articles 20 and 21 of the WA apply;

   (2) if not in scope of the WA, the definition of deportation order is such that only one which is justified by reference to reg. 27 of the EEA Regulations makes the EEA citizen ineligible for a grant of status under the EUSS.

(G) There is a distinction between (1) and (2) because under the definition of deportation order under the EUSS, only 5 years continuous residence (as opposed to lawful residence under the EEA Regulations) is needed to acquire enhanced protection.

(H) The effect of a finding that the deportation is not justified by reference to reg. 27 of the EEA Regulations is that Exception 7 under section 33 of the United Kingdom Borders Act 2007 is met, and the Secretary of State's policy is then to revoke any deportation order, at which point leave to remain under the EUSS can be granted.

(I) If the deportation decision against an EEA citizen arises in a human rights appeal under section 82 of the 2002 Act, then that appeal should be stayed pending resolution of any outstanding application under the EUSS to allow an appeal against a negative decision to be determined as the same time as a human rights appeal.

(J) Where an appeal has been allowed under the EEA Regulations; or, in an appeal under the CRA Regulations on the basis the deportation decision is not justified by reference to reg. 27 of the EEA Regulations, it follows that any linked appeal against the same decision under section 82 of the 2002 Act will be allowed on the basis that the decision under appeal was not in accordance with the law.

[106] We then turn to the specific cases.

ZA [Abdullah]

[107] As noted in the Error of Law decision, ZA's case is that he had acquired permanent residence in accordance with the EEA regulations, prior to 31 December 2020, and that he had applied under the EUSS on 30 June 2021, and thus within the time limit. He was asked to provide evidence of his status, his solicitors replying to that request on 15 November 2021. On 3 May 2022, the Secretary of State signed a deportation order pursuant to section 32(5) of the 2007 Act, refused his human rights claim and refused his application under the EUSS, having not accepted that he had been resident in the United Kingdom for a continuous period of five years and had so not acquired permanent residence, nor was he satisfied that he had been lawfully resident immediately prior to 31 December 2020. He was not satisfied either that ZA met the suitability requirements as he was subject to a deportation order, concluding also by reference to reg. 27 of the EEA Regulations that this was justified.

[108] The judge found that ZA had not acquired permanent residence; that the decision to refuse the EUSS application was correct; and, nonetheless, deportation was disproportionate in article 8 terms.

[109] Judge Kebede set that decision aside in its entirety, observing at [22] that the legal position was unclear.

[110] In this case there were two rights of appeal: one under the 2002 Act against the decision to refuse the Human Rights claim consequent on the deportation order; and, the other under the CRA Regulations against the decision under the EUSS.

[111] Applying the reasoning set out above, the correct sequence should have been to consider, in the context of the EUSS decision, whether ZA's conduct was such that his deportation was justified by reference to reg. 27 of the EEA Regulations. That will require first a consideration of when or if he was exercising Treaty Rights (and whether he had acquired permanent residence) prior to 31 December 2020. If either of those were made out, then he would come within the scope of the Withdrawal Agreement. If he does not meet either of those conditions it is necessary to ask whether he was resident prior to 31 December 2020 and if that is so, was it for a continuous period of 5 years. If either of those is correct, then he falls within the EUSS. And, if he had acquired 5 years continuous residence, he benefits from enhanced protection.

[112] Once those facts have been established, and decision made on the deportation issue, and thus on the EUSS appeal, then the section 82 appeal will need to be considered as ZA has rights of appeal under both.

[113] While we accept that it may follow from the findings as to exercise of Treaty Rights that ZA fell within the scope of the WA, and that a decision should have been made under the EEA Regulations, that makes no material difference to the conduct of the appeal as the test would be the same.

[114] We accept that the section 82 appeal will involve a consideration of whether the decision was "in accordance with the law" as part of the five-step process set out in *Razgar* [2004] UKHL 27. In the light of our findings, the appeal under section 82 would fall to be allowed on that basis, if ZA succeeds under the EEA Regulations.

[115] Turning then to the list of issues in this appeal, we answer them as follows:

(i) ZA has a right of appeal under the CRA Regulations on both available grounds and a right of appeal under section 82 of the 2002 Act.

(ii) ZA does not have a right of appeal under the EEA Regulations as there is no decision under those regulations made. That would have been the case had he fallen within the scope of the WA at the relevant time, due to exercise of Treaty Rights as at 31 December 2020, a matter that needs to be resolved. But, in any event, the issue on appeal under the CRA Regulations is whether the test in reg. 27 of the EEA Regulations is met, and thus the result is the same.

(iii) Whether ZA benefits from the imperative grounds test, or serious grounds level of protection turns on findings of fact to be made as to his residence in the United Kingdom, and whether during that period he was exercising Treaty Rights.

(iv) Whether the decision to deport ZA ought to have been done under the EEA Regulations turns on the answers to (iii) above.

(v) For the reasons set out at (ii) above, it makes no difference whether ZA's deportation was regulated by the EEA Regulations or not, given the same test applies under the CRA Regulations. Nor would there be any material difference between the two appeals.

(vi) ZA's appeal should be allowed under section 82 on the basis that it was not in accordance with the law if he succeeds in demonstrating that the decision to deport him is not justified by reference to reg. 27.

[116] The following issues therefore need still to be determined:

(i) whether ZA had acquired permanent residence prior to 31 December 2020

(ii) Or, alternatively whether he was exercising Treaty rights as at that date

[117] The directions as to how the appeal will proceed are set out below.

AS (Szuba)

[118] On 14 October 2020, Mr Szuba was convicted on a guilty plea of possession with intent to supply Class A drugs for which on 28 January 2021 he was sentenced to 5 years and 3 months' imprisonment. On 23 October 2021, the Secretary of State took a decision to deport him pursuant to the Immigration Act 1971 as he was a foreign criminal and none of the exceptions set out in section 33 of the 2007 Act applied. His then solicitors wrote to the Secretary of State on 9 November 2021, submitting that the decision should have been taken pursuant to the EEA Regulations, not domestic law. The Secretary of State replied on 7 March 2022, seeking evidence that he had made an EUSS application in February 2020 as claimed.

[119] On 23 May 2022, the Secretary of State, having treated AS's representations as a human rights claim, refused it, giving rise to a right of appeal, and serving on him a deportation order dated 23 May 2022.

[120] On appeal, the judge noted at [8] that AS appealed on the basis that his case is governed by the EEA Regulations, recording at [10] that he had confirmed with the representatives that the appeal is governed by those regulations.

[121] The judge directed himself at [16] that by operation of the CRA regulations at reg. 7 the substantive law governing the appeal is the EEA Regulations. Having heard evidence and submissions, the judge went on to find:

(i) AS had made an application under the EUSS in February 2020 [27];

(ii) AS had acquired permanent residence under the EEA Regulations [28], [29];

(iii) AS qualifies for the highest level of protection – imperative grounds of public policy [30];

(iv) AS did not present a sufficiently serious current threat [31];

(v) Removal would not be proportionate [32].

[122] The Secretary of State sought permission to appeal on the grounds that the judge had erred as he:

(i) had no jurisdiction to consider the appeal under the EEA Regulations, the appeal being solely an appeal on human rights grounds under section 82 of the 2002 Act, the Grace Period Regulations not applying;

(ii) had given inadequate reasons for finding that AS had made an EUSS application in February 2020;

[123] Permission to appeal was granted on 24 February 2023.

[124] In his response pursuant to rule 24, AS avers that the judge did not err in his approach to the law, and that if he did, it was immaterial, observing at [13] that the Secretary of State had not challenged many relevant findings. It is also averred that the judge had, having had regard to all the evidence, given sufficient reasons for concluding that AS had made an application under the EUSS in February 2020.

[125] The relevant issues in this appeal were agreed.

[126] The decision under appeal was a human rights decision and thus the right of appeal was under section 82 of the 2002 Act. There was no decision under the EEA Regulations or under the EUSS and so there was no appeal under the CRA or the EEA Regulations. On that basis, the FtT made a significant error [16] in concluding that the substantive law governing the appeal was the EEA Regulations, an error compounded at [17]. Even had AS made an application under the EUSS in February 2020, there was no decision under those regulations which gave rise to an appeal.

[127] In the circumstances, we agree with Ms Smyth that the judge should have considered the appeal under section 82(1) of the 2002 Act. He did not do so. Had he applied the five-step *Razgar* analysis, then he would have had to consider

whether the decision was in accordance with the law, before considering whether it was proportionate. He did neither.

[128] Whether that error was material turns primarily on whether the judge erred in finding that AS had made an application under the EUSS in February 2020. It is to that issue that we turn next.

[129] With regard to the finding that AS had made an EUSS application in February 2020, we remind ourselves that as an appellate tribunal we should be reluctant to overturn a finding of fact made by a lower tribunal.

[130] AS's evidence is that he had made an application for settlement at the same time as his mother and stepfather in February 2020, a point put to the Secretary of State in representations made on 9 November 2021. On 7 March 2022, he wrote to AS's solicitors seeking further information about that application. There is no indication in the bundle that there was a response to that letter, and in its Notice of Decision dated 23 May 2022, the Home Office stated [2] that AS had not provided documentary evidence of his application, nor that he had an outstanding application to the EUSS. There is, however, an email dated 7 June 2022 from AS's stepfather, stating that they do not have the confirmation email as Yahoo mail deletes the account after 12 months' inactivity. That email address is not specified. There is, further, an email from UK Visas sent Wednesday 15 June (presumably 2022), stating that they had closed a UK Visas and Immigration account registered to that address as a result of a phone call and that as a result, any applications linked to that account were deleted.

[131] It appears from the Certificate of Application dated 11 July 2022 that AS had made an application under the EUSS on 30 June 2022.

[132] There is no mention in AS's Witness statement of having made any application. The judge summarised his evidence as follows:

> "12. In summary, having adopted his witness statement, the appellant confirmed that he has made an application under the EUSS together with his mother and stepfather in February 2020 and that it had been indicated that that application had been pending but he did not receive a reference in respect of it. He contacted the Home Office from prison to enquire about the status of that application and was advised that the pending application would be deleted and that he should resend the application by paper which he has done. The outcome of that application is pending."

[133] Here, there was no documentary evidence that an application under the EUSS had been made. The email from the Home Office states simply that any application that had been made would be deleted which is not confirmation than an application had been made. On a proper analysis, it is the oral evidence, not the documents that indicate an application had been made then deleted.

[134] Further, as Ms Smyth submitted, the judge does not engage with the letters from the Secretary of State which concluded that there was no evidence of an application being made. We accept that the Secretary of State's representative did not suggest that AS was not a credible witness (see decision at [28]) but it was still for AS to prove on the balance of probabilities that he had made an application in February 2020.

[135] We do not consider that the reasoning in this case is adequate in the circumstances of the case, given the lack of any documentary evidence that an application was made and we note this is a case in which it is said that it was

received but can no longer be found. AS's solicitors wrote to the Home Office on 9 November asking them to check their records. But the judge did not engage with this, or why the Home Office could find no record of the application.

[136] Accordingly, we find that ground 2 is made out, and the finding that AS had made an application under the EUSS in February 2020 is unsustainable.

[137] We accept that, in considering a human rights appeal under section 82 of the 2002 Act, it will be necessary, following *Razgar* to consider whether the decision was in accordance with the law, and whether the requirements of the Immigration Rules (including EUSS) had been met, that being relevant to proportionality. Here, having directed himself wrongly according to the law, and having reached an unsustainable finding of fact as to the making of an EUSS application, the judge did not address the issue of proportionality with reference to the law applicable to human rights appeals. Taking these factors together, we conclude that the error was material, given the fundamental error in approach to the relevant law.

[138] For these reasons, we answer the issues raised in AS's appeal as follows:

(i) The scope of the appeal is confined to section 82 of the 2002 Act, a human rights appeal.

(ii) The judge erred in applying the EEA Regulations as they were not directly applicable, there being no decision under those Regulations.

(iii) The error in doing so is material for the reasons set out above.

(iv) The FtT did err in concluding that AS had made an application under the EUSS.

(v) The reasons for doing so were inadequate.

(vi) The FtT was entitled to consider the EEA Regulations but only indirectly in considering Appendix EU, given how deportation order is defined under that by reference to reg. 27 of the EEA Regulations. Whether AS fell within the scope of the WA depends on whether he had made an EUSS application before 30 June 2021, an issue to be determined.

[139] We have given directions for the remaking of this appeal below.

RR [Rudokas]

[140] RR did not attend the hearing, nor was he represented. The panel is still unaware of any explanation for this. We are, however, satisfied that he was given due notice of the time, date and venue of the appeal and in all the circumstances of the case, we were satisfied that, bearing in mind the overriding objective, it would be fair and in the interests of justice to proceed to determine the appeal.

[141] On 21 January 2020, RR was granted indefinite leave to remain under the EUSS. On 13 July 2022 he was sentenced to 2 years imprisonment in respect of acquiring, using, or possessing criminal property, an offence with a start date of 12 October 2021. He was at the same time sentenced to a month's imprisonment in

respect of each of two counts of possession of a prohibited weapon, all three sentences to be served concurrently.

[142] On 9 August 2022, the Secretary of State wrote to RR, informing him that she had decided to make a deportation decision against him as a foreign criminal, pursuant to the 1971 Act and the 2007 Act as he had not shown that any of the exceptions set out in section 33 of that Act applied to him. He was also informed of his right of appeal under reg. 6 of the CRA and of the possible grounds of appeal.

[143] In his grounds of appeal, RR, said that the deportation order breached his right to private and family life under article 8 of the Human Rights Convention, and that his deportation is not conducive to the public good.

[144] On 17 October 2022, RR was served with a section 120 notice. On 25 October 2022, his solicitors wrote to the Secretary of State, explaining that he has lived in the United Kingdom since 2005, has a subsisting relationship with his partner who has ILR and that they have two British Citizen children.

[145] RR's appeal was heard on 8 February 2023. In a decision dated 14 February 2023, the judge set out reg. 27 and parts of Schedule 1 to the EEA Regulations and gave a self-direction with respect to article 8 of the Human Rights Convention. At [16] and [17], the judge wrote this:

"16. Mr McBride and Mr Hussain both made helpful submissions that the test for proportionality in this case is to be found in Regulation 27 of the EEA Regulations 2016. Mr McBride accepted that the evidence in the Appellant's bundle showed that he was working in the UK back to April 2005, that he had attained permanent residence under the EEA Regulations 2016 and was resident in the UK for more than ten years before his offence. On this basis, the Respondent must show imperative grounds of public security, the highest level, in order to deport the Appellant.

17. In considering the factors that weigh for and against the Appellant, I take into account Regulation 27(5)-(6) and Schedule 1 of the EEA Regulations 2016."

[146] The judge concluded at [22]:

"There is no indication that the Appellant represents a significant future threat to the fundamental interests of society. I find that deportation in these circumstances is a disproportionate interference with his right to a private and family life, and the rights to a family life of Ms Paredinyte and their children. It follows from my findings that I allow the appeal."

[147] The Secretary of State sought, and was granted permission to appeal on the grounds that the judge had erred by:

(i) Misdirecting himself in law as to the basis of the appeal which was under reg. 6 of the CRA, the EEA Regulations having no relevance and exception 7 with section 33 of the 2007 Act not being applicable;

(ii) Failing properly to apply section 117C of the 2002 Act in assessing article 8 of the Human Rights Act.

[148] Permission to appeal was granted on 29 March 2023.

[149] As with any appeal, the starting point for any consideration is the decision made. In this case, it is a decision to make a deportation order pursuant to section 5(1) of the 1971 Act which, by operation of reg. 6 of the CRA Regulations grants a right of appeal on the grounds set out in reg. 8 of those regulations.

[150] The decision is manifestly not a decision under the EEA Regulations, and it is not a refusal of a human rights claim. Although, arguably, the grounds of appeal do raise such a claim, there is no decision on that issue. That said, the human rights issue was raised in response to a section 120 notice, and is thus potentially a new matter. The decision under appeal is not, however, a human rights decision for the purposes of section 113 of the 2002 Act.

[151] Mr Buley had nothing to say about whether the decision in this case involved the making of an error of law but relied on his skeleton argument, arguing that by operation of section 7(1) of the Human Rights Act, the First-tier Tribunal had the jurisdiction to consider the compatibility of the Secretary of State's actions, and to consider if the actions were unlawful in terms of section 6 of that Act.

[152] Regrettably, we conclude that the judge's decision in this appeal was fundamentally misconceived. There is no reference to the CRA Regulations, nor any indication why, wrongly, it was thought that the EEA Regulations were relevant given that they had been revoked. Given that the criminal conduct that gave rise to the decision post-dated 31 December 2020, RR could not benefit from the protections offered by article 20 of the WA. Similarly, at best, the raising of human rights issues was a new matter, an issue not addressed, and the correct procedure was not followed; there was no written consent to the issue being raised and so as a matter of law, it could not be considered.

[153] We turn next to section 7 of the Human Rights Act which, materially provides:

"**7 Proceedings**

(1) A person who claims that a public authority has acted (or proposes to act) in a way which is made unlawful by section 6(1) may –

    (a) bring proceedings against the authority under this Act in the appropriate court or tribunal, or

    (b) rely on the Convention right or rights concerned in any legal proceedings,

but only if he is (or would be) a victim of the unlawful act.

(2) In subsection (1)(a) 'appropriate court or tribunal' means such court or tribunal as may be determined in accordance with rules; and proceedings against an authority include a counterclaim or similar proceeding.

…

(6) In subsection (1)(b) 'legal proceedings' includes –

    (a) proceedings brought by or at the instigation of a public authority; and

(b) an appeal against the decision of a court or tribunal."

[154] RR cannot rely on sub-section (1)(a) because it is restricted to the "appropriate court or tribunal", defined in subsection (2) to mean "such court or tribunal as may be determined in accordance with rules ...". The only tribunals upon which section 7(1)(a) jurisdiction has been conferred by rules are the Special Immigration Appeals Commission and the Proscribed Organisations Appeals Commission. No provision has been made for the First-tier Tribunal.

[155] In *R (A) v B* [2009] UKSC 12 the Supreme Court addressed that subsection, and how it differs from sub-section 1(a). Lord Brown held [45]:

"In *R v Kansal (No 2)* [2002] 2 AC 69, 105–106 I said that section 7(1)(a) and section 7(1)(b) are designed to provide two quite different remedies. Section 7(1)(a) enables the victim of the unlawful act to bring proceedings under the Act against the authority. It is intended to cater for free-standing claims made under the Act where there are no other proceedings in which the claim can be made. It does not apply where the victim wishes to rely on his Convention rights in existing proceedings which have been brought against him by a public authority. His remedy in those proceedings is that provided by section 7(1)(b), which is not subject to the time limit on proceedings under section 7(1)(a) prescribed by section 7(5); see also *Wilson v First County Trust Ltd (No 2)* [2004] 1 AC 816, para 90. *The purpose of section 7(1)(b) is to enable persons against whom proceedings have been brought by a public authority to rely on the Convention rights for their protection.*" [emphasis added].

[156] It is perhaps surprising that the AIRE Centre's submissions on section 7 simply do not engage with this decision or *R v Kansal*, let alone seek to distinguish Supreme Court authority. Section 7(i)(b) operates as a shield, not a sword. There is thus no question of any rights under section 7 being infringed by the CRA.

[157] It follows from this that the decision of the First-tier Tribunal involved the making of an error of law, as the judge applied the wrong law, and failed to identify the relevant legislation under which the appeal could be brought, nor did he identify the relevant ground of appeal. On that basis alone, it must be set aside. Further, there is no arguable basis on which he could have considered whether the deportation decision was a disproportionate interference with Mr RR's article 8 rights.

[158] Accordingly, we answer the issues raised in RR's appeal as follows:

(i) The right of appeal was under the CRA Regulations, the grounds being set out in reg. 8, subject to reg. 9.

(ii) The FtT did not have jurisdiction to decide the appeal by reference to the EEA Regulations, as they did not apply.

(iii) There being no human rights decision, the permissible grounds of appeal did not allow the FtT to reach a decision on article 8 grounds.

[159] We therefore set it aside, and remit the appeal to the FtT as it will be necessary to remake the decision. In doing so, we note Ms Smyth's request that the human rights claim raised under the section 120 notice should be considered by the First-tier Tribunal.

ABDULLAH & ORS (EEA; DEPORTATION; PROCEDURE) (Rintoul UTJ)

Directions

The three appeals are to be de-linked and will be remade in separate hearings. We therefore set out below separate directions in respect of each appeal.

ZA

[1] The appeal will be listed to be remade in the Upper Tribunal on a date to be fixed.

[2] The Upper Tribunal will need to determine whether ZA had been residing in the United Kingdom as at 31 December 2020, if so for what continuous period; whether he had acquired permanent residence prior to then; and, the extent to which he had been exercising Treaty Rights prior to 31 December 2020. It may also need to determine whether ZA was continuously resident after 31 December 2020, and on what basis.

[3] The parties are therefore directed to prepare and serve 10 working days before the next hearing in electronic form:

  a. An agreed bundle including any further witness statements in respect of any witness including the appellant, it is intended to call in respect of ZA

  b. a bundle of authorities

[4] Skeleton arguments are to be exchanged 5 working days before the hearing

SA

1 The appeal will be listed to be remade in the Upper Tribunal on a date to be fixed.

2 A CMR will be held prior to that to determine what findings made by the FtT can be preserved, and to determine whether the appeal should be stayed pending a decision on AS' EUSS application.

RR

1 The Secretary of State has stated in his email of 14 February 2024 that: *"Mr Rudokas' human rights appeal can be dealt with by the FTT as a new matter in his existing appeal under the CRA Regulations as provided for in regulation 9.*

2 In the circumstances, we remit RR's appeal to the First-tier Tribunal for a fresh decision on all issues.

ANNEX 1: LIST OF ISSUES IN ABDULLAH

CHRONOLOGY & LIST OF ISSUES

Chronology

References (e.g., [327]) are to page numbers in the FTT Hearing Bundle unless otherwise specified

8 Sept 1992:	Abdullah ('A') born in Saudi Arabia. Family – parents (originally from Iraq) and siblings – later relocated to Netherlands as refugees and obtained citizenship there.
2008:	A claims to have moved with his family move to the United Kingdom.
	A claims to have studied and worked in the United Kingdom between 2008 to 2017.
	His parents and siblings have settled status in the United Kingdom under the EU Settlement Scheme ('EUSS').
4 Jan 2010:	A reprimanded for possession of Class B drug (cannabis) [327]
29 June 2010:	A convicted of assault with intent to rob [328]
	Sentenced to 12 months Community Rehabilitation Order ('CRO'), 60 hours Community Punishment Order ('CPO') [NB revised to 70 hours]
22 Sept 2010:	A convicted of failing to comply with CRO/CPO (unpaid work requirement imposed) [328]
5 Jan 2011:	A convicted of failing to comply with CRO/CPO (order revoked) [328]
5 May 2011:	A's application for EEA residence card refused [338]
16 March 2014:	A's daughter born (a British National)
3 Oct 2017:	A convicted of restraining/obstructing PC (12-month conditional discharge) [328]
25 Oct 2017:	A convicted of battery [328]
	Restraining order, 15 days rehabilitation and 120 hours unpaid work imposed
28 Nov 2019:	A involved in incident where he is alleged to have assaulted a third-party during a traffic dispute
30 June 2021:	A made a EUSS application [320]
30 July 2021:	A convicted of offence (inflicting GBH without intent) in connection with the 28 Nov 2019 incident and is sentenced to 18 months imprisonment (reduced on appeal to 12 months) [343]
	A is described in sentencing remarks as having a previous conviction for assaulting his girlfriend in the United Kingdom [NB This is presumably the 25 Oct 2017 incident.]
	A is also described as having a conviction for assault in the Netherlands.
	A had pleaded not guilty to the offence.

9 Sept 2021:	A begins prison sentence
11 Oct 2021:	SSHD notify A of intention to deport due to his conviction **[348] [360]** Decision stated to be made in accordance with the Immigration (European Economic Area) Regulations 2016 (the "2016 Regs") or the Immigration Act 1971 / United Kingdom Borders Act 2007 (s.32) (i.e., on the basis A was a foreign criminal).
15 Nov 2021:	A's solicitors submit representations resisting deportation **[361]** A argued that: ○ He is an EU citizen in the United Kingdom with a right to permanent residence under the 2016 Regs acquired pre-31 December 2020. ○ He does not meet the threshold for deportation having acquired a right to permanent residence in the United Kingdom ○ He is an EU national who does not meet the threshold for deportation because he has lived and exercised treaty rights in the United Kingdom for a continuous period of at least 10-years and there are no imperative public security reasons for deportation. ○ It would be disproportionate interference with A's Article 8 rights (family/private life in the United Kingdom).
31 Jan 2022:	SSHD issues decision to detain A
25 March 2022:	A released from prison **[207]**
3 May 2022:	SSHD notifies A of decision to: ○ Refuse A's EUSS application on the basis of (i) suitability (Appendix EU Immigration Rules, Rule 15), because A was subject to a deportation order of even date in connection with his criminal conviction(s) and (ii) inability to show continuous qualifying period of residence because he cannot include time spent in prison (Rule 14) and could not show any other conditions for ILR applied **[309]**. Letter notifies A of a right of appeal (at para 43). ○ Refuse A's human rights claim and make a deportation order **[481]**. Letter notifies A of right of appeal against decision to refuse his human rights claim pursuant to s.82 of the Nationality, Immigration and Asylum Act 2002 (the "2002 Act"). ○ Deportation order stated to be made under the United Kingdom Borders Act 2007 and Immigration Act 1971 on the basis that the SSHD was not satisfied that A was a person to whom the 2016 Regs applied (no evidence lawfully resident in United Kingdom pre-31 December 2020): see paras. 10 and 11 of letter.

9 May 2022:	A served with deportation decision/order
9 May 2022:	A files appeal on basis that the SSHD's decision [15]:
	o In respect of his human right's claim was unlawful because it breached his Art. 8 rights (private/family life).
	o In respect of his EUSS application was (i) not in accordance with Appendix EU to the Immigration Rules (Rules 11–15) or the Withdrawal Agreement (the "WA") and (ii) breached A's rights under the 2016 Regs (regs. 23(6)(b) and 27)
2 Nov 2022:	Appeal heard by FTT (Judge Coutts) against both the human rights and EUSS decisions
	o Appellant's case set out at paras 7–12 and 19 of the FTT judgment: (i) acquired permanent right of residence in the United Kingdom by reason of being a national of the Netherlands and by exercising treaty rights since he arrived in the United Kingdom in or about 2008; (ii) this continued uninterrupted until he was convicted for assault on 30 July 2021 and sentenced to prison term; (iii) the SSHD was wrong to consider his deportation on conducive grounds and should have applied a test of public policy, public security or public health grounds which were relevant to his status as an EEA citizen; (iv) the decision breached his Article 8 rights (genuine and subsisting relationship with daughter).
20 Dec 2022:	FTT decision handed down
	o Human rights appeal succeeds (breach of Art.8 rights because of relationship with daughter meaning exception to deportation applied / deportation would be unduly harsh (paras 37–39))
	o EUSS appeal does not succeed. FTT not satisfied that A had been exercising treaty rights for a continuous period of five years and concluded he had not acquired permanent right of residence in the United Kingdom. the SSHD therefore entitled to take forward deportation on conducive grounds. FTT not entitled to look behind the deportation order (paras 28–31).
23 Dec 2022:	The SSHD seeks permission to appeal the human rights decision on basis of (i) material error of law in and (ii) failure to give adequate reasons for finding that deportation would be unduly harsh

11 Jan 2023:	Permission to appeal granted by FTT in respect of both human rights and EUSS decisions but on alternative ground: Did judge err in failing to consider whether deportation capable of being justified in accordance with the 2016 Regs rather than considering deportation solely under domestic deportation regime given criminal conduct took place pre-31 December 2020? ○ Judge's explanation for this set out at paras 4–11 of the PTA Decision. In summary: (i) the SSHD had conceded in her human rights' decision letter that A's proposed deportation falls to be considered under 2016 Regs; (ii) additionally Article 20.1 of the WA and [7.3] of the Explanatory Memorandum to the 2020 Regulations both confirm in broad terms that the 2016 Regs will continue to apply to EEA Citizens in respect of conduct predating end of the transition period (the "TP"); (iii) A's conduct pre-dated the TP; (iv) the 2016 Regs therefore apply, not the domestic deportation regime. The FTT therefore arguably erred in failing to consider whether A's proposed deportation was capable of being justified under the 2016 Regs. Permission to appeal granted against both decisions because FTT's consideration of the human rights appeal was arguably tainted consideration of the conjoined EUSS appeal (para 11). ○ A raised this issue in Rule 24 response (citing *Smith* [2019] UKUT 00216 (IAC)) and agreed permission to appeal should be granted *("the* [FTTJ] *failed to properly consider the relevant provisions under* [regs 23(6)(b) and 27 of the 2016 Regs] *and Article 20.1 of the* [WA] *and 7.3 of the Explanatory Memorandum to the Citizens Rights (Applicant Deadline and Temporary Protection) (EU Exit) Regulations 2020").* ○ SSHD agreed that this argument could be raised on appeal.
4 May 2023:	UT (Judge Kebede) grants SSHD's appeal on basis that: ○ Judge's decision on the human rights appeal was devoid of proper reasoning (para 21) ○ UT considered it had not been able to resolve the issue of whether the 2016 Regs or domestic deportation regime should have been applied because parties unable to clarify applicable law (paras 20 and 22). Judge Coutts did not deal with this issue. FTT's decision set aside in its entirety (para 23) Directed that the decision be remade in the UT (including possible further oral evidence) and that legal position vis what deportation regime applied needed to be determined as part of this process (para 24) UT identified what it considers to be the issues in dispute (para 27)

List of issues

1. For the Home Office (pursuant to para. 27(a)(i) of the UT's decision): the SSHD to provide *"confirmation of the relevant decision made in relation to the appellant's deportation, given the apparent inconsistency between the documents at Annex K and M of the Home Office bundle, both dated 3 May 2022."*

2. What are the relevant rights of appeal arising from the SSHD's decision?

3. In respect of A's appeal under s.82 of the 2002 Act:

   a. Should A's human rights claim be allowed, and if so, on what basis?

4. In respect of A's appeal under the Immigration (Citizens' Rights Appeals) (EU Exit) Regulations 2020 ("the Appeals Regs"):

   a. What were the available grounds of appeal?

   b. Did A's deportation have to be considered by reference to the EU law test in Chapter VI of the Directive pursuant to the WA, and if so, why?

   c. In order to answer that question, does it need to be determined whether or not A was exercising Treaty rights before the end of the transition period, and if so, was A exercising such rights?

   d. If the EU law test applied:

      i. What level of protection did A enjoy against deportation under that test (which includes consideration of whether A enjoyed a right of permanent residence)?; and

      ii. Is his deportation justified by reference to the EU law test?

   e. As to the Immigration (European Economic Area) Regulations 2016 ("the 2016 Regs"):

      i. Is it relevant to consider whether A's deportation was regulated by the 2016 Regs, and if so, why?

      ii. If it is relevant, was A's deportation regulated by the 2016 Regs (including the relevant statutory provisions which apply the 2016 Regs notwithstanding their revocation)?

      iii. What are the consequences, if any, of the 2016 Regs applying in A's case?

ANNEX 2: LIST OF ISSUES AND CHRONOLOGY IN SSHD V SZUBA

CHRONOLOGY & LIST OF ISSUES

Chronology

References in the form **[A/pg.no]** *(e.g., [A/78]) are to page numbers in the Appellant's FTT Hearing Bundle unless otherwise specified*

References in the form **[R/pg.no]** *(e.g., [R/78]) are to page numbers in the Respondent's FTT Hearing Bundle unless otherwise specified*

1 Feb 1996:	Szuba (Polish national) ('S') born
Aug 2007:	S moved to the United Kingdom aged 11 and has lived continuously in United Kingdom since
2007–2014:	S was in education and acquired permanent residence as a student
17 Sept 2013:	S convicted of intimidating witness/juror with intent to obstruct/pervert/interfere with justice (9 months referral order) **[A/78]**
10 Jan 2014:	S convicted on 3 counts of resisting/obstructing a PC (offence committed while on bail) (one month added to existing referral order)
13 Aug 2014:	S convicted of Class A drug possession (12-month community order)
11 Sept 2014:	S cautioned for Class B drug possession
5 Feb 2015:	S convicted of assault occasioning ABH (3 months imprisonment suspended for 18 months, 60 hours unpaid work and 12-month supervision requirement)
7 Sept 2017:	S convicted on 2 counts of driving under the influence (fine and 15-month driving disqualification ('DQ'))
26 Jan 2018:	S's daughter born (British national as S's partner is a British national) **[A/489]**
2 Aug 2018:	S convicted of driving while DQ (fine and 8-month DQ)
24 Sept 2018:	S convicted on two counts of driving under the influence and while DQ (1-year Community Order ('CO'), unpaid work requirement, 3-year DQ)
19 Dec 2018:	S convicted of failing to comply with CO (CO continued and fine)
17 May 2019:	S convicted of failing to comply with CO (CO continued and fine)
13 Sept 2019:	S convicted of failing to comply with CO (CO continued and fine)
10 Oct 2019:	S arrested in connection with drug dealing (Class A and B drugs)
Feb 2020:	S made application under EU Settlement Scheme ('EUSS') [NB This was a finding of fact in the FTT but is challenged by the SSHD (see below)]
2 Aug 2020:	S again arrested in connection with drug dealing (Class A) while released under investigation in connection with 10 Oct 2019 arrest

3 Aug 2020:	S detained in prison(?) **[A/22]**
14 Oct 2020:	S convicted on 3 counts of intent to supply Class A, 2 counts of intent to supply Class B drugs and acquiring/using criminal property **[A/79] [R/8]**
28 Jan 2021:	S sentenced to prison (five years and three months imprisonment) **[A/529] [R/14]**
4 May 2021:	S sentenced to three months imprisonment in default of fine **[A/529]**
24 Oct 2021:	S served notice of decision to deport **[R/57]**
	o Decision made under the United Kingdom Borders Act 2007/Immigration Act 1971
9 Nov 2021:	S's sols provide submissions in response to deportation decision, including raising human rights claim **[A/39]**
7 March 2022:	S asked to provide evidence of EUSS application / documents in support of status **[R/481]**
24 March 2022:	S makes SAR request to HMRC **[R/487]**
6 April 2022:	S responds to 7 March 2022 request but not considered to have provided sufficient evidence of EUSS application
23 May 2022:	SSHD decision to:
	o Make a deportation order, including because of convictions. SSHD made decision under domestic regime (United Kingdom Borders Act 2007/Immigration Act 1971) **[A/97]**
	o Refuse A's human rights claim **[A/75]**.
	o Letter notes that while S claims to have submitted an online application for the EUSS, the relevant evidence had not been provided to show that this had been done. Therefore, there was no evidence that S had an outstanding application to the EUSS.
30 May 2022:	S appealed against (i) human rights claim refusal and (ii) deportation order on the basis that **[A/67]**:
	o It breached his rights under EU law. S claimed he benefitted from protection under the Immigration (European Economic Area) Regulations 2016 (the "2016 Regs") on the basis he had exercised treaty rights for at least five years and had been continuously resident for at least ten years, with the date of the offence being pre-31 Dec 2020.
	o It would breach his Article 8 rights (relationship with daughter and partner)
30 June 2022:	S applies under EUSS again allegedly on SSHD advice (previous application deleted)

21 Dec 2022:	Appeal heard (Judge Dixon)
	○ Proceeded on the basis that the 2016 Regs applied (para 10)
20 Jan 2023:	Appeal allowed on basis imperative grounds for deportation not shown and deportation to Poland would not be proportionate
3 Feb 2023:	SSHD appeals on basis that:
	○ The FTT erred in disposing of the appeal under the 2016 Regs when the only appeal brought was against the SSHD's refusal of S's human rights claim
	○ The FTT gave inadequate reasons for finding that S had made a EUSS application in Feb 2020
24 Feb 2023:	PTA granted on both grounds (Judge Curtis)
	○ S has filed Rule 24 Response opposing appeal, including on the basis that (i) even if the judge erred in disposing of the appeal under the 2016 Regs, that error made no material difference to the outcome of the hearing because of the findings of fact made by the FTT and (ii) the FTT gave adequate reasons for its decision vis the Feb 2020 EUSS application
18 March 2023:	S released from prison(?) [A/22]

List of issues

1. What is the source and scope of S's right of appeal to the FTT?

2. In light of the above, did the FTT err in deciding, for the reasons it gave at [16]–[17], that the substantive law governing S's appeal was the Immigration (European Economic Area) Regulations 2016 ("2016 Regs"), as saved?

3. If so, is the error material such that the FTT decision is required to be set aside and re-made?

4. Did the FTT materially err in deciding that S had made an application under the EUSS in February 2020?

5. Did the FTT give adequate reasons for its finding of fact that S made an EUSS application in February 2020?

6. Without prejudice to the above, in deciding the appeal additional potential issues are:

   a. Was the FTT entitled to apply the 2016 Regs when determining an appeal on human rights grounds, and if so, why?

   b. Even if the FTT did not err in respect of its decision that S had made an application under the EUSS in February 2020, would that have entitled the FTT to decide the appeal by reference to the 2016 Regs absent a relevant decision from the SSHD giving rise to a right of appeal in which those 2016 Regs (or the underpinning requirements in the Withdrawal Agreement) fell to be considered?

c. Was the FTT entitled to consider S's appeal and deportation by reference to the EU law test in Chapter VI of the Directive 2004/38EC pursuant to the Withdrawal Agreement or otherwise, and if so, on what basis? In particular, what is the scope and relevance of Article 20 and 21 of the Withdrawal Agreement?

d. Whether the position under the Withdrawal Agreement, including appeal rights, is reflected in relevant domestic legislation?

e. Was S required to have taken any steps, such as making an EUSS application, to benefit from the Withdrawal Agreement?

ANNEX 3: LIST OF ISSUES AND CHRONOLOGY IN SSHD V RUDOKAS

CHRONOLOGY & LIST OF ISSUES

Chronology

References (e.g., [65]) are to page numbers in the SSHD Appeal Bundle unless otherwise specified

16 Dec 1985:	Rudokas ('R') born (Lithuanian national)
2005:	R moves to United Kingdom
26 Feb 2013:	R's son (British citizen) born to R and his partner, also a Lithuanian national who has EU settled status [65]
26 Nov 2016:	R's daughter (British citizen) born
21 Jan 2020:	R granted indefinite leave to remain under EU Settlement Scheme ('EUSS')
13 July 2022:	R convicted of money laundering/weapons possession offences (2-year prison sentence and POC (£384,120.19)) [8] R pleaded guilty to the offences of which he was convicted, on one occasion only doing so after the jury had been sworn in.
9 Aug 2022:	SSHD gives notice of Stage 1 decision to deport under United Kingdom Borders Act 2007 / Immigration Act 1971 [11]
23 Aug 2022:	R appeals 9 August 2022 Stage 1 decision to deport on (i) human rights grounds (Art. 8) and (ii) that his deportation is not conducive to the public good (Immigration Act 1971 and United Kingdom Borders Act 2007) [47] Also stated that his EU right to free movement is being restricted. R does not provide substantive representations in support
13 Oct 2022:	R placed in immigration detention [71]
18 Oct 2022:	SSHD confirms decision to deport in Stage 2 decision and makes deportation order under s.32(5) United Kingdom Borders Act 2007 [27] [NB R did not seek to appeal Stage 2 decision]
25 Oct 2022:	R provides representations in support of Stage 1 decision appeal [63] These are not received by SSHD until 4 Jan 2023 [4]
11 Nov 2022:	Service of Stage 2 decision and deportation order on R confirmed [71]
25 Jan 2023:	R granted immigration bail
27 Jan 2023:	R released from immigration detention
8 Feb 2023:	R's appeal against the Stage 1 decision heard by FTT (Judge Ficklin) Dealt with on the basis of EEA Regulations 2016
12 Feb 2023:	Appeal allowed Held that deportation would be a disproportionate interference with Article 8 rights (para 22)

Feb 2023: SSHD applies for permission to appeal on two grounds:
- The FTT erred in law in determining the appeal on the basis of EEA Regulations 2016. It should have been dealt with under the Immigration (Citizens' Rights Appeals) (EU Exit) Regulations 2020 since the decision was made under the United Kingdom Borders Act 2007/Immigration Act 1971 because R was convicted post-31 December 2020.
- The decision on the human rights issue was inadequately reasoned/infected by a misdirection in law, including failure to consider/apply the unduly harsh test.

29 March 2023: Permission to appeal granted (Judge Sills)
Considered that the decision appears confused as to whether the appeal was under the EEA Regulations 2016 or on human rights grounds.

List of issues – To be determined at Error of Law hearing unless parties agree there was an Error of Law

1. What was the scope of R's right of appeal against the decision of 9 August 2022?

2. In light of the above, did the FTT have jurisdiction to decide the appeal by reference to the test for removal on public policy grounds under the Immigration (European Economic Area) Regulations 2016? If so, on what basis?

3. If, which is unclear, the FTT decided the appeal on Article 8 grounds, did the FTT have jurisdiction to determine the appeal on that basis, and if so, why?

4. If the answer to that question is yes, did the FTT nonetheless materially err in its approach to Article 8, in particular because:

    a. It misdirected itself in relation to the facts, or failed to have proper regard to all relevant factors (para. 10 of SSHD's grounds)? and/or

    b. It erred in its approach to s.117A of Nationality, Immigration and Asylum Act 2002 (para. 11 of SSHD's grounds)? and/or

    c. It failed correctly to direct itself, or to apply, the "unduly harsh" test (paras. 12 to 14 of SSHD's grounds)?

5. Did the FTT give proper reasons for its decision?